INVARIANT MEASUREMENT WITH RATERS AND RATING SCALES

The purpose of this book is to present methods for developing, evaluating, and maintaining rater-mediated assessment systems. This book addresses the following topics: (1) introduction to the principles of invariant measurement, (2) application of the principles of invariant measurement to rater-mediated assessments, (3) description of the lens model for rater judgments, (4) integration of principles of invariant measurement with the lens model of cognitive processes of raters, (5) illustration of substantive and psychometric issues related to rater-mediated assessments in terms of validity, reliability, and fairness, and (6) discussion of theoretical and practical issues related to rater-mediated assessment systems.

Invariant measurement is fast becoming the dominant paradigm for assessment systems around the world, and this book provides an invaluable resource for graduate students, measurement practitioners, substantive theorists in the human sciences, and other individuals interested in invariant measurement when judgments are obtained with rating scales.

George Engelhard, Jr. is currently at the University of Georgia. He is a professor emeritus at Emory University. He is the author or co-author of over 200 journal articles, book chapters, and monographs. His research addresses a variety of topics including invariant measurement, the role of assessment in improving education, and Rasch Measurement Theory.

Stefanie A. Wind is an assistant professor of educational measurement at the University of Alabama. Her research includes the development and application of psychometric methods for examining a variety of issues in educational measurement, with an emphasis on rating scales and performance assessments.

INVARIANT MEASUREMENT WITH RATERS AND RATING SCALES

Rasch Models for Rater-Mediated Assessments

George Engelhard, Jr.
Stefanie A. Wind

Routledge
Taylor & Francis Group

NEW YORK AND LONDON

First published 2018
by Routledge
711 Third Avenue, New York, NY 10017

and by Routledge
2 Park Square, Milton Park, Abingdon, Oxon, OX14 4RN

Routledge is an imprint of the Taylor & Francis Group, an informa business

© 2018 Taylor & Francis

The right of George Engelhard, Jr. and Stefanie A. Wind to be identified
as authors of this work has been asserted by them in accordance with
sections 77 and 78 of the Copyright, Designs and Patents Act 1988.

All rights reserved. No part of this book may be reprinted or reproduced
or utilised in any form or by any electronic, mechanical, or other
means, now known or hereafter invented, including photocopying and
recording, or in any information storage or retrieval system, without
permission in writing from the publishers.

Trademark notice: Product or corporate names may be trademarks
or registered trademarks, and are used only for identification and
explanation without intent to infringe.

Library of Congress Cataloging-in-Publication Data
A catalog record for this book has been requested

ISBN: 978-1-84872-549-2 (hbk)
ISBN: 978-1-84872-550-8 (pbk)
ISBN: 978-1-31576-682-9 (ebk)

Typeset in Bembo
by Apex CoVantage, LLC

To the loves of my life: Judy Monsaas, David Monsaas Engelhard, Emily Monsaas Engelhard, Shimby McCreery, and Dashiell Engelhard McCreery (GE)

To my excellent husband: Jesse Fred Bickel, and my parents: Nancy Wind and Mike Wind (SAW)

CONTENTS

ACKNOWLEDGMENTS

George Engelhard, Jr.

The original vision and groundwork for creating this book emerged during a sabbatical leave from Emory University (Fall of 2012). During my sabbatical leave, I had the pleasure of working with colleagues at the College Board. I am indebted to Wayne Camara who arranged for me to have an office near Columbus Circle in Manhattan. I also had the distinct pleasure of sharing a third-floor walkup in the Bowery with a very talented jazz musician: my son, David Monsaas Engelhard. Colleagues and friends in my new home at the University of Georgia have been very supportive of my scholarly work. A number of graduate students at the University of Georgia helped in numerous ways to support the completion of this book. In particular, I would like to mention Jue Wang and J. Kyle Jennings. I would also like to thank the peer reviewers who provided detailed and helpful suggestions for improvement.

Stefanie A. Wind

I think it is best to first acknowledge my co-author, George Engelhard, Jr. I am grateful to Professor Engelhard for taking me on as his student at Emory, and for his unwavering dedication to the education of new measurement scholars. Thank you for teaching me, and for setting an example of what it means to be a generous scholar, careful thinker, and friend. I am also fortunate to have many other mentors whose support has helped me to begin my career in academia. Likewise, I am fortunate to have many loving and supportive friends and family members who have helped me along the way. I also appreciate the peer reviewers for their thoughtful comments that helped to improve this book.

PREFACE

Major Themes

Rating scales are a popular approach for collecting human judgments in numerous situations. In fact, it is fair to say that rating scales in the human sciences are ubiquitous. Rating scales appear in applied settings that range from high-stakes performance assessments in education through personnel evaluations in assessment of language proficiency. This book utilizes both the principles of invariant measurement and the lens model from cognitive psychology as theoretical frameworks for examining judgmental processes based on rating scales. In essence, this book focuses on guiding principles that can be used for the creation, evaluation, and maintenance of invariant assessment systems based on human judgments.

The main themes examined in this book include (1) an introduction to the principles of invariant measurement, (2) the application of the principles of invariant measurement to rater-mediated assessments, (3) a description of the lens model for rater judgment and decision processes, (4) an integration of principles of invariant measurement with the lens model of cognitive processes for raters, (5) considerations and illustrations of substantive and psychometric issues related to rater-mediated assessments in terms of validity, reliability, and fairness, and (6) theoretical and practical issues related to the development and improvement of rater-mediated assessments.

Much of our research has focused on applying the principles of invariant measurement to issues and problems encountered with rater-mediated assessment systems in a variety of situations. Rater-mediated assessments place the rater in a key position to judge and evaluate performances using rating scales (Engelhard, 2002). Among the many applications involving rater-mediated assessments are large-scale writing assessments, teacher-evaluation systems, and licensure and certification examinations for employment in various occupations. In all of these situations, rater-mediated assessments create numerous measurement and conceptual issues that are different from the problems encountered with traditional assessment systems based on selected-response format examinations such as the familiar multiple-choice items. One of the main concerns with rating scales is that human judgments can be fallible, and that they also can be deliberately biased and misleading. There are several key questions that must be addressed when ratings are used based on human judgments:

- How can we evaluate the quality and accuracy of the ratings?
- How can we detect and correct inaccuracies in ratings?
- How do the foundational issues of validity, reliability, and fairness as defined in the *Standards for Educational and Psychological Testing* (American Educational Research Association, American Psychological Association, and National Council on Measurement in Education, 2014) apply to rater-mediated assessments?
- How can we develop fair systems of rater-mediated assessments based on the principles of invariant measurement?

An earlier book on invariant measurement (Engelhard, 2013) primarily focused on dichotomous data ($x = 0, 1$), while this book describes measurement models for rating scales that yield ordered polytomous data ($x = 0, 1, 2, \ldots k$). The current book extends and augments this earlier research. It extends the principles of invariant measurement to data based on raters and rating scales. Interested readers should consider reading both *Invariant Measurement: Using Rasch Models in the Social, Behavioral, and Health Sciences* and the current book in order to get a more complete picture of invariant measurement with dichotomous and polytomous data. The overall goal of both books is to improve research, theory, and practice related to measurement in the human sciences.

Audiences for the Book

The intended audiences for this book are graduate students, measurement practitioners, substantive theorists in the human sciences, and other individuals interested in invariant measurement when judgments are obtained with rating scales. The issues raised in this book should assist people who are interested in developing psychometrically sound and legally defensible assessment systems that employ rating scales and utilize human raters within a variety of contexts within the human sciences. The book is written to be accessible to undergraduate, graduate, and postgraduate audiences who are motivated to improve measurement in the human sciences. Readers with a minimal background in statistics (equivalent to an introductory course in statistics) should be able to access the content. This book can also be used as a supplementary textbook in a variety of courses on research methodology in social, behavioral, and health sciences (e.g., anthropology, communication, economics, education, health sciences, psychology, public policy, and sociology). It can also serve as a reference work for social scientists. Invariant measurement is fast becoming the dominant paradigm for assessment systems around the world, and this book should be of interest to scholars in numerous countries because of the widespread use of rating scales and rater-mediated assessments.

Note to Students

This book is fundamentally different from other volumes on measurement and psychometrics. We start with a clear and unifying philosophical position on measurement theory (invariant measurement). These principles are used as a guide for the reader to integrate and evaluate the plethora of apparently discon-nected and conflicting theories of measurement utilized in the human sciences. This approach makes it distinct from current books on psychometrics that pres-ent lists of apparently disjointed testing and measurement topics to readers. In order to increase the didactic value of the book, draft versions of most of the chapters were used in seminars and graduate courses at both Emory University and the University of Georgia. This book also features several applications and case studies drawn from several areas including large-scale writing assessments. The Facets computer program (Linacre, 2015) is used frequently because it is the primary package for examining rating quality from the perspective of Rasch Measurement Theory. A useful website for obtaining a free version of Facets (MINIFAC) is as follows: www.winsteps.com/minifac.htm. MINIFAC is limited to 2,000 responses. A website has been created with resources freely available to support the quest for invariant measurement: www.GeorgeEngelhard.com.

Overall Structure and Preview

The book is organized into six major parts:

- Part I provides an introduction, overview, and discussion of the foundational issues encountered in measurement in the social sciences. Specifically, this part introduces key concepts used throughout the book including invariant measurement, rating scales, and Wright maps. It also briefly discusses the idea of progress in the social sciences related to measurement that includes a view of science as problem solving and progress in social science measure-ment defined as problem-solving effectiveness.
- Part II describes two major paradigms in measurement theory that are useful for organizing our thinking about rating scales: test-score and scaling tradi-tions. It describes selected theoretical models for human judgment that have implications for raters, and describes a lens model for social judgments that is promising for conceptualizing rater-mediated assessments.

- Part III includes chapters that are organized around the three foundational areas of testing identified in the *Standards for Educational and Psychological Testing* (AERA, APA, & NCME, 2014): validity, reliability, and fairness. The focus is on understanding these foundational issues within the context of rater-mediated assessments. The principles of rater-invariant measurement are also stressed in terms of how to conceptualize and empirically examine rating quality in rater-mediated assessment systems. This part concludes with a chapter reporting on a case study in which procedures for evaluating the quality of rater-mediated assessments in terms of validity, reliability, and fairness are illustrated using data from a large-scale, rater-mediated writing assessment.
- In Part IV, the emphasis turns to measurement models within the scaling tradition. Detailed analyses are provided of the major measurements models used for rating scales based on the Rasch models (Rating Scale Model, Partial Credit Model, and Facets Model). Technical issues related to the estimation of the parameters in these models are discussed.
- Part V begins with a chapter on the examination of model-data fit. This part also includes a chapter on designing rater-mediated assessment systems, as well as approaches for examining and maintaining the quality of rating scale functioning in ongoing assessment systems.
- The final part (Part VI) offers a summary and suggestions for future directions in research related to invariant measurement with raters and rating scales in the social sciences.

References

American Educational Research Association [AERA], American Psychological Association [APA], and National Council on Measurement in Education [NCME]. (2014). *Standards for educational and psychological testing.* Washington, DC: AERA.

Engelhard, G. (2002). Monitoring raters in performance assessments. In G. Tindal & T. Haladyna (Eds.), *Large-scale assessment programs for ALL students: Development, implementation, and analysis* (pp. 261–287). Mahwah, NJ: Erlbaum.

Engelhard, G. (2013). *Invariant measurement: Using Rasch models in the social, behavioral, and health sciences.* New York: Routledge.

Linacre, J. M. (2015). *Facets Rasch Measurement* (Version 3.71.4). Chicago, IL: Winsteps.com.

PART I

Introduction

1

INTRODUCTION AND OVERVIEW

> The essence of all forms of rating devices is the same. Some particular psychological continuum is defined . . . landmarks or guideposts [cues] are supplied along this continuum to aid a judge in the evaluations of samples to be placed on that continuum . . . a straight horizontal line is drawn to represent the continuum . . . the judge merely checks . . . that point on the continuum where he believes the sample should fall.
>
> *(Guilford, 1936, p. 263)*

This chapter provides a general introduction to the principles of invariant measurement within the context of rating scales and rater judgments. As noted by Guilford (1936), there is a very simple underlying structure for all rating scales; however, the creation of a continuum to represent meaningful and useful constructs in the social, behavioral, and health sciences is far from simple. This book describes some of the key components to consider in the development of invariant measures obtained from raters within a variety of ecological contexts. Guilford (1936) highlighted several essential steps in the development of rating scales:

- Identify a continuum,
- Select cues (landmarks or guideposts) to define the continuum,
- Create a structure for the rating scale,
- Ask raters to evaluate the location of persons on the continuum by comparison with the cues on the continuum using a rating scale, and
- Assign ratings to persons based on their judged locations on the continuum.

These essential aspects of rating-scale methods must be addressed whenever rating scales are used to collect judgments in a variety of settings. The idea of a continuum is a very powerful way to represent constructs in the social sciences that are difficult to measure and to conceptualize. Figure 1.1 gives a visual representation of rating scales embodied in the opening quote. In this figure, the

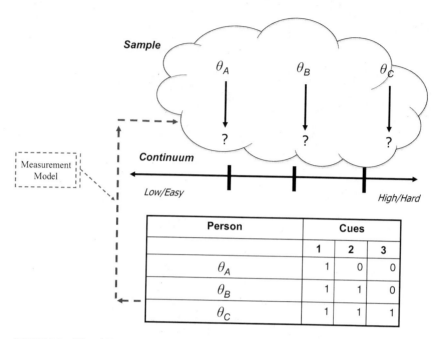

FIGURE 1.1   Visual Representation of Rating-Scale Methods Based on Guilford (1936)

sample consists of three persons (A, B, and C) with true locations on the continuum (θ_s). The continuum ranges from low/easy to high/hard going from left to right on the line. The rater's judgmental task is to locate the three persons on the continuum based on three cues (shown as short vertical lines on the continuum) that represent "cues," such as performance-level descriptions. A rater judges that Person A is above the first cue and below the other two cues, and the rater assigns a rating pattern of [1 0 0] to Person A. The observed ratings are summarized in a similar fashion for Persons B and C in the table. The next step is to connect the observed rating patterns using a measurement model (dashed arrows between table and sample) to infer the location of persons on the continuum. In this simple illustration, the observed responses patterns suggest that Person C has the highest location on the continuum because the response pattern [1 1 1] suggests that this person is above the three cues. In this very simple example, the measurement model is called Guttman scaling. This book introduces and describes a variety of other measurement models that were created to aid researchers in linking observations to infer person locations on a continuum.

As will be seen later in this chapter, Guilford's concept of a continuum can be operationally defined in the form of a *Wright map* that can be used to represent a latent variable or construct. In earlier work, the Wright map has also been called a variable map, item map, and curriculum map (Wilson, 2011).

This chapter provides an overview and introduction to many of the themes that undergird this book on rater-invariant measurement. It lays the foundation for building a framework for invariant measurement with rating scales and raters. The following specific questions and issues are introduced in this chapter:

- What is invariance?
- What is measurement?
- What is invariant measurement?
- What is invariant measurement with raters?
- What are rating scales?
- What are rater-mediated Wright maps?
- Case study: Middle School Writing Assessment
- Summary and discussion

The questions and the underlying concepts are briefly illustrated with a small case study that examines the assessment of writing achievement among a group of middle-school students. The chapter concludes with a summary and discussion.

What Is Invariance?

> Einstein, however, was not truly a relativist . . . beneath all of his theories, including relativity, was a quest for invariants . . . and the goal of science was to discover it.
>
> *(Isaacson, 2007, p. 3)*

Invariance can be viewed as a fundamental concept in the physical and social sciences. As the subtitle of Nozick's book (2001) on invariance suggests, the *structure of the objective world* can be viewed through the lens of the concept of invariance. A variety of definitions have been proposed for thinking about invariance. There is the commonsense notion that invariance is a property of attributes that includes relationships among other attributes that remain fixed within a stable and consistent framework for guiding research, theory, and practice. Within philosophy, invariance relates to objectivity and its twin concept of subjectivity, and it also has implications in the search for *truths* that endure beyond the details of a particular context. In addressing the concept of invariance in general, there is also an implicit concern with variance—if an attribute is determined not to be invariant, then it begs the question of *how variant is it?* As pointed out by Fisher (2008), "anomalous failures of invariance . . . [prompt] the search for explanations of consistent inconsistencies that might lead to discoveries of new variables" (p. 190). Nozick (2001) argues that almost all philosophers have "sought to establish permanent truth in an enduring framework of thought; these truths were supposed to be absolute, objective and universal . . . [and] to stand firm for all time" (p. 1). When the search for invariant "truths" fails, then the quest for invariance has still provided a useful philosophical framework for understanding the journey and discussing the aspects of relevant variance.

Turning from philosophy to science, the general concept of invariance also plays an important role in scientific endeavors. As indicated in the opening quote for this section, Einstein was not truly a relativist, and within the field of physics he considered labeling his ideas a theory of invariance (Isaacson, 2007). Stevens (1951) stressed that "the scientist is usually looking for invariance whether he knows it or not" (p. 20). Nozick (2001) points out that to understand something means that "we want to know the transformations it is invariant under and also the transformations it is variant under" (p. 78). Science can be viewed as a systematic examination and search for these invariances.

Invariance is important as a scientific concept because it reflects what researchers are seeking in order to provide a stable framework and structure for understanding the world around us. We recommend reading Nozick (2001) for a thoughtful discussion of invariance, and its implications for philosophy and the sciences. In this book, an important lesson for the reader is to recognize that invariance and variance are essentially two sides of the same coin. Scientists may seek invariance in the attributes that are being studied, but if invariance is not found it becomes important to identify sources of variance. It seems to us that frequently the importance of invariance as a goal for science is not recognized by researchers who tend to stress the noise, variance, and uncertainty in our activities rather than the messages conveyed in invariant relationships between attributes that we are seeking to discover. Everything is not invariant, but it is important for scientists to sort out what facets are stable and consistent from the facets that are ephemeral, unpatterned, and variant in the world around us.

The word *invariance* has been widely used in several different disciplines that range from mathematics and physics to philosophy. Each discipline has slightly different denotations and connotations of the term. In this book, invariance is viewed in a fairly commonsensical way as stability and consistency across different contexts that can be defined and studied from different perspectives. Fisher (2008) stresses the use of "the metaphysical status of invariance as the criterion hallmark of meaningfulness and existence, and so of validity," (p. 190) across many scientific disciplines.

What Is Measurement?

MEASUREMENT consists in the assignment of numerals to things or properties. But not every assignment of numerals is measurement. A street is not measured when numerals are assigned to the houses in it; a dyer does not measure his colours when he assigns numerals to them in his catalogue. To understand in what circumstances the assignment of numerals is measurement, we must ask what is the significance of numerals as distinct from other symbols, such as hieroglyphics or the letters of our alphabet.

(*Campbell & Jeffreys, 1938, p. 121, capitalization in the original*)

Measurement, in its broadest sense, is defined as the assignment of numerals to objects or events according to rules.

(Stevens, 1946, p. 677)

There are a variety of different definitions of measurement that have been proposed over the years. Many of the definitions echo the quotes above regarding the assignment of numbers or numerals on the basis of rules. In many ways, the essence of this definition still stands, but it leaves open the question of how to define the *rules*. The rules define the conditions (requirements and assumptions) that must be met in order to achieve the important implications of invariant measurement for theory and practice. Some researchers have tried to define measurement in a theoretical and ecological vacuum. However, measurement at the end of the day is about the development of meaningful scores that locate persons on a continuum (latent variable or construct) that can be used to make decisions about each person. Measurement and the development of various instruments and scales occur within theoretical and purposive contexts that cannot be ignored. For example, Chang (2004) has described how measurement issues played an integral part in the invention of the concept of temperature. He offers an instructive example that captures many of the challenges researchers also face in developing scales in the social sciences.

As pointed out by the sociologist Paul Lazarsfeld, measurement theories are important because they define

problems of concept formation, of meaning, and of measurement necessarily fuse into each other . . . measurement, classification and concept formation in the behavioral sciences exhibit special difficulties. They can be met by a variety of procedures, and only a careful analysis of the procedure and its relation to alternative solutions can clarify the problem itself, which the procedure attempts to solve.

(Lazarsfeld, 1966, p. 144)

This perspective on measurement can be extended to highlight the more inclusive perspective that measurement theories in the social sciences serve the following functions (Engelhard, 2013):

- Define the aspects of quantification that are defined as problematic,
- Determine the statistical models and appropriate methods used to solve these problems,
- Determine the impact of our research in the social, behavioral, and health sciences,
- Frame the substantive conclusions and inferences that we draw, and ultimately
- Delineate and limit the policies and practices derived from our research work in the social, behavioral, and health sciences, and

- Provide a framework for evaluating the correspondence between our theoretical views and empirical data.

Measurement is the systematic process of locating both persons and items on a continuum that represents a construct. This definition of measurement is similar to the one used by Engelhard (2013). The major purpose of this book is to explore the extension of this definition of measurement to rater-mediated assessments. Questions of invariance revolve around the stability and consistency of the scale (the instrument), as well as the stability and consistency of the location of raters, items, persons, and other facets of assessment systems on the scale. In the context of rater-mediated assessments, invariance relates to the properties of ratings obtained from raters.

What Is Invariant Measurement?

> The scientist seeks measures that will stay put while his back is turned.
>
> *(Stevens, 1951, p. 21)*

The views of invariant measurement that are developed in this book are primarily, but not exclusively, based on the philosophy of measurement developed by Georg Rasch (1960/1980, 1961, 1977). Rasch (1961) was motivated by his observation that "present day statistical methods are entirely group-centered, so that there is a real need for developing individual-centered statistics" (p. 321). Rasch began his inquiry into developing individual-centered statistics by exploring

> the possibilities for just comparing individuals and comparing stimuli. In doing so, I shall, however, formulate four requirements that to my mind seem indispensable for well-defined comparisons. Preliminarily, it may be noted that in order to compare stimuli we have to apply them to some adequately chosen individuals, and similarly, that in order to compare individuals in a given respect, we must use some adequate stimuli.
>
> *(Rasch, 1961, p. 331)*

He specified these requirements as follows:

> The comparison between two stimuli should be independent of which particular individuals were instrumental for the comparison; and it should also be independent of which other stimuli within the considered class were or might also have been compared.
>
> Symmetrically, a comparison between two individuals should be independent of which particular stimuli within the class considered were instrumental for the comparison; and it should also be independent of

which other individuals were also compared, on the same or on some other occasion.

(Rasch, 1961, pp. 331–332)

The basic measurement problem in the first section of this quote deals with person-invariant calibration of items (stimuli). The goal of person-invariant item calibration is to locate items on a continuum and to minimize the unwanted influences of person subgroups. Person-invariant item calibration has been called *measurement invariance* by Millsap (2011). The second part of Rasch's quote refers to item-invariant measurement of persons or individuals. The basic problem is to estimate a person's location on the same continuum or construct without undue dependence on the particular set of test items used or other persons.

Rasch (1961) proposed a simple and an elegant equation for representing response probabilities that supports this view of comparisons and invariant measurement (specific objectivity) with separation of items and persons. According to Rasch, the probability of a correct response ($a_{vi} = 1$) or incorrect response ($a_{vi} = 0$) can be presented as:

$$P\{a_{vi}\} = \frac{(\theta_v \sigma_i)^{a_v i}}{1 + \theta_v \sigma_i}$$

(Rasch, 1961, p. 324)

where θ is the person parameter for person v and σ is an item parameter for item i. In current usage, the Rasch model is typically presented in exponential form:

$$Pr\{a_{vi} = 1\} = \frac{\exp(\theta_v - \delta_i)}{1 + \exp(\theta_v - \delta_i)}$$

where $Pr\{a_{vi} = 1\}$ is the probability of observing a correct response. The Rasch model is an example of a measurement theory that can be used to connect observed responses and items (cues) to infer person locations on a continuum or latent variable.

Rasch's requirements for specific objectivity can be stated in terms of five requirements for invariant measurement related to person measurement, item calibration, and Wright maps (Engelhard, 2013). These five requirements are summarized in Figure 1.2.

When the requirements of invariant measurement are approximated with empirical data, then meaningful and useful Wright maps can be constructed to represent focal constructs in the social sciences.

Concerns related to invariant measurement have a long history in measurement within the social sciences. Engelhard (2008) described the history of this concept in terms of item-invariant person measurement and person-invariant

Requirements for Invariant Measurement (IM)

Person measurement:

1. The measurement of persons must be independent of the particular items that happen to be used for the measuring: Item-invariant measurement of persons.

2. A more able person must always have a better chance of success on an item than a less able person: Non-crossing person response functions.

Item calibration:

3. The calibration of the items must be independent of the particular persons used for calibration: Person-invariant calibration of test items.

4. Any person must have a better chance of success on an easy item than on a more difficult item: Non-crossing item response functions.

Wright map:

5. Persons and items must be simultaneously located on a single underlying latent continuum: Wright map.

FIGURE 1.2   Five Requirements of Invariant Measurement

Note: These requirements are based on Engelhard (2013).

calibration of items. Some of the key measurement theorists who have used the concept of invariant measurement in different forms include Thorndike (1904); Thurstone (1925, 1926); Guttman (1944); Rasch (1960/1980); Lazarsfeld (1959); and Mokken (1971). What has not been explicitly recognized is that other measurement theories including Classical Test Theory (Spearman, 1904), Generalizability Theory (Cronbach et al., 1972), and factor analysis (Thurstone, 1947) can also be viewed through the lens of invariant measurement. This book contributes to the creation of a system based on the principles of invariant measurement for rating scales used by raters.

What Is Invariant Measurement with Raters?

> [M]ost of the reservations, regardless of how elegantly phrased, reflect fears that rating scale data are subjective (emphasizing, of course, the undesirable connotations of subjectivity), biased, and at worst, purposefully distorted.
>
> *(Saal, Downey, & Lahey, 1980, p. 413)*

In earlier research on raters, Engelhard (2002) introduced the idea of *rater-mediated assessments* in order to stress the concept that scores are assigned by raters to person responses to constructed-response items, and that the ratings are mediated and interpreted through the cognitive lens of raters. It is important to stress that the data being modeled are the obtained ratings from raters based on the essays, portfolios, and other performances (Engelhard, 2002). This early work did not explicitly extend the models to different classical and modern theories of measurement. Furthermore, it was not recognized that each model for ratings included an implicit model of social judgment. This book highlights that both measurement theories, as well as theories of social judgment, are needed to more fully conceptualize, model, and evaluate rater-mediated assessments. The basic structure of rater-mediated assessments should include an explicit consideration of two theoretical frameworks: a conceptual model of the judgmental processes of the raters and a measurement model for the ratings within the assessment system. The basic process of rater-mediated assessments includes most of the following facets: A rater judges the quality of a person's response to a task using one or more domains defined by a rubric designed to represent a construct using a rating scale.

In this book, the model for judgmental processes is based on the lens model first proposed by Brunswik (1952). A variety of classical and modern measurement theories are described for examining judgments based on the extension of key concepts of invariant measurement to rating scales. The basic model representing a lens model perspective on invariant measurement is shown in Figure 1.3.

This figure suggests that the location of a person (θ_p) is mediated and interpreted through a set of cues (e.g., domains, benchmarks, and rating categories) by a rater who assigns a judged value using a rating scale to this person's location

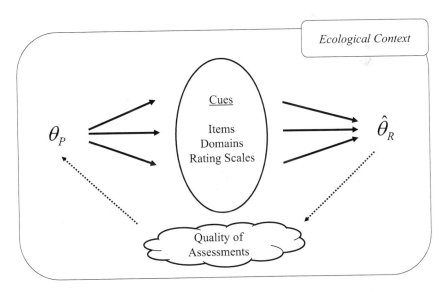

FIGURE 1.3   Lens Model for Rater-Mediated Assessments

(θ_R) based on the cues. As described by Cooksey (1996), cues are defined as any information that is available to a rater for use in informing a judgment (rating) regarding person location on the continuum. This lens model also indicates that the match between the person's true theta (θ_p) and the rater's judged theta (θ_R) should be evaluated for its accuracy through various indicators of rating quality (e.g., rater agreement, detection of rater errors and biases). As pointed out by Landy and Farr (1980), ratings must be interpreted in light of the fact that "all information must ultimately pass through a cognitive filter represented by the rater" (p. 100). Figure 1.3 also suggests that the whole process occurs within a particular ecological context.

The five requirements for invariant measurement described in the previous section (Figure 1.2) can be extended to measurement with raters. Figure 1.4 lists the extension of these requirements for invariant measurement with raters.

These requirements can be viewed as step-by-step extensions of the original five requirements with four components:

- Rater-invariant person measurements,
- Rater-invariant calibrations of cues and rating scales,
- Invariant locations of raters, and
- Rater-invariant Wright maps.

Each of these components is addressed in detail in other sections of the book. Briefly, rater-invariant person measurement reflects the overall goal of building an assessment system that supports rater independent assessment of persons. The next two components highlight the need for invariant cues and rating scales in building a stable and consistent framework for measurement. It is essential for invariant measurement to have a high degree of agreement and consistency regarding the interpretation and use of the cues and structure of the rating scale. The next component reflects invariant locations (calibrations) of raters in terms of rater severity/leniency. The last component emphasizes the importance of creating a rater-invariant Wright map to provide a visual definition of the construct that is being measured. In many ways, the rater-invariant Wright map can be viewed as the main outcome of building a rater-mediated assessment system that meets the requirements of invariant measurement. Each of these components is illustrated below in the case study. Figure 1.5 shows a simple example of the importance of invariant measurement of persons.

In Figure 1.5, three subsets of items (cues) are shown with their locations on the underlying continuum. The person (θ) has an invariant position on the continuum that cuts across the item subsets. However, the item subsets differ in their locations (or judged item difficulties), and therefore the observed scores of the person are not invariant—although the person's location has not changed, the scores range from 1 to 3 depending on the difficulties of the subsets of items. One of the major goals of invariant measurement is to estimate the invariant

---

Requirements for Invariant Measurement with Raters

Rater-invariant measurement of persons

1. The measurement of persons must be independent of the particular raters that happen to be used in the assessment.

- A more able person must always have a better chance of a higher rating than a less able person: Non-crossing person response functions.

Rater-invariant calibration of cues

2. The calibration of the cues must be independent of the particular raters used in the assessment.

- Any person must have a better chance of a higher rating on an easy cue than on a more difficult cue: Non-crossing cue response functions.

Rater-invariant calibration of rating scales

3. The structure of the rating categories must be independent of the particular raters used in the assessment.

- Any person should have a better chance of receiving a low rating than high rating: Non-crossing category response functions.

Invariant locations of raters

4. The locations of raters must be independent of the particular persons, cues, and rating scales used in the assessment.

- Any person must have a better chance of success from a lenient rater than a more severe rater: Non-crossing rater response functions.

Rater-invariant Wright map

5. Persons, cues, rating scales and raters must be simultaneously located on an underlying latent continuum used in an assessment system.

- All raters must share a common understanding and use of the Wright map: Rater-invariant calibration of assessment system.

FIGURE 1.4 Requirements of Invariant Measurement with Raters

Note: Cues are defined as sources of information that raters use in forming their judgments (e.g., items and domains) regarding person locations on the construct represented by the Wright map.

location of the person on the continuum that is independent of the particular set of cues or items that are used in the process.

In order to build a framework for invariant measurement with raters and rating scales, at least two theories are needed: a theory of judgment for rating processes and a suitable measurement theory that can support invariant measurement. In addition, there is usually a substantive theory of social behavior in the background that drives the conceptualization of the underlying construct.

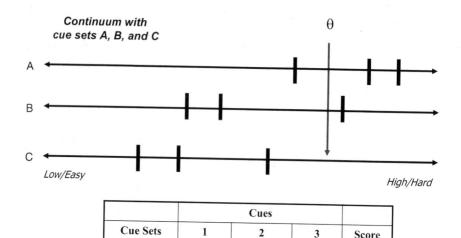

FIGURE 1.5 Invariant Location of Person (θ) on the Continuum with Cue-Dependent Scores on Three Cue Subsets (A, B, and C)

There are close connections between these theoretical frameworks, and this book focuses primarily on measurement and judgment theories. The underlying substantive theories will be evident in the examples and case studies.

What Are Rating Scales?

Guilford (1936) provided a historical sketch of the early use of rating-scale methods. He suggested that Galton (1883) was one of the first researchers to use rating-scale methods. Figure 1.6 shows the format of the rating scale used by Galton (1883) for measuring vividness of mental representations of sensations.

Guilford (1936) identified four major structures for rating scales that with minor modifications can still be used to classify modern rating-scale structures. These rating-scale formats are (using Guilford's labels):

- Numerical rating scale,
- Graphic rating scale,
- Defined-group scale, and
- Standards-based scale.

Each of these formats connects back to Guilford's notion of a continuum with landmarks to assist the rater in understanding and judging the meaning of the

F.—Questions on Visualizing and Other Allied Faculties

12. Call up before your imagination the objects specified in the six following paragraphs, numbered A to F, and consider carefully whether your mental representation of them generally, is in each group very faint, faint, fair, good, or vivid and comparable to the actual sensation:

A. *Light and colour.*—An evenly clouded sky (omitting all landscape), first bright, then gloomy. A thick surrounding haze, first white, then successively blue, yellow, green, and red.

B. *Sound.*—The beat of rain against the window panes, the crack of a whip, a church bell, the hum of bees, the whistle of a railway, the clinking of tea-spoons and saucers, the slam of a door.

C. *Smells.*—Tar, roses, an oil-lamp blown out, hay, violets, a fur coat, gas, tobacco.

D. *Tastes.*—Salt, sugar, lemon juice, raisins, chocolate, currant jelly.

E. *Touch.*—Velvet, silk, soap, gum, sand, dough, a crisp dead leaf, the prick of a pin.

F. *Other sensations.*—Heat, hunger, cold, thirst, fatigue, fever, drowsiness, a bad cold.

FIGURE 1.6   Early Rating Scale

Source: Galton (1883, p. 256).

continuum. The *numerical rating scale* appears today in the format used by Likert and his colleagues (Likert, 1932; Likert, Roslow, & Murphy, 1934). They suggested the following structure for obtaining responses from persons related to attitude statements:

If you agree with a statement, put a plus (+).
If you strongly agree with a statement, put a plus with a circle around it (⊕).
If you disagree with a statement, put a minus (−).
If you strongly disagree with a statement, put a minus with a circle around it (⊖).
If you are undecided, put a question mark (?).

Likert et al. (1934, p. 229)

These responses are scored as ratings 4, 5, 2, 1, and 3 (undecided), respectively. A rating of "5" is defined as most favorable, while "1" is defined as the least favorable attitude regarding the content of the attitude statement. A person's score is obtained by adding the ratings corresponding to how the person rated each statement.

The *graphic rating scale* is similar to the numerical rating scale with the rater actually seeing a horizontal line representing the continuum, and then locating persons on this continuum (Myford, 2002). The *defined-group format* is not as commonly used today, but for some measurement applications it may be necessary to group persons into categories with pre-determined proportions. One example of this format is grading-on-a-curve with pre-determined proportions of letter grades (As, Bs, Cs, Ds, and Fs). Grading-on-a-curve is still used in some educational settings to address issues such as grade inflation in which too many high grades are assigned to students. A *standards-based scale* uses a map of benchmarks and other illustrative performances to define the continuum. Guilford (1936) cites Thorndike's work (1910, 1913) on developing scales of handwriting and drawing as early examples of standards-based scales. This rating format fell out of favor during the 20th century, but the fundamental idea of a Wright map undergirding invariant measurement used in this book would be categorized by Guilford as a standards-based scale.

There are numerous examples in the literature of rating-scale formats that yield ordered or graded responses. Figure 1.7 provides a few examples of numerical, graphic, and standards-based ratings scales.

The continuum in this case is based on the creation of an instrument to measure levels of teacher caring. Each of these formats yields a rating that can be used to provide data regarding the location of teachers on the continuum. Johnson, Penny, and Gordon (2009) provide examples of rubrics and scoring guides based on holistic and analytic rating scales that can also be used to obtain rater judgments of performance assessments.

It should be recognized that early discussions of rating-scale methods were grounded in psychophysical methods (Guilford, 1936). Rating scales were viewed as one of several methods for collecting judgments in early work by psychologists. Other methods that were used to collect judgments included the constant method, paired comparisons, and the method of successive categories (Bock & Jones, 1968). It was not until Thurstone (1927) argued persuasively for the use of psychophysical methods to scale attitudes that rating scales began to assume their familiar form seen today and to appear frequently in modern measurement work across the social sciences.

What Are Rater-Mediated Wright Maps?

> The map of a variable is the beginning and end of assessment . . . the map of a variable is a visual representation of the current status of variable construction . . . it is a pictorial representation of the "state of the art" in constructing a variable.
>
> *(Stone, Wright, & Stenner, 1999, p. 309)*

Numerical rating scale

Indicate beside each of the following statements how caring the teacher is based on a scale from 1 to 4 with 1=Not at all caring and 4=Very caring.

      The teacher is very caring.   _____

How caring is the teacher? (Circle one)

      Very caring   4
      Caring   3
      Not caring   2
      Not at all caring   1

Graphic rating scale

How caring is the teacher? (Indicate response on the line)

```
|----------------------|----------------------|----------------------|----------------------|
      Not at                  Not                 Caring                  Very
    all caring                caring                                     caring
```

Standards-based rating scale

Indicate the portfolio that best represents the level of teacher caring.

```
|----------------------|----------------------|----------------------|----------------------|
```

     A   B   C   D

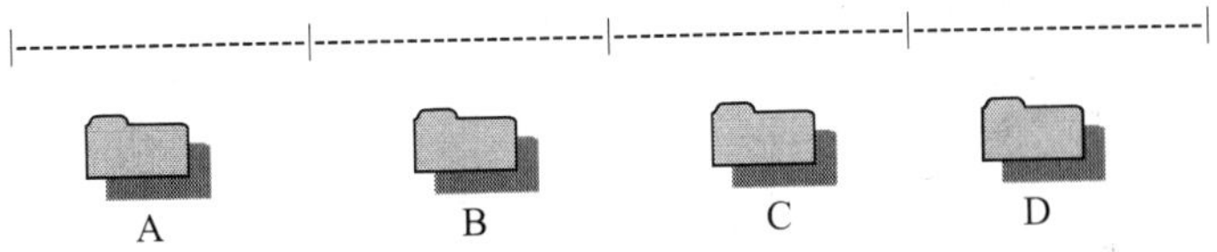

FIGURE 1.7   Examples of Rating Scales That Yield Graded Responses from Raters: Level of Teacher Caring

A Wright map is a major outcome of a well-developed and useful assessment system. The Wright map provides a visual display that provides a framework for understanding the meaning of scores obtained from the assessment. The idea of a continuum described by Guilford (1936) in the opening quote to this chapter can be extended and operationally viewed as a Wright map. Guilford's *scale of standards* defines a continuum as illustrated by Thorndike (1910, 1913) in the areas of handwriting and drawing. This format bears a remarkable resemblance to the methods advocated in this book. This resemblance is not coincidental because Thorndike was an early proponent of a scaling tradition in measurement theory that supports the creation of Wright maps and invariant measurement (Engelhard,

2013). Recent advances in measurement theory have stressed the development of Wright maps to convey the meaning of the constructs being measured, and also to provide clear displays that can increase the utility of the measures. In essence, we are creating communities of meaning and use for the key constructs that have been theoretically identified as having relevance in our substantive theories in the social sciences. Wright maps play an important role by serving as "invariantly calibrated instruments . . . through which research communities acquire common languages, [and] common points of reference" (Fisher, 2008, p. 190).

In this book, *Wright maps* are viewed as an instantiation of an operational definition mediated and interpreted by a set of raters of a continuum designed to represent a construct. The first step in the creation of a Wright map is to develop an initial conceptualization of the construct that is being measured and represented by the Wright map. This *intended Wright map* represents a set of hypotheses regarding how to make an unobservable or latent variable visible. Once the intended map is created, the researcher can develop and define a study for implementing the intentions embodied in the Wright map. The *implemented Wright map* provides empirical information regarding how well observed data matches the intended map. In assessment practices, there is an ongoing interaction between our understanding of a variable as embodied in the intended map and the model–data fit to real data visualized with the implemented map. The Wright map becomes a catalyst of increasing our knowledge and understanding about the construct being measured. Wright maps help to clarify and serve as the plan or blueprint for assessment development. If good model–data fit is obtained between the intended and implemented Wright map, then this provides an important source of validity evidence for the use of the scores obtained on the scale. It is important to recognize that "maps by their very nature, invite improvement . . . a map calls attention to its accuracy and inaccuracy" (Stone, Wright, & Stenner, 1999, p. 309). Where appropriate, we will affix the prefix "rm" for rater mediated to remind the reader that aspects of the assessment process are rater-mediated.

CASE STUDY: MIDDLE SCHOOL WRITING ASSESSMENT

In order to anchor the ideas presented in this introductory chapter, a case study that focuses on the rating of essays written by middle-school students is introduced. This middle school writing assessment is used for illustrative purposes. The Middle School Writing (MSW) Assessment provides information regarding the writing proficiency of students in the middle grades in the United States. In this case study, the underlying continuum represents writing proficiency. In order to define writing proficiency, several cues are identified in the MSW Assessment. These cues are domains, benchmarks, and rating categories. These cues define the intended lens that raters are asked to use in assigning persons a location of the writing proficiency scale. Figure 1.8 shows the intended representation of the rater-mediated Wright map for writing proficiency that drives the MSW Assessment. The first column of the Wright map indicates the true locations of three students (θ_A, θ_B, and θ_C) on the writing proficiency scale. Column two provides the metric in logits (Ludlow & Haley, 1995) that underlies the scale. Columns three to five represent the cues that are also located on the continuum and serve to guide rater judgments in rating the three students. Table 1.1 describes the four domains of writing (conventions, organization, ideas, and style) that receive separate ratings (analytic-scoring design). Figure 1.9 shows excerpts from three benchmarks or exemplars that serve to illustrate the quality of

Rater uses cues (domain, benchmarks, and rating categories)
to judge person locations on the logit scale.

True Person Locations	Logit Scale	CUES *(hard)*			Rater	Judged Person Locations
High	4.00	**Domains**	**Benchmarks**	**Rating Categories**		**High**
	3.00	*Conventions*	High Proficiency	*High*		
$\theta_A \rightarrow$	2.00		[*There are many goals in life ...*]			$\leftarrow \theta_{rm\text{-}A}$ Essay A
	1.00	*Ideas*				
$\theta_B \rightarrow$	.00		Medium Proficiency [*I'm a cheerleader ...*]	*Medium*	Raters	$\leftarrow \theta_{rm\text{-}B}$ Essay B
	-1.00	*Organization*				
$\theta_C \rightarrow$	-2.00		Low Proficiency [*Hi, my goals in life ...*]	*Low*		$\leftarrow \theta_{rm\text{-}C}$ Essay C
	-3.00	*Style*				
Low	-4.00	**CUES** *(easy)*				**Low**

FIGURE 1.8 Intended Wright Map for Writing Proficiency (Rater-Mediated Wright Map)

Note: Figure 1.9 provides longer excerpts from the three benchmark essays.

TABLE 1.1 Description of Domains for Writing Proficiency

Domain	Description	Key elements
Conventions (C)	The writer controls sentence formation, usage, and mechanics.	• Sentence formation • Usage • Mechanics
Ideas (I)	The writer establishes a controlling idea and elaborates the main points with examples.	• Controlling idea/focus • Supporting ideas • Depth of development
Organization (O)	The writer arranges ideas in a clear order, and the overall structure of the response is consistent.	• Overall plan • Introduction/body/conclusion • Sequence of ideas
Style (S)	The writer controls language to engage the reader.	• Audience awareness • Voice • Strategies appropriate to genre

writing that students exhibit for these areas along the logit scale. Students responded to a prompt or writing task that asked them to *describe their goals in life.*

The last cue is the rating categories that define regions along the logit scale that indicate low, medium, and high writing proficiency. The next column indicates the location of the expert raters who interpret the cues and make judgments regarding the locations of the persons. The penultimate column shows the location of raters on the continuum. The final column represents the judged person locations on the Wright map by the rater based on the three essays written by students A, B, and C.

Based on the data presented in Table 1.2, the parameters of the Rasch model were estimated using the Facets computer program (Linacre, 2015). The Wright map in Figure 1.8 for writing proficiency serves to identify a continuum with illustrative benchmarks and cues that define the continuum. Raters are asked to judge and evaluate the location of each person's essay on the writing continuum by comparison with the cues. These judgments are collected as ratings in four domains using the Wright map as the frame of reference to define the writing continuum.

The implemented Wright map is shown in Figure 1.10. This Wright map is based a dataset consisting of four raters evaluating 40 essays on four domains using a three-category rating scale (1 = *low*; 3 = *high*). It is beyond the scope of this introductory chapter to provide exhaustive analyses of these data, but there are a few preliminary observations that can be made

A: HIGH WRITING PROFICIENCY

There are many goals in life that I would like to accomplish. There are many goals everyone would like to accomplish, but they usually have a main goal and worry about the other goals later. I too have a main goal to accomplish and that goal is to become an astronaut! But I have to apply myself with thing like: school work, my education, and doing whatever else I can to become an astronaut. Making steps to achieve my goal is the only way to obtain what I most desire.

B: MEDIUM WRITING PROFICIENCY

I'm a cheerleader and I have a sports goal. I'm on a level four team and our goal is to be a level five cheer team by the end of the year. If you're on a level five you can go and compete at the worlds competition in Florida. The worlds competition is like no other because you get to spend time and compete with other cheer teams from around the world, which is worth fighting for.

C: LOW WRITING PROFICIENCY

Hi my goals in life are better then 1c year early. Befer I whente be a prenesie or whell. But now I see the real wrcld pculcun't be bcllesc prenesie. My recil Gcal in life cure finishing schccl sc nc cne can take me what I ccn't bc cure Why Sc I ccn be Semebcay in the wcrld

FIGURE 1.9 Benchmarks for Writing Proficiency (Task for Student: My goals in life are . . .)

Note: These are excerpts from longer essays.

TABLE 1.2 Observed Ratings of Essays Written by 40 Persons Obtained from Four Raters Using Three Categories (1 = Low, 2 = Medium, and 3 = High Quality of Writing)

Person	Rater 1				Rater 698				Rater 2509				Rater 2606			
	C	O	I	S	C	O	I	S	C	O	I	S	C	O	I	S
1	1	2	2	2	2	2	2	1					1	1	1	1
2	3	2	3	3	2	3	3	3					2	3	3	3
3	2	1	2	1	2	2	2	2					1	2	2	1
4	2	3	3	3	3	3	3	2					2	3	3	2
5	1	2	1	1	1	1	1	1					1	1	1	1
6	2	2	1	1	1	2	1	2					2	2	1	2
7	2	3	3	2	2	2	2	2					2	2	2	2
8	1	2	3	1	2	2	2	2					2	2	2	2
9	1	1	1	2	1	2	2	2					1	2	2	1
10	2	3	1	1	2	2	2	2					2	2	2	2
11	1	1	2	1	2	2	1	2					2	2	1	2
12	3	1	1	1					2	2	2	2	1	2	2	2
13	1	3	2	1					2	2	2	2	2	2	2	2
14	1	2	2	2					2	2	2	2	2	2	2	2
15	1	1	1	3					1	2	2	2	1	2	1	1
16	2	1	3	2					2	1	1	2	2	2	1	2
17	2	1	2	2					2	2	1	2	2	2	2	2
18	2	2	2	2					1	2	2	2	1	2	2	2
19	1	1	1	2					1	1	1	1	2	1	1	2
20	2	3	2	2					2	2	1	2	2	2	1	2
21	1	2	1	2					2	2	1	1	2	2	2	2
22	1	1	2	2					1	2	1	1	1	2	1	1
23	1	1	2	2	2	1	2	2					2	2	1	2
24	2	1	1	1	2	2	2	2					2	2	2	2
25	2	2	2	3	2	3	3	3					2	3	3	2
26	3	2	2	3	1	1	1	1					1	1	1	1
27	2	2	3	3	2	2	3	3					1	2	3	2
28	2	1	3	2	2	2	2	2					2	2	2	2
29	1	1	1	3	2	2	2	2					1	2	1	1
30	2	2	1	3	1	2	1	2					1	2	1	2
31	2	1	2	2	3	2	3	3					2	3	3	2
32	3	1	3	3	2	2	2	2					1	2	2	2
33	1	2	2	1					3	2	3	2	2	2	3	2
34	3	3	3	2					1	1	1	1	1	1	1	1
35	1	2	1	1					2	3	2	3	3	3	2	3
36	2	3	3	3					2	1	1	1	1	1	1	1
37	2	3	1	2					2	2	2	2	3	2	2	3
38	1	3	3	3					2	1	1	2	2	1	1	2
39	1	1	1	2					1	1	1	2	2	1	1	2
40	1	2	1	2					1	1	1	1	1	1	1	1

Note: Empty cells are missing by design. Domains: C = Conventions, I = Ideas , O = Organization, and S = Style.

to begin the story about the MSW Assessment. The implemented Wright map suggests that the empirical order of the writing domains is congruent with the intended ordering (the style domain is relatively easy compared to the conventions domain, which is relatively hard). The raters appear to vary in severity with Rater 2509 relatively severe compared to Rater 698. The reliability of separation for persons is .81, and this value is comparable to coefficient alpha. The analyses of these data are continued in future chapters.

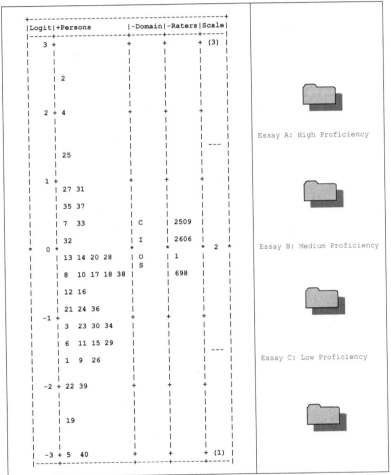

```
+---------------------------------------+
|Logit|+Persons        |-Domain|-Raters|Scale|
|-----+----------------+-------+-------+-----|
|  3  +                +       +       +  (3) |
|     |                |       |       |      |
|     |                |       |       |      |
|     | 2              |       |       |      |
|     |                |       |       |      |
|     |                |       |       |      |
|  2  + 4              +       +       +      |
|     |                |       |       |      |
|     |                |       |       |  --- |
|     | 25             |       |       |      |
|     |                |       |       |      |
|  1  +                +       +       +      |
|     | 27 31          |       |       |      |
|     | 35 37          |       |       |      |
|     | 7  33          | C     | 2509  |      |
|     | 32             | I     | 2606  |      |
*  0  *                *       *       * 2  * |
|     | 13 14 20 28    | O     | 1     |      |
|     | 8  10 17 18 38 | S     |       |      |
|     |                |       | 698   |      |
|     | 12 16          |       |       |      |
|     | 21 24 36       |       |       |      |
| -1  +                +       +       +      |
|     | 3  23 30 34    |       |       |      |
|     | 6  11 15 29    |       |       |      |
|     | 1  9  26       |       |       |  --- |
|     |                |       |       |      |
| -2  + 22 39          +       +       +      |
|     |                |       |       |      |
|     | 19             |       |       |      |
|     |                |       |       |      |
| -3  + 5  40          +       +       +  (1) |
|-----+----------------+-------+-------+-----|
```

Essay A: High Proficiency

Essay B: Medium Proficiency

Essay C: Low Proficiency

Domains: C = Conventions, I = Ideas , O = Organization, and S = Style

FIGURE 1.10 Implemented Wright Map (Rater-Mediated) for Four Domains by Four Raters Using Three Categories Based on the Many-Facet Rasch Model

Summary and Discussion

> Einstein briefly considered calling his creation Invariance Theory.
>
> *(Isaacson, 2007, p. 132)*

This chapter introduced some of the key concepts related to invariance. These themes are expanded and illustrated throughout the book with a specific focus on invariant measurement with raters. One of the focal points of this chapter and the entire book is the view of measurement as defining a continuum or line that operationally defines a construct. Invariant measurement can be understood as a philosophy that seeks the creation of scales that have a certain degree of consistency and stability across various facets of assessment situations. Invariance is a set of hypotheses that can be critically examined by researchers in order to produce meaning and useful scales. If invariance is not achieved within a particular context, then sources of variance can be explored to gain a deeper understanding of the construct that is represented by the scale.

Invariance is an important concept that cuts across many disciplines. This chapter has started a path towards the use of the concept of invariance to highlight commonalities across different issues encountered in measurement in the social sciences. It is beyond the scope of a single chapter to fully define invariance and measurement in general, but the goal was to introduce the reader to these ideas that ebb and flow throughout the book. This chapter also serves to provide a preliminary introduction to rating scales, and to invite readers to begin imagining the role that raters and judgments play within the context of rater-mediated assessments.

References

Bock, R. D., & Jones, L. V. (1968). *The measurement and prediction of judgment and choice.* San Francisco: Holden-Day.

Brunswik, E. (1952). *The conceptual framework of psychology.* Chicago: University of Chicago Press.

Campbell, N. R., & Jeffreys, H. (1938). Symposium: Measurement and its importance for philosophy. *Proceedings of the Aristotelian Society,* Supplementary volumes, *17,* 121–151.

Chang, H. (2004). *Inventing temperature: Measurement and scientific progress.* Oxford: Oxford University Press, Inc.

Cooksey, R. W. (1996). *Judgment analysis: Theory, methods and applications.* Bingley, UK: Emerald.

Cronbach, L. J., Gleser, G. C., Nanda, H., & Rajaratnam, N. (1972). *The dependability of behavioral measurements: Theory of generalizability for scores and profiles.* New York: Wiley.

Engelhard, G. (2002). Monitoring raters in performance assessments. In G. Tindal & T. Haladyna (Eds.), *Large-scale assessment programs for all students: Development, implementation, and analysis* (pp. 261–287). Mahwah, NJ: Erlbaum.

Engelhard, G. (2008). Historical perspectives on invariant measurement: Guttman, Rasch, and Mokken [Focus article]. *Measurement: Interdisciplinary Research and Perspectives, 6,* 1–35.

Engelhard, G. (2013). *Invariant measurement: Using Rasch models in the social, behavioral, and health sciences.* New York: Routledge.

Fisher, W. F. (2008). Other historical and philosophical perspectives on invariance in measurement. *Measurement: Interdisciplinary Research and Perspectives, 6*(3), 190–194.

Galton, F. (1883). *Inquiries into social faculty and its development.* London: Macmillan & Company, Ltd.

Guilford, J. P. (1936). *Psychometric methods.* New York: McGraw Hill.

Guttman, L. (1944). A basis for scaling qualitative data. *American Sociological Review, 9*(2), 139–150.

Isaacson, W. (2007). *Einstein: His life and universe.* New York: Simon & Shuster.

Johnson, R. L., Penny, J. A., & Gordon, B. (2009). *Assessing performance: Designing, scoring, and validating performance tasks.* New York: Guilford Press.

Landy, F. J., & Farr, J. L. (1980). Performance rating. *Psychological Bulletin, 87*(1), 72–107.

Lazarsfeld, P. (1966). Concept formation and measurement in the behavioral sciences: Some historical observations. In G. J. Direnzo (Ed.), *Concepts, theory, and explanation in the behavioral sciences* (pp. 144–202). New York: Random House.

Lazarsfeld, P. F. (1959). Latent structure analysis. In S. Koch (Ed.), *Psychology: A study of a science, volume three: Formulation of the person and the social context* (pp. 476–543). New York: McGraw-Hill.

Likert, R. (1932). A technique for the measurement of attitudes. *Archives of Psychology, 22*(140), 5–55.

Likert, R., Roslow, S., & Murphy, G. (1934). A simple and reliable method of scoring the Thurstone attitude scales. *Journal of Social Psychology, 5*, 228–238.

Linacre, J. M. (2015). *Facets Rasch Measurement* (Version 3.71.4). Chicago, IL: Winsteps.com.

Ludlow, L., & Haley, S. M. (1995). Rasch model logits: Interpretation, use, and transformation. *Educational and Psychological Measurement, 55*(6), 967–975.

Millsap, R. E. (2011). *Statistical approaches to measurement invariance.* New York: Routledge.

Mokken, R. J. (1971). *A theory and procedure of scale analysis.* The Hague/Mouton/Berlin: De Gruyter.

Myford, C. M. (2002). Investigating design features of descriptive graphic rating scales. *Applied Measurement in Education, 15*(2), 187–215.

Nozick, R. (2001). *Invariances: The structure of the objective world.* Cambridge, MA: The Belknap Press of Harvard University Press.

Rasch, G. (1960/1980). *Probabilistic models for some intelligence and attainment tests.* Copenhagen: Danish Institute for Educational Research. (Expanded edition, Chicago: University of Chicago Press, 1980).

Rasch, G. (1961). On general laws and meaning of measurement in psychology. In J. Neyman (Ed.), *Proceedings of the fourth Berkeley Symposium on mathematical statistics and probability* (pp. 321–333). Berkeley: University of California Press.

Rasch, G. (1977). On specific objectivity: An attempt at formalizing the request for generality and validity of scientific statements. *Danish Yearbook of Philosophy, 14*, 58–94.

Saal, F. E., Downey, R. G., & Lahey, M. A. (1980). Rating the ratings: Assessing the psychometric quality rating data. *Psychological Bulletin, 88*(2), 413–428.

Spearman, C. (1904). The proof and measurement of association between two things. *American Journal of Psychology, 15*, 72–101.

Stevens, S. S. (1946). On the theory of scales of measurement. *Science, 103*(2684), 677–680.

Stevens, S. S. (1951). Mathematics, measurement and psychophysics. In S. S. Stevens (Ed.), *Handbook of experimental psychology* (pp. 1–49). New York: Wiley.

Stone, M. H., Wright, B. D., & Stenner, J. A. (1999). Mapping variables. *Journal of Outcome Measurement, 3*(4), 308–322.

Thorndike, E. L. (1904). *An introduction to the theory of mental and social measurements.* New York: Teachers College, Columbia University.

Thorndike, E. L. (1910). Handwriting: Introduction. *The Teachers College Record, 11*(2), 1–3.

Thorndike, E. L. (1913). A scale for measuring achievement in drawing. *Teachers College Record, 14*, 345–382.

Thurstone, L. L. (1925). A method of scaling psychological and educational tests. *Journal of Educational Psychology, 16*, 433–451.

Thurstone, L. L. (1926). The scoring of individual performance. *Journal of Educational Psychology, 17*, 446–457.

Thurstone, L. L. (1927). A law of comparative judgment. *Psychological Review, 34*(4), 273–286.

Thurstone, L. L. (1947). *Multiple factor analysis.* Chicago: University of Chicago Press.

Wilson, M. (2011). Some notes on the term: "Wright map". *Rasch Measurement Transactions, 25*(3), 1331.

2

PROGRESS IN THE SOCIAL SCIENCES

An Historical and Philosophical Perspective

> We must explain why science—our surest example of sound knowledge—progresses as it does, and we first must find out how, in fact, it does progress.
>
> *(Kuhn, 1970, p. 20)*

One of the major themes of this book is that measurement in general, and invariant measurement in particular, is essential for supporting progress in the social sciences. Measurement is a technology that plays a key role in both the theory and practice of numerous social science disciplines including education, psychology, and the health sciences. In particular, this book argues that progress within measurement theory is based on methodological advances that support the quest for invariant measurement. Progress broadly conceived defines an essential link between our measurement theories, the quality of the substantive theories utilized in our research, and the resultant problem-solving systems that are created. Theories provide conceptual frameworks for understanding and seeking improvements in the social world around us.

As an example of this perspective, the director of the Institute of Educational Statistics has stressed the power of measurement within the context of educational research and practice:

> We know that *good measurement is the cornerstone of all scientific research*. I believe it is especially important in a social science like education that depends heavily on the interactions and communication among and between key stakeholders, whether they are parents, students, teachers, principals, researchers, superintendents, school board members or newspaper reporters. Good *measurement brings conceptual clarity by precisely defining the phenomena* that we are trying to change. It enables researchers to build frameworks or theories that

integrate multiple concepts. It helps us better test and then understand the mechanisms and pathways to improved outcomes. Good measurement also gives educators frameworks to help them place the phenomenon in context as they plan or seek improvement strategies.

(Easton, 2012, p. 7, italics added)

This chapter provides a brief discussion of the philosophical and historical grounding that has guided our research on invariant measurement. This discussion transitions to a consideration of the persistent measurement issues and foundational areas that undergird measurement in the social sciences. The motivation for introducing these measurement issues is to identify the measurement problems and questions that measurement theories are created to address. Measurement theories are designed to provide solutions to problems, and progress is evaluated by examining their problem-solving effectiveness. A consideration of the history and philosophy of science provides a focus for (1) identifying key measurement problems, and (2) considering various theories of measurement as contributing to progress in the social science methodology related to quality of the solutions provided for empirical and conceptual problems.

There are three important ideas underlying our current research on the history and philosophy of measurement: complementary science, epistemic iterations, and thought experiments with ideal types. This book uses organizing principles from invariant measurement to cover a variety of apparently disparate measurement issues and topics with a coherent set of underlying philosophical principles. Our approach includes proposing a complementary science of measurement. Chang (2004) introduced the idea of complementary science, and he utilized this idea in his instructive analyses of the invention of temperature as a variable in the physical sciences. Very briefly, complementary science is a hybrid of principles from both history and philosophy of science that can illuminate facets of a disciplinary area that are not examined within the context of what Kuhn (1970) has called *normal science*. Kuhn (1970) defined normal science as "research firmly based upon one or more past scientific achievements, achievements that some particular scientific community acknowledges for a time as supplying the foundation for its further practice" (p. 10). Normal science is defined by the paradigms that are found for example in various handbooks and textbooks that serve to guide scientific practice. A complementary science can guide us in reconsidering the underlying assumptions that are frequently taken for granted in the current practice of measurement.

Next, the issues and problems that measurement theories are designed to address are presented based on a consideration of the persistent methodological questions in educational testing identified by Hattie, Jaeger, and Bond (1999), and the *Standards for Educational and Psychological Testing* (American Educational Research Association, American Psychological Association, and National Council on Measurement in Education, 2014).

The following topics are briefly addressed in this chapter:

- History and philosophy of science

  o   What is science?
  o   How is progress defined in science?
  o   What is a complementary science?
  o   What are epistemic iterations?
  o   What are thought experiments with ideal types?
  o   Summary

- Measurement problems in the social sciences

  o   What are the persistent measurement issues in the social sciences?
  o   What are the foundational areas of testing?

- Summary and discussion

History and Philosophy of Science

> Philosophy of science without history of science is empty; history of science without philosophy of science is blind.
>
> *(Lakatos, 1971, p. 91)*

The sections in this part focus on describing the fundamental perspectives of science underlying this book, as well as our perspective on progress in the human sciences.

What Is Science?

> Science fundamentally aims at the solution of problems [and] the rationality and progressiveness of a theory are most closely linked . . . with its problem solving effectiveness.
>
> *(Laudan, 1977, pp. 4–5)*

There are a variety of views on how to define science. Following Laudan (1977), we define science as an inquiry system that embodies a set of procedures for solving a variety of problems. In this book, the focus is on the solution of measurement problems that arise in the interpretation and use of test scores within social science research, and also within the context of several applied fields, such as education and health sciences. We embrace the following perspective on the nature of science described by the National Research Council:

> At its core, scientific inquiry is the same in all fields. Scientific research, whether in education, physics, anthropology, molecular biology, or economics, is a continual process of rigorous reasoning supported by a dynamic interplay among methods, theories, and findings. It builds understandings in the form of models or theories that can be tested. Advances in scientific

> knowledge are achieved by the self-regulating norms of the scientific community over time, not, as sometimes believed, by the mechanistic application of a particular scientific method to a static set of questions.
>
> *(Shavelson & Towne, 2002, p. 2)*

The National Research Council identifies six guiding principles that underlie all scientific inquiry:

1. Pose significant questions that can be investigated empirically,
2. Link research to relevant theory,
3. Use methods that permit direct investigation of the questions,
4. Provide a coherent and explicit chain of reasoning,
5. Replicate and generalize across studies, and
6. Disclose research to encourage professional scrutiny and critique.

These principles clearly stress the idea that questions and problems are at the core of science. These principles also highlight that theories are inevitably related to the solution of problems. For the purposes of this book, Principle 5 directly highlights the importance of examining the limits of invariance across multiple studies within the context of measurement in the social sciences.

How Is Progress Defined in Science?

Progress in science and the methodology of science can be viewed as directly related to how well problems are solved. In evaluating progress from a scientific perspective, it is important to consider and identify persistent problems, and then to identify the adequacy of the proposed solutions. Laudan (1977) suggests that the "the central cognitive test of any theory involves assessing its adequacy as a solution of certain empirical and conceptual problems" (p. 70).

One process for evaluating the adequacy of problem solution involves epistemic iterations. Epistemic iteration is defined as "a process in which successive stages of knowledge, each building on the preceding one, are created in order to enhance the achievement of certain epistemic goals" (Chang, 2004, p. 253). For example, Behizadeh and Engelhard (2014) have analyzed the role of epistemic iterations in the dialectic between the measurement and writing communities within the context of developing valid writing assessments.

We argue in this book that the key epistemic goal in measurement theory should be based on the quest for invariance, and that this includes a detailed framework for addressing both the range and limits of invariance. We also argue that epistemic iterations play an important role in defining progress through the interplay between measurement theory and practice between and within various scientific communities. It is essential to identify the significant questions and measurement issues, and then to share research results in order to encourage professional scrutiny and critique (Principle 6).

What Is a Complementary Science?

> Complementary science—history and philosophy of science as a continuation of science by other means.
>
> *Chang (2004, p. 235)*

History of science can be defined as a narrative regarding the role of science in the accumulation of knowledge. The standard perspective on the history of science according to Laudan (1977) is that "the historian . . . is dealing with facts and data, seeking to arrange them into a convincing and coherent tale about how scientific ideas have evolved" (p. 156). George Sarton (1957) who is considered a founder of the history of science (Garfield, 1985) stated that "the history of science is the only history which can illustrate the progress of mankind. In fact, *progress* has no definite and unquestionable meaning in other fields than the field of science" (p. 5).

In contrast, Thomas Kuhn (1970) portrays the history of science in more nuanced terms. For Kuhn, the history of science is a story based on competing paradigms, conceptual systems, and world views. Paradigms are defined as "universally recognized scientific achievements that for a time provide model problems and solutions to a community of practitioners" (1970, p. viii). In many ways, Kuhn (1970) and his view of paradigms introduce many aspects of a philosophy of science into the history of science. Philosophy of science according to Laudan (1977) is "a normative, evaluational and largely *a priori* investigation of how science ought to proceed" (p. 156).

In contrast to Kuhn (1970), complementary sciences as envisioned by Chang (2004) do not stress the idea of competing paradigms, conceptual systems, and world views. Instead, complementary sciences highlight the conceptual continuity of perspectives within different scientific disciplines. Chang (2004) has proposed the idea of a complementary science based on guiding principles from the two fields of history and philosophy of science. According to Chang (2004), complementary science combines "reclamation of past science, a renewed judgment on past and present science, and an exploration of alternatives" (p. 250). In his view of complementary science,

> philosophy and history work together in identifying and answering questions about the world that are excluded from current specialist science. Philosophy contributes its useful habits of organized skepticism and criticism, and history serves as the supplier of forgotten answers and questions.
>
> *(Chang, 2004, p. 240)*

A complementary science can examine aspects of an area of scientific inquiry that are not the focus of current practices in the area. For example, current work in measurement research that would be labeled normal science by Kuhn (1970) focuses on pressing problems ranging from the operational use of computer adaptive testing (van der Linden & Glas, 2010) to issues related to rater cognition in performance assessments (Myford, 2012). A complementary science of measurement can guide a reconsideration of underlying assumptions and requirements that are taken for granted in the current practice of measurement. It can also seek out original and historical doubts that can be used to reassess the past arguments. A complementary science of measurement can utilize past and current paradigms and research traditions to frame a narrative regarding progress in measurement within the social sciences. In some cases, it is informative to focus on paradoxes to illuminate differences between competing measurement theories that have not been resolved. One example in educational and psychological measurement is the attenuation paradox (Loevinger, 1954). Basically, the attenuation paradox appears when the psychometric guidelines of maximizing reliability coefficients yield a decrease in validity coefficients (Engelhard, 1993).

What Are Epistemic Iterations?

> Certain methods of mathematical computation correct themselves, so that if an error be committed, it is only necessary to keep right on, and it will be corrected in the end. . . . This calls to mind one of the most wonderful features of reasoning . . . namely, that reasoning tends to correct itself.
>
> *(Charles Sanders Pierce, as cited in Chang, 2004, p. 45)*

Charles Sanders Pierce introduced the idea that progress in reasoning and theory can be improved iteratively. As pointed out earlier, epistemic iterations can be viewed as a process for evaluating progress in science (Chang, 2004). In mathematics and numerical methods, an iteration is a problem-solving method in which an initial guess at the correct answer is used to start a set of successive approximations that are used to solve an equation or problem with a certain level of accuracy. Basically, Pierce extended this principle to include scientific theories with his proposal that progress can also take place iteratively in the area of ideas. This process is similar to a Hegelian dialectic in which a thesis provokes an antithesis and opposing ideas generate a synthesis superior to either of the original ideas.

Within the context of measurement theory, the idea of epistemic iterations has been briefly explored by Engelhard and Behizadeh (2012) in their consideration of consensus definitions of validity. Progress in clarifying foundational concepts in measurement and selecting competing measurement theories can be achieved through an iterative process that is evaluated in terms of key goals, such as the following five values for theory choice: accuracy, consistency, scope, simplicity, and fruitfulness (Kuhn, 1977). Of course, the evaluative criteria for these key values are a matter of judgment and choice among a community of scholars. We suggest the use of the principles of invariant measurement as the source of key epistemic goals (Chang, 2004). In the development of a complementary science of measurement, it is also important to recognize that other choices for key epistemic goals might be used to judge progress in measurement.

What Are Thought Experiments with Ideal Types?

> The dreamer, the builder of castles in the air, the poet of social or technological utopias all experiment in thought. Even the respectable merchant as well as the devoted inventor or researcher does the same thing.
>
> *(Mach, 1926/1976, p. 451)*

Einstein is famous for his use of thought experiments in the formulation of his theories of general and specific relativity. Isaacson (2007) points out that

> One thing that we can note with some confidence is Einstein's main starting point . . . he repeatedly said that his path toward the theory of relativity began with his thought experiment at age 16 about what it would be like to ride at the speed of light alongside a light beam.
>
> *(p. 114)*

A thought experiment (*Gedankenexperiment* in German) can be literally viewed as an experiment conducted in the "laboratory of the mind" (Brown, 1991, p. 122). As pointed out by Norton (1991), Einstein's thought experiments are grounded in a particular philosophical perspective that stresses that "a theory should not use theoretical terms which have no observational support" (p. 135).

What are the functions of thought experiments? For example, Kuhn (1981) has argued that thought experiments can provide scientists with ways to retrieve memories of anomalies that have been ignored. This view fits very nicely with the idea that a complementary science of measurement can revisit various paradoxes, such as the attenuation paradox (Loevinger, 1954), that were not resolved in a satisfying manner or that the underlying principles were not clarified to an adequate extent.

We view thought experiments as related to the concept of ideal types. It is close to the use of the term by the physicist Ernest Mach (1926/1976). In essence, Mach suggested articulating imaginary scenarios and models that are idealized in some fashion, and then he suggested the design of experiments to examine the observable consequences of these studies. A key component of a thought experiment for Mach is the comparison between these imaginary scenarios viewed as ideal types based on a theoretical perspective and the actual results of the experimental studies. It is clear that this epistemological strategy is similar to the use of ideal types in the social sciences by the German sociologist Max Weber. Coser (1977) described Weber's ideal type as follows:

> an ideal type is an analytical construct that serves the investigator as a measuring rod to ascertain similarities as well as deviations in concrete cases. It provides the basic method for comparative study . . . Ideal types enable one to construct hypotheses linking them with the conditions that brought the phenomenon or event into prominence.
>
> *(pp. 223–224)*

According to Mach (1926/1976),

> it can be seen that the basic method of the thought experiment is just like that of a physical experiment, namely, the method of variation. By varying the circumstances (continuously, if possible) the range of validity of an *idea* (expectation) related to these circumstances is increased. Through modification and specialization of the circumstance the *idea* is modified and specialized and these procedures vary.
>
> *(p. 453, italics added)*

Cooper (2005) has argued that thought experiments can be viewed in terms of a set of ideal scenarios created in terms of a series of *what if statements*. In measurement for example, Lazarsfeld (1959) proposed the concept of reliability within an individual with the following thought experiment:

> Suppose we ask an individual, Mr. Brown, repeatedly whether he is in favor of the United Nations; suppose further that after each question we "wash his brains" and ask him the same question again. Because Mr. Brown is not certain as to how he feels about the United Nations, he will sometimes give a favorable and sometimes an unfavorable answer. Having gone through this procedure many times, we then compute the proportion of times Mr. Brown was in favor of the United Nations
>
> *(Lazarsfeld, 1959, p. 493)*

Summary

In summary, it is important in creating a complementary science of measurement in the social sciences that researchers begin to build a framework with a common language guided by the epistemic goals of invariant measurement. Measurement theories for raters and ratings within the test-score and scaling traditions are discussed in Chapter Three. In some cases, it is useful to treat Classical Test Theory as synonymous with the test-score tradition and modern test theory as represented by Item Response Theory with the scaling tradition. For the purposes of this book, we classify measurement theories into test–score and scaling traditions with the potential for viewing theories from both traditions as contributing to the creation of measures in the human sciences that meet the requirements of invariant measurement. The two traditions are described in detail in Chapter Three.

The creation of a complementary science of measurement for the social sciences can be used to gauge progress in the solution of persistent problems in assessment systems. The concepts of complementary science, epistemic iterations, and thought experiments with ideal-type models can be used to view the history and philosophy of measurement, and to examine the development of the science of measurement in the social sciences over time. Complementary sciences are "at once historical, philosophical, and scientific" (Chang, 2004, p. 235). A complementary science of measurement is a *science* that can contribute to improvement in measurement theory and use with broader implications for the measurement community.

History and philosophy of science support the identification of various paradigms (Kuhn, 1970), programs of research (Lakatos, 1971), and research traditions (Laudan, 1977) that dominate research, theory, and practice within an area of study, such as measurement in the social sciences. Research traditions define world views that articulate the problems, provide guidance for problem solution, and define the epistemic goals (e.g., invariance) used in the evaluation of progress. Complementary sciences offer several methods including epistemic iterations and thought experiments that aid researchers in understanding current dominant research traditions and fostering progress in the solution of measurement problems. One of the purposes of this book is to suggest the creation of a complementary science of measurement that builds on history and philosophy of the field with a critical eye on fostering progress in social science research based on the principles of invariant measurement. As with other areas of measurement, this book focuses primarily on the implications of these ideas for rater-mediated assessments.

Measurement Problems in the Social Sciences

> One can only understand a system of ideas when one knows, in detail, the problems to which it is addressed.
>
> *(Laudan, 1977, p. 176)*

What Are the Persistent Measurement Issues in the Social Sciences?

Since science is defined here in terms of problem solving, it is important to consider the major problems that have motivated the creation and use of various measurement theories in the social sciences. Recently, Engelhard (2013) discussed a set of perennial measurement issues that appear repeatedly in the history of measurement and assessment systems. The measurement issues that are identified are based on an earlier list of persistent issues in educational testing described by Hattie, Jaeger, and Bond (1999). Hattie and his colleagues identified five categories for thinking about persistent measurement issues: conceptual models of measurement, test and item development, test administration, test use, and test evaluation. We modified these general categories, and used them in the last chapter of Engelhard (2013) to summarize and suggest future areas of research related to invariant measurement. The five general categories that we use for thinking about persistent measurement issues are:

1. Measurement models,
2. Use of assessments,
3. Assessment development,
4. Administration of assessments, and
5. Evaluation of assessments.

These issues are shown in Figure 2.1. We have placed the three foundational areas in the center of the figure in order to suggest that addressing the five

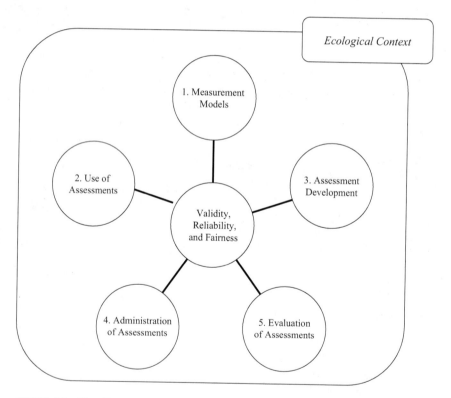

FIGURE 2.1 Five Persistent Measurement Issues and Three Foundational Areas of Measurement in the Social Sciences

Note: Guiding principles based on the requirements of invariant measurement.

issues interacts with the three foundational areas from the *Standards for Educational and Psychological Testing*. These three foundational areas are discussed in the next section. Procedures and practices related to the five issues buttress the warrants related to the reliability, validity, and fairness of an assessment system. We have also tried to suggest in this figure that ecological context plays a role in understanding the measurement issues and three foundational areas. The ecological context includes the purpose of the assessment system, as well as the intended meaning and uses of the scores obtained from the assessments. Context also includes the decision context, such as whether test scores are used for high-stakes decisions, and the ecological validity of the overall assessment system.

Measurement models provide the underlying conceptual and theoretical frameworks that guide the theory and practice of assessment in the social sciences. Measurement models function as paradigms in the sense of Kuhn (1970). In this book, we group measurement models into broad paradigms or research traditions called the *test-score* and *scaling traditions*. As will be shown in later chapters, measurement models and the research tradition within which the program of research is grounded serve to focus the attention of researchers on a particular set of problems, solutions, and criteria for determining the psychometric quality of an assessment system. In some cases, the two research traditions have diametrically opposing perspectives on an issue. For example, rating quality from the perspective of the test-score tradition evaluates ratings primarily in terms of rater agreement indices, while the scaling tradition views ideal raters as experts who are consistent in their interpretation and judgments of human performance. These two paradigms (test-score and scaling traditions) provide a way to organize our thinking about a set of apparently dissimilar measurement models that share some common underlying features related to their historical and philosophical roots. The test-score and scaling traditions share a concern regarding invariant measurement, although they approach the issues and problems from different perspectives. A careful consideration of each tradition is conducted in later chapters with the goals of clarifying the differences and highlighting similarities that may form a basis for the next epistemic iteration in our views of invariant measurement and progress in the social sciences.

The intended and appropriate *use of assessments* includes recognizing that assessment systems are not built in a vacuum—they are designed to serve a variety of purposes and inform key decisions in a variety of contexts. As suggested in Figure 2.1, the intended interpretations and uses of test scores by users are closely linked to every phase of the assessment process from the specification of content, through choices regarding measurement models, to criteria used to examine the psychometric quality of the assessment. The use of assessments reflects the purposes and intended uses of the scores obtained from an assessment system, and each component should form an integral aspect to warrant the appropriate interpretations and uses. As Haertel (2013) has pointed out, it is also important to consider both *direct and indirect* uses of the test scores. The use of assessments includes a careful consideration of how to create Wright maps and other ways to enhance the communicative value of the scores for the intended purposes. In the *Standards for Educational and Psychological Testing*, four application areas (educational testing and assessment, psychological testing and assessment, policy uses of test results, and workplace testing and assessment) are discussed in detail.

Assessment development functions to provide guidance for the design of items, tasks, and other opportunities to observe behavior from persons in order to draw inferences about person locations on an underlying continuum. Items can be broadly conceived as situations designed to obtain systematic information about person locations on a construct including various forms of selected- and constructed-response items or tasks. Assessment development includes a consideration of the purpose of the assessment system along with the development of test specifications based on the intended interpretations and uses of the scores. Assessment development includes field testing, selection, and evaluation of items including scoring rubrics and overall evaluation of the assessment system. The four building blocks defined by Wilson (2005) highlight the close connections between measurement models and the assessment development process. Recent research on the principles of universal design (Johnstone, Altman, & Thurlow, 2006) and evidence-centered design (Huff, Steinberg, & Matts, 2010; Mislevy & Haertel, 2006) hold promise for connecting the principles of invariant measurement and sound guidance for assessment development.

Administration of assessments addresses issues regarding how persons provide responses to the items, tasks, and other aspects of the assessment systems. Traditionally, most assessments have used a paper-and-pencil format with the tests administered in large group settings. The primary item type has been some form of a selected-response item. The classical group administration of assessments is being replaced with computer-administered assessments, and also in some cases adaptive assessments that provide a targeted set of items based on earlier estimates of a person's location on the underlying continuum. Frequently, the proper administration of an assessment includes considerations such as maintaining a level of standardization of processes in order to maintain invariance of score meaning across various settings for different persons. Recent research on accommodations related to test fairness have moved from the definition of a fair administration based on all students taking the test in exactly the same way to a perspective that suggests that a fair assessment provides appropriate accommodations that allow each student to demonstrate what they know and can do without a strict adherence to standardized administrations for everyone.

The *evaluation of assessments* depends in a critical way on the three foundational areas of validity, reliability, and fairness. As discussed later in this chapter, these three foundational areas are defined and evaluated in different ways depending on the measurement model and research tradition used to guide the evaluative process. There are discontinuities and conflicting recommendations coming from different research traditions. For example, the test-score tradition defines reliability in a way that can lead to an attenuation paradox when an increase in the reliability of test scores leads to decreases in the validity of the test scores (Loevinger, 1954). The attenuation paradox is not necessarily observed when assessment systems are evaluated from the perspective of the scaling tradition.

What Are the Foundational Areas of Testing?

During the preparation of this book, the new edition of the *Standards for Educational and Psychological Testing* (AERA, APA, & NCME, 2014) was being discussed and revised with a new set of test standards published in 2014. The *Standards for Educational and Psychological Testing* reflect a consensus definition of psychometrically sound and legally defensible measurement principles and practices. In many ways, the *Standards for Educational and Psychological Testing* serve to guide the communities of practice in evaluating the problem-solving effectiveness of an assessment system. We have systematically tied many facets of this book on invariant measurement to these new *Standards for Educational and Psychological Testing*. In particular, the *Standards for Educational and Psychological Testing* identify three foundational areas for testing:

- Validity,
- Reliability, precision, and errors of measurement, and
- Fairness in testing.

The three foundational areas primarily map into the criteria that are used to define measurement quality. These three foundational areas interact with the procedures and processes that reflect how measurement issues are framed, addressed, and evaluated by the measurement community. The next few paragraphs briefly summarize the three foundational issues based on the *Standards for Educational and Psychological Testing*. The *Standards for Educational and Psychological Testing* state that the guiding principles are applicable to all tests and test users. The perspectives on the three foundational issues embodied in the *Standards for Educational and Psychological Testing* are very important because they represent consensus definitions used by the measurement community. Part III of this book describes the foundational areas for ratings scales with Chapters Five, Six, and Seven focusing on validity, reliability, and fairness issues, respectively. Chapter Eight provides a detailed case study on middle grades writing assessments related to evidence regarding the validity, reliability, and fairness of ratings.

1. How Is Validity Defined in Test Standards?

In many ways, current views of validity have been so broadly defined that the concept is on the verge of becoming irrelevant to many of the historical and philosophical concerns that have emerged over the past century. From the perspective of the development of a complementary science of measurement, it is clearly time for the next epistemic iteration (Engelhard & Behizadeh, 2012). Early views of validity had a great deal of intuitive appeal. For example, validity for Guilford (1936) "pertains to the truth of the ratings—how nearly they represent evaluations of the trait" (p. 279). Later evidence-centered definitions of validity defined the concept in an empirical manner as the relationship between test scores and an agreed-upon criterion measure. The current consensus view of validity as represented in the *Standards for Educational and Psychological Testing* (2014) is as follows:

> Validity refers to the degree to which evidence and theory support the interpretations of test scores for proposed uses of tests. Validity is, therefore, the most fundamental consideration in developing and evaluating tests. The process of validation involves accumulating relevant evidence to provide a sound scientific basis for the proposed score interpretations.
>
> *(p. 11)*

The guiding principle related to validity is that a "clear articulation of each intended test interpretation for a specified use should be set forth, and appropriate validity evidence in support of each intended interpretation should be provided" (AERA, APA, & NCME, 2014, p. 13). It is important to note that the focus in the first half of the 20th century on reliability of test scores was in fact a remnant of philosophical views of test scores embodied in Classical Test Theory (Stigler, 1992). As pointed out earlier, the mean of a set of repeated observations was viewed as a valid indicator of a person's true score on the variable being measured. It seems that validity was not viewed as an analytically separate concept from reliability. This section provided a preliminary introduction to the area of validity. The choice of measurement model also plays a crucial role in determining the indices that are used to evaluate the warrants for the proposed meaning and use of the test scores related to validity evidence related to the intended purposes of the assessment system. Chapter Five provides more detail on the concept of validity for rater-mediated assessments.

2. How Are Reliability, Precision, and Errors of Measurement Defined in the Test Standards?

This foundational area focuses on reliability, precision, and errors of measurement. The authors of the *Standards for Educational and Psychological Testing* argue that reliability has been defined in two major ways:

> First, the term has been used to refer to the reliability coefficients of classical test theory, defined as the correlation between scores on two equivalent forms . . .

Second the term has been used in a more general sense, to refer to the consistency or precision of scores across replications of a testing procedure, regardless of how this consistency is estimated or reported (e.g., in terms of standard errors, reliability coefficients per se, generalizability coefficients, error/tolerance ratios, information functions, or various indices of classification consistency).

(AERA, APA, & NCME, 2014, p. 33)

In order to reduce the ambiguity among different definitions, the authors of the *Standards for Educational and Psychological Testing* suggest using the term *reliability/precision* to denote "consistency of the scores across instances of the testing procedure" (p. 33), and the term *reliability coefficient* to refer to the "reliability coefficients of classical test theory" (p. 33). This book argues that the concepts of consistency and dependability across replications related to this foundational area (reliability, precision, and errors of measurement) can be productively viewed through the lens of invariant measurement. Essentially, research on reliability mirrors many if not most of the issues encountered in the quest for invariant measurement in the social sciences. The guiding principle related to reliability is stated as follows: "Appropriate evidence of reliability/precision should be provided for the interpretation for each intended score use" (AERA, APA, & NCME, 2014, p. 42). In evaluating this foundational area, as well as the areas related to validity and fairness, the choice of measurement model plays a crucial role in determining the indices that are used to evaluate psychometric quality of the assessment system. Chapter Six provides more detail on the concept of reliability for rater-mediated assessments.

3. How Is Fairness Defined in the Test Standards?

The last foundational area addresses issues related to fairness in testing. In many ways fairness is embedded within the broader view of validity; however, a variety of issues that emerged in the late 20th century related to social justice drove a justifiable concern with fairness as a dominant area of psychometric research. Fairness is defined as related to the appropriate uses of assessment results usually in the form of test scores. The guiding principle related to fairness is stated as follows:

All steps in the testing process, including test design, validation, development, administration, and scoring procedures, should be designed in such a manner as to minimize construct irrelevant variance and to promote valid score interpretations for the intended uses for all examinees in the intended population.

(AERA, APA, & NCME, 2014, p. 63)

There are four clusters related to fairness in assessment identified in the *Standards for Educational and Psychological Testing*. The recommendations include the following considerations in the creation of fair assessments:

1. Test design, development, administration, and scoring procedures that minimize barriers to valid score interpretations for the widest possible range of individuals and relevant subgroups.
2. Validity of test score interpretations for the intended uses for intended examinee population.
3. Accommodations to remove construct-irrelevant and support valid interpretations of scores for their intended uses.
4. Safeguards against inappropriate score interpretations for intended uses.

(p. 63)

Chapter Seven provides more detail on the concept of fairness for rater-mediated assessments.

In summary, each of these three foundational areas from the *Standards for Educational and Psychological Testing* is developed in more detail throughout the book. As pointed out earlier, one of main themes of this book is that most (if not all) of the foundational issues and concerns about measurement can be productively viewed through the lens of invariant measurement. A second theme is that the definition of the problem, as well as the strategies for posing and answering measurement questions, are embedded within the different measurement traditions or paradigms. Different measurement theories play a key role in framing both the issues and evidence used for evaluating the psychometric quality of a measurement system. For example, the test-score tradition has focused almost exclusively on issues related to reliability and errors of measurement, while the scaling tradition has sought the identification and creation of a continuum to represent constructs in the social sciences.

The three foundational areas of validity, reliability, and fairness are deeply intertwined with the research paradigm underlying the measurement models being used in assessment systems. Both research traditions (test-score and scaling) have implicit and explicit implications for conceptualizing the three foundational areas relative to invariant measurement. Each of these foundational issues is closely examined in future chapters from the perspective of invariant measurement with raters using rating scales.

Summary and Discussion

> The solution of a maximum number of empirical problems, and the generation of a minimum number of conceptual problems and anomalies is the central aim of science.
>
> *(Laudan, 1977, p. 111)*

This chapter has provided a brief overview of a perspective on progress in the social sciences. Following the approach of Laudan (1977), we define progress in terms of improvements in the problem-solving capabilities of various theoretical perspectives. Measurement theories play defining roles in research and practices in the social sciences, and it is our contention that it is essential for social scientists to develop an understanding and appreciation for how major measurement theories have evolved over time. In order to track progress in measurement theories over time, we propose developing a complementary science of measurement based on Chang (2004).

Another theme running throughout this chapter is that it is essential to consider the persistent measurement problems and foundational issues undergirding assessment systems. We have briefly discussed five categories for thinking about measurement issues (Measurement models, Use of assessments, Assessment development, Administration of assessments, and Evaluation of assessments) that guide forthcoming chapters and comparisons of measurement theories. Since measurement theories are defined from a scientific perspective as providing solutions for a variety of persistent assessment issues, it is essential to identify the problems and research questions that our theories are designed to address. It is also important to acknowledge that measurement theories not only provide solutions to measurement problems, but measurement theories also provide definitions of the problems and identify evaluative criteria that are used to provide warrants regarding progress and success in defining measurement challenges in our social science research and praxis.

References

American Educational Research Association [AERA], American Psychological Association [APA], & National Council on Measurement in Education [NCME]. (2014). *Standards for educational and psychological testing.* Washington, DC: AERA.

Behizadeh, N., & Engelhard, G. (2014). *What is a valid writing assessment?* Paper presented at the International Objective Measurement Workshop, Philadelphia, PA.

Brown, J. R. (1991). Thought experiments: A platonic account. In T. Horowitz & G. Massey (Eds.), *Thought experiments in science and philosophy* (pp. 119–128). Lanham, MD: Rowman and Littlefield.

Chang, H. (2004). *Inventing temperature: Measurement and scientific progress.* Oxford: Oxford University Press, Inc.

Cooper, R. (2005). Thought experiments. *Metaphilosophy, 36*(3), 328–347.

Coser, L. A. (1977). *Masters of sociological thought: Ideas in historical and social context* (2nd ed.). Fort Worth, TX: Harcourt Brace Jovanovich.

Easton, J. Q. (2012). *How the testing community can help advance education policy and practice.* Presentation at the annual meeting of the National Council on Measurement in Education, Vancouver, BC, Canada.

Engelhard, G. (1993). What is the attenuation paradox? *Rasch Measurement Transactions, 6*(4), 257.

Engelhard, G. (2013). *Invariant measurement: Using Rasch models in the social, behavioral, and health sciences.* New York: Routledge.

Engelhard, G., & Behizadeh, N. (2012). Epistemic iterations and consensus definitions of validity. *Measurement: Interdisciplinary Research and Perspectives, 10*(1), 55–58.

Garfield, E. (1985). The life and career of George Sarton: The father of the history of science. *Journal of the History of the Behavioral Sciences, 21*(2), 107–117.

Guilford, J. P. (1936). *Psychometric method.* New York: McGraw-Hill.

Haertel, E. (2013). How is testing supposed to improve schooling? *Measurement: Interdisciplinary Research and Perspectives, 11*, 1–18.

Hattie, J., Jaeger, R. M., & Bond, L. (1999). Persistent methodological questions in educational testing. In A. Iran-Nejad & P. D. Pearson (Eds.), *Review of research in education* (Vol. 24, pp. 393–446). Thousand Oaks, CA: Sage.

Huff, K., Steinberg, L., & Matts, T. (2010). The promises and challenges of implementing evidence-centered design in large-scale assessment. *Applied Measurement in Education, 23*(4), 310–324.

Isaacson, W. (2007). *Einstein: His life and universe.* New York: Simon & Shuster.

Johnstone, C., Altman, J., & Thurlow, M. (2006). *A state guide to the development of universally designed assessments.* Minneapolis: University of Minnesota, National Center on Educational Outcomes.

Kuhn, T. S. (1970). *The structure of scientific revolutions* (2nd ed.). Princeton, NJ: Princeton University Press.

Kuhn, T. S. (1977). *The essential tension: Selected studies in scientific tradition and change.* Chicago: University of Chicago Press.

Kuhn, T. S. (1981). A function for thought experiments. In I. Hacking (Ed.), *Scientific revolutions* (pp. 6–27). Oxford: Oxford University Press.

Lakatos, I. (1971). History of science and its rational reconstructions. *Boston Studies in the Philosophy of Science, 8*, 91–136.

Laudan, L. (1977). *Progress and its problems: Toward a theory of scientific change.* Berkeley: University of California Press.

Lazarsfeld, P. F. (1959). Latent structure analysis. In S. Koch (Ed.), *Psychology: A study of a science* (Vol. 3, pp. 476–543). New York: McGraw-Hill.

Loevinger, J. (1954). The attenuation paradox in test theory. *Psychological Bulletin, 51*(5), 493–504.

Mach, E. (1926/1976). On thought experiments. In E. Mach (Ed.), *Knowledge and error: Sketches on the psychology of enquiry* (pp. 449–457). Dordrecht: D. Reidel Publishing Company [Translation of *Erkenntnis und Irrtum* (5th edition, 1926)].

Mislevy, R. J., & Haertel, G. D. (2006). Implications of evidence-centered design for educational testing. *Educational Measurement: Issues and Practice, 25*(4), 6–20.

Myford, C. M. (2012). Rater cognition research: Some possible directions for the future. *Educational Measurement: Issues and Practice, 31*(3), 48–49.

Norton, J. (1991). Thought experiments in Einstein's work. In T. Horowitz & G. Massey (Eds.), *Thought experiments in science and philosophy* (pp. 129–148). Lanham, MD: Rowman & Littlefield.

Sarton, G. (1957). *The study of the history of science.* New York: Dover Publications.

Shavelson, R. J., & Towne, L. (Eds.). (2002). *Scientific research in education.* Washington, DC: National Academy Press.

Stigler, S. M. (1992). A historical view of statistical concepts in psychology and educational research. *American Journal of Education, 101*(1), 60–70.

van der Linden, W. J., & Glas, C. A. W. (2010). *Elements of adaptive testing.* New York, NY: Springer.

Wilson, M. (2005). *Constructing measures: An item response modeling approach* (2nd ed.). Mahwah, NJ: Erlbaum.

PART II

Theories of Measurement and Judgment for Rating Scales

3

MEASUREMENT MODELS FOR RATER-MEDIATED ASSESSMENTS

A Tale of Two Research Traditions

> A successful research tradition is one which leads, via its component theories, to the adequate solution of an increasing range of empirical and conceptual problems.
> *(Laudan, 1977, p. 82)*

Current measurement practices and research within the context of rater-mediated assessments tend to be dominated by two measurement theories: Generalizability (G) Theory and Rasch Measurement Theory. This chapter provides a comparison of these two measurement theories viewed as component theories within two broader research paradigms—the test-score and scaling research traditions, respectively. Chapter Two sketched a set of issues related to progress in measurement in the social sciences from a historical and philosophical perspective. This chapter examines two key research traditions that have been found to be useful for organizing our thinking about measurement theories during the 20th century: test-score and scaling traditions (Engelhard, 2013). Further, this chapter considers how the major underlying considerations in rater-mediated assessments can be considered within the two research traditions. As the name implies, the test-score tradition guides psychometric analyses based primarily on scores (such as the sum of correct responses), while the scaling tradition seeks to define and map an underlying continuum to represent a construct.

Overall, this book stresses measurement theories within the scaling tradition, and the roles that these measurement theories play in the development of rater-mediated assessment systems that can support invariant measurement. However, a comparison of research traditions currently used to model raters and ratings provides a context for stressing the advantages of modern measurement theory based on the scaling tradition. Researchers in both traditions are concerned with invariance, although from different theoretical perspectives using different measurement models with different approaches and strategies.

The specific issues and questions addressed in this chapter are organized as follows:

- Research traditions in measurement for rater-mediated assessments
  1. What is the test-score tradition?
  2. What is the scaling tradition?

- Comparative perspective on the two traditions for rater-mediated assessments
  1. What is Generalizability (G) Theory?
  2. What is Rasch Measurement Theory?
  3. Summary and discussion

After describing the two research traditions, we describe two component theories within these research traditions with implications for evaluating rater-mediated assessments. We illustrate the theories with a common dataset that examines help-seeking behavior in mathematics (Kenderski, 1983). The illustrative analyses highlight how rater-mediated assessments can be evaluated within the test-score and scaling traditions.

Research Traditions in Measurement for Rater-Mediated Assessments

> What we need, if our appraisals of [alternative theories] are to be at all reliable, is serious historical scholarship devoted to the various research traditions in a given field of inquiry.
>
> *(Laudan, 1977, p. 194)*

Classical and modern measurement theories can be viewed as representing distinct paradigms or research traditions (Andrich, 2004; Kuhn, 1970; Laudan, 1977). In previous work on measurement theory (Engelhard, 2013), it has been found useful to organize theories into two paradigms called the test-score and scaling traditions. The test-score tradition aligns with classical measurement theories. Modern measurement traditions on the other hand tend to more closely align with the scaling tradition and recent advances to Item Response Theory. The distinctions between test-score and scaling traditions go back to early work by Mosier (1940, 1941) who highlighted the potential for overlap between psychophysics and mental test theory. The distinction also appears in a review chapter by Torgerson (1961) that stressed the distinctions between test theory and scaling. These two research traditions share a common concern with various aspects of invariant measurement. One goal of this chapter is to encourage readers to see the connections between test-score and scaling traditions, and to consider the advantages and disadvantages of each of these traditions for building assessment systems in the human sciences based on the principles of invariance.

The two research traditions (test-score and scaling) function like paradigms. As pointed out by Kuhn (1970), paradigms can be conceptualized as "universally recognized scientific achievements that for a time provide model problems and solutions to a community of practitioners" (p. viii). According to Kuhn (1970), paradigms include laws, theories, applications, and instrumentation, and "the paradigm functions by permitting the *replication* of examples" (p. 23, emphasis added). Laudan (1977) argued that the concept of paradigms can also be applied to social sciences, and he called them *research traditions*—we use Laudan's term in this book. This chapter challenges the reader to consider two different research traditions in measurement within the social sciences in terms of their applications in the context of rater-mediated assessments. The major goal of this chapter is to foster a deeper conceptual understanding of invariant measurement for rater-mediated assessments grounded across research traditions.

Engelhard (2013) identified the essential features of the test-score tradition as consisting of a test-score focus using linear models with the major goal of estimating variance components (error components) related to a variety of aspects of an assessment system. Examples of component measurement theories within the test-score tradition include Classical Test Theory (Gulliksen, 1950), G theory (Cronbach et al., 1972), traditional factor analysis (Thurstone, 1947), and structural equation modeling (Bollen, 1989; Joreskog, 1974).

On the other hand, the essential features of the scaling tradition (Engelhard, 2013) include a focus on the person-cue rating process based on non-linear models using a logistic function with the goal of locating persons, raters, and cues on an underlying latent variable or continuum. It cannot be stressed enough that a distinctive feature of the scaling tradition is the creation of a line to represent a latent variable or construct. Measurement research in the scaling tradition includes early work in psychophysics and absolute scaling (Torgerson, 1958), Rasch Measurement Theory (Rasch, 1960/1980), Item Response Theory (Lord, 1980), Nonparametric Item Response Theory (Mokken, 1971), and modern factor analyses in the form of Multidimensional Item Response Theory (Reckase, 2009).

1. What Is the Test-Score Tradition?

> The investigator who tests a person twice is likely to obtain scores that differ . . . the observed score is seen as the sum of a "true score" and a purely random "error."
>
> *(Cronbach et al., 1972, p. 1)*

The test-score tradition starts from the definition of an observed score as being decomposable into two parts: a true score and an error score. Assuming that the *true score* is invariant over replications, then any difference in observed scores is attributable to random and systematic variation in error scores. Classical Test Theory is driven by this idea, and the same basic decomposition drives how observed scores are typically modeled from the perspective of measurement theories within the test-score tradition.

Scores can be defined in a variety of ways. One purpose of a test score is to provide a summary index of performances from a person across various samples of behavior under different conditions. Most people are familiar with the calculation of a test score based on a simple summation of correct responses to a set of dichotomously scored multiple-choice items (incorrect = 0, correct = 1). Higher counts of correct responses imply higher levels of achievement on the construct represented by items on the test. A similar process can be used when a person's responses are summarized with a rating scale. It is possible to sum the ratings from each observation or performance, and define this as the person's score. It is also possible to summarize scores and ratings as mean scores for both person and items. In some cases, it is also useful to define a person's score as a percentage of the total possible points. As pointed out by Edgeworth (1890) within the context of ratings and rater-mediated assessments:

> the *true or standard mark* of any piece of work, is the average of the marks given by a large number of competent examiners equally proficient in the subject, and instructed as to the character and purpose of the examination . . . The error committed is the difference between the mark in question and the ideal mean above described . . . If any one denies that the mean of a great number of judgments constitutes a true standard of taste, he is free to indulge his own philosophical views.
>
> *(p. 461, italics added)*

This quote embodies a continuing theme within the test-score tradition that an average across assessment opportunities defined by cues represents a true score. This may be one of the reasons why measurement theories in the test-score tradition blur the important distinction between precision and accuracy. For example, Shewhart (1939) within the context of quality control stressed that increasing precision is conceptually distinct from increasing the accuracy of a measurement process. As pointed out in numerous introductory textbooks on measurement, reliability is necessary but not sufficient for supporting inferences about the validity of test scores for the intended uses. This point is also evident within the test-score tradition as shown in the attenuation paradox. Briefly, the attenuation paradox (Loevinger, 1954) illustrates how increasing reliability can lead to a concomitant decrease in the validity of the scores for the intended purposes of the assessment system.

It is well known that there is variability within persons, and that this variation may lead to different observed scores over multiple observations and occasions even when the underlying true score is invariant. The measurement theories within the test-score tradition trace their historical roots to Classical Test Theory (CTT). CTT makes use of the foundational idea that there are observed scores for a person that may or may not vary over replications, and that there is an underlying and stable true score, T_n, that is invariant over replications. The basic equation of CTT can be written as follows:

$$X_n = T_n + E_n \qquad (3.1)$$

where

X_n = the observed score for person n,
T_n = the true score for person n, and
E_n = the error score for person n.

The error score reflects measurement error that is attributed to within-person random variation over replications. If the measurement errors are random with a mean of zero, then

$$\hat{T}_n = \frac{\sum_{i=1}^{r} X_r}{r}$$

(3.2)

and the mean observed scores over r replications is defined as an estimate of an invariant true score for person n. This simple tautology (Brennan, 2011; Lord, 1980; Traub, 1997) has dominated much of the work in measurement during most of the 20th century. It also underlies the measurement theories that we classify within the test-score tradition.

Early work on rating scales within the test-score tradition did not distinguish between ratings and test scores. Ratings were typically obtained from raters who recorded their judgments with some form of rating scale. The role of errors of measurement in judgments is captured in historical narratives that detail the discrepancies in observations between astronomers and their assistants that led to the notion of a personal equation. Stigler (1986) provides an informative narrative of these historical events that we recommend for the interested reader.

Gulliksen (1950) derived the basic equations of Classical Test Theory from two different perspectives with one derivation based on random errors and the second derivation based on true scores. Novick (1966) should also be consulted for other approaches to deriving the basic equations underlying Classical Test Theory. As pointed out by Traub (1997), Equation 3.1 is a

> tautology, which is to say the sum of the two quantities on the right-hand side of the equation equal the single quantity on the left-hard side *by definition*. Consequently, the fundamental equation of classical reliability theory can never be proven false as a way of representing or modeling observed scores.
>
> *(p. 19, italics in the original)*

What can we do with this definition? As pointed out by Brennan (2011), measurement theories in the test-score tradition, such as Classical Test Theory and G theory, are tautological—they cannot be empirically tested and refuted with observed data. Even though the measurement models within the test-score tradition cannot be empirically tested and empirically refuted, they do provide useful descriptive and conceptual frameworks. For example, the clarification of the role of replications and the idea of sampling from a larger universe of potential observations are powerful ideas that are related to invariant measurement.

At the end of the day, many of the measurement models within the test-score tradition yield a single coefficient that ranges between .00 and 1.00 that represents the reliability or precision of a measurement procedure. These generalizability coefficients include Cronbach's coefficient alpha. These coefficients are interpreted as estimates of the ratio of true score variance to observed score variance. As pointed out above, using the term *true or universe score* may lead to confusion in interpreting these coefficients as being validity coefficients rather than indices of generalizability across replications. It may be preferable to recast the interpretation of these coefficients as *replication coefficients* as suggested by Mellenbergh (1977).

Reliability and generalizability coefficients provide an oversimplification of the measurement process by focusing on limited aspects of the psychometric properties of a rater-mediated assessment system. This simplification has been overwhelmingly attractive to practitioners in the social and behavioral sciences that desire a single index for their scales that provides evidence of the quality of the measures that they have constructed. Unfortunately, this has led to the proliferation of a single index (e.g., coefficient alpha) as the *only index* of measurement quality widely known and used by many practitioners. As pointed out by Cronbach and Shavelson (2004), "I no longer regard the alpha formula as the most appropriate way to examine most data" (p. 403). Cronbach and Shavelson (2004) suggested the use of G theory as an extension of Classical Test Theory. G theory is widely used to examine ratings obtained in rater-mediated assessments, and it is described in more detail later in this chapter.

Table 3.1 provides a comparison between the test-score and scaling traditions on selected topics. The second column includes the key aspects of the test-score tradition. G theory is defined as a component theory within the test-score tradition. The focus on test scores leads to an emphasis on group-level and nomothetic interpretations within G theory with a major goal of estimating error variances used to calculate generalizability coefficients. G theory also can examine in detail the variance of person ordering across replications. G theory also embodies what Embretson and her colleagues (Embretson, 1996; Embretson & Reise, 2000) have called the *old rules of measurement,* such as fixed standard errors of measurement for all scores, score meaning obtained by comparison to a person's position in a norm group, and the sample dependence of item properties. As pointed out earlier, G theory is a tautological model that cannot be refuted by data.

2. What Is the Scaling Tradition?

> The objective of the analysis is . . . to represent the item locations and the respondent values as points on the scale of the quantitative variable.
>
> *(Bock, 1997, p. 21)*

TABLE 3.1 Comparison of Test-Score and Scaling Traditions on Selected Topics

Topics	Test-Score Tradition	Scaling Tradition
Essential Features	Focus on test scores Linear Observed ratings and scores Person is not a facet in the model Goal: Estimate errors variances in order to calculate a generalizability coefficient	Focus on person–cue ratings Non-linear (logits) Latent variable Person is a facet in the model Goal: Locate persons, raters, and cues on a Wright map to define latent construct
Component Measurement Theory	Generalizability Theory	Rasch Measurement Theory
Level of Measurement	Ordinal Scores	Interval Measures
Level of Analysis	• Group level: Nomothetic • Relative standing in a group • Invariance of person ordering across replications • Between-person variability (individual differences)	• Individual level: Idiographic • Invariant location of a person on Wright map • Invariance of person locations over raters and cues • Within- and between-person variability
Philosophical Focus	• Variance (inconsistency) • Identify sources of error variance • Minimize noise • Weak assumptions • Tautology (not refutable by data) • Normal distribution assumed	• Invariance (consistency) • Create a continuum to represent construct • Maximize signal • Strong requirements • Does the data fit the *model?* • No distributional assumptions
Principles of Measurement	Old Rules of Measurement	New Rules of Measurement

(Continued)

TABLE 3.1 (Continued)

Topics	Test-Score Tradition	Scaling Tradition
Model	$X_{nmi} = \mu + \theta_n + \lambda_m + \delta_i + E_{nmi}$	$pr(x = k \mid \theta, \lambda, \delta, \tau) = \pi_{nmij} = \dfrac{\exp\left[\displaystyle\sum_{j=0}^{k}(\theta - \lambda_m - \delta_i - \tau_k)\right]}{\displaystyle\sum_{r=0}^{m_i}\exp\left[\displaystyle\sum_{j=0}^{r}(\theta_n - \lambda_m - \delta_i - \tau_k)\right]}$
Major Outcomes	G Study D Study	Wright Map Model–Data Fit Analyses
Model–Data Fit	No evaluation of model–data fit (tautological)	Good model–data fit is necessary to achieve invariant measurement
Key Computer Program	GENOVA Crick and Brennan (1983)	FACETS (Linacre, 1989)
Representative Theorists	Cronbach et al. (1972)	Rasch (1960/1980)

The scaling tradition starts with the idea of an underlying continuum that can be used to represent an attribute or latent variable. This line provides a definition and useful visual representation of the construct being measured. Component measurement theories within the scaling tradition have their roots in 19th-century psychophysics and continue with modern theories such as the Item Response Theory (Baker & Kim, 2004). Measurement models within the scaling tradition share an emphasis on the construction of an underlying latent variable based on person–item responses for selected-response items (e.g., multiple-choice items), as well as extensions to model person–cue ratings (e.g., writing tasks) for constructed-response items used in rater-mediated assessments.

Measures can be defined in a variety of ways. Within the scaling tradition, measures represent locations on a continuum defined by a set of items or cues that represent assessment opportunities for collecting information about a person's location on the line. This continuum within the context of rater-mediated assessments is illustrated by the Wright map (Figure 1.8) that was presented in Chapter One.

In terms of ratings and rater-mediated assessments, measurement theories within the test-score tradition view ratings and scores as essentially equivalent. The underlying view is that rating points are equidistant on the continuum, and that ratings can be summed to create a total score for each person. This view of uniform categories widths may not match empirical use of a rating scale. Within the scaling tradition, distances may vary between thresholds or category coefficients are empirically estimated to define the size of each rating category. For example, Engelhard and Wind (2013, p. 21) illustrate the distinction between theoretical and empirical rating categories as shown below:

Theoretical and Empirical Rating Categories				
Panel A: Theoretical rating categories				
Ratings	1	2	3	4
Labels	Inadequate	Minimal	Good	Very Good
Theoretical mapping on latent variable	Low $\quad$ (τ_1) $\quad$ (τ_2) $\quad$ (τ_3) $\quad$ High ⭐			
Panel B: Empirical rating categories				
Ratings	1	2	3	4
Labels	Inadequate	Minimal	Good	Very Good
Empirical mapping on latent variable	Low $\quad$ (τ_1) $\quad$ (τ_2) $\quad$ (τ_3) $\quad$ High			

Panel A represents the theoretical mapping that views the rating categories of equal width on the latent variable, while Panel B indicates empirically that a rater may conceptualize and map the rating categories differently from the intended and theoretical perspective. The impact of differential thresholds for defining categories is that some persons are misclassified as Good (persons located near the star) when the accurate rating should be Very Good. Measurement models within the scaling tradition explicitly examine the assumption that the categories are equally spaced on an underlying continuum.

The essential process underlying most scaling models for ratings is to dichotomize the categories in some fashion. For example, models based on Rasch Measurement Theory parameterize the probability of moving across adjacent categories as shown below:

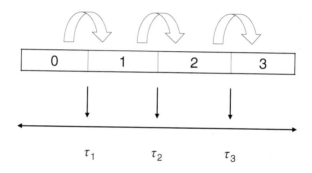

The equation for adjacent categories (ϕ is the conditional probability of moving from x-1 to x) based on the Rasch model is

$$\phi_{nik} = \frac{\pi_{nik}}{\pi_{nik-1} + \pi_{nik}} = \frac{\exp\left[\theta_n - \delta_i - \tau_k\right]}{1 + \exp\left[\theta_n - \delta_i - \tau_k\right]}, \quad k = 1, \ldots, m \tag{3.3}$$

where

π_{nix} = conditional probability of person n on item i being in category x shown in Equation 3.2,
θ_n = location of person n on the latent variable,
δ_i = location of item i on the latent variable, and
τ_m = location of threshold m on the latent variable,

and m is the number of thresholds (number of categories minus one). This is the operating characteristic function that defines the conditional probability of moving across adjacent categories.

The category response function defines the conditional probability of person n being rated in category x on item i. It can be written as:

$$\pi_{nix} = \frac{\exp\left[\sum_{j=0}^{x}(\theta - \delta_i - \tau_k)\right]}{\sum_{k=0}^{m}\exp\left[\sum_{j=0}^{k}(\theta_n - \delta_i - \tau_k)\right]} \,, \, x = 0, \ldots, m \qquad (3.4)$$

where $\tau_0 = 0$, and x is the category index (coded $0, \ldots, m$). Equations 3.1 and 3.2 are called the *Rating Scale Model* (Andrich, 1978; Wright & Masters, 1982).

As pointed out earlier, Table 3.1 provides a comparison between the test-score and scaling traditions on selected topics. The third column includes the key aspects of the scaling tradition. Measurement theories in the scaling tradition focus on person-cue ratings with the goal of locating persons, raters, and cues on a Wright map that is used to define the latent construct. The focus on rater-cue ratings provides the opportunity for idiographic interpretations of ratings. Rasch Measurement Theory as a component theory within the scaling tradition provides the opportunity to obtain invariant measurement within rater-mediated assessments. Rasch Measurement Theory embodies what Embretson and her colleagues (Embretson, 1996; Embretson & Reise, 2000) have called the *new rules of measurement*, such as standard errors of measurement that vary based on information in the ratings, criterion-referenced interpretation of scores based on person locations on the Wright map, and invariant item properties when there is good model-data fit.

In summary, much of the work on rating scales within the test-score tradition views ratings and scores as essentially equivalent. The underlying view is that rating points are equidistant on the continuum, and this view may not be accurate. Distances may vary between the rating categories and thresholds (Bock & Jones, 1968; Engelhard & Wind, 2013), and the measurement models within the scaling tradition explicitly examine and address this particular measurement problem. In essence, modern extensions of the scaling tradition are grounded in psychophysics (Mosier, 1940, 1941) with the explicit inclusion of a person parameter and the recognition that category boundaries may vary. Other models, such as Samejima's Graded Response Model, dichotomize ratings in alternative ways. These alternative scaling models are described and compared in Chapter Nine.

Comparative Perspective on the Two Traditions for Rater-Mediated Assessments

> A research tradition is thus a set of ontological and methodological "do's" and "don'ts."
>
> *(Laudan, 1977, p. 82)*

The two major measurement theories used extensively to evaluate the psychometric quality of rater-mediated assessments are G theory and Rasch Measurement

Theory. In the next few sections, these two measurement theories are described and viewed as component theories of the test-score and scaling traditions, respectively.

It is important to recognize that different measurement research traditions reflect different ways of seeing and understanding the psychometric quality of a rater-mediated assessment. In essence, they represent different stories about the data grounded in different philosophical perspectives. One way to conceptualize G theory is in terms of Venn diagrams. This approach was used in Cronbach et al. (1972), and Venn diagrams continue to reflect an iconic representation of the G theory in current work (Brennan, 2001), because they illustrate the decomposition of variance across various sources of error. Panel A in Figure 3.1 shows how a rater-mediated assessment might be viewed from the perspective of G theory.

On the other hand, Rasch Measurement Theory can be represented by a line displayed in a Wright map that graphically represents the construction of a continuum to represent a construct or latent variable. Panel B in Figure 3.1 shows how a rater-mediated assessment might be viewed from the perspective of Rasch Measurement Theory.

1. What Is Generalizability (G) Theory?

> To ask about rater agreement is to ask how well we can generalize from a set of ratings to ratings by other raters. To ask about the reliability of an essay-examination grade is to ask how representative this is of a grade that might be given to the same paper by other markers, or of grades on another paper by the same subject.
>
> (Cronbach, Rajaratnam, & Gleser, 1963, p. 144)

Classical Test Theory has been a dominant force in psychometrics with its influences continuing into the 21st century. Classical Test Theory is classified within the test-score tradition with a focus on measurement errors. This emphasis on sources of error variance has been extended and elaborated upon within the context of G theory. In essence, G theory can be viewed as an application of fixed, mixed, and random effects models (analysis of variance models) with multiple sources of error. G theory can be viewed as the merging of Classical Test Theory and analysis of variance (Brennan, 1997). One of its first applications was within the context of rater-mediated assessments by Ebel (1951) on the reliability of ratings. Cronbach, Rajaratnam, and Gleser (1963) and Brennan (1983, 2001) are key references regarding G theory. Interest in G theory has waxed and waned since its early development, but there has been a resurgence of interest in applications of G theory within the context of rater-mediated assessment of various performances in the human sciences. The model for G theory is an extension of Classical Test Theory with a decomposition of the undifferentiated error component in Classical Test Theory. The underlying model is shown below for n persons rated by m raters using i items:

$$X_{nmi} = \mu + \theta_n + \lambda_m + \delta_i + E_{nmi}$$

(3.5)

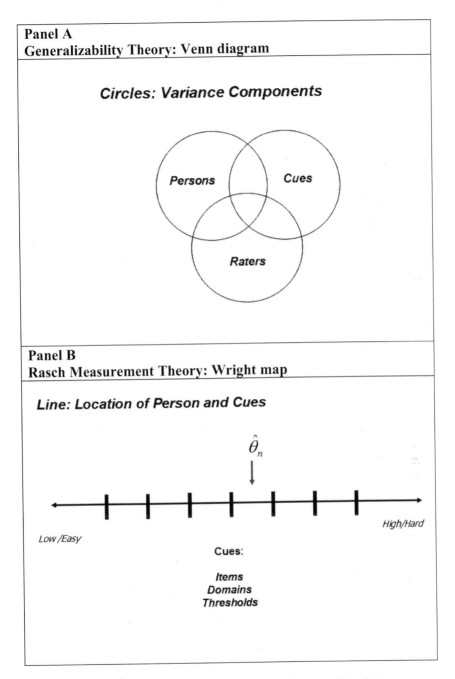

Panel A
Generalizability Theory: Venn diagram

Circles: Variance Components

Persons   *Cues*

Raters

Panel B
Rasch Measurement Theory: Wright map

Line: Location of Person and Cues

$\hat{\theta}_n$

Low /Easy   *High/Hard*

Cues:

Items
Domains
Thresholds

FIGURE 3.1   Iconic Representations of Generalizability Theory and Rasch Measurement Theory

The decomposition of the sum score can also be written as follows:

$$X_{pmi} = \mu + (\mu_p - \mu) + (\mu_m - \mu) + (\mu_i - \mu)$$
$$+ (X_{pmi} - \mu_p - \mu_m - \mu_i + \mu) \tag{3.6}$$

with each of the parameters defined as follows:

μ = grand mean rating,
$\mu_p - \mu$ = person effect (θ),
$\mu_m - \mu$ = rater effect (λ),
$\mu_i - \mu$ = item effect (δ), and

a residual term. In G theory, the observed test score for person n (X_n) is defined as the sum of grand mean of the ratings and a set of deviation scores associated with person, rater, and item effects as shown above. The focus of G theory is on the analysis of sources of error variance. G theory uses the statistical methodology underlying fixed, random, and mixed effects ANOVA models to solve psychometric issues, including the development of efficient measurement procedures. G coefficients can be interpreted as the ratio of true score (corrected for various sources of error variance) to observed score variance.

G theory continues the tradition of Classical Test Theory with a focus on summed ratings rather than the person-cue ratings. The major historical publications on G theory are by Hoyt (1941) and Cronbach et al. (1972). Brennan (1983) provided computer programs (GENOVA) that have enhanced the practical utility of G theory. In essence, G theory extends Classical Test Theory in order to examine systematic and error sources of variation that can be identified from undifferentiated error scores. The essential steps in conducting G theory analyses are described in Briesch et al. (2014). Hendrickson and Yin (2010) provide criteria that can be used for evaluating studies conducted within this research tradition.

In order to illustrate G theory, a small dataset is used. These data are shown in Table 3.2. Shavelson and Webb (1991) used G theory to analyze these data based on a dissertation by Kenderski (1983). This dataset was also analyzed with the Rasch model by Linacre (1996), and it provides the opportunity to examine a common dataset with two different measurement theories representing different research traditions. Shavelson and Webb (1991) described the Kenderski dataset as

an example of the data generated by behavior observation. Nine-year-old children were observed while solving mathematics problems in class. The children's conversations while doing the work were tape-recorded. Raters read transcript of the tapes and counted the number of times each child asked for help from other children. All children were observed (taped) on the same two occasions 3 weeks apart. The same two raters coded all transcripts.

(p. 8)

TABLE 3.2 Counts of Help-Seeking Behaviors in Solving Mathematics Problems

Raters	1		2		
Occasions ·	1	2	1	2	Sum Score
Persons					
1	0	1	1	2	4
2	3	4	1	2	10
3	2	2	1	0	5
4	1	2	0	1	4
5	1	2	2	1	6
6	4	4	3	4	15
7	1	1	2	1	5
8	2	2	0	0	4
9	1	1	1	2	5
10	1	1	1	0	3
11	1	2	1	1	5
12	1	2	1	1	5
13	2	1	1	1	5

Note: The judged counts can be viewed as ratings for the purposes of the illustrative analyses. This is a persons × raters × occasions design.

Source: Kenderski (1983).

The Kenderski study focuses on individual differences in requests for help in solving mathematics problems. Furthermore, it reflects differences in rater judgments in interpreting students' requests. The Kenderski data are shown in Table 3.2.

The first step in analyzing the Kenderski data is to specify the variance components. This initial step is described as a Generalizability study (G study). Results from the G study are used to explore the consequences of varying sample sizes for a measurement procedure on reliability estimates in a follow-up procedure called a Decision study (D study; described further below). We view the G study design as a two-facet design with persons as the object of measurement. Persons are not considered a facet in G theory, and this translates into persons × raters × cues design that can be analyzed as a three-way ANOVA with one rating per cell. The definitions of the variance components are shown in Table 3.3. It is beyond the scope of this chapter to describe the construction of this table in detail, and Shavelson and Webb (1991) should be consulted for additional details. However, we would like to highlight the last column that provides the underlying questions that guide the interpretation of these variance components.

A small R program (Appendix 3.A) was written to analyze the Kenderski data, and Table 3.4 presents the results of the G study for these data. First of all, it is important to note that about 35% of the variance in the total scores is attributable to persons, and this supports the inference that the persons varied in how the raters judged their help-seeking behaviors. Because persons are defined

TABLE 3.3 Estimates of Variance Components for Random Effects: G Study Design (persons × raters × cues)

Source of Variation	Mean Square	Expected Mean Square	Estimated Variance Component	Interpretation
Persons (P)	MS_p	$\sigma_{res}^2 + n_c\sigma_{pr}^2 + n_r\sigma_{pc}^2 + n_r n_c\sigma_p^2$	$\hat{\sigma}_p^2 = \left[MS_p - MS_{pr} - MS_{pc} - MS_{res}\right]/n_r n_c$	Do person scores vary on the construct?
Raters (R)	MS_r	$\sigma_{res}^2 + n_p\sigma_{rc}^2 + n_c\sigma_{pr}^2 + n_p n_c\sigma_r^2$	$\hat{\sigma}_r^2 = \left[MS_r - MS_{pr} - MS_{rc} - MS_{res}\right]/n_p n_c$	Do raters vary in severity/leniency?
Cues (C)	MS_c	$\sigma_{res}^2 + n_p\sigma_{rc}^2 + n_r\sigma_{pc}^2 + n_p n_r\sigma_c^2$	$\hat{\sigma}_c^2 = \left[MS_c - MS_{pc} - MS_{rc} - MS_{res}\right]/n_p n_r$	Do cues vary in judged difficulty?
P × R	MS_{pr}	$\sigma_{res}^2 + n_c\sigma_{pr}^2$	$\hat{\sigma}_{pr}^2 = \left[MS_{pr} - MS_{res}\right]/n_c$	Is person order invariant over raters?
P × C	MS_{pc}	$\sigma_{res} + n_r\sigma_{pc}^2$	$\hat{\sigma}_{pc}^2 = \left[MS_{pc} - MS_{res}\right]/n_r$	Is person order invariant over cues?
R × C	MS_{rc}	$\sigma_{res}^2 + n_p\sigma_{rc}^2$	$\hat{\sigma}_{rc}^2 = \left[MS_{rc} - MS_{res}\right]/n_p$	Is cue order invariant over raters?
Residual	MS_{res}	σ_{res}^2	$\hat{\sigma}_{res}^2 = MS_{res}$	Residual variance (pro)
Relative Error			$\hat{\sigma}_{Rel}^2 = \dfrac{\hat{\sigma}_{pr}^2}{n_r} + \dfrac{\hat{\sigma}_{pc}^2}{n_c} + \dfrac{\hat{\sigma}_{res}^2}{n_r n_c}$	Norm-referenced (rank order) interpretations
Generalizability Coefficient			$\hat{\rho}^2 = \dfrac{\hat{\sigma}_p^2}{\hat{\sigma}_p^2 + \hat{\sigma}_{Rel}^2}$	A "generalizability coefficient is approximately equal to.... the squared correlation between observed scores and universe scores" (Brennan, 1983, p. 17)

Note: Cues (e.g., items, occasions, and cues) are the assessment opportunities that raters used make their judgments about persons. Variance components in G and D studies are based on expected variance components. A G coefficient is called *coefficient alpha* in a person by cue (one-facet) design.

TABLE 3.4 G Study for Kenderski Data

	ANOVA			G Study	
Source of Variation	Sum of Squares	df	Mean Square	Estimated Variance Components	Percent of Variance
Persons	30.9231	12	2.5769	.3974	35%
Raters	3.7692	1	3.7692	.0096	1%
Occasions	0.6923	1	0.6923	.1090	10%
pr	10.2308	12	0.8526	.0673	6%
po	4.3077	12	0.3590	.3141	28%
ro	0.3077	1	0.3077	.0064	1%
Residual	2.6923	12	.2244	.2244	20%

as the object of measurement, the variance attributed to persons is described as "universe score variance" in the language of Generalizability Theory. Essentially, universe score variance reflects variance related to the construct or latent variable. The next-largest variance component reflects the person-by-occasion interaction, and this value suggests that the order of persons in help-seeking behaviors was not replicated over occasions. In other words, the relative ordering of students was not consistent over occasions. According to Shavelson and Webb (1991), "the child who sought the most help on one occasion did not necessarily seek the most help on another occasion" (p. 35). Finally, we want to note that almost 20% of the variance was not accounted for by this model as shown by the residual variance defined as the three-way interaction between persons, raters, and occasions. The estimated Generalizability coefficient for the G study is low (G coefficient is approximately .62).

One of the distinctive features of G theory is that it provides a framework for predicting changes in G coefficients based on alternative designs called Decision (D) studies. These estimated variance components are related to the Spearman-Brown prophecy formula used in Classical Test Theory (Crocker & Algina, 1986). Table 3.5 shows how the results of the G study can be used to estimate expected G coefficients based on changing the number of raters and occasions. For example, it is predicted that the use of one rater on one occasion will yield a G coefficient of .3961, and as pointed out by Shavelson and Webb (1991), "these levels of reliability are too low for decision-making purposes" (p. 102). Increasing the number of raters to two and number of occasions to four yields an estimated value of .7392 as shown in the last column in Table 3.5. The estimated G coefficients can also be shown graphically (Figure 3.2). It is clear in this display that increasing both the number of raters and occasions increases the estimated G coefficients, and that these increases in estimated G coefficients tend to yield diminishing returns at some point.

The next section describes Rasch Measurement Theory, and also includes an analysis of the Kenderski data using the Rasch model.

TABLE 3.5 D Studies for Kenderski Data

	G Study	Alternative D Studies						
Raters	1	1	1	1	2	2	2	2
Occasions	1	2	3	4	1	2	3	4
Source		Estimated Variance Components						
Person (p)	0.3974	0.3974	0.3974	0.3974	0.3974	0.3974	0.3974	0.3974
Rater (r)	0.0096	0.0096	·0.0096	0.0096	0.0048	0.0048	0.0048	0.0048
Occasion (o)	0.1090	0.0545	0.0363	0.0273	0.1090	0.0545	0.0363	0.0273
pr	0.0673	0.0673	0.0673	0.0673	0.0337	0.0337	0.0337	0.0337
po	0.3141	0.1571	0.1047	0.0785	0.3141	0.1571	0.1047	0.0785
po	0.0064	0.0032	0.0021	0.0016	0.0032	0.0016	0.0011	0.0008
Residual	0.2244	0.1122	0.0748	0.0561	0.1122	0.0561	0.0374	0.0281
Relative Variance	0.6058	0.3366	0.2468	0.2019	0.4600	0.2468	0.1758	0.1402
Generalizability Coefficient	0.3961	0.5415	0.6169	0.6631	0.4635	0.6169	0.6934	0.7392

Note: G study variance components are based on estimated values from Table 3.4. D study coefficients focus on predicting coefficients if features of the rating design are changed (e.g., increase in number of occasions and/or raters. D study coefficients increase with number of occasions, and also increase with number of raters.

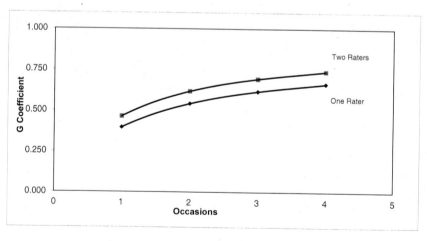

FIGURE 3.2 Kenderski Data: Decision Study Estimates for Raters and Occasions (p × r × o)

2. What Is Rasch Measurement Theory?

> The purpose of a measurement model is to extract from suitable data a useful definition of an intended variable and then to measure persons on this variable.
>
> *(Wright & Masters, 1982, p. 91)*

Rasch Measurement Theory is a component theory within the scaling tradition. Rasch developed a measurement model based on the cumulative logistic distribution (1960/1980). Rasch (1977) started with a set of requirements that he labeled *specific objectivity*. In his words,

> The comparison between two stimuli should be independent of which particular individuals were instrumental for the comparison; and it should also be independent of which stimuli within the considered class were or might also have been compared.
>
> Symmetrically, a comparison between two individuals should be independent of which particular stimuli with the class considered were instrumental for the comparison; and it should also be independent of which other individuals were also compared on the same or on some other occasion.
>
> *(Rasch, 1961, pp. 331–332)*

Rasch's concept of specific objectivity supports the view of invariant measurement developed in this book. Rasch's approach allowed the conceptual separation of items and persons. As shown in this book, the basic principles of Rasch Measurement Theory can be extended to rater-mediated assessments in order to yield the advantages of invariant measurement.

Although the Rasch model has a similar form to other IRT models (van der Linden & Hambleton, 1997), Rasch developed his work on measurement theory independently of this other research in psychometrics. Rasch clearly stated his quest for invariant measurement based on his concept of specific objectivity. Invariant measurement was the salient theme in his measurement work. As pointed out numerous times in this book, invariant measurement forms the basis for the new rules of measurement (Embretson, 1996) that support sound measurement practices in the 21st century. It should be stressed that Rasch described an elegant approach that provides the opportunity to meet the requirements for invariant measurement in the human sciences described in Chapter One.

A major proponent of Rasch models was Professor Ben Wright of the University of Chicago. He was instrumental in the development of computer programs and the application of Rasch models to solve a host of practical measurement problems. In his words, "The Rasch model is so simple that its immediate relevance to contemporary measurement practice and its extensive possibilities for solving measurement problems may not be fully apparent" (Wright, 1977, p. 104).

The Kenderski data can be used to illustrate how an approach based on Rasch Measurement Theory differs from an approach based on G theory. A general version of the Many-Facet (MF) model based on the extension of the Rasch models (Linacre, 1989) shown in Equations 3.1 and 3.2 for analyzing rater-mediated assessment can be written as

$$\phi_{nmik} = \frac{P_{nmik}}{P_{nmik} - 1 + P_{nmik}} = \frac{\exp\left(\theta_n - \lambda_m - \delta_i - \tau_k\right)}{1 + \exp\left(\theta_n - \lambda_m - \delta_i - \tau_k\right)} \tag{3.7}$$

and the category response function as follows:

$$\pi_{nmij} = \frac{\exp\left[\sum_{j=0}^{k}\left(\theta_n - \lambda_m - \delta_i - \tau_k\right)\right]}{\sum_{r=0}^{m_i}\exp\left[\sum_{j=0}^{r}\left(\theta_n - \lambda_m - \delta_i - \tau_k\right)\right]} \tag{3.8}$$

This can be presented in log-odds format for the Kenderski data that highlights the linear structure of the logistic model:

$$Ln\left(\frac{P_{nmik}}{P_{nmik-1}}\right) = \theta_n - \lambda_m - \delta_i - \tau_k \tag{3.9}$$

where

P_{nmik} = probability of person n being rated k on occasion i by rater m,
P_{nmik-1} = probability of person n being rated $k-1$ on occasion i by rater m,
θ_n = judged location of person n,
λ_m = severity of rater m,
δ_i = judged difficulty of occasion i, and
τ_k = judged difficulty of rating category k relative to category $k-1$.

In contrast to Generalizability Theory, persons are treated as a facet in the MF model. The rating category coefficient, τ_k, is not considered a facet in the model. Rather, it represents the threshold value of moving between adjacent rating categories (category k and category $k-1$). The syntax for conducting an MF model analysis of the Kenderski data using the Facets computer program (Linacre, 2015) is shown in Appendix 3.B.

First of all, one of the distinctive features of Rasch Measurement Theory as a component theory within the scaling tradition is the construction of a line to represent the latent variable. Figure 3.3 provides the Wright map for the Kenderski data. In the context of a rater-mediated assessment, the Wright map reflects rater judgments related to each of the facets in the measurement model. The first column represents the logit scale used to map the construct of perceived helping behaviors. Column 2 indicates the judged locations of persons on the scale, with Person 6 seeking the most help and Person 10 seeking the least help. Column 3 represents the rater facet, and the display indicates

```
+----------------------------------------------------------+
|Logit|+Person                  |+Rater|+Occasion|Scale|
|-----+-------------------------+------+---------+-----|
|  4 + Asks the most            + More + More     + (4) |
|     | 6                       |      |          |      |
|     |                         |      |          |      |
|     |                         |      |          |      |
|  3 +                          +      +          +      |
|     |                         |      |          | --- |
|     |                         |      |          |      |
|     |                         |      |          |      |
|     |                         |      |          |      |
|  2 +                          +      +          +  3  |
|     |                         |      |          |      |
|     |                         |      |          |      |
|     | 2                       |      |          | --- |
|     |                         |      |          |      |
|  1 +                          +      +          +      |
|     |                         |      | 1        |      |
|     |                         |      |          |  2  |
|     |                         | B    |          |      |
|     |                         |      |          |      |
*  0 *                          *      *          *      *
|     |                         |      |          |      |
|     |                         | A    |          |      |
|     | 5                       |      |          | --- |
|     |                         |      | 2        |      |
| -1 +                          +      +          +      |
|     | 3   7   9   11 12 13     |      |          |      |
|     |                         |      |          |      |
|     |                         |      |          |      |
|     |                         |      |          |      |
| -2 + 1   4   8                +      +          +  1  |
|     |                         |      |          |      |
|     |                         |      |          |      |
|     |                         |      |          |      |
|     | 10                      |      |          |      |
| -3 +                          +      +          +      |
|     |                         |      |          |      |
|     |                         |      |          |      |
|     |                         |      |          | --- |
|     |                         |      |          |      |
| -4 + Asks the least           + Less + Less     + (0) |
|-----+-------------------------+------+---------+-----|
```

FIGURE 3.3   Wright Map for Kenderski Data

that Rater 1 tends to judge students as seeking more helping behaviors as compared to Rater 2. The persons seem to request more help on Occasion 1 as compared to Occasion 2 as shown in Column 4. The final column shows the structure of the rating scale based on the counts of observed helping behaviors.

The summary statistics for the Kenderski data are shown in Table 3.6. There are several features to note in this table. First of all, two out of the three facets (Raters and Occasions) are centered with a mean of zero. This centering is done in order to anchor the measure. In most applications of the Facets Model, the object of measurement is allowed to float (i.e., the facet is not centered), and the other facets are centered. Next, it is important to note that both the Infit and Outfit statistics with values less than the expected value of one indicate that the ratings may have some dependences because of the use of raters (additional details about the interpretation of model-data fit statistics for raters are presented in Chapter Eleven). Finally, the reliability of separation for persons is .75, and this statistic is comparable to coefficient alpha when data fit the model.

We can also examine in detail the differences within each facet. Table 3.7 shows the summary table for persons. As shown in the Wright map, Person 6 is judged to seek the most help, while Person 10 is judged to seek the least help while solving mathematics problems in the classroom. We also have an index of how well the person ratings matched the theoretical structure of the Rasch model. We interpret the Outfit MS to indicate that Person 1 had the highest level of misfit (Outfit MS = 2.19).

Table 3.8 provides similar levels of detail for occasions and raters. The persons were perceived to ask for more help on Occasion 1 (1.7 behaviors) as compared to Occasion 2 (1.2), and this difference was statistically significant (*Rel* = .90,

TABLE 3.6 Rasch Measurement Theory: Summary Table for Kenderski Data

Measures	Persons	Raters	Occasions
M	−.92	.00	.00
SD	1.71	.45	1.06
N	13	2	2
Infit			
M	.88	.86	.87
SD	.58	.03	.20
Outfit			
M	.89	.89	.89
SD	.62	.04	.23
Reliability of Separation	.75	~ .00	.90
χ^2 Statistic	46.8*	1.9	10.4*
Degrees of Freedom	12	1	1

* $p < .05$

chi-square = 10.4, $df = 1$, $p < .001$). Rater A observed fewer helping behaviors as compared to Rater B, but the difference was not statistically significant. Table 3.9 gives the summary statistics for the rating categories. This dataset is very small, and most of the ratings (or counts) were scores of one. One of the thresholds is

TABLE 3.7 Rasch Measurement Theory: Person Summary Table for Kenderski Data (ordered by measures)

Person	Count	Mean Count	Measure(Logits)	SE	Infit MS	Outfit MS
6	4	3.75	3.76	0.96	0.25	0.18
2	4	2.50	1.34	0.63	0.55	0.64
5	4	1.50	−0.60	0.81	0.86	0.95
3	4	1.25	−1.27	0.85	1.24	1.28
7	4	1.25	−1.27	0.85	1.28	1.33
9	4	1.25	−1.27	0.85	0.99	0.99
11	4	1.25	−1.27	0.85	0.22	0.21
12	4	1.25	−1.27	0.85	0.22	0.21
13	4	1.25	−1.27	0.85	0.57	0.53
1	4	1.00	−2.01	0.87	2.15	2.19
4	4	1.00	−2.01	0.87	0.68	0.67
8	4	1.00	−2.01	0.87	1.78	1.80
10	4	0.75	−2.80	0.90	0.59	0.62

TABLE 3.8 Occasion and Rater Summary Tables for Kenderski Data

Occasion	Count	Mean	Measure	SE	Infit MS	Outfit MS
1	26	1.7	.75	.32	.73	.73
2	26	1.2	−.75	.33	1.00	1.05
Rater						
A	26	1.2	−.32	.33	.88	.92
B	26	1.6	.32	.33	.84	.86

TABLE 3.9 Summary Statistics for the Rating Categories

Score	Count	%	Average Measure	Outfit MS	Threshold	SE
0	6	12	−2.52	.9	—	—
1	26	50	−1.52	1.2	−3.51	.48
2	14	27	−.90	1.1	−.52	.36
3	2	4	2.23	.1	2.22	.78
4	4	8	3.68	.4	1.82*	.93

* Disordered threshold in judged counts. See category response and test characteristic displays in Table 3.10.

TABLE 3.10 Visual Diplays for Rasch Analyses of Kenderski Data

Panel A: Category Response Functions

Panel B: Test Characteristic Function

Panel C: Category Response Functions for Rater 1

Panel D: Category Response Functions for Rater 2

disordered (Category 3 to Category 4), and this suggests the raters are not using the categories in the same way. Additional details related to the interpretation of rating scale thresholds are provided in Chapter Thirteen.

Several graphical displays for these data are summarized in Table 3.10. Panel A shows the disordered threshold noted above. Panels C and D in Table 3.10 also reveal that Raters 1 and 2 did not use the *count scale* in the same way. These observations about rating scale structure remain hidden in the G theory analyses.

Summary and Discussion

> The tradition of psychometrics in the early twentieth century seems to have been held together by little more than the conviction that mental phenomena could be mathematically represented.
>
> *(Laudan, 1977, p. 105)*

This chapter provided an overview of two broad research traditions that can be used to classify and examine measurement theories for rater-mediated assessments: the test-score and scaling traditions. The dominant approaches for examining rater-mediated assessments within these two frameworks are Generalizability Theory (test-score tradition) and Rasch Measurement Theory (scaling tradition). A small illustrative data analysis of help-seeking behavior in mathematics (Kenderski, 1983) was used to highlight the major characteristics of each approach. This chapter highlighted differences in the essential features of the test-score and scaling traditions. As the name implies, measurement theories within the test-score tradition include a focus on scores, the use of linear models, and an emphasis on the estimation of components of error variance. In contrast, the essential features of the scaling tradition include an item-person response focus, the use of non-linear models, and an emphasis on creating a continuum. Later in this book (Chapter Nine), we provide detailed comparative analyses of several other major measurement models within the scaling tradition for ordered rating categories: Rating Scale (Andrich, 1978), Partial Credit (Masters, 1982), Many-Facet (Linacre, 1989), Generalized Partial Credit (Muraki, 1992), Graded Response Model (Samejima, 1969), and Modified Graded Response Model (Muraki, 1990).

Within the context of rater-mediated assessments, the major distinction between the test-score and scaling traditions is related to the emphasis on total observed ratings within the test-score tradition and the emphasis on person–cue ratings within the scaling tradition. Within the test-score tradition, rating scale categories are treated as equidistant, such that ratings can be summed to create a total score for each person. On the other hand, the scaling tradition allows for flexibility in the distance between rating scale categories and requires a transformation of ratings to a linear scale in order to describe person locations on a construct. The perspective presented in this book is that the score obtained from summing the number of ordered guideposts (i.e., rating scale categories) above which a person is located on a construct is not an item-invariant scoring system. Rather, a measurement model is needed to estimate a person's location (theta) that does not depend on the particular guideposts or cues used to define the continuum. Item Response Theory offers an approach for accomplishing this task under appropriate circumstances.

It is helpful to think of the concept of the ideal rater-mediated assessment system from each research tradition. First of all, the ideal raters within the test-score tradition should exhibit high consistency between raters with raters viewed as *scoring machines* such as the current use of automated or machine scoring of essays (Shermis & Burstein, 2013). The test-score tradition also seeks cue difficulties that are approximately equal in order to reduce cues as a source of error variance in the model. The estimation of category coefficients is ignored, and ratings are treated as exhibiting equal and fixed units on the score scale.

The scaling tradition is shown in Column 3 in Table 3.11. The ideal raters within the scaling tradition exhibit high internal consistency, and variation in

TABLE 3.11 Theoretical Conceptualization of Rater-Mediated Assessments for Test-Score and Scaling Traditions

Topics	Test-Score Tradition	Scaling Tradition
Ideal raters	High consistency (agreement) between raters	High consistency within a rater
	Random effects	Estimate rater locations on continuum
	Raters as source of error variance	Model-data fit for each rater
	Key idea: Raters are scoring machines	Key idea: Raters are experts
Ideal cues	Equal cue difficulties	Range of cue difficulties
	Cues as sources of error variation	Cue locations define the continuum
	Item-sampling model (Shavelson quote)	Assessment opportunities used to measure persons
Ideal thresholds	Defined as equal units on score scale	Thresholds estimated to define units
	Fixed units based on ratings	Units are not fixed based on ratings
	Estimation of thresholds is ignored	Thresholds are estimated for rating categories
	Not explicitly included in the model	Ratings are not equivalent to test scores with estimated locations of rating categories on continuum
	Ratings are equivalent to test scores with equal units	
Ideal rater-mediated assessment system	Rater differences are minimized and rater agreement maximized to control for rater effects	Raters are trained and calibrated to interpret rating scale and cues to define continuum

rater severity is estimated by rater locations on a Wright map. Raters are viewed as experts who judge the location of cues on the latent variable. Cue locations define the meaning of the latent variable, and assessment opportunities provided information for estimating person location on the line used to measure persons. Category coefficients and thresholds are estimated, and then used to define units in the assessment system. Units are not fixed based on ratings, and ratings are not viewed as equivalent to test scores.

In summary, it is important to consider what these two theoretical perspectives illuminate about the psychometric quality of an assessment system. Each perspective views the assessment process differently, and it is important to recognize that the criteria used to evaluate psychometric quality, as well as recommendations for improving the assessment system, can vary depending on the research tradition that guides the researcher.

References

Andrich, D. A. (1978). A rating formulation for ordered response categories. *Psychometrika, 43*, 561–573.

Andrich, D. A. (2004). Controversy and the Rasch model: A characteristic of incompatible paradigms? *Medical Care, 42*(1), 1–7.

Baker, F. B., & Kim, S. (2004). *Item response theory: Parameter estimation techniques* (2nd ed., Revised and Expanded). New York: Marcel Dekker.

Bock, R. D. (1997). A brief history of item theory response. *Educational Measurement: Issues and Practice, 16*(4), 21–33.

Bock, R. D., & Jones, L. V. (1968). *The measurement and prediction of judgment and choice.* San Francisco: Holden-Day.

Bollen, K. A. (1989). *Structural equations with latent variables.* New York, NY: Wiley.

Brennan, R. L. (1983). *Elements of Generalizability Theory.* Iowa City, IA: Act Publications.

Brennan, R. L. (1997). A perspective on the history of generalizability theory. *Educational measurement: Issues and practice, 16*(4), 14–20.

Brennan, R. L. (2001). *Generalizability theory.* New York: Springer-Verlag.

Brennan, R. (2011). Generalizability theory and classical test theory. *Applied Measurement in Education, 24*, 1–21.

Briesch, A. M., Swaminathan, H., Welsh, M., & Chafouleas, S. M. (2014). Generalizability theory: A practical guide to study design, implementation, and interpretation. *Journal of School Psychology, 52*(1), 13–35.

Crick, J. E., & Brennan, R. L. (1983). *Manual for GENOVA: A generalized analysis of variance system (ACT Technical Bulletin No. 43).* Iowa City, IA: ACT, Inc.

Crocker, L., & Algina, J. (1986). *Introduction to classical and modern test theory.* Orlando, FL: Holt, Rinehart and Winston.

Cronbach, L. J., Gleser, G. C., Nanda, H., & Rajaratnam, N. (1972). *The dependability of behavioral measurements: Theory of generalizability for scores and profiles.* New York: Wiley.

Cronbach, L. J., Rajaratnam, N., & Gleser, G. C. (1963). Theory of generalizability: A liberalization of reliability theory. *British Journal of Statistical Psychology, 16*(2), 137–163.

Cronbach, L. J., & Shavelson, R. J. (2004). My current thoughts on coefficient alpha and successor procedures. *Educational and Psychological Measurement, 64*(3), 391–418.

Ebel, R. L. (1951). Estimation of the reliability of ratings. *Psychometrika, 16,* 407–424.

Edgeworth, F. Y. (1890). The element of chance in competitive examinations. *Journal of the Royal Statistical Society, 53,* 460–475, 644–663.

Embretson, S. E. (1996). The new rules of measurement. *Psychological Assessment, 8*(4), 341–349.

Embretson, S. E., & Reise, S. P. (2000). *Item response theory for psychologists.* Mahwah, NJ: Erlbaum.

Engelhard, G. (2013). *Invariant measurement: Using Rasch models in the social, behavioral, and health sciences.* New York: Routledge.

Engelhard, G., & Wind, S. A. (2013). *Rating quality studies using Rasch measurement theory.* College Board Research Report 2013–3. New York: The College Board.

Gulliksen, H. (1950). *Theory of mental tests.* New York: Wiley.

Hendrickson, A., & Engelhard, G. (2011). *Evaluating the quality of rater-mediated assessments with a multi-method approach.* Paper presented at the International Meeting of the Psychometric Society (IMPS), Hong Kong.

Hendrickson, A., & Yin, P. (2010). Generalizability theory. In G. R. Hancock & R. O. Mueller (Eds.), *The reviewer's guide to quantitative methods in the social sciences* (pp. 115–122). New York: Routledge.

Hoyt, C. J. (1941). Test reliability estimated by analysis of variance. *Psychometrika, 6,* 153–160.

Joreskog, K. G. (1974). Analyzing psychological data by structural analysis of covariance matrices. In D. H. Krantz, R. C. Atkinson, R. D. Luce, & P. Suppes (Eds.), *Contemporary developments in mathematical psychology* (Vol. 2, pp. 1–56). San Francisco: W. H. Freeman.

Kenderski, C. M. (1983). *Interaction process and learning among third-grade black and Mexican-American students in cooperative small groups.* Unpublished doctoral dissertation, University of California, Los Angeles.

Kuhn, T. S. (1970). *The structure of scientific revolutions* (2nd ed.). Princeton, NJ: Princeton University Press.

Laudan, L. (1977). *Progress and its problems: Toward a theory of scientific change.* Berkeley: University of California Press.

Linacre, J. M. (1989). *Many-facet Rasch measurement.* Chicago: MESA Press.

Linacre, J. M. (1996). Generalizability theory and many-facet Rasch measurement. In G. Engelhard & M. Wilson (Eds.), *Objective measurement: Theory into practice* (pp. 85–98). Norwood, NJ: Ablex Publishing Company.

Linacre, J. M. (2015). *Facets Rasch Measurement* (Version 3.71.4). Chicago, IL: Winsteps.com.

Loevinger, J. (1954). The attenuation paradox in test theory. *Psychological Bulletin, 51*(5), 493.

Lord, F. M. (1980). *Applications of item response theory to practical testing problems.* Hillsdale, NJ: Erlbaum.

Masters, G. N. (1982). A Rasch model for partial credit scoring. *Psychometrika, 47,* 149–174.

Mellenbergh, G. J. (1977). The replicability of measures. *Psychological Bulletin, 84*(2), 378–384.

Mokken, R. J. (1971). *A theory and procedure of scale analysis.* The Hague/Mouton/Berlin: De Gruyter.

Mosier, C. I. (1940). Psychophysics and mental test theory: Fundamental postulates and elementary theorems. *Psychological Review, 47,* 355–366.

Mosier, C. I. (1941). Psychophysics and mental test theory II: The constant process. *Psychological Review, 48,* 235–249.

Muraki, E. (1990). Fitting a polytomous item response model to Likert-type data. *Applied Psychological Measurement, 14,* 59–71.

Muraki, E. (1992). A generalized partial credit model: Application of an EM algorithm. *Applied Psychological Measurement, 16,* 159–176.

Novick, M. R. (1966). The axioms and principal results of classical test theory. *Journal of Mathematical Psychology, 3*(1), 1–18.

Rasch, G. (1960/1980). *Probabilistic models for some intelligence and attainment tests.* Copenhagen: Danish Institute for Educational Research. (Expanded edition, Chicago: University of Chicago Press, 1980).

Rasch, G. (1961). On general laws and meaning of measurement in psychology. In J. Neyman (Ed.), *Proceedings of the fourth Berkeley Symposium on mathematical statistics and probability* (pp. 321–333). Berkeley: University of California Press.

Rasch, G. (1977). On specific objectivity: An attempt at formalizing the request for generality and validity of scientific statements. *Danish Yearbook of Philosophy, 14,* 58–94.

Reckase, M. D. (2009). *Multidimensional item response theory.* New York: Springer.

Samejima, F. (1969). *Estimation of latent ability using a response pattern of graded scores* (Psychometric Monograph No. 17). Richmond, VA: Psychometric Society.

Shavelson, R. J., & Webb, N. M. (1991). *Generalizability theory: A primer.* Newbury Park, CA: Sage Publications.

Shermis, M., & Burstein, J. (Eds.). (2013). *Handbook of automated essay evaluation: Current applications and new directions.* New York: Routledge.

Shewhart, W. A. (1939). *Statistical method from the viewpoint of quality control.* Washington, DC: Graduate School of the Department of Agriculture.

Stigler, S. M. (1986). *The history of statistics: The measurement of uncertainty before 1900.* Cambridge, MA: The Belknap Press of Harvard University Press.

Thurstone, L. L. (1947). *Multiple factor analysis.* Chicago: University of Chicago Press.

Torgerson, W. F. (1961). Scaling and test theory. *Annual Review of Psychology, 12,* 51–70.

Torgerson, W. S. (1958). *Theory and methods of scaling.* New York: Wiley.

Traub, R. (1997). Classical test theory in historical perspective. *Educational Measurement: Issues and Practice, 16*(10), 8–13.

van der Linden, W. J., & Hambleton, R. K. (Eds.). (1997). *Handbook of modern item response theory.* New York: Springer.

Wright, B. D. (1977). Solving measurement problems with the Rasch model. *Journal of Educational Measurement, 14*(2), 97–116.

Wright, B. D., & Masters, G. N. (1982). *Rating scale analysis: Rasch measurement.* Chicago: MESA Press.

APPENDIX 3.A

R syntax

```
#Clear variables
rm(list = ls())
```

```
#Load XLConnect in order to read Excel files
library(XLConnect)
```

```
# Load workbook
wb <- loadWorkbook("C:/Users/George/Dropbox/Data/Kenderski.xls", create =
TRUE)
```

```
x = readWorksheet(wb, sheet = "Kenderski")
x
```

```
x$Person <- as.factor(x$Person)
x$Occasion <- as.factor(x$Occasion)
x$Rater <- as.factor(x$Rater)
```

```
results <- aov(Rating~Person*Occasion*Rater, data = x)
```

```
anova(results)
```

R output

Analysis of Variance Table

Response: Rating

	Df	Sum Sq	Mean Sq	F value	Pr (> F)
Person	12	30.9231	2.5769		
Occasion	1	3.7692	3.7692		
Rater	1	0.6923	0.6923		
Person: Occasion	12	10.2308	0.8526		
Person: Rater	12	4.3077	0.3590		
Occasion: Rater	1	0.3077	0.3077		
Person: Occasion: Rater	12	2.6923	0.2244		
Residuals	0	0.0000			

APPENDIX 3.B

Facets Syntax	Data (cont.)	Data (cont.)
Title = Kenderski (1983)	10,1,1,1	1,2,2,2
Facets = 3	11,1,1,1	2,2,2,2
Barchart = No	12,1,1,1	3,2,2,0
Pt-biserial = Yes	13,1,1,2	4,2,2,1
Iterations = 50	1,1,2,1	5,2,2,1
Arrange = m	2,1,2,4	6,2,2,4
Positive = 1,2	3,1,2,2	7,2,2,1
Model = ?,?,#,r4	4,1,2,2	8,2,2,0
*	5,1,2,2	9,2,2,2
Labels =	6,1,2,4	10,2,2,0
1,Person	7,1,2,1	11,2,2,1
1-13 =	8,1,2,2	12,2,2,1
*	9,1,2,1	13,2,2,1
2,Occasion	10,1,2,1	
1-2 =	11,1,2,2	
*	12,1,2,2	
3,Rater	13,1,2,1	
1 = A	1,2,1,1	
2 = B	2,2,1,1	
*	3,2,1,1	
Data =	4,2,1,0	
1,1,1,0	5,2,1,2	
2,1,1,3	6,2,1,3	
3,1,1,2	7,2,1,2	
4,1,1,1	8,2,1,0	
5,1,1,1	9,2,1,1	
6,1,1,4	10,2,1,1	
7,1,1,1	11,2,1,1	
8,1,1,2	12,2,1,1	
9,1,1,1	13,2,1,1	

4

LENS MODELS OF HUMAN JUDGMENT FOR RATER-MEDIATED ASSESSMENTS

> The expert must identify information or cues from the multidimensional stimulus he encounters. These cues are diagnostic (i.e., contain information) about the final decision or judgment. The expert's ability to identify cues can be seen as a problem of extracting weak signals from a background of noise.
>
> *(Einhorn, 1974, p. 562)*

This chapter stresses the use of lens models (Brunswik, 1952) as a conceptual framework for examining human judgment and decision-making. Lens models offer a promising framework for guiding our views of human judgment within the context of rater-mediated assessments. One of the major themes of this book is that when raters score performance assessments, it is critically important to recognize that the scores and inferences drawn about persons are based on *judgments*. It is also important to recognize that the judgments being examined are obtained from *experts*. In rater-mediated assessments, the "experts" are defined as highly trained raters who have a deep understanding of the assessment system.

Numerous models have been proposed for examining human judgment and decision-making. For example, Cooksey (1996a) describes and compares 14 different theoretical perspectives on judgment and decision-making. It is not our goal in this chapter to provide a comprehensive new model, or to critically evaluate a particular theoretical perspective on human judgment. Rather our goals are to briefly reflect on human judgment using lens models, and to selectively borrow, modify, and adapt aspects of alternative theories and perspectives that we believe hold the most promise for understanding, improving, and monitoring rater-mediated assessments.

Brunswik (1952, 1955a, 1955b, 1956) proposed a new perspective in psychology called *probabilistic functionalism* (Athanasou & Kaufmann, 2015; Postman &

Tolman, 1959). An important aspect of Brunswik's research was the concept of a lens model (Hammond, 1955; Postman & Tolman, 1959). The structure of Brunswik's lens models varied over time and application areas. Figure 4.1 presents a lens model for perception proposed by Brunswik (1955a).

In this case, a person utilizes a set of cues (proximal-peripheral cues) to generate a response (central response). The accuracy of a person's response can be evaluated (functional validity) by its relationship to the distal variable. Ecological validities represent the relationships between the distal variable and the cues, while utilization validities reflect the relationship between the cues and the central response. In both cases, higher values of correspondence are viewed as evidence of validity. The diagram shown in Figure 4.1 is called a *lens model* because it resembles the way light passes through a lens defined by cues.

Another way to conceptualize the lens model is to view the distal variable in Figure 4.1 as a latent variable that is made visible by cues (intervening variables) that are used by a rater to generate a response. In rater-mediated assessments, the accuracy of a rater's response (observed rating) is evaluated by its correspondence or relationship to the latent variable (distal variable). Engelhard (1992, 1994, 2013) adapted the lens model as a conceptual framework for rater judgments in writing assessment as shown in Figure 4.2. The basic idea is that a latent variable, such as writing competence, is made visible through a set of cues or intervening variables (rater, domains, and rating scale). The goal is to have a close correspondence between the latent variable (writing competence) and the observed ratings. It is also important to note that the ecological context plays a role in the conceptual framework.

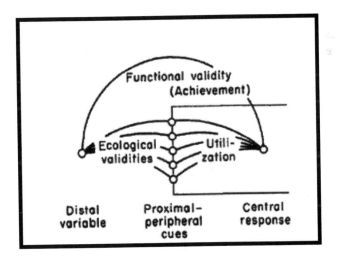

FIGURE 4.1   Lens Model for Perception Constancy

Source: Brunswik (1955a, p. 206).

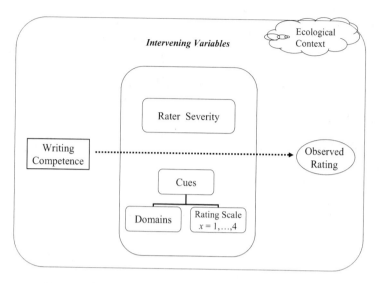

FIGURE 4.2   Lens Model for Measuring Writing Ability

Source: Engelhard (2013, p. 194).

This chapter focuses on the following questions and issues:

- What is human judgment?
- What are lens models for human judgment?
- How have lens models been used for rater-mediated assessments of student performance?
- Summary and discussion

What Is Human Judgment?

> Judgement and choice are pervasive activities . . . judgement is an inevitable aspect of living.
>
> *(Hogarth, 1987, p. 1)*

There are a variety of definitions of judgments. Shulman and Elstein (1975) used Johnson's (1955) definition to define human thought in terms of three key functions and processes: preparation, production, and judgment. Specifically, judgment is the

> evaluation or categorizing of an object of thought. This is logically differentiated from productive thought in that typically nothing is produced. The material is merely judged; i.e., put into one category or another. Many of the subjective analyses of thinking have included a concluding phase of hypothesis testing or verification during which the thoughts previously

produced are judged. In experimental psychology, judgment is a well developed topic, studied chiefly under the headings of psychophysics, aesthetics, attitudes and rating of personnel.

(Johnson, 1955, p. 51, cited in Shulman & Elstein, 1975, p. 14)

Shulman and Elstein (1975, p. 14) summarize Newell's (1968) perspective on judgment as follows:

Inputs

* The main inputs to the process are given and available; obtaining, discovering, or formulating them is not part of judgment.

Outputs

* The output is simple and well defined prior to the judgment; the judgment itself is one of a set of admissible responses; where classes or categories are given, it is usually called *selection, estimation,* or *classification.*

Process

* The process is not simple transduction of information; judgment goes beyond the information given, adding information to the output.
* Judgment is not simply a calculation or the application of a given rule.
* The process of judgment concludes or occurs at the end of a more extended process.
* The process is immediate, not extended through time with subprocesses, in which case we would refer to preparation for judgment.
* The process is distinguished from searching, discovering, or creating, as well as from musing, browsing, or idly observing.

Each of these points has implications for rater-mediated assessments. First of all, the inputs to a rater-mediated assessment system include a set of given cues that raters use to guide their judgments. Next, the output tends to be simplified in terms of a holistic rating or a set of analytic ratings (e.g., domains in writing assessment). Finally, the aspects of the process in rater-mediated assessments are not simple because raters must process a set of intended and unintended aspects that may affect rater judgments; this typically occurs at the end of a training session with immediate processing once the assessment system becomes operational.

Research on human judgment has also been influenced by several general trends in 20th-century psychology. Two dominant research traditions emerged in psychology in the past century: behaviorism and cognitive science. In the first part of the 20th century, behaviorism was the dominant paradigm (Skinner, 1938; Watson, 1919). Essentially, behaviorism emphasizes the study of observable behaviors, and stresses that the study of the mind is too vague to be the focus of an objective science of human behavior. The second half of the 20th century marked the emergence of cognitive sciences that include the study of a variety of topics such as decision-making and judgment, thought processes, memory, information processing, and language (Barsalou, 1992; Neisser, 1967). The transition from behavorism to cognitive psychology is often marked by a book review written by Chomsky (1959) who reviewed a book entitled *Verbal Behaviors* (Skinner, 1957). Chomskey (1959) argued that language cannot be learned and understood solely from a behaviorist perspective. Chomsky argued for internal mental structures that are avoided from a classical behaviorist perspective. In essence, cognitive sciences stress that internal cognitive representations can lead to changes in behavior.

Currently, cognitive psychology provides guidance for thinking about human judgment. It is of historic interest to recall that the early roots of psychology in the 19th century stressed cognition. Psychology in the late 19th century was dominated by psychophysics. In particular, the work of Fechner (1860) was very influential. Psychophysics was defined by Fechner as "an exact science of the functional relations of dependencies between body and mind" (quoted in Torgerson, 1958, p. v). Fechner's Law models the relationship between sensation and stimulus intensity. Fechner's Law can be written as follows:

$$S = K \log R$$

where S represents a sensation intensity, R refers to the stimulus intensity, and K represents a constant. Fechner's Law can also be shown graphically:

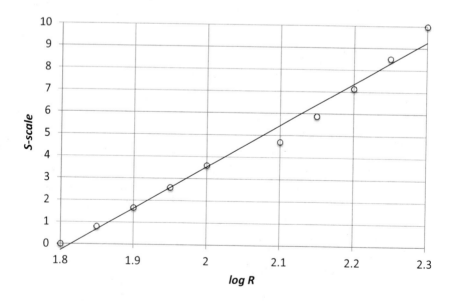

Fechner's Law is important because it connects an observable variable (log R) to an unobservable or latent variable of perceived sensation (S-scale). Fechner's work provided the basis for Thurstone's (1959) seminal research on the measurement of attitudes and values that includes the application of measurement principles in psychophysics to problems in psychometrics related to the prediction of judgment and choice (Bock & Jones, 1968).

The early work in psychophysics as represented by Fechner (1860) is congruent with many of the fundamental ideas of cognitive psychology. The research in psychophysics has evolved in psychometrics, and it recognizes the connection between *mind and body* sought by Fechner. A seminal event in measurement was the recognition by Thurstone (1959) that the methodology of psychophysics can be used to develop scaling models for unobserved variables, such as judgments, values, attitudes, and beliefs. In fact, much of the current work on latent variable models including Item Response Theory within the scaling tradition has its roots in earlier frameworks in psychology that essentially made judgments observable. These ideas have great potential for improving measurement in the social, behavioral, and health sciences.

This chapter utilizes cognitive psychology in general to conceptualize judgmental processes. Specifically, the lens model provides a framework for guiding our thinking related to rater-mediated assessments. Another important development in research on human judgment, choice, and decision-making is the emergence of research on expert judgments. In our work on raters, the focus is on trained raters, and the research on expert judgments has implications for informing research, theory, and practice on rater-mediated assessments.

It should be stressed that the judgments being considered in this chapter do not reflect everyday and routine types of judgments, but reflect judgments of experts and trained raters (Einhorn, 1974). This is an important distinction because everyday judgments have been characterized with phrases such as *thinking fast and slow* (Kahneman, 2011). Raters in assessment contexts are trained to operate as experts who have been prepared for their judgments. In making a distinction between judgment in general and expert judgment, Einhorn (1974) has identified several features of expert judgment that we should keep in mind related to rater-mediated assessments.

Einhorn (1974) addressed the issues of how raters deal with multidimensional information. He argued for the use of psychometric criteria as an indication of expert judgment. Specifically, he highlighted three criteria:

- Experts should tend to cluster variables in the same way when identifying and organizing cues,
- Expert judgment should be highly reliable within individual raters (intra-judge reliability), show both convergent and discriminant validity, and be relatively free of judgmental bias when measuring cues, and
- Experts should weight and combine information in similar ways.

Each of these criteria is relevant for defining and evaluating raters within the context of rater-mediated assessment. For example, a rater who scores an essay has to address multidimensional information, and to determine if the rubrics that define the domains are relevant. The rater has to judge the relative weight of each cue including intended evaluative aspects as well as unintended aspects that may or may not be construct relevant for assessing competence in writing.

What Are Lens Models for Human Judgment?

> The simple beauty of Brunswik's lens model lies in recognizing that the person's judgment and the criterion being predicted can be thought of as two separate functions of cues available in the environment of the decision.
>
> *(Karelaia & Hogarth, 2008, p. 404)*

The underlying model of judgmental processes used in this book is based on Brunswik's (1952) lens model. Lens models have been modified to examine human judgments by Hammond (1955), and they have been used extensively across social science research contexts. For example, there are two important meta-analyses of research organized around lens models. First, Karelaia and Hogarth (2008) conducted a meta-analysis of five decades of lens models studies ($N =$ 249) that included a variety of task environments. More recently, Kaufmann, Reips, and Wittmann (2013) conducted a meta-analysis based on 31 lens model studies including applications from medicine, business, education, and psychology. An important resource for recent work on lens models is the website of the Brunswik Society (www.brunswik.org/) that provides yearly abstracts of current research utilizing a lens model perspective.

Gibson (1979/2014) has used Brunswik's lens model within the context of perception, while Hammond and his colleagues (1975; Hammond, 1980, 1996; Hammond & Stewart, 2001) adapted Brunswik's ideas to the analysis of human judgments and decision-making. Cooksey (1996a) built on this earlier work, and developed a theoretical perspective that he called *Judgment Analysis*. Cooksey has used Judgment Analysis in several studies for evaluating rater-mediated performance assessments in reading (Cooksey, Freebody, & Davidson, 1986) and writing assessments (Cooksey, Freebody, & Wyatt-Smith, 2007). Cooksey (1996b) described in detail the methodology of social judgment theory. It should be pointed out that Hammond (1955) referred to the lens-model framework as social judgment theory, while Cooksey (1996a) called this framework judgment analysis. For our purposes, both perspectives are illustrative of Brunswik's lens model, and represent adaptation of the lens model for the study of human judgment. Later in this chapter, we use an example from Cooksey, Freebody, and Wyatt-Smith (2007) to illustrate the application of the lens models within the context of writing assessment.

As pointed out earlier, Engelhard (2013) adapted a lens-model perspective for the assessment of writing competence. This is shown in Figure 4.2. The lens model can be used to represent assessments that are based on both selected-response items (e.g., multiple-choice items) and constructed-response items (e.g., written essays). Figure 4.3 illustrates the lens-model perspective for the two item

Selected-response items (e.g., multiple-choice items)

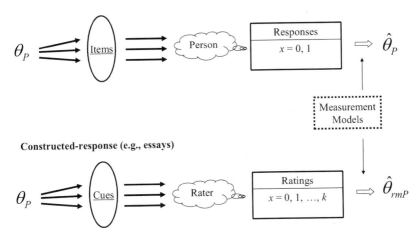

Constructed-response (e.g., essays)

FIGURE 4.3 Lens Model for Selected- and Constructed-Response Items

types. For selected-response items, person p responds to a set of items designed to reveal his or her location on the line (θ_p) representing the latent variable. The person's dichotomous responses ($0 =$ incorrect, $1 =$ correct) are mediated through the person's cognitive processes with a measurement model (e.g., Rasch model) connecting the observed response to an estimate of the location of person p $(\hat{\theta}_p)$ on the line.

The situation is not as direct with constructed-response items because the person's responses are mediated through a rater, and the measurement model is used to model ratings. In this case, person p creates a response (e.g., essay) that is scored on the basis of a set of pre-specified cues (these are analogous to items in the selected-response situation) by a rater to reveal the person's location on the line (θ_p) representing the latent variable. The polytomous ratings are mediated through a rater who infers the person's cognitive processes. An appropriate measurement model (e.g., Rasch model) is used to connect the observed rating from a rater to a rater-mediated estimate of the location of person p (θ_{rm-p}) on the line.

How Have Lens Models Been Used for Rater-Mediated Assessments of Student Performance?

In this section, we present two applications of lens models in order to illustrate the utility of this approach to human judgment. The first study is based on assessment of writing, and the second study examines the judgments of nurses. These two studies show the potential of Brunswik's lens model for understanding judgmental processes within educational settings.

Teacher Evaluations of Student Writing

> The assessment of students' writing is a high-stakes activity that has for decades sparked debates in professional, research, policy, and community settings.
>
> (Cooksey, Freebody, & Wyatt-Smith, 2007, p. 402)

Cooksey conducted several studies examining judgmental processes using the lens model. This section briefly describes an application of judgment analysis to a study of writing by Cooksey, Freebody, and Wyatt-Smith (2007). In the selected application, Cooksey et al. describe teachers' assessment of student writing as a judgmental process that is shaped by a variety of cues, including the assessment context, the nature of the judgmental task, and characteristics of student essays. Specifically, the lens model was used as a theoretical and analytic framework for considering differences in teacher judgments related to the use of various cues, as well as differences across individual teachers.

In order to explore teacher assessment of writing as a judgmental task, a group of 20 teachers scored a set of essays composed by their own students and a set of essays composed by unfamiliar students. Each teacher provided two sets of ratings on the familiar and unfamiliar essays. First, the teachers were asked to provide an overall rating of the essay using a five-category rating scale; this task was intended to reflect typical classroom assessment practices. Next, the teachers were asked to provide a rating using the national benchmark scale, which has three categories; this task was intended to reflect an external assessment system. Both ratings were assigned to the set of familiar essays first, followed by the unfamiliar essays. During each of the scoring activities, the teachers provided concurrent think-aloud narrations of their decision-making processes. Further, each composition was analyzed for text features, including features related to essay length, complexity, mechanics, form, and evidence of revision.

Transcripts from the think-aloud interviews and results from the text analysis were used to obtain a set of cues for teacher judgments of writing achievement in the lens model. Specifically, variation in teacher judgment was examined in terms of four major categories of cues: assessment context (familiar or unfamiliar students), cues based on qualitative analyses of think-aloud interview transcripts, coded text features, and interactions between assessment context and think-aloud interview results. These sets of cues were entered as blocks in hierarchical regression models to predict teacher judgments. Separate models were specified for the classroom assessment and benchmark standards judgment tasks for each teacher, such that a total of 40 regression models were estimated. Variation among cue weights, along with the change in model fit (R^2), was examined following each block.

Regression results were examined in terms of the individual teachers and across the set of cues. Findings revealed variation in the degree to which individual teachers emphasized the cues across the group of teachers, and across the classroom assessment and benchmark standards judgmental tasks. Overall, these results highlighted the usefulness of the lens model approach for exploring judgmental processes across assessment contexts and comparing these processes across judgmental tasks. Cooksey, Freebody, and Wyatt-Smith (2007) discussed these findings in terms of frequently used agreement statistics as indicators of rating quality, and noted that these group-level statistics do not reveal the complexity involved in teacher judgment that reflects a variety of cues specific to an assessment context. Further, results from this study highlight the usefulness of the lens model as an approach to exploring the complex nature of the judgmental task associated with evaluating student writing that may be masked by group-level summaries of rater judgment. Cooksey et al. observed that detailed, individual teacher level (i.e., idiographic) analyses, such as those illustrated in the present analysis, can provide insight into judgmental processes that can be used to inform group-level (i.e., nomothetic) summaries of these judgments. In their words, "Once an *idiographic* level of understanding has been achieved, focus can then shift toward seeking defensible *nomothetic* trends or generalisations across a sample of teachers (Cooksey, 1988, p. 279)" (p. 404, emphasis in the original).

Use of Clinical Information by Nurses

> At the heart of modern professional clinical practice are nurses as "knowledgeable doers" (Department of Health, 1999) exercising their clinical judgment in the context of evidence based decisions made for the benefit of patients.
>
> *(Thompson et al., 2005, p. 69)*

The second illustrative application of lens models to explore human judgment is based on an examination of nurses' judgments when making diagnoses in clinical settings. Nursing provides an example of an authentic context in which expert judges (nurses) use a variety of cues (symptoms) in order to make judgments (diagnoses) that guide decisions (treatments). Specifically, Thompson et al. (2005) illustrated the use of the lens model as a conceptual and analytic approach for exploring nurses' use of clinical information when diagnosing hypovolemic shock, along with differences in judgments following instruction and across individual nurses.

In order to explore this judgmental process, a group of nurses was presented with a series of simulated medical scenarios in which clinical information related to six symptoms was presented based on advice from expert clinicians. Each scenario included variations on the level of normality of each symptom among patients who are not experiencing hypovolemic shock: normal, equivocal, and abnormal. For each scenario, the nurses were asked to estimate the likelihood that the simulated patient was in shock (0–100 scale), and provide a dichotomous judgment regarding the patient's status as not in shock (0) or in shock (1). The nurses completed the judgmental procedure prior to and immediately following the presentation of a lecture related to clinical diagnosis. Using these judgments, analyses focused on examining nurses' judgmental accuracy, along with differences in the weights assigned to clinical information across individual and groups of nurses.

Major findings suggested reduced variability in the weights assigned to the clinical cues following instruction, where the overall group of nurses appeared to attach similar weights to most of the symptoms prior to instruction, but placed greater emphasis on a smaller subset of symptoms following instruction. Despite this change, analyses at the level of individual nurses revealed that the variability in weights assigned to the clinical information persisted following instruction. As pointed out by Thompson et al. (2005), this idiographic lens model approach provides insight into variation among individual nurses' judgments and the relative importance of clinical cues when making diagnoses. Information about this variation can be used to guide instruction in order to improve accuracy in clinical settings. In their words, social judgment theory approaches "reveal this complexity, which would be lost if we used group-averaged learning needs as a start point for planning or evaluating teaching and learning" (p. 75).

Summary and Discussion

> As we enter our next phase of work *[on rater cognition]*, our primary goal must remain the same as it has in the past—to do all that we can to help ensure that the ratings that raters assign are accurate, reliable, and fair.
>
> *(Myford, 2012, p. 49)*

This chapter presented a short and selective framework for thinking about human judgments within the context of rater-mediated assessment. This review was not intended to be comprehensive. Rather, it was intended to highlight key features of lens models with the potential to aid our understanding of human judgment in the context of rater-mediated assessment. Psychological theories of judgment are important because they contribute to the development of perspectives on how to select, train, evaluate, and monitor the quality of ratings obtained in rater-mediated assessment systems. Lens models provide a useful starting point for understanding various facets of the rating process. We do not directly use the regression and correlational approach used by several researchers (Cooksey, 1996a, 1996b; Hammond, 1955; Tucker, 1964). Our approach is to use the conceptual and theoretical components of the original lens model proposed by Brunswik (1952) to lay the foundation for our thinking about human judgment within the context of rater-mediated assessments. Historically, judgments in psychology have been typically studied under the areas of psychophysics, attitude measurement, and personnel ratings. In this chapter, we illustrated the application of judgment analysis in the context of rater-mediated assessments using a lens model framework.

Brunswik's lens model also had the goal of discovering unobserved variables that would be viewed as latent variables today. Brunswik and others based the methodological analyses of the lens model on the extant statistical methods of their historical period. Although ANOVA models based on Fisher's contributions (1925, 1935) were emergent in psychological methodology, Brunswik argued that concerns with ecological validity did not fit the experimental approach underlying ANOVA models. Brunswik preferred regression and correlational analyses for examining lens models because the statistical methodology matched his theoretical and conceptual focus on probabilistic functionalism. In this book, we make the link between lens models and modern scaling theories based on Item Response Theory and structural equation models informed by a concern with the goals of invariant measurement. It is important to note that rater-mediated assessments should include a theory of human judgment, as well as a measurement theory that is congruent with the theory of human judgment.

References

Athanasou, J. A., & Kaufmann, E. (2015). Probability of responding: A return to the original Brunswik. *Psychological Thought, 8*(1), 7–16.

Barsalou, L. W. (1992). *Cognitive psychology: An overview for cognitive scientists.* New York: Psychology Press.

Bock, R. D., & Jones, L. V. (1968). *The measurement and prediction of judgment and choice.* San Francisco: Holden-Day.

Brunswik, E. (1952). *The conceptual framework of psychology.* Chicago: University of Chicago Press.

Brunswik, E. (1955a). Representative design and probabilistic theory in a functional psychology. *Psychological Review, 62*(3), 193–217.

Brunswik, E. (1955b). In defense of probabilistic functionalism: A reply. *Psychological Review, 62*(3), 236–242.

Brunswik, E. (1956). *Perception and the representative design of psychological experiments* (2nd ed.). Berkeley, CA: University of California Press.

Chomsky, N. (1959). A review of B. F. Skinner's *Verbal Behavior. Language, 35*(1), 26–58.

Cooksey, R. W. (1988). Social judgment theory in education: Current and potential applications. In B. Brehmer & C.R.B. Joyce (Eds.), *Human judgment: The SJT view* (pp. 273–316). Amsterdam: North Holland Elsevier.

Cooksey, R. W. (1996a). *Judgment analysis: Theory, methods, and applications.* Bingley, UK: Emerald Press.

Cooksey, R. W. (1996b). The methodology of social judgement theory. *Thinking and Reasoning, 2*(2/3), 141–173.

Cooksey, R. W., Freebody, P., & Davidson, G. R. (1986). Teachers' predictions of children's early reading achievement: An application of social judgment theory. *American Educational Research Journal, 23*(1), 41–64.

Cooksey, R. W., Freebody, P., & Wyatt-Smith, C. (2007). Assessment as judgment-in-context: Analyzing how teachers evaluate students' writing. *Educational Research and Evaluation, 13*(5), 401–434.

Einhorn, H. J. (1974). Expert judgment: Some necessary conditions and an example. *Journal of Applied Psychology, 59*(5), 562–573.

Engelhard, G. (1992). The measurement of writing ability with a many-faceted Rasch model. *Applied Measurement in Education, 5*(3), 171–191.

Engelhard, G. (1994). Examining rater errors in the assessment of written composition with a many-faceted Rasch model. *Journal of Educational Measurement, 31*(2), 93–112.

Engelhard, G. (2013). *Invariant measurement: Using Rasch models in the social, behavioral, and health sciences.* New York: Routledge.

Fechner, G. T. (1860). *Elemente der psychophysik* [Elements of psychophysics]. Leipzig, Germany: Breitkopf & Hartel.

Fisher, R. A. (1925). *Statistical methods for research workers.* Edinburgh: Oliver & Boyd.

Fisher, R. A. (1935). *The design of experiments.* Edinburgh/London: Oliver and Boyd.

Gibson, J. J. (1979/2014). *The ecological approach to visual perception: Classic edition.* New York: Psychology Press.

Hammond, K. R. (1955). Probabilistic functioning and the clinical method. *Psychological Review, 62*(4), 255.

Hammond, K. R. (1980). Introduction to Brunswikian theory and methods. In K. R. Hammond & N. E. Wascoe (Eds.), *Realizations of Brunswik's representative design* (pp. 1–12). San Francisco: Jossey-Bass.

Hammond, K. R. (1996). *Human judgment and social policy: Irreducible uncertainty, inevitable error, unavoidable injustice.* New York: Oxford University Press.

Hammond, K. R., & Stewart, T. R. (2001). *The essential Brunswik: Beginnings, explications, applications.* New York: Oxford University Press.

Hammond, K. R., Stewart, T. R., Brehmer, B., & Steinmann, D. (1975). Social judgment theory. In M. Kaplan & S. Schwartz (Eds.), *Human judgment and decision processes* (pp. 271–312). New York: Academic Press.

Hogarth, R. M. (1987). *Judgement and choice: The psychology of decision* (2nd ed.). New York: John Wiley & Sons.

Johnson, D. M. (1955). *The psychology of thought and judgment.* New York, NY: Harper & Row.

Kahneman, D. (2011). *Thinking, fast and slow.* New York: Farrar, Straus and Giroux.

Karelaia, N., & Hogarth, R. (2008). Determinants of linear judgment: A meta-analysis of lens studies. *Psychological Bulletin, 134*(3), 404–426.

Kaufmann, E., Reips, U. D., & Wittmann, W. W. (2013). A critical meta-analysis of lens model studies in human judgment and decision-making. *PLoS One, 8*, e83528.

Myford, C. M. (2012). Rater cognition research: Some possible directions for the future. *Educational Measurement: Issues and Practice, 31*(3), 48–49.

Neisser, U. (1967). *Cognitive psychology: Classic edition.* New York, NY: Psychology Press.

Newell, A. (1968). Judgment and its representation: An introduction. In B. Kleinmuntz (Ed.), *Formal representation of human judgment* (pp. 1–16). New York, NY: Wiley.

Postman, L., & Tolman, E. C. (1959). Brunswik's probabilistic functionalism. *Psychology: A Study of a Science, 1*, 502–564.

Shulman, L. S., & Elstein, A. (1975). Studies of problem solving, judgment, and decision making: Implications for educational research. In F. N. Kerlinger (Ed.), *Review of research in education* (Vol. 3, pp. 3–42). Itasca, NY: Peacock.

Skinner, B. F. (1938). *The behavior of organisms.* New York: Appleton-Century-Crofts.

Skinner, B. F. (1957). *Verbal behavior.* New York: Appleton-Century-Crofts.

Thompson, C. A., Foster, A., Cole, I., & Dowding, D. W. (2005). Using social judgment theory to model nurses' use of clinical information in critical care education. *Nurse Education Today, 25,* 68–77.

Thurstone, L. L. (1959). *The measurement of values.* Chicago: University of Chicago Press.

Torgerson, W. S. (1958). *Theory and methods of scaling.* New York: Wiley.

Tucker, L. R. (1964). A suggested alternative formulation in the developments by Hursch, Hammond, and Hursch, and by Hammond, Hursch, and Todd. *Psychological Review, 71*(6), 528–530.

Watson, J. B. (1919). *Psychology: From the standpoint of a behaviorist.* Philadelphia, PA: Lippincott.

PART III

Foundational Areas for Rating Scales

5

VALIDITY, INVARIANT MEASUREMENT, AND RATER-MEDIATED ASSESSMENTS

> Validity refers to the degree to which evidence and theory support the interpretations of test scores for proposed uses of tests.
>
> *(AERA, APA, & NCME, 2014, p. 11)*

Chapter Two provided a brief overview of the three foundational areas described in the *Standards for Educational and Psychological Testing* (AERA, APA, & NCME, 2014): Validity, reliability, and fairness. This chapter addresses the foundational area of validity with an emphasis on the implications of this foundational area for rater-mediated assessments. Figure 2.1 in Chapter Two suggests the three foundational areas are fundamental for all aspects of an assessment system including the measurement models, use of the assessment, assessment development, administration, and evaluation of the assessment. At their base, topics related to validity are about the meaning, interpretation, and appropriate uses of test scores.

The purposes of this chapter are to provide a brief overview of changes in the definitions of validity over time, to describe the current consensus definition of validity provided by the *Standards for Educational and Psychological Testing* (AERA, APA, & NCME, 2014), and to discuss the concept of validity as it applies specifically to rater-mediated assessments.

The chapter is organized around the following questions and issues:

- What is validity?
- What is the current consensus definition of validity?
- How is validity defined for rater-mediated assessments?
- What constitutes validity evidence to support the interpretation and use of rater-mediated assessments?
- Summary and discussion

This chapter emphasizes how validity can be viewed within the context of rater-mediated assessments.

What Is Validity?

One of the major topics of current discussion and debate in measurement is related to the concept of validity. There is general agreement regarding the importance of validity for measurement in the human sciences; however, the definition of this concept and the methods used for documenting the validity of test scores has been a contentious topic over time. Further, there is disagreement within the educational measurement community regarding the history of the development and definition of validity (Engelhard & Behizadeh, 2012; Borsboom, Mellenbergh, & van Heerden, 2004; Kane, 2013; Newton, 2012; Newton & Shaw, 2015). Although it is beyond the scope of this chapter to provide a thorough discussion of the historical development and current discussions of validity, this section provides a brief overview of highlights in the development of validity theory, followed by a discussion of the current consensus definition of validity, as reflected in the *Standards for Educational and Psychological Testing*.

Summary of Historical Views of Validity

Early definitions of validity within the measurement community were based on objectivity in the interpretation of scores. For example, Thorndike (1919) described a valid scale as one "in respect to whose meaning all competent thinkers agree" (p. 11). The concept of agreement is also reflected in Kelley's (1927) proposition that validity is indicated by agreement about what a scale is intended to measure. Later discussions of validity focused on the role of empirical evidence of the relationship between observed scores and relevant external variables (Gulliksen, 1950; Thurstone, 1931). For example, according to Gulliksen (1950), "the validity of a test is the correlation of the test with some criterion" (p. 88). The definition of objectivity as agreement among a group of experts who are members of a community of practice reflects the quest for invariance more generally in the social, behavioral, and health sciences. As pointed out by Nozick (2001) in his book *Invariances: The Structure of the Objective World*, objective facts yield intersubjective agreement within a community of practice; they are invariant from different perspectives, and they exist independent of our beliefs, desires, and observations—they are refutable. Early measurement theorists searched for objectivity defined as agreement and invariance.

During the second half of the 20th century, the concept of validity evolved such that it was viewed in terms of a *validation process*, where interrelated types of validity evidence could be used to support particular interpretations and uses of test scores (Cronbach, 1971; Cronbach & Meehl, 1955). Specifically, the first version of the *Standards for Educational and Psychological Testing* (APA, 1954) described four types of validity to evaluate a test for distinct purposes: content, predictive, concurrent, and construct. Depending on the intended use of a test, different types of validity evidence were viewed as more or less essential. This view of distinct categories or *types of validity* was also promoted in the subsequent edition of the *Standards for Educational and Psychological Testing* (AERA, APA, & NCME, 1974), where three types of validity were described: criterion, content, and construct.

Soon after the publication of the 1954 edition of the *Standards for Educational and Psychological Testing*, Loevinger (1957) expressed her concerns over the scientific usefulness of the classifications of validity evidence into distinct categories. Instead, she proposed a unified view of construct validity as encompassing all of validity. Loevinger described her unified view of validity as follows: "There is only one kind of validity which exhibits the property of transposability or *invariance* under changes in administrative setting which is the touchstone of scientific usefulness: that is *construct validity*" (p. 641, italics added).

As evidenced by the 1974 *Standards for Educational and Psychological Testing* and other authoritative texts on educational measurement (e.g., Cronbach, 1971), Loevinger's unified view of validity as construct validity was not immediately adopted. However, discussions of validity in the 1980s began to reflect an emphasis on construct validity as a unifying theme (e.g., Anastasi, 1986; Cronbach, 1980, 1984; Linn, 1980). In particular, Messick (1989) echoed Loevinger's unified view in his influential discussion of validity. Specifically, he presented a broad view of construct validity that included a consideration of consequential validity evidence. In his words:

> The testing field . . . is moving toward recognition of validity as a unitary concept, in the sense that score meaning as embodied in construct validity underlies all score-based inferences. But for a fully unified view of validity, it must also be recognized that the appropriateness, meaningfulness, and usefulness of score-based inferences depend as well on the social consequences of testing.
>
> *(p. 19)*

Kane (1992, 2006, 2013) proposed a slightly different view based on an argument-based approach to validity. This approach to validity can be described as an iterative process based on articulating arguments and testing warrants for claims related to the interpretation and use of tests. In essence, Kane's framework is based on the specification of interpretative arguments for test score interpretations and uses, where justification is needed to support inferences.

Recent discussions of validity have highlighted the notion that validity is defined within communities of practice (Behizadeh & Engelhard, 2015), and that content-area researchers may have unique definitions of validity and procedures for validation that reflect values within their communities. In order to improve the validity of assessment systems, communication is needed between content-area and measurement communities of practice. Along the same lines, Sireci (2013) pointed out that communication and agreement about *purpose* of assessment systems across communities of practice is essential in order to inform the validation process. Speaking to the educational measurement community, he observed:

> Tests are developed to fulfill one or more intended purposes. It is incumbent upon us as psychometricians to help those who commission these tests to articulate the intended purposes. Once these purposes are articulated, we know what we need to validate. We also know what it is we need to measure!
>
> *(p. 100)*

The next section describes the current consensus definition of validity within the measurement community, as defined in the *Standards for Educational and Psychological Testing*. The consensus definition and related standards for validity are then considered as they apply specifically to rater-mediated assessments.

What Is the Current Consensus Definition of Validity?

The *Standards for Educational and Psychological Testing* (AERA, APA, & NCME, 2014) provide guidance for evaluating assessment systems that reflect a consensus definition within the measurement community regarding psychometrically sound and legally defensible measurement principles and practices. The most recent version of the *Standards for Educational and Psychological Testing* defines validity as "the degree to which accumulated evidence and theory support a specific interpretation of test scores for a given use of a test" (AERA, APA, & NCME, 2014, p. 11). The corresponding standards reflect the argument-based approach advocated by Kane (1992, 2006, 2013). Although current discussions within the measurement community include other views of validity than the argument-based approach (e.g., Borsboom, 2005; Borsboom & Markus, 2013; Borsboom, Mellenbergh, & van Heerden, 2004), our discussion of validity for rater-mediated assessments is driven by the current consensus definition given in the *Standards for Educational and Psychological Testing*.

For each foundational area described in the *Standards for Educational and Psychological Testing*, an overarching standard is presented to highlight the guiding principles that reflect best practices for the development, interpretation, and use of educational and psychological tests. Following the overarching standard, clusters of individual standards are presented with comments that describe more specific guidelines related to various stages in the assessment process. The overarching standard for validity is as follows.

STANDARD 1.0

Clear articulation of each intended test score interpretation for a specified use should be set forth, and appropriate validity evidence in support of each intended interpretation should be provided.

AERA, APA, and NCME (2014, p. 23)

This overarching standard is followed by three clusters of individual standards:

  I. Establishing intended uses and interpretations,
 II. Issues regarding samples and settings used in validation, and
III. Specific forms of validity evidence.

These three thematic clusters are shown in Figure 5.1 (Panel A). The first cluster emphasizes the idea that validity cannot be evaluated in a *vacuum* without specifically considering the intended uses and interpretations for an assessment system. Standards within this cluster highlight the importance of clearly articulating the intended purpose(s) of assessment systems and considering potential intended and unintended consequences associated with each interpretation and use of test scores. Standards in the second cluster emphasize the importance of considering the context for assessment systems during the validation process. This idea is illustrated in Figure 2.1, which emphasizes the role of the assessment context in informing all aspects of an assessment system. Different validity concerns may be applicable to different assessment contexts. The third cluster of validity standards describes five specific sources of evidence to support the interpretation and use of test scores. Panel B in Figure 5.1 shows the specific forms of validity evidence in Cluster III. Sources for validity evidence are classified as evidence based on (A) test content, (B) response processes, (C) internal structure, (D) relations to external variables, and (E) consequences of testing. Although five separate sources of validity evidence are presented, the *Standards for Educational and Psychological Testing* emphasize a unified conceptualization of validity, where the different sources of evidence

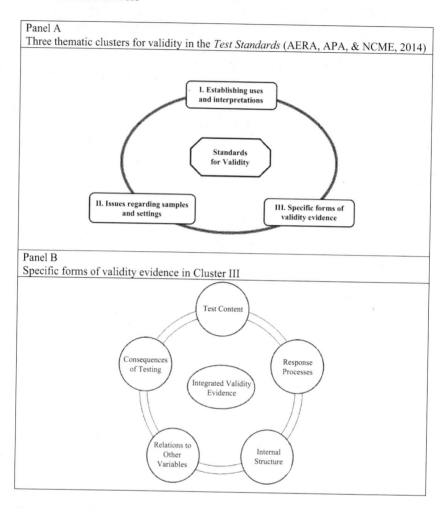

Panel A
Three thematic clusters for validity in the *Test Standards* (AERA, APA, & NCME, 2014)

I. Establishing uses
and interpretations

Standards
for Validity

II. Issues regarding samples
and settings

III. Specific forms of
validity evidence

Panel B
Specific forms of validity evidence in Cluster III

Test Content

Consequences
of Testing

Response
Processes

Integrated Validity
Evidence

Relations to
Other
Variables

Internal
Structure

FIGURE 5.1   Validity Standards from the *Standards for Educational and Psychological Testing*

"may illuminate different aspects of validity, but they do not represent distinct types of validity. Validity is a unitary concept" (pp. 13–14). Table 5.1 lists the five sources of evidence, along with a short definition from the *Standards for Educational and Psychological Testing*.

Drawing upon the current consensus definition for validity, the next section includes a discussion of the concept of validity as it applies specifically to rater-mediated assessments. First, an overview of validity discussions for performance assessments in general is provided. A discussion of the five sources of validity evidence from the *Standards for Educational and Psychological Testing* as they apply to raters follows.

TABLE 5.1 Three Thematic Clusters of Validity Standards from the *Standards for Educational and Psychological Testing*

Cluster		*Description from the Standards for Educational and Psychological Testing*
I. Establishing intended uses and interpretations		"Statements about validity should refer to particular interpretations for specified uses. It is incorrect to use the unqualified phrase 'the validity of the test'" (p. 11)
II. Issues regarding samples and settings used in validation		"Validation is the joint responsibility of the test developer and test user. The test developer is responsible for furnishing relevant evidence and a rationale in support of any test score interpretations for specified uses intended by the developer. The test user is ultimately responsible for evaluating the evidence in the particular setting in which the test is to be used" (p. 13)
III. Specific forms of validity evidence	A. Test content	Evidence related to the "relationship between the content of a test and the construct it is intended to measure" (p. 14)
	B. Response processes	"Evidence concerning the fit between the construct and the detailed nature of the performance or response actually engaged in by test takers" (p. 15)
	C. Internal structure	"The degree to which the relationships among test items and test components conform to the construct on which the proposed test score interpretations are based" (p. 16)
	D. Relations to other variables	"Evidence based on relationships to other variables provides evidence about the degree to which these relationships are consistent with the construct underlying the proposed test score interpretations" (p. 16)
	E. Consequences of testing	"Decisions about test use are appropriately informed by validity evidence about the intended test score interpretations for a given use, by evidence evaluating additional claims about consequences of test use that do not follow directly from test score interpretations, and by value judgments about unintended positive and negative consequences of test use" (p. 21)

How Is Validity Defined for Rater-Mediated Assessments?

One of the major themes of this book is that rater-mediated assessment systems involve an additional layer associated with the judgmental processes that function as a lens to interpret cues regarding person performances. As a result, validity considerations for rater-mediated assessments must include a close examination of the judgmental processes used by raters to mediate assessment opportunities and inferences about other aspects of the assessment system. Several scholars have discussed validity issues as they apply specifically to performance assessments; however, many of these previous studies have not stressed strongly enough the key roles of raters in these assessment systems. The next section provides a brief summary of general discussions of validity for performance assessments, followed by a consideration of validity as it applies specifically to raters.

Validity Issues for Performance Assessments in General

As large-scale performance assessments were very popular in the 1980s and 1990s, research around this time included an emphasis on validity concerns related to unique characteristics of these assessments. Specifically, several researchers expressed concerns that traditional validity criteria were not sufficient for the unique challenges associated with performance assessments. For example, Moss (1992) observed:

> Performance assessments present a number of validity problems not easily handled with traditional approaches and criteria for validity research. These assessments typically permit students substantial latitude in interpreting, responding to, and perhaps designing tasks; they result in fewer independent responses, each of which is complex, reflecting integration of multiple skills and knowledge; and they require expert judgment for evaluation. Consequently, meeting criteria related to such validity issues as reliability, generalizability, and comparability of assessments—at least as they are typically defined and operationalized—becomes problematic.
>
> *(p. 230)*

Sharing these concerns about the adequacy of traditional validation methods, several researchers proposed sets of validity criteria and suggestions for validation processes specifically aimed at performance assessments. For example, arguing that the adoption of a performance assessment format was itself a method for improving the validity of an assessment system, Frederiksen and Collins (1989) considered validity in terms of the ability for an assessment to contribute to positive changes to educational systems—what they called the *systemic validity* of an assessment. They proposed a set of principles for the design of systemically valid assessments that included four standards for evaluating the validity of a performance assessment that included directness, scope, reliability, and transparency. Frederiksen and Collins claimed that a "systemically valid test is one that induces in the education system curricular and instructional changes that foster the development of the cognitive skills that the test is designed to measure" (p. 27).

In a similar way, Linn, Baker, and Dunbar (1991) claimed that traditional validity criteria were not sufficient for the evaluation of performance assessments, observing:

> The traditional [validity] criteria need to be expanded. . . . This expansion is needed not just as a theoretical nicety but because judgments about the relative merits of the many efforts now under way to move assessments 'beyond the bubble' will depend on the criteria that are used and the relative weight that is given to them.
>
> *(p. 20)*

Linn et al. proposed a set of eight criteria for evaluating performance-based assessments, such as evidence regarding intended and unintended consequences, transfer, fairness, cognitive complexity, meaningfulness, content quality, comprehensiveness of content coverage, and cost.

Other discussions of validity for performance assessments during the 1990s included issues related to task-centered versus construct-centered assessments (Messick, 1994), authenticity of assessment tasks (Linn, Baker, & Dunbar, 1991; Messick, 1994; Moss, 1994), and others. More recently, Lane and Stone (2006) identified another set of validity issues that they claimed were especially relevant for performance assessments including cognitive complexity, directness and meaningfulness, consequences, and group performance differences. Finally, Johnson, Penny, and Gordon (2009) presented a practical guide to the design, scoring, and validation of performance tasks, where they suggested that performance tasks should be evaluated in terms of eight criteria: (1) authenticity, (2) context, (3) cognitive complexity, (4) in-depth content coverage, (5) examinee-structured response, (6) credibility, (7) costs, and (8) reform. It is beyond the scope of this chapter to describe in detail each of the sets of criteria, and the reader should consult the original sources for a more thorough discussion.

In contrast to sets of validity criteria specifically for performance assessments as described above, Messick (1994) argued that all assessments should be evaluated by the same validity criteria:

> Performance assessments must be evaluated by the same validity criteria, both evidential and consequential, as are other assessments. Indeed, such basic assessment issues as validity, reliability, comparability, and fairness need to be uniformly addressed for all assessments because they are not just measurement principles, they are *social values* that have meaning and force outside of measurement wherever evaluative judgments and decisions are made.
>
> *(p. 13)*

When evaluating rater-mediated assessments, it is essential to recognize that the interpretation of each of these issues is directly tied to the quality of the ratings that are mediated through a group of raters. Although several recent discussions of validity for performance assessments mention the involvement of raters in the assessment process, including rater training procedures, concerns with rater biases, and rater consistency (e.g., Lane & Stone, 2006; Slomp, Corrigan, & Sugimoto, 2014), specific validity concerns and issues related to raters have not been fully explored. Rather, the role of raters and rating quality in these assessments is generally featured in discussions of reliability and generalizability issues.

It cannot be stressed enough that many of the earlier criteria for evaluating performance assessment ignore the crucial distinction that we make in this book—all aspects of rater-mediated assessment of performances are defined in terms of the lens that undergirds rater judgments. It is essential to have validity criteria that reflect this key idea.

What Constitutes Validity Evidence to Support the Interpretation and Use of Rater-Mediated Assessments?

This chapter contributes to the existing literature related to validity for performance assessments by providing a discussion of validity issues for rater-mediated assessments that emphasizes raters as a key factor in the assessment process. In this section, the three thematic clusters of validity standards from the *Standards for Educational and Psychological Testing* are considered from the perspective of rater-mediated assessments, with an emphasis on the underlying issues related to invariant measurement. Table 5.1 summarizes the themes emphasized in the standards within each cluster. Table 5.2 summarizes the major concerns related to the three thematic clusters for validity using questions that highlight concerns related to selected-response assessments and rater-mediated assessments. Whereas the underlying questions for selected-response assessments are specified to reflect the underlying concerns emphasized in the *Standards for Educational and Psychological Testing* for assessments in general, the questions presented for rater-mediated assessments are formulated to reflect the perspective of rater-invariant measurement.

1. Establishing Intended Uses and Interpretations

The first cluster of validity standards focuses on the clear specification of intended interpretations and uses for test scores. Standards in this cluster caution test developers and test users that validity evidence cannot be evaluated without a clear specification of the particular interpretation and use that it is intended to support. As given in the *Standards for Educational and Psychological Testing* (AERA, APA, & NCME, 2014):

> Statements about validity should refer to particular interpretations for specified uses. It is incorrect to use the unqualified phrase "the validity of the test."

(p. 11)

As given in Table 5.2, the validity standards in this cluster reflect the following underlying question for selected-response assessments:

* *What is the intended interpretation and use of test scores?*

Essentially, the first cluster of validity standards emphasizes the need to provide rationale for each intended interpretation and use of test scores that is supported by appropriate evidence. Further, the *Standards for Educational and Psychological Testing* call test users to consider the alignment between the intended interpretation and use specified by test developers and their own intended interpretation and use in order to determine whether additional validity evidence is needed for the particular assessment context.

From the perspective of rater-invariant measurement, the underlying concerns related to minimizing barriers to valid test interpretations can be summarized using the following question:

* *What is the intended interpretation and use of ratings?*

The underlying questions for rater-mediated assessments in Table 5.2 reflect essentially the same concerns as those identified for constructed-response items, with an emphasis on the role of raters' judgmental process for evaluating student responses in terms of the construct. Specifically, when rater judgment is involved in scoring procedures, it is necessary to consider how ratings will be interpreted as indicators of student standing on the construct. Depending on the intended interpretation and use of ratings, different scoring designs (i.e., how many raters score each student), rater training and qualification procedures, and rater monitoring procedures may be necessary to support a particular interpretation and use.

2. Issues Regarding Samples and Settings Used in Validation

The second cluster of validity standards focuses on the clear specification of the samples and settings from which validity evidence is gathered to support a particular interpretation and use. The standards in this cluster focus on the documentation of sample and setting characteristics. These standards allow test users to determine the relevance of validity evidence provided by a test developer across a variety of assessment contexts. As given in the *Standards for Educational and Psychological Testing* (AERA, APA, & NCME, 2014):

> Validation is the joint responsibility of the test developer and test user. The test developer is responsible for furnishing relevant evidence and a rationale in support of any test score interpretations for specified uses intended by the developer. The test user is ultimately responsible for evaluating the evidence in the particular setting in which the test is to be used.
>
> *(p. 13)*

TABLE 5.2 Underlying Questions for the Three Validity Clusters Based on Selected–Response and Rater-Mediated Assessments

Cluster	Selected-Response Assessments	Rater-Mediated Assessments
I. Establishing intended uses and interpretations	What is the intended interpretation and use of test scores?	What is the intended interpretation and use of ratings?
II. Issues regarding samples and settings used in validation	What samples and settings were used to collect validity evidence to support the intended interpretation and use of test scores?	What samples and settings were used to obtain rater training materials (e.g., benchmark papers)?
III. Specific forms of validity evidence		
A. Test content	What is the latent variable being measured?	What is the rater–mediated latent variable?
B. Response processes	How are observations and responses categorized to represent person locations and levels on the latent variable?	How do rater interpretations of rubrics and performance-level descriptors lead to ratings of student achievement that define the rater-mediated latent variable?
C. Internal structure	How are person and item responses mapped onto the latent variable?	How are rater interpretations of person locations, domain difficulties, and rating-scale categories mapped onto the rater-mediated latent variable?
D. Relations to other variables	How does the alignment between observed scores and relevant external variables support the interpretation of test scores in terms of the latent variable?	How does the alignment between ratings and relevant external variables support the interpretation of ratings in terms of the latent variable?
E. Consequences of testing	What is the range of possible intended and unintended consequences of the assessment system?	What is the range of possible intended and unintended consequences of the rater-mediated assessment system?

As given in Table 5.2, the validity standards in this cluster reflect the following underlying question for selected-response assessments:

- *What samples and settings were used to collect validity evidence to support the intended interpretation and use of test scores?*

Essentially, the second cluster of validity standards describes the joint responsibilities of test developers and test users to ensure that sufficient evidence is gathered to evaluate the appropriateness of a particular assessment for a given interpretation and use.

In the context of rater-mediated assessments, considerations related to samples and settings must also include consideration of the context in which rater training and monitoring procedures take place. These considerations are summarized in the underlying question for rater-mediated assessments related to the second cluster of validity standards:

- *What samples and settings were used to obtain rater training materials (e.g., benchmark papers)?*

In addition to information about the samples and settings used to collect information from students that is used in validity studies, it is essential to also consider the nature of the materials presented during rater training. For example, many operational assessment systems require raters to complete training exercises in which they learn how to apply rubrics or scoring guides based on exemplar performances that serve as benchmarks for scoring. Further, scoring procedures often include interspersed "validity checks," where benchmark papers are inserted into operational scoring in order to compare observed ratings with criterion ratings. Information related to the characteristics of students from whom these benchmarks are obtained, as well as the characteristics of assessment settings, is needed in order to inform the interpretation of ratings.

3. Specific Forms of Validity Evidence

The third cluster of validity standards focuses on the integration of various sources of relevant validity evidence to support a given interpretation and use for test scores. The standards in this cluster are described separately as they apply to the five sources of validity evidence identified in the *Standards for Educational and Psychological Testing*: (A) test content, (B) response processes, (C) internal structure, (D) relations to external variables, and (E) consequences of testing. Following this structure, Table 5.2 presents the underlying questions related to the third cluster of validity standards separately for each of the five sources of validity evidence.

A. Evidence Based on Test Content

The first source of validity evidence described in the *Standards for Educational and Psychological Testing* is evidence based on test content. This form of evidence is based on "an analysis of the relationship between the content of a test and the construct it is intended to measure" (p. 14). From the perspective of invariant measurement, this source of validity evidence can be conceptualized in terms of the Wright map. As noted in Chapter One, Wright maps are visual representations of the latent variable that facilitate the interpretation of locations of individual persons, items, and other facets in terms of this underlying continuum. For selected-response items, the key underlying question related to test content is:

• *What is the latent variable being measured?*

When constructing a measure, researchers must begin by conceptualizing the underlying continuum in terms of a qualitative order from low to high (i.e., fail/pass; strongly disagree/disagree/agree/strongly agree; etc.). Examination of the alignment between observed and expected ordering of persons, items, or other facets on the Wright map can be used to support the interpretation of logit-scale locations as representing locations on the latent variable based on observations collected during the measurement process.

For raters, the key underlying question related to this source of validity evidence is:

• *What is the rater-mediated latent variable?*

In the context of rater-mediated assessments, it is important to recognize that locations on the Wright map represent rater judgments of student achievement, cue difficulties, and the difficulty of rating scale categories. As a result, it is important to recognize that raters' decision-making processes mediate all of the information about these facets. In a rater-mediated assessment, cues may take on the form of tasks, prompts, or domains in analytic scoring. Accordingly, the Wright map for a rater-mediated assessment can be seen as a summary of rater judgment regarding students, items, and other facets across a set of raters. Good model-data fit suggests adherence to the requirements for rater-invariant measurement—that is, the locations of raters, students, and other facets may be compared on the same linear scale.

B. Evidence Based on Response Processes

The second major source of validity evidence is evidence based on response processes. According to the *Standards for Educational and Psychological Testing,* validity evidence in this category includes "Evidence concerning the fit between the construct and the detailed nature of the performance or response actually engaged in by test takers" (AERA, APA, & NCME, 2014, p. 15). In practice, theoretical and empirical analyses of student responses to assessment tasks are used to gather evidence about the match between the cognitive processes used by students and the construct the assessment is intended to measure. For selected-response assessments, underlying concerns related to this source of validity evidence can be summarized as follows:

- *How are observations and responses categorized to represent person locations and levels on the latent variable?*

For selected-response assessments, student responses are categorized according to scoring rules used to distinguish the range of responses that indicate a correct response (e.g., a response that warrants a score of "1") from those that indicate an incorrect response (e.g., a response that warrants a score of "0"). In the context of educational achievement tests, the range of responses often includes the selection of a pre-specified response alternative (e.g., A, B, C, or D). Evidence related to response processes may be gathered using retrospective or concurrent think-aloud interviews, where students narrate their thought processes while responding to assessment tasks (Ericsson & Simon, 1980); this technique has been widely used during assessment development (Ercikan et al., 2010; Kaliski, France, & Huff, 2011; Leighton, 2004).

When assessments involve raters, it is also necessary to gather evidence related to the response processes of raters. As noted in the *Standards for Educational and Psychological Testing*:

> Relevant validity evidence includes the extent to which the processes of observers or judges are consistent with the intended interpretation of scores . . . Thus, validation may include empirical studies of how observers or judges record and evaluate data along with analyses of the appropriateness of these processes to the intended interpretation or construct definition.
>
> *(pp. 15–16)*

Evidence based on response processes is related to rater interpretations of the performance tasks (i.e., prompts), scoring rubric(s), performance-level descriptors (i.e., PLDs), and rating scale categories. Essentially, the goal in collecting evidence based on rater response processes is to support the inference that the raters share a common understanding of components of the assessment system and their alignment with elements of student responses that facilitates a community of meaning and use for an assessment instrument. The underlying concerns related to this source of validity evidence for rater-mediated assessments can be summarized as follows:

- *How do rater interpretations of rubrics and performance-level descriptors lead to ratings of student achievement that define the rater-mediated latent variable?*

In practice, validity evidence in this category may be collected using think-aloud studies with raters during training procedures or operational scoring (e.g., Lumley, 2002; Wolfe, Kao, & Ranney, 1998).

C. Evidence Based on Internal Structure

The third major source of validity evidence is based on internal structure. According to the *Standards for Educational and Psychological Testing*, this source of evidence is based on "the degree to which the relationships among test items and test components conform to the construct on which the proposed test score interpretations are based" (p. 16). For selected-response items, concerns related to this source of validity evidence can be summarized as follows:

- *How are person and item responses mapped onto the latent variable?*

Essentially, validity evidence related to internal structure includes evidence about relationships among tasks, and relationships between tasks and the total score. Within the framework of Rasch Measurement Theory, this alignment between tasks can be empirically investigated by comparing scores on a given item or task with mean locations of students within score groups. Evidence of a positive relationship between item scores and mean locations can support the interpretation of test scores in terms of the construct. Within the test-score tradition, similar indices have been investigated using the point-biserial correlation between raw scores on items and total raw scores on instruments (Crocker & Algina, 1986). Consistency of item ordering across subgroups of respondents also provides evidence related to the internal structure of an assessment. In particular, indices of differential item functioning (DIF) can be used to collect evidence that the assessment tasks function similarly across subgroups, such as best language, gender, and race/ethnicity. From the perspective of invariant measurement, DIF indices describe the degree to which the requirements of invariant measurement hold across student subgroups.

In the context of rater-mediated assessments, validity evidence related to the internal structure of an assessment is used to support the interpretation of ratings as indices of the construct intended to be measured by the assessment. Underlying concerns related to internal structure for rater-mediated assessments can be summarized using the following question:

- *How are rater interpretations of person locations, domain difficulties, and rating-scale categories mapped onto the rater-mediated latent variable?*

Within the framework of rater-invariant measurement, validity evidence in this category generally includes indicators of a positive relationship between observed ratings and measures of student achievement, where evidence of a positive relationship provides support for the interpretation of item scores in terms of the construct. Specifically, a *test response function* can be plotted that shows the correspondence between observed ratings on the raw-score and Rasch-based estimates of student achievement. Evidence that increasing observed ratings corresponds to increasing estimates of student achievement suggest that observed ratings support the interpretation of observed ratings as indices of student locations on the latent variable. Additional evidence based on Rasch Measurement Theory related to the internal structure of rater-mediated assessments includes indicators of model-data fit and differential facet functioning; these indices will be described further in Chapter Six (Reliability) and Chapter Seven (Fairness), respectively.

D. Evidence Based on Relations to Other Variables

The fourth source of validity evidence listed in the *Standards for Educational and Psychological Testing* is evidence based on relations between test scores and other relevant variables. Evidence in this category is used to support the hypothesis that relationships among test scores and relevant variables "are consistent with the construct underlying the proposed test score interpretations" (AERA, APA, & NCME, 2014, p. 16). As noted in the *Standards for Educational and Psychological Testing*, this type of validity evidence includes evidence of both *convergent relationships* that indicate that a test is measuring what it is intended to measure, as well as *divergent relationships* (i.e., null relationships) that indicate that a test is not measuring what it is not intended to measure. As given in Table 5.2, the underlying question for this source of validity evidence is:

- *How does the alignment between observed scores and relevant external variables support the interpretation of test scores in terms of the latent variable?*

The selection of relevant criteria for examining convergent and divergent relationships depends on the theoretical framework for the assessment, which specifies expected relationships with operationally distinct variables from the test score. Relevant relationships may include predictive or concurrent relationships with external variables. The *Standards for Educational and Psychological Testing* also emphasize the importance of examining the generalizability of relations to other variables across relevant subgroups and contexts.

In the context of rater-mediated assessments, relations to other variables may be examined through comparisons between observed ratings and scores on other relevant variables. Essentially, these correlational analyses are used to explore the alignment between rater judgments of student achievement and indices based on other measures. The underlying question for this source of validity evidence for rater-mediated assessments is:

- *How does the alignment between ratings and relevant external variables support the interpretation of ratings in terms of the latent variable?*

Depending on the intended interpretation and use of the assessment, correspondence between rater-assigned scores and scores from selected-response assessments of the same or similar domains may be relevant. However, several studies of the relationship between rater-assigned scores and scores from selected-response assessments in the same or similar domains suggest differences in the underlying construct measured by the two assessment formats (e.g., Rodriguez, 2003). Further, differences have been observed in the correspondence between selected-response and constructed-response formats across student subgroups, including gender and race/ethnicity (Pomplun et al., 1992).

When the quality of ratings is of interest, it may also be informative to examine the alignment between observed ratings and ratings that are assumed to be valid for a particular interpretation and use. In operational settings, rater training and monitoring procedures often include methods for checking the alignment between operational ratings and ratings assigned by individual or groups of expert raters. These ratings are considered a standard against which to evaluate operational ratings, where the match between operational and expert ratings serves as an indicator of rater accuracy. The conceptualization of accuracy as a function of the difference between observed and operationally defined *true ratings* is evident throughout research on rating quality. For example, Sulsky and Balzer (1988) reviewed research between the 1970s and 1980s that used indices of rater accuracy as a method for monitoring rating quality, and recognized a common conceptualization and operational definition of accuracy as "a term used to describe both the strength and kind of relation between one set of measures and a corresponding set of measures (e.g., true scores) considered to be an accepted standard for comparison (Guion, 1965)" (pp. 497–498). Similarly, Woehr and Huffcutt (1994) claimed that the evaluation of rater accuracy requires a "comparison of an individual rater's rating across performance dimensions and/or ratees with corresponding evaluations provided by expert raters (i.e. 'true score'). With these measures then, the closer the raters' ratings are to the 'true scores', the more accurate they are believed to be" (p. 192).

In practice, two major approaches are used to obtain the criterion ratings that represent *true* or *expert* scores: (1) the arithmetic average of operational ratings for a particular student is calculated as the criterion (e.g., Wolfe, 2004; Wolfe & McVay, 2012); or (2) ratings are obtained from one or more expert raters who are selected based on their familiarity with the assessment context, experience assigning ratings, training, or other qualifications (Engelhard, 1996; Johnson, Penny, & Gordon, 2009; Wind & Engelhard, 2012, 2013). The first approach is applied as an indicator of precision or reliability. When the second approach is used, practical constraints often limit the availability of expert ratings for every performance. As a result, individual rater alignment with expert ratings is often calculated using read-behind procedures, where selected performances are scored by both operational and expert raters and the scores are compared (Johnson, Penny, & Gordon, 2009).

E. Evidence Based on Consequences of Testing

The final category of validity evidence in the *Standards for Educational and Psychological Testing* is based on the consequences of testing. As given in the standards:

> Decisions about test use are appropriately informed by validity evidence about intended test score interpretations for a given use, by evidence evaluating additional claims about consequences of test use that do not follow directly from test score interpretations, and by value judgments about unintended positive and negative consequences of test use.
>
> *(p. 21)*

Reflecting Messick (1989) and others, the *Standards for Educational and Psychological Testing* related to evidence based on the consequences of testing emphasize the importance of considering the range of possible intended and unintended consequences of assessment systems. Accordingly, the underlying concerns related to this source of validity evidence for selected-response assessments are summarized using the following question:

- *What is the range of possible intended and unintended consequences of the assessment system?*

The *Standards for Educational and Psychological Testing* highlight the importance of looking beyond the interpretation of a test score as an indicator of student achievement to also consider how tests may be used to inform decisions about educational systems, policy decisions, and other potential consequences not directly related to the construct being measured.

In the context of rater-mediated assessments, underlying concerns related to the consequences of testing can be summarized using the following question:

- *What is the range of possible intended and unintended consequences of the rater-mediated assessment system?*

Discussions of the consequences of testing related specifically to performance assessments often focus on the potential for *curricular and instructional washback* (Hamp-Lyons, 2002; Messick, 1996), or positive changes to curriculum and teaching methodologies as a result of the use of performance assessments. However, Messick (1994, 1995) cautioned that washback should not be an assumed positive consequence of performance assessments, such that the assessment format itself is viewed as a solution to the negative consequences of selected-response tests. Rather, both positive and negative consequences may result from performance assessments, and empirical evidence is needed to evaluate the consequences of all assessments, regardless of their format. In his words:

> It is not just that some aspects of multiple-choice testing may have adverse consequences for teaching and learning, but that *some aspects of all testing, even performance testing, may have adverse as well as beneficial educational consequences.* And if both positive and negative aspects, whether intended or unintended, are not meaningfully addressed in the validation process, then the concept of validity loses its force as a social value.
>
> *(Messick, 1994, p. 22, italics added)*

When raters are considered specifically, evidence related to the consequences of testing is often discussed in terms of the potential consequences of differences in rater severity and reliability. Essentially, these concerns stem from practical considerations in assessment systems, where resources limit the number of ratings that can be assigned to student artifacts such that differences among individual raters result in potential fairness issues. Within the context of writing assessment, Slomp, Corrigan, and Sugimoto (2014) observed:

> Historically, consequential validity concerns related to scoring procedures have focused on the issue of interrater reliability. The validity concern here is that a student's score should not be a function of who scored the test, but rather a reflection of a student's performance in relation to the construct measured, as expressed through the scoring criterion.
>
> *(p. 282)*

Despite efforts during rater training procedures to establish a common framework for interpreting student achievement within an assessment context, research on performance assessments indicates that differences in rater severity persist beyond training (e.g., Lunz & Stahl, 1990; Lunz, Stahl, & Wright, 1996; O'Neill & Lunz, 2000; Raymond, Webb, & Houston, 1991). As a result, differences in rater severity could result in differential consequences for students, depending on *the luck of the rater draw.*

Rather than focusing on indices of rater agreement and reliability to support validity arguments for the interpretation and use of rater-assigned scores, indices of rating quality based on the requirements for invariant measurement can be used to identify the degree to which ratings are invariant across individual raters.

As a result, evidence of rater-invariant measurement can be used to support the claim that measures of student achievement are independent of the particular raters who scored their work, and that calibrations of raters are independent of the particular students they happened to score. A detailed discussion of indices of rating quality that can be used to support the hypothesis of rater-invariant measurement is provided in Chapter Twelve.

Summary and Discussion

Validation was once a priestly mystery, a ritual behind the scenes, with the professional elite as witness and judge. Today it is a public spectacle combining the attractions of chess and mud wrestling.

(Cronbach, 1988, p. 3)

This chapter briefly described (1) the evolution of the concept of validity during the 20th century, (2) the current consensus definition of validity as represented by the *Standards for Educational and Psychological Testing*, and (3) the implications of these guiding principles of validity for rater-mediated assessments. According to the *Standards for Educational and Psychological Testing*, validity is defined as "the degree to which evidence and theory support the interpretations of test scores for proposed uses of tests" (AERA, APA, & NCME, 2014, p. 11). In this chapter, this guiding principle was discussed in terms of measurement issues that arise within the context of rater-mediated assessments. When raters are used in an assessment system, it is essential that researchers and practitioners evaluate the quality of judgments obtained from these raters, and recognize that all of the validity evidence is mediated through the judgmental lens that raters bring to the process. The ratings that are modeled and used to inform decisions about persons are based on rater *perceptions* and *judgments* regarding a set of cues that are selected to guide how raters interpret not only the latent variable of interest, but also the locations of other facets in the model that serve to define the latent variable.

This chapter described how the five sources of validity evidence listed in the *Standards for Educational and Psychological Testing* for Cluster III (Table 5.1) could be conceptualized to guide the collection of validity evidence related to rater-mediated assessments. As pointed out by Wilson (2005), the collection of validity evidence for any measurement procedure should not be viewed as a checklist item that is only relevant during the initial iteration of instrument development. Rather,

The purpose of validity evidence in instrument development is to help the measurer make the instrument work in a way that is more consistent with the intent, and evidence that the instrument is not doing so it is not a dead end in this process . . . The trick is to find a way to make that evidence useful in the next iteration of the process.

(p. 156)

When an assessment system involves raters, it is necessary to collect evidence related to the unique challenges associated with the judgmental processes used to interpret cues and to obtain ratings in rater-mediated assessments. It is important to evaluate and incorporate validity evidence regarding all aspects of the rater-mediated assessment system that includes rater judgments.

The key idea in this chapter is that validity evidence for rater-mediated assessments should reflect the complex nature of these assessments that depend in a fundamental way on raters' engagement in judgmental processes. The raters interpret and make connections among student artifacts, prompts, rubrics, rating scales, and other variables unique to the ecological context in which the assessment is situated. Further, in order to inform the interpretation and use of these assessments, validity evidence based on a coherent measurement perspective provides a frame of reference for evaluating the quality of the assessment system and informing future iterations of assessment development. In particular, Rasch Measurement Theory (Rasch, 1960/1980) provides a useful framework for evaluating the quality of ratings. Evidence of good model-data fit provides support for the interpretation of the Wright map as an illustration of rater-invariant person measures and person-invariant rater calibrations on the logit scale.

It is important to note that although we have treated the three foundational areas of validity, reliability, and fairness as separate chapters in this book, each foundational area provides scientific support for the inferences regarding the meaning, interpretation, and use of test scores within an assessment system. The concluding chapter of the *Standards for Educational and Psychological Testing* sums up this perspective with a consensus view of validity as follows:

> Ultimately, the validity of an intended interpretation of test scores relies on all the available evidence relevant to the technical quality of a testing system. Different components of validity evidence are described in subsequent chapters of the [*Test*] *Standards*, and include evidence of careful test construction; adequate score reliability; appropriate test administration and scoring; accurate score scaling, equating, and standard setting; and careful attention to fairness for all test takers, as appropriate to the test interpretation in question.
>
> *(AERA, APA, & NCME, 2014, p. 22)*

Following the general structure presented in this chapter, the next two chapters provide an introduction to the foundational areas of reliability and fairness. The emphasis is again on how these concepts can be considered from the perspective of rater-mediated assessments. Using a case study approach, Chapter Eight illustrates the major ideas presented in Chapters Five to Seven using empirical data from a rater-mediated assessment of writing.

References

American Educational Research Association [AERA], American Psychological Association [APA], & National Council on Measurement in Education [NCME]. (2014). *Standards for educational and psychological testing.* Washington, DC: AERA.

American Psychological Association. (1954). Technical recommendations for psychological tests and diagnostic techniques. *Psychological Bulletin, 51*(2, suppl.).

American Psychological Association [APA], American Educational Research Association [AERA], & National Council on Measurement in Education [NCME]. (1974). *Standards for educational and psychological tests and manuals.* Washington, DC: AERA.

Anastasi, A. (1986). Evolving concepts of test validation. *Annual Review of Psychology, 37,* 1–15.

Behizadeh, N., & Engelhard, G. (2015). Valid writing assessment from the perspectives of the writing and measurement communities. *Pensamiento Educativo. Revista De Investigación Educacional Latinoamericana, 52*(2), 34–54.

Borsboom, D. (2005). *Measuring the mind: Conceptual issues in contemporary psychometrics.* Cambridge: Cambridge University Press.

Borsboom, D., & Markus, K. A. (2013). Truth and evidence in validity theory. *Journal of Educational Measurement, 50*(1), 110–114.

Borsboom, D., Mellenbergh, G. J., & Van Heerden, J. (2004). The concept of validity. *Psychological Review, 111,* 1061–1071.

Crocker, L., & Algina, J. (1986). *Introduction to classical and modern test theory.* New York: Holt, Rinehart and Winston.

Cronbach, L. J. (1971). Test validation. In R. L. Thorndike (Ed.), *Educational measurement* (2nd ed., pp. 443–507). Washington, DC: American Council on Education.

Cronbach, L. J. (1980). Validity on parole: How can we go straight? *New Directions for Testing and Measurement: Measuring Achievement, Progress Over a Decade, 5,* 99–108.

Cronbach, L. J. (1984). *Essentials of psychological testing* (4th ed.). New York: Harper & Row.

Cronbach, L. J. (1988). Five perspectives on validity argument. In H. Wainer & H. I. Braun (Eds.), *Test validity* (pp. 3–17). Hillsdale, NJ: Lawrence Erlbaum Associates, Publishers.

Cronbach, L. J., & Meehl, P. E. (1955). Construct validity in psychological tests. *Psychological Bulletin, 52,* 281–302.

Engelhard, G., Jr. (1996). Evaluating rater accuracy in performance assessments. *Journal of Educational Measurement, 33*(1), 56–70.

Engelhard, G., Jr., & Behizadeh, N. (2012). Epistemic iterations and consensus definitions of validity. *Measurement: Interdisciplinary Research and Perspectives, 10*(1), 55–58.

Ercikan, K., Arim, R., Law, D., Domene, J., & Lacroix, S. (2010). Application of think aloud protocols for examining and confirming sources of differential item functioning identified by expert reviews. *Educational Measurement: Issues and Practice, 29,* 24–35.

Ericsson, K. A., & Simon, H. A. (1980). Verbal reports as data. *Psychological Review, 87*(1), 215–251.

Frederiksen, J. R., & Collins, A. (1989). A systems approach to educational testing. *Educational Researcher, 18*(9), 27–32.

Guion, R. M. (1965). *Personnel testing.* New York, NY: McGraw-Hill.

Gulliksen, H. (1950). *Theory of mental tests.* New York: Wiley.

Hamp-Lyons, L. (2002). The scope of writing assessment. *Assessing Writing, 8*(1), 5–16.

Johnson, R. L., Penny, J. A., & Gordon, B. (2009). *Assessing performance: Designing, scoring, and validating performance tasks.* New York: Guilford Press.

Kaliski, P. K., France, M., & Huff, K. (2011, March). *Using think aloud interviews in evidence-centered assessment design for the AP World History exam.* Paper presented at the annual meeting of the American Educational Research Association, New Orleans.

Kane, M. T. (1992). An argument-based approach to validity. *Psychological Bulletin, 112,* 527–535.

Kane, M. T. (2006). Validation. In R. L. Brennan (Ed.), *Educational measurement* (4th ed., pp. 17–64). Westport, CT: American Council on Education and Praeger.

Kane, M. T. (2013). Validating the interpretations and uses of test scores. *Journal of Educational Measurement, 50*(1), 1–73.

Kelley, T. (1927). *Interpretation of educational measurements.* Yonkers, NY: World Book Company.

Lane, S., & Stone, C. (2006). Performance assessment. In R. Brennan (Ed.), *Educational measurement* (4th ed., pp. 387–431). Westport, CT: American Council on Education and Praeger.

Leighton, J. P. (2004). Avoiding misconception, misuse, and missed opportunities: The collection of verbal reports in educational achievement testing. *Educational Measurement: Issues and Practice, 23*(4), 6–15.

Linn, R. L. (1980). Issues of validity for criterion-reference measures. *Applied Psychological Measurement, 4,* 547–561.

Linn, R. L., Baker, E. L., & Dunbar, S. B. (1991). Complex performance assessment: Expectations and validation criteria. *Educational Researcher, 20*(8), 15–21.

Loevinger, J. (1957). Objective tests as instruments of psychological theory. *Psychological Reports, 3,* 635–694. Monograph Supplement 9.

Lumley, T. (2002). Assessment criteria in large-scale writing tests: What do they really mean to the raters? *Language Testing, 19*(3), 246–276.

Lunz, M. E., & Stahl, J. A. (1990). Judge consistency and severity across grading periods. *Evaluation and the Health Professions, 13,* 425–444.

Lunz, M. E., Stahl, J. A., & Wright, B. D. (1996). The invariance of rater severity calibrations. In G. Engelhard, Jr. & M. Wilson (Eds.), *Objective measurement: Theory into practice* (Vol. 3, pp. 99–112). Norwood, NJ: Ablex.

Messick, S. (1989). Validity. In R. L. Linn (Ed.), *Educational measurement* (3rd ed.). New York, NY: Macmillan Publishing Company.

Messick, S. (1994). The interplay of evidence and consequences in the validation of performance assessments. *Educational Researcher, 23*(2), 13–23.

Messick, S. (1995). Validity of psychological assessment: Validation of inferences from persons' responses and performances as scientific inquiry into score meaning. *American Psychologist, 50*(9), 741–749.

Messick, S. (1996). Validity and washback in language testing. *Language Testing, 13,* 241–256.

Moss, P. A. (1992). Shifting conceptions of validity in educational measurement: Implications for performance assessment. *Review of Educational Research, 62,* 229–258.

Moss, P. A. (1994). Can there be validity without reliability? *Educational Researcher, 23*(2), 5–12.

Mullis, I. (1984). Scoring direct writing assessments: What are the alternatives? *Educational Measurement: Issues and Practices, 3,* 16–18.

Newton, P. E. (2012). Clarifying the consensus definition of validity. *Measurement: Interdisciplinary Research and Perspectives, 10*(1), 1–29.

Newton, P. E., & Shaw, S. D. (2015). Disagreement over the best way to use the word "validity" and options for reaching consensus. *Assessment in Education: Principles, Policy & Practice, 23*(2), 1–19.

Nozick, R. (2001). *Invariances: The structure of the objective world*. Cambridge, MA: Harvard University Press.

O'Neill, T. R., & Lunz, M. E. (2000). A method to study rater severity across several administrations. In M. Wilson & G. Engelhard, Jr. (Eds.), *Objective measurement: Theory into practice* (Vol. 5, pp. 135–146). Stamford, CT: Ablex.

Pomplun, M., Wright, D., Oleka, N., & Sudlow, M. (1992). *An analysis of English composition test essay prompts for differential difficulty*. New York: College Entrance Examination Board.

Rasch, G. (1960/1980). *Probabilistic models for some intelligence and attainment tests*. Copenhagen: Danish Institute for Educational Research. (Expanded edition, Chicago: University of Chicago Press, 1980).

Raymond, M. R., Webb, L. C., & Houston, W. M. (1991). Correcting performance-rating errors in oral examinations. *Evaluation and the Health Professions, 14*(1), 100–122.

Rodriguez, M. C. (2003). Construct equivalence of multiple-choice and constructed-response items: A random effects synthesis of correlations. *Journal of Educational Measurement, 40*(2), 163–184.

Sireci, S. G. (2013). Agreeing on validity arguments. *Journal of Educational Measurement, 50*(1), 99–104.

Slomp, D. H., Corrigan, J. A., & Sugimoto, T. (2014). A framework for using consequential validity evidence in evaluating large-scale writing assessments: A Canadian study. *Research in the Teaching of English, 48*(3), 276–302.

Sulsky, L. M., & Balzer, W. K. (1988). Meaning and measurement of performance rating accuracy: Some methodological and theoretical concerns. *Journal of Applied Psychology, 73*, 497–506.

Thorndike, E. L. (1919). *An introduction to the theory of mental and social measurements* (Revised and Enlarged ed.). New York, NY: Teachers College, Columbia University.

Thurstone, L. L. (1931). *The reliability and validity of tests*. Ann Arbor, MI: Edwards.

Wilson, M. R. (2005). *Constructing measures: An item response theory approach*. Mahwah, NJ: Lawrence Erlbaum.

Wind, S. A., & Engelhard, G. (2012). Examining rating quality in writing assessment: Rater agreement, error, and accuracy. *Journal of Applied Measurement, 13*(4), 321–335.

Wind, S. A., & Engelhard, G. (2013). How invariant and accurate are domain ratings in writing assessment? *Assessing Writing, 18*(4), 278–299. https://doi.org/10.1016/j.asw.2013.09.002

Woehr, D. J., & Huffcutt, A. I. (1994). Rater training for performance appraisal: A quantitative review. *Journal of Occupational and Organizational Psychology, 67*, 189–205.

Wolfe, E. W. (2004). Identifying rater effects using latent trait models. *Psychology Science, 46*, 35–51.

Wolfe, E. W., Kao, C. W., & Ranney, M. (1998). Cognitive differences in proficient and nonproficient essay scorers. *Written Communication, 15*, 465–492.

Wolfe, E. W., & McVay, A. (2012). Application of latent trait models to identifying substantively interesting raters. *Educational Measurement: Issues and Practice, 31*(3), 31–37.

6

RELIABILITY, PRECISION, AND ERRORS OF MEASUREMENT FOR RATINGS

All knowledge—beyond that of bare isolated occurrence—deals with uniformities.
(Spearman, 1904, p. 72)

This chapter continues the discussion of the foundational areas described in the *Standards for Educational and Psychological Testing* (AERA, APA, & NCME, 2014). In particular, this chapter addresses the foundational area of reliability with an emphasis on the role and implications of reliability in the context of rater-mediated assessments. At their base, topics related to reliability are focused on the consistency and stability of measures over various replications of an assessment process.

The purposes of this chapter are to provide a brief summary of historical views of reliability, to describe the current consensus definition of reliability provided by the *Standards for Educational and Psychological Testing* (AERA, APA, & NCME, 2014), and to discuss the concept of reliability as it applies specifically to rater-mediated assessments.

Following the same structure as Chapter Five, the current chapter is organized around the following questions and issues:

- What is reliability?
- What is the current consensus definition of reliability?
- How is reliability defined for rater-mediated assessments?
- What constitutes reliability evidence to support the interpretation and use of rater-mediated assessments?
- Summary and discussion

This chapter emphasizes how reliability can be viewed within the context of rater-mediated assessments.

What Is Reliability?

> The investigator who tests a person twice is likely to obtain scores that differ. Determination of the magnitude of such inconsistencies in measurement has been recognized as important.
>
> *(Cronbach et al., 1972, p. 1)*

Much of the work on reliability has its genesis in an early paper by Spearman (1904), who suggested that the observed correlation coefficient between two variables is under-estimated by measurement errors when no corrections are made for attenuation. As demonstrated in the opening quote for this chapter, Spearman's research on reliability was motivated by a quest for identifying *uniformities* over replications of measurement procedures. In focusing on uniformities, Spearman's work highlights the key role of invariance in evaluating reliability. Following Spearman's original observations, a variety of methods for evaluating reliability have been proposed that vary in terms of what aspects of a measurement procedure are treated as replications and what aspects constitute measurement error. In a sense, the process of establishing what constitutes a replication is also focused on establishing those aspects of a measurement procedure that are expected to remain invariant. Despite this early focus on invariance, subsequent reliability research, particularly within the test-score tradition, is characterized by a focus on identifying and quantifying sources of error that reduce the precision of scores—in a sense, focusing on the "noise" rather than the "signal."

Similar to validity (see Chapter Five), the definition of reliability, along with the methods used for investigating it in the human sciences, has been a contentious topic since Spearman's initial efforts. In particular, this chapter highlights the idea that the underlying concern in much of the research on reliability can be productively viewed as a concern with the invariance of measures over a variety of circumstances and varying conditions used to locate a person on the continuum of interest. In this book, we argue that reliability can be viewed as the flip side of invariance—when items, persons, and raters are not invariant, then it is important to examine the sources that contribute to this lack of invariance.

Although it is beyond the scope of this chapter to provide a thorough discussion of the historical development and current discussions of reliability, the next section provides a brief overview of highlights in the development of methods for examining reliability, with an emphasis on the conceptualization of reliability in terms of replications. A discussion in the next section of the current consensus definition of reliability, as reflected in the *Standards for Educational and Psychological Testing*, follows.

Summary of Historical Views of Reliability

Spearman's initial (1904) work on disattenuated correlations laid the foundation for the development of a variety of reliability coefficients based on correlations between variables defined as replications of measurement procedures, where higher correlations indicated a higher degree of reliability. In particular, Spearman (1910) and Brown (1910) proposed a formula for calculating reliability based on the correlation between halves of a composite test score that shared the same mean and variances of observed scores (i.e., parallel halves); this coefficient provided a method for evaluating reliability in a single test administration. Essentially, the two halves used to calculate the reliability coefficients can be viewed as replications over which consistency is evaluated.

As pointed out by Brennan (2001), the reliability indices that followed the Spearman-Brown formula reflect an "argument over what should be considered a replication of a measurement procedure" that "resonates to this day" (p. 297). Specifically, disagreement emerged over the definition of what constituted "comparability" in order to define replications of the measurement procedure. Whereas Brown (1910) required that reliability be calculated using repeated administrations of the *same* test, Kelley (1923) proposed the use of the correlation between "comparable tests" as an indicator of reliability, where comparable tests were defined in terms of the underlying "attitude or set," and similar levels of difficulty, while also being sufficiently different in order to "lead to a memory transfer of correlation between errors" (p. 203, as cited in Brennan, 2001).

Gulliksen's *Theory of Mental Tests*, which is often regarded as the key source on Classical Test Theory, includes a chapter on reliability titled "Experimental Methods for Obtaining Test Reliability" that describes several approaches for calculating reliability coefficients, including techniques based on halves of tests, repeated testing procedures, parallel forms, and KR-20. As pointed out by Brennan (2001), Gulliksen did not explicitly discuss the role of replications in his discussion of reliability but rather focused on the selection between several approaches for obtaining an estimate of reliability. However, Gulliksen's definition of reliability reflects a view of replications in terms of parallel test forms. In his words: "Reliability has been regarded as the correlation of a given test with a parallel form" (Gulliksen, 1950, p. 88).

Using a somewhat different view of replications, Kuder and Richardson (1937) proposed the use of the KR-20 and KR-21 coefficients as a solution to the fact that differences in the method by which *halves* were created resulted in different split-half reliability estimates. Specifically, Kuder and Richardson proposed two formulas for calculating reliability for a test composed of dichotomous items based on the number of items in a test, the total test variance, and the individual item variances. In a somewhat similar fashion, Cronbach's (1951) alpha coefficient was presented as an extension of KR-20/KR-21, where replications were defined as subsets of items within a single test administration. The alpha coefficient is equivalent to the split-half coefficient based on all possible "halves," and it can be calculated for both dichotomous and polytomous items.

Marked by Cronbach et al.'s (1972) *The Dependability of Behavioral Measurements*, the development of Generalizability Theory (G theory) represents the next major development in reliability research within the test-score tradition. Cronbach and his colleagues developed what they considered to be a "liberalization" of Classical Test Theory. Cronbach recognized that the typical statistical methods for estimating reliability coefficients based on correlation coefficients were limited, and that the emerging work by R. A. Fisher (1925) on the analysis of variance (ANOVA) might provide a coherent framework for structuring the key questions typically addressed under the topic of reliability. According to Cronbach et al. (1972):

> Fisher (1925) revolutionized statistical thinking with the concept of the factorial experiment in which the conditions of observation are classified in several respects. Investigators who adopt Fisher's line of thought must abandon the concept of undifferentiated error. The error formerly seen as amorphous is now attributed to multiple sources, and a suitable experiment can estimate how much variation arises from each controllable source.
>
> *(p. 1)*

The main points are that ANOVA models can be used to systematically explore error variance, and that researchers can "learn far more by allocating variation to facets than by carrying the conventional reliability analysis" (p. 2). They argue for the following advantages of G theory over the Classical Test Theory model:

1. Explicit consideration of the several facets of a measurement operational dispels ambiguities that were present in, and concealed by, the classical model.
2. The multifacet study can appraise interactions inaccessible to the older methods, and so can improve one's understanding of the measure.
3. One multifacet study answers questions that formerly required several separate sets of data.
4. Multifacet information enables one to design more efficient procedures for collecting data, either for the measurement of individuals or for the determination of group means.

> *(p. 2)*

In examining the dependability of measures, it is interesting to note that Cronbach and his colleagues did not simply view G theory as a methodology for examining reliability. The concept of *dependability* or *accuracy* clearly goes beyond what would typically be considered "reliability" by most researchers. As pointed out by Brennan (2001),

> Cronbach and his colleagues abandoned any attempt at answering the question, "What is *the* reliability of a test?" Rather, their work dramatically reveals that there is no such thing as *the* reliability of a test; there are as many reliabilities as there are specifications of a universe of generalization that one or more investigators is (are) willing to assert as meaningful for

some purpose. In this sense, it can be argued that reliability is not a unitary concept, and the concept of reliability is tied inextricably to notions of replications of a measurement procedure, as specified by an investigator.

(p. 301, italics in original)

Also drawing upon the use of ANOVA techniques to evaluate reliability, Mellenbergh (1977) presented another perspective on replications. Mellenbergh discussed the use of coefficients that reflect a variety of specifications of replications within the design of measurement procedure that can be viewed as a more general presentation of Generalizability Theory. Specifically, coefficients for estimating reliability were derived based on the concept of complete and incomplete replications. Whereas a complete replication includes a duplication of the measurement procedure with the same facets of interest (e.g., the same students, same items, and same raters), an *incomplete replication* is a replication in which only some subsets of the facets are replicated. Mellenbergh distinguished between *reliability coefficients*, which reflect coefficients calculated based on complete replications, and *generalizability coefficients*, which include replicability coefficients for all possible coefficients except the complete replication. Together, the reliability and generalizability coefficients were described as a set of *replicability coefficients*, which includes all possible coefficients for a given measurement procedure.

On the other hand, research in the scaling tradition, such as Item Response Theory, provides a more nuanced view of reliability. In particular, many of the key differences highlighted in comparisons between the test-score and scaling traditions are related to the concept of reliability. For example, Embretson (1996) contrasted Classical Test Theory (CTT) with Item Response Theory (IRT) through a set of six "old and new rules for measurement." Embretson and Reise (2000) expanded the initial set into a list of 10 rules that illustrate "principles by which tests and measures of individual differences are developed" (p. 39). A major theme in the comparison is the emphasis on the precision of measurement as a function of the match (i.e., targeting) between persons and items within the framework of IRT, where the size of error varies depending on the "appropriateness" of items for persons. Because calibrations for items and persons are on the same scale, it is possible to make direct comparisons between the two in order to ensure adequate targeting—and thus maximize the precision of a measurement procedure. This feature of IRT is highlighted in contrast to estimates of reliability and precision within the framework of CTT, which depend on the characteristics of samples of persons, items, and test forms. As noted by Embretson and Reise, estimates of measurement precision within the framework of IRT are characterized by information functions for measurement procedures, which illustrate the degree to which targeting between items and persons can be maximized to yield optimal levels of "information" or precision in the estimation of achievement levels.

What Is the Current Consensus Definition of Reliability?

As noted in Chapter Five, the *Standards for Educational and Psychological Testing* (AERA, APA, & NCME, 2014) can be viewed as a summary of the current consensus definition within the measurement community regarding psychometrically sound and legally defensible measurement principles and practices. The most recent version of the *Standards for Educational and Psychological Testing* defines reliability as follows:

> The general notion of reliability/precision is defined in terms of *consistency over replications* of the testing procedure. Reliability/precision is high if the scores for each person are consistent over replications of the testing procedure and is low if the scores are not consistent over replications.
>
> *(p. 35, italics added)*

This definition echoes previous conceptualizations of reliability in terms of consistency over replications. According to the *Standards for Educational and Psychological Testing*, evidence of consistency is needed to support the interpretation and use of scores. This view is further emphasized in the overarching and individual standards that are included in the reliability chapter:

STANDARD 2.0

Appropriate evidence of reliability/precision should be provided for the interpretation for each intended score use.

AERA, APA, and NCME (2014, p. 42)

The subsequent standards presented for reliability are organized in eight thematic clusters of individual standards. Figure 6.1 illustrates the eight clusters, which are named as follows:

I. Specifications for replications of the testing procedure
II. Evaluating reliability/precision
III. Reliability/Generalizability coefficients
IV. Factors affecting reliability/precision
V. Standard errors of measurement
VI. Decision consistency
VII. Reliability/precision of group means
VIII. Documenting reliability/precision

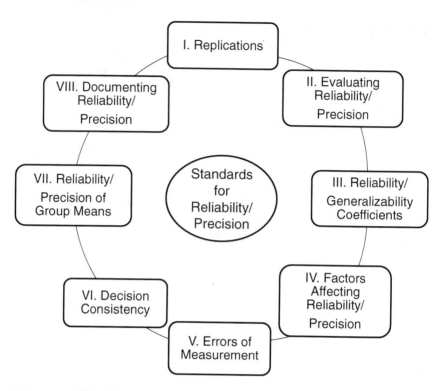

FIGURE 6.1 Eight Thematic Clusters of Reliability Standards from the *Standards for Educational and Psychological Testing*

Whereas the individual standards for validity were organized into only three clusters that presented broad views related to the conceptualization of validity evidence, each of the eight reliability clusters provides a somewhat more specific treatment of various concerns related to calculating and reporting evidence of reliability across measurement applications. Table 6.1 summarizes the major themes of each cluster; these themes will be discussed in more detail later in this chapter.

The emphasis on errors of measurement and inconsistencies is prevalent across the reliability standards. Although the *Standards for Educational and Psychological Testing* briefly mention the use of information functions and the distribution of the latent variable in Item Response Theory, the discussion of reliability is generally centered on the decomposition of observed scores into sources of error variance using G-theory procedures. In this chapter, we discuss the reliability concerns that are highlighted in the eight clusters from the perspective of invariant measurement, particularly as they apply to rater-mediated assessments.

The next section provides a brief overview of conceptualizations of reliability specifically related to rater-mediated assessments within the *Standards for Educational and Psychological Testing* and within performance assessment research

TABLE 6.1 Eight Thematic Clusters of Reliability Standards from the *Standards for Educational and Psychological Testing*

Cluster	Description from the Standards for Educational and Psychological Testing
I. Specifications for Replications of the Testing Procedure	"Replications involve independent administrations of the testing procedure, such that the attribute being measured would not be expected to change" (p. 35)
II. Evaluating Reliability/Precision	"For most testing programs, scores are expected to generalize over alternate forms of the test, occasions (within some period), testing contexts, and raters (if judgment is required in scoring). To the extent that the impact of any of these sources of variability is expected to be substantial, the variability should be estimated in some way" (p. 37)
III. Reliability/ Generalizability Coefficients	"Different reliability (and generalizability) coefficients may appear to be interchangeable, but the different coefficients convey different information. A coefficient may encompass one or more sources of error" (p. 38)
IV. Factors Affecting Reliability/Precision	"A number of factors can have significant effects on reliability/precision, and in some cases, these factors can lead to misinterpretations of the results, if not taken into account" (p. 38)
V. Standard Errors of Measurement	"The [SEM] can be used to generate confidence intervals around reported scores. It is therefore generally more informative than a reliability or generalizability coefficient" (p. 39)
VI. Decision Consistency	"*Decision consistency* refers to the extent to which the observed classifications of examinees would be the same across replications of a testing procedure. *Decision accuracy* refers to the extent to which observed classifications of examinees based on the results of a single replication would agree with their true classification status" (p. 40, italics in original).
VII. Reliability/Precision of Group Means	"In evaluating group performance by estimating the mean performance or mean improvement in performance for samples from the group, the variation due to the sampling of persons can be a major source of error . . . . Standard errors for individual scores are not appropriate measures of the precision of group averages" (p. 40)
VIII. Documenting Reliability/ Precision	"Typically, developers and distributors of tests have primary responsibility for obtaining and reporting evidence for reliability/precision . . . Reported evaluations of reliability/precision should identify the potential sources of error for the testing program, given the proposed uses of the scores" (pp. 40–41)

in general. Then, each of the eight clusters of reliability standards is explored from the perspective of rater-invariant measurement. The case study in Chapter Eight illustrates techniques based on Rasch Measurement Theory (Rasch, 1960/1980) that can be used to evaluate reliability within the framework of invariant measurement.

How Is Reliability Defined for Rater-Mediated Assessments?

As noted in the discussion of validity for rater-mediated assessments (Chapter Five), a major theme emphasized throughout this book is the importance of considering the role of raters' judgmental process when evaluating the quality of rater-mediated assessments in terms of validity, reliability, and fairness. Somewhat in contrast to general discussions of validity for performance assessments, in which the role of raters was rarely included in validity considerations, general discussions of reliability for performance assessments often directly consider the role of raters and rating quality. However, the general view of reliability as it relates to raters reflects the persistent emphasis on identifying the proportion of measurement error that can be attributed to raters, rather than focusing on rating quality in terms of the requirements for a measurement model with useful properties. The next section provides a brief summary of general discussions of reliability for performance assessments, followed by a consideration of reliability as it applies specifically to raters.

Reliability Issues for Performance Assessments in General

In Chapter Five, we noted that many researchers concerned with validity issues for performance assessments in general did not explicitly focus on the role of the rater in terms of validity. Rather, any discussions of raters were presented in terms of reliability issues. These discussions of reliability issues for performance assessments in the past several decades reflect a persistent concern with the variation among raters that remains consistent with the view in the current *Standards for Educational and Psychological Testing* that "if raters are used to assign scores to responses, the variability in scores over qualified raters is a source of error" (AERA, APA, & NCME, 2014, p. 33). This view reflects the test-score tradition, where high levels of rater agreement and reliability are used as evidence of psychometric quality.

In his summary of persistent issues and concerns related to the scoring of performance assessment, Clauser (2000) observed:

> Highly reliable ratings are possible even in large-scale testing programs, but they typically come at considerable cost. This *limiting factor* in the use of raters

has recently been examined in some detail (Hardy, 1995; Wainer & Thissen, 1993), but it is not a new issue (e.g., Coffman, 1971; Stalnaker, 1951).

(p. 317, italics added)

Along the same lines, Brookhart and Nitko's (2014) recent introductory textbook on educational assessment includes an overview of various item formats, including performance assessments. Describing essay-based assessments as a classic example of performance assessments, the authors' advice for test construction reflects an emphasis on inconsistency among raters as a potential source of measurement error that could negatively affect the quality of an assessment. In their words:

> The essay format often has very low inter-rater reliability. You can make a deliberate effort to overcome some of the *negative factors that lower the reliability* of essay scoring . . . . Attending to these factors will reduce the measurement errors in your evaluations of students' work.
>
> *(pp. 233–234, emphasis added)*

The emphasis on identifying levels of rater inconsistency is also evident in Johnson, Penny, and Gordon's (2009) practical guide for designing, implementing, scoring, and evaluating performance assessments. In particular, their discussion of methods for evaluating the reliability of performance assessments includes six types of reliability estimates that reflect the test-score tradition: (1) Cronbach's alpha, (2) Kuder-Richardson 20, (3) split-half, (4) parallel forms, (5) test-retest, and (6) Generalizability Theory analyses. The first five coefficients are presented as techniques for evaluating the overall influence of measurement error on the psychometric quality of a performance assessment, where the structure of the available data dictates the selection of an appropriate reliability coefficient. Generalizability Theory techniques are presented as methods for exploring sources of measurement error in more detail.

A major theme across these general treatments of reliability issues for performance assessments is concern with variation among raters as a source of measurement error. In this book, we emphasize the need to go beyond these indicators of consistency or agreement and evaluate the quality of ratings based on the requirements for invariant measurement. In contrast to analyses based on decomposing error variance into overall sources of measurement error, we highlight the importance of examining the precision of measurement associated with individual elements within facets—such as individual raters, students, or rubric domains. In particular, we present the Many-Facet Rasch (MFR) model as a useful framework in which it is possible to explore indicators of reliability and precision related to various facets in an assessment procedure while still maintaining a focus on rater-invariant measurement. Chapter Eight provides an illustrative case study that demonstrates the application of the MFR model as a tool for exploring the requirements for rater-invariant measurement, along with indicators of validity, reliability, and fairness. The next section includes a discussion of the thematic clusters of reliability standards from the recent revision of the *Standards for Educational and Psychological Testing*, with an emphasis on how the underlying reliability concerns can be considered from the perspective of rater-invariant measurement.

What Constitutes Reliability Evidence to Support the Interpretation and Use of Rater-Mediated Assessments?

This chapter contributes to the existing literature related to reliability for performance assessments through the exploration of a variety of concerns related to reliability from the perspective of rater-invariant measurement, particularly as these concerns relate to the reliability/precision standards in the recent revision of the *Standards for Educational and Psychological Testing*. In this section, the eight thematic clusters of reliability standards from the *Standards for Educational and Psychological Testing* are considered from the perspective of rater-mediated assessments, with an emphasis on the underlying issues related to invariant measurement. Table 6.1 summarizes the themes emphasized in the standards within each cluster. Table 6.2 summarizes the major concerns related to the eight thematic clusters for reliability using questions that highlight concerns related to selected-response assessments and rater-mediated assessments. Whereas the underlying questions for selected-response assessments are specified to reflect the underlying concerns emphasized in the *Standards for Educational and Psychological Testing* for assessments in general, the questions presented for rater-mediated assessments are formulated to reflect the perspective of rater-invariant measurement.

1. Specifications for Replications of the Testing Procedure

The first cluster of reliability standards (Specifications for replications of the testing procedure) focuses on the clear articulation of what constitutes a replication. The *Standards for Educational and Psychological Testing* define replications as follows:

> Replications involve independent administrations of the testing procedure, such that the attribute being measured would not be expected to change.
> *(AERA, APA, & NCME, 2014, p. 35)*

Accordingly, the standards included in the first cluster emphasize the need for reliability evidence related to the specific facet(s) of the assessment system that are treated as replications. In other words, standards in the first cluster require researchers to establish those aspects of a testing procedure that are expected to

TABLE 6.2 Underlying Questions for the Eight Reliability Clusters Based on Selected-Response and Rater-Mediated Assessments

Cluster	Selected-Response Assessments	Rater-Mediated Assessments
I. Specifications for Replications of the Testing Procedure	Which aspects of the assessment system are fixed, and which aspects can vary?	Which aspects of the rater-mediated assessment system must be invariant?
II. Evaluating Reliability/Precision	Which reliability estimates are needed in order to inform score interpretations and uses?	Which cues in the judgmental process should be included in the measurement model?
III. Reliability/ Generalizability Coefficients	What is defined as measurement error?	What is the reliability/ precision of rater judgments related to various cues?
IV. Factors Affecting Reliability/Precision	What types of variation are expected to influence reliability/ precision? What is the nature of the effect of this variation on estimates of reliability/precision?	Is there evidence to support the inference of rater-invariant measurement?
V. Standard Errors of Measurement	What is the standard error of measurement that can be used to generate standard errors around reported scores?	What is the precision of estimates on the rater-mediated Wright map?
VI. Decision Consistency	What does a test-retest procedure reveal about consistency in classifications?	Is there sufficient evidence of adequate linking between raters and model-data fit to adjust student achievement estimates for differences in rater severity?
VII. Reliability/Precision of Group Means	What are the characteristics of samples and procedures from which estimates of reliability/precision are obtained?	What are the characteristics of raters whose judgments are used to obtain scores?
VIII. Documenting Reliability/Precision	What methods are used to collect data and report reliability/ precision estimates?	What type of rating design was used to collect rater judgments?

remain invariant. As given in Table 6.2, the reliability standards in this cluster reflect the following underlying question for selected-response assessments:

Which aspects of the assessment system are fixed, and which aspects can vary?

As pointed out above, much of the work on reliability, particularly within the test-score tradition, is focused on the use of replications to decompose observed variation into various sources of error. The standards within this cluster are concerned with specifying the aspects of an assessment system for which variation would suggest measurement error. This process lays the foundation for additional analyses to quantify the influence of error as an indicator of the reliability/ precision of a measurement procedure.

On the other hand, when reliability is considered from the perspective of invariant measurement, concerns related to the first cluster can be framed in terms of specifying the aspects of the measurement system that must be evaluated in terms of the requirements for invariant measurement. More specifically, when rater-mediated assessments are of interest, reliability considerations that correspond to the first cluster of standards reflect the following underlying question:

Which aspects of the rater-mediated assessment system must be invariant?

Typically, rater-mediated assessments involve the combination of a variety of facets, such as raters, students, prompts, domains, and rating scales. As will be illustrated in Chapter Eight, it is possible to directly model these facets using the Many-Facet Rasch (MFR) measurement model (Linacre, 1989). In a sense, specifying these facets in an MFR model is analogous to conducting generalizability studies for a set of facets of interest in that separate estimates of reliability/precision can be calculated for each facet. However, rather than emphasizing the influence of measurement error, MFR model procedures are based on evaluating each facet in terms of the requirements for invariant measurement.

When MFR model indices suggest departures from the requirements for invariant measurement (see Chapter Thirteen), it is possible to examine individual elements within each facet, such as individual raters or domains, in order to identify possible substantive explanations for the violations and inform the next iteration of the assessment procedure.

2. Evaluating Reliability/Precision

Standards in the second cluster call for alignment between the methods used to evaluate reliability/precision and the intended score interpretations and uses for a particular assessment system. Specifically, if a particular aspect of the assessment system is predicted to result in substantial variability, the *Standards for Educational and Psychological Testing* call for reliability indices that quantify this variation:

> For most testing programs, scores are expected to generalize over alternate forms of the test, occasions (within some period), testing contexts, and raters (if judgment is required in scoring). To the extent that the impact of any of these sources of variability is expected to be substantial, the variability should be estimated in some way. ·
>
> *(AERA, APA, & NCME, 2014, p. 37)*

According to the *Standards for Educational and Psychological Testing*, test developers and users must not only identify the aspects of the measurement procedure that are expected to vary (see Cluster I), but must also evaluate the degree to which this variation could impact the generalizability of the results. The underlying concerns reflected in this cluster of standards can be summarized as follows for selected-response assessments:

Which reliability estimates are needed in order to inform score interpretations and uses?

These standards call for reliability analyses that will provide test users with sufficient information regarding the generalizability of the assessment procedure. Specifically, the *Standards for Educational and Psychological Testing* require information about reliability/precision that reflects intended uses of scores, including reliability/precision estimates for subscores, change scores, or, in the case of adaptive testing, model-based conditional standard errors.

From the perspective of rater-invariant measurement, the underlying concerns related to evaluating reliability/precision can be summarized in terms of the following underlying question:

Which cues in the judgmental process should be included in the measurement model?

This underlying question reflects the view that rater-mediated assessments do not provide direct measures of student achievement; rather, all of the information obtained from these assessments can be seen as the result of rater judgment regarding student achievement, domain difficulty, rating scale categories, and other facets of interest. As noted above, these cues can be directly incorporated into the measurement model in order to explore the degree to which the requirements for invariant measurement hold across various aspects of the judgmental process. The specification of facets in the measurement model reflects the unique set of cues of interest for a particular measurement procedure. Information about rating quality in terms of these judgmental cues should be provided in order to inform the interpretation and use of rater-assigned scores. When there is evidence of adequate fit to the model, the Wright map can be conceptualized as a summary of rater judgments related to each cue of interest.

3. Reliability/Generalizability Coefficients

The third cluster of standards emphasizes the lack of equivalence between different types and specifications of reliability coefficients. Reflecting the emphasis on the test-score tradition that characterizes the *Standards for Educational and Psychological Testing* for reliability, these standards highlight differences between G-theory coefficients that are calculated for different facets (e.g., items or raters), and emphasize the fact that these coefficients convey unique information about sources of measurement error, depending on their specification. As given in the *Standards for Educational and Psychological Testing*, the standards in this cluster caution test developers and users in the interpretation of reliability/generalizability coefficients:

> Different reliability (and generalizability) coefficients may appear to be interchangeable, but the different coefficients convey different information. A coefficient may encompass one or more sources of error.
> *(AERA, APA, & NCME, 2014, p. 38)*

These cautions are particularly relevant within the context of the G-theory framework, in which indices of reliability/precision can be calculated for numerous facets that reflect the unique characteristics of an assessment procedure. Examination of the suite of coefficients for a particular assessment procedure provides a broader picture of reliability in terms of the specific facets of interest.

For selected-response items, the underlying concerns reflected in the third cluster of standards can be summarized using the following question (Table 6.2):

What is defined as measurement error?

Essentially, differences among reliability/generalizability coefficients are based on the types of variation that are treated as measurement error. For example, reliability coefficients specific to occasions are based on a conceptualization of differences among scores across occasions as measurement error, and consistency across occasions is viewed as evidence of reliability/precision. Values of reliability/generalizability coefficients describe the degree to which measurement error can be attributed to a particular facet.

On the other hand, underlying concerns related to the third cluster of standards related to rater-mediated assessments can be conceptualized as indices of reliability/precision related to rater judgments. It should be noted that the *Standards for Educational and Psychological Testing* specifically address rater-mediated assessments in Standard 2.7, which is included in the third cluster:

Standard 2.7

When subjective judgment enters into test scoring, evidence should be provided on both *inter-rater consistency* in scoring and *within-examinee consistency* over repeated measurements. A clear distinction should be made among reliability data based on (a) independent panels of raters scoring the same performances or products, (b) a single panel scoring successive performances or new products, and (c) independent panels scoring successive performances or new products.

(AERA, APA, & NCME, 2014, p. 44)

In the discussion for this standard, the *Standards for Educational and Psychological Testing* recommend the use of G-theory analyses in order to distinguish among sources of measurement error related to variability among tasks, raters, and students that reflect unique components of the assessment procedure. Specifically, the following guidance is provided:

Task-to-task variations in the quality of an examinee's performance and rater-to-rater inconsistencies in scoring represent independent sources of measurement error . . . . Generalizability studies and variance component analyses can be helpful in estimating the error variances arising from each source of error.

(AERA, APA, & NCME, 2014, p. 44)

This standard reflects the view of variability in rater judgment as a source of measurement error that must be minimized in order to obtain trustworthy scores. Again, the focus in this cluster of standards illustrates the emphasis on variability and measurement error, rather than invariance.

It is also possible to examine different aspects of reliability/precision related to rater judgment from the perspective of rater-invariant measurement. The underlying concerns for rater-mediated assessments related to the third cluster can be summarized using the following question:

What is the reliability/precision of rater judgments related to various cues?

As noted above, it is possible to formulate an MFR model that includes facets unique to a particular assessment procedure. When the MFR model is used to calculate indices of reliability for various facets, these reliability indices reflect the reliability/precision of rater judgment related to each facet. Specifically, reliability indices based on the Rasch model can be calculated separately for each facet in the model. Two indices of reliability are typically used: (1) Reliability of separation (*Rel*), and (2) A chi-square statistic (χ^2). When data fit the model, the reliability of separation statistic for the student facet (θ) has a similar interpretation to Cronbach's alpha coefficient. For other facets, the reliability of separation statistic describes the spread of differences in individual locations of elements within the facet (in this case, individual raters and items). The chi-square statistic can be calculated to determine whether the differences among logit-scale locations are statistically significant.

4. Factors Affecting Reliability/Precision

Standards in the fourth cluster call for consideration of potential variations on administration procedures or forms, as well as various subgroups of test takers. In light of these potential variations in testing conditions or participants, it is necessary to collect data that reflects anticipated variations and reports the resulting influence on reliability. The fourth cluster of standards can be summarized as follows (Table 6.1):

> A number of factors can have significant effects on reliability/precision, and in some cases, these factors can lead to misinterpretations of the results, if not taken into account.
>
> *(AERA, APA, & NCME, 2014, p. 38)*

In the language of G-theory, the standards in this cluster require the careful specification of the universe of generalization for an assessment procedure, such that the influence of measurement error can be investigated related to each relevant aspect of the assessment.

For selected-response assessments, the underlying concerns related to the fourth thematic cluster can be summarized in terms of two questions (Table 6.2):

- *What types of variation are expected to influence reliability/precision?*
- *What is the nature of the effect of this variation on estimates of reliability/precision?*

These questions reflect the ongoing emphasis within the *Standards for Educational and Psychological Testing* on variance, rather than invariance, in the conceptualization of reliability.

For rater-mediated assessments, factors influencing reliability/precision are related to variations in rating quality across and within groups of raters. Reflecting this concern, the second rater-specific standard for reliability/precision is included in Cluster IV:

Standard 2.8

> When constructed-response tests are scored locally, reliability/precision data should be gathered and reported for the local scoring when adequate size samples are available.
>
> *(AERA, APA, & NCME, 2014, p. 44)*

This standard is particularly relevant for rater-mediated assessments in which scoring is conducted across different settings. The *Standards for Educational and Psychological Testing* emphasize the importance of evaluating and reporting reliability/precision across these settings.

Concerns related to the influence of various factors on the reliability/precision of a measurement procedure can be considered in terms of invariance. For rater-mediated assessments, these concerns can be conceptualized in terms of the following question:

Is there evidence to support the inference of rater-invariant measurement?

Within the framework of rater-invariant measurement, indices of fit to an ideal-type model can be evaluated in order to support the inference that rater judgments are invariant as they relate to a variety of facets. Specifically, indicators of model-data fit for Rasch models include statistical and graphical summaries of residuals that describe differences between model-expected and observed responses. The case study in Chapter Eight will illustrate the use of indices of model-data fit that can be used to evaluate the requirements of rater-invariant measurement related to various facets of interest in a rater-mediated assessment. Specifically, the illustrative analyses focus on two commonly used fit statistics: Infit and Outfit mean square error (MSE), along with their standardized counterparts. Because it is unweighted, the Outfit statistic is useful because it is particularly sensitive to "outliers," or extreme unexpected observations. On the other hand, Infit statistics are weighted by statistical information; as a result, they are not as sensitive to extreme outliers. Both unstandardized and standardized versions of these statistics are available.

5. Standard Errors of Measurement

Standards in the fifth cluster highlight the value of calculating and reporting confidence intervals around reported scores as an indicator of reliability/precision. Specifically, these standards note that both overall and conditional standard errors of measurement should be reported in the units of the test score scale, particularly when cut scores are used. As given in Table 6.1, these standards are based on the idea that:

> The [SEM] can be used to generate confidence intervals around reported scores. It is therefore generally more informative than a reliability or generalizability coefficient.
>
> *(AERA, APA, & NCME, 2014, p. 39)*

For selected-response assessments, the underlying concerns for the standards in this cluster can be summarized as follows:

What is the standard error of measurement that can be used to generate standard errors around reported scores?

Standard errors are informative in the interpretation and use of individual scores. Reflecting the test-score tradition, the *Standards for Educational and Psychological Testing* emphasize the interpretation of the SEM as an index of the influence of various sources of measurement error, where "a more comprehensive standard error (i.e., one that includes the most relevant sources of error, given the definition of the testing procedure and the proposed interpretation) tends to be more informative than a less comprehensive standard error" (AERA, APA, & NCME, 2014, p. 39).

On the other hand, reliability considerations related to this cluster can be summarized from the perspective of rater-invariant measurement in terms of the following question:

What is the precision of estimates on the rater-mediated Wright map?

Just as distinct indices of model-data fit and reliability can be obtained for individual facets specified in the MFR model, it is also possible to obtain standard error estimates for each element within a facet (e.g., individual raters, students, or domains). Specifically, it is possible to calculate standard error (*SE*) estimates for each facet that describe the range within which element (i.e., individual performance, rater, and item) would be expected to fall over replications of the assessment procedure. Smaller values of *SE* indicate more precise estimates, such that the logit-scale locations would be expected to remain stable across repeated administrations of an assessment. The use of SE estimates as an indicator of reliability/precision will be illustrated in the case study in Chapter Eight.

6. Decision Consistency

Cluster VI only includes one standard, which calls for the use of a test-retest approach to investigate decision consistency and decision accuracy (when possible) in classifications. As can be seen in the description of this cluster in Table 6.1, the *Standards for Educational and Psychological Testing* distinguish between *decision consistency* and *decision accuracy* as follows:

> *Decision consistency* refers to the extent to which the observed classifications of examinees would be the same across replications of a testing procedure. *Decision accuracy* refers to the extent to which observed classifications of examinees based on the results of a single replication would agree with their true classification status.
>
> (*AERA, APA, & NCME, 2014, p. 40, italics in original*)

This cluster is particularly relevant for assessments whose purpose is classification within distinct categories. Further, the *Standards for Educational and Psychological*

Testing emphasize the fact that both the degree of decision consistency/accuracy and the consequences for classification errors vary across the range of test scores. In light of this inconsistency, the standards call for the calculation of conditional standard errors and/or decision consistency/accuracy indices that reflect the variation in reliability/precision across the score scale.

For selected-response items, the underlying concerns in the *Standards for Educational and Psychological Testing* related to the decision consistency cluster can be summarized as follows:

What does a test-retest procedure reveal about consistency in classifications?

Examination of the *Standards for Educational and Psychological Testing* reveals a view of classification consistency based on the view of repeated administrations as replications over which consistency is examined. Specifically, the following recommendations are provided:

> Although decision consistency is typically estimated from the administration of a single form, it can and should be estimated directly through the use of a test-retest approach, if consistent with the requirements of test security and if the assumption of no change in the construct is met and adequate samples are available.
>
> *(AERA, APA, & NCME, 2014, p. 46)*

In the context of rater-mediated assessments, decision consistency is based on the degree to which different classifications would result from differences in rater severity. As will be discussed in the next chapter, differences in rater severity are essentially a fairness issue related to the exchangeability of raters when these differences persist despite rater training.

In previous research on rater-mediated assessments, the MFR model has been applied as a method for adjusting estimates of student achievement across raters who exhibit different severity levels (Engelhard & Myford, 2003; Lunz & Suanthong, 2011; Myford & Mislevy, 1995). Specifically, when the rating design contains sufficient links between raters (see Chapter Twelve), the resulting student achievement estimates (θ) are adjusted for differences in rater severity. However, the degree to which these adjustments can be interpreted depends on the degree to which model-data fit is observed for raters (Wind, Wesolowski, & Engelhard, 2015). As a result, decision consistency concerns within the framework of rater-invariant measurement can be summarized in terms of concerns related to rating designs and model-data fit. As given in Table 6.2, the underlying question for rater-mediated assessments can be stated as follows:

Is there sufficient evidence of adequate linking between raters and model-data fit to adjust student achievement estimates for differences in rater severity?

The next chapter will provide a more detailed discussion of the fairness concerns related to adjustments for differences in rater severity, and the consequences of model-data misfit for raters will be illustrated in the case study in Chapter Eight. Chapter Twelve provides additional details related to rater linking designs.

7. Reliability/Precision of Group Means

Standards in the seventh cluster are focused on reliability concerns for assessment situations in which group means are of interest. Specifically, these standards call for the use of the standard error for the estimates of group means, rather than standard errors for individual scores. In particular, the *Standards for Educational and Psychological Testing* related to this cluster describe unique concerns related to the role of measurement error for assessments in which the group mean is of interest:

> In evaluating group performance by estimating the mean performance or mean improvement in performance for samples from the group, the variation due to the sampling of persons can be a major source of error . . . . Standard errors for individual scores are not appropriate measures of the precision of group averages.
>
> *(AERA, APA, & NCME, 2014, p. 40)*

Essentially, this cluster of standards reflects a view that differences among samples constitute measurement error when group means are of interest. In order to account for the potential influence of measurement error due to differences among samples, the *Standards for Educational and Psychological Testing* emphasize the need to collect data about sample characteristics and procedures from which reliability estimates are obtained.

Accordingly, the underlying concerns for selected-response items can be summarized in terms of the following question:

> *What are the characteristics of samples and procedures from which estimates of reliability/ precision are obtained?*

In the context of rater-mediated assessments, details about the samples of students from which estimates of reliability/precision are obtained are not sufficient to inform the interpretation and use of rater-assigned scores. In addition to these details, information is also needed regarding characteristics of the raters, including background information and details about training and monitoring. As given in Table 6.2, these concerns can be summarized using the following question:

> *What are the characteristics of raters whose judgments are used to obtain scores?*

Although the documentation of rater background characteristics and training is essential to inform the interpretation and use of scores, evidence of fit to the MFR model supports the inference of rater-invariant measurement, such that estimates of student achievement do not depend on information about the particular raters who scored each student, and estimates of rater severity do not depend on the particular students whose work was evaluated.

8. Documenting Reliability/Precision

Finally, the standards in Cluster VIII deal with appropriate documentation and reporting of information about reliability/precision. These standards emphasize the shared responsibility of test developers *as well as* local test users to gather and evaluate information related to reliability/precision specific to particular test uses and interpretations. The standards in this cluster reflect the following recommendations:

> Typically, developers and distributors of tests have primary responsibility for obtaining and reporting evidence for reliability/precision. . . . Reported evaluations of reliability/precision should identify the potential sources of error for the testing program, given the proposed uses of the scores.
> *(AERA, APA, & NCME, 2014, pp. 40–41)*

Whereas standards in earlier clusters emphasized the importance of identifying and evaluating the potential impact of different sources of measurement error, the standards in this cluster emphasize the importance of adequate documentation to inform score interpretation and use across settings. As given in Table 6.2, the underlying concerns related to this cluster can be summarized in terms of the following question for selected-response assessments:

What methods are used to collect data and report reliability/precision estimates?

In the context of rater-mediated assessments, it is essential that information related to data collection for reliability/precision analyses also include information regarding the rating design. Specifically, details related to the number of raters who scored each student, along with the degree to which raters are linked, are necessary in order to interpret estimates of student achievement based on rater-assigned scores. Accordingly, the underlying concerns related to this cluster can be summarized in terms of the following question:

What type of rating design was used to collect rater judgments?

As noted in the discussion for Cluster VI, Rasch models can be used to obtain estimates of student achievement that are adjusted for differences in rater severity, along with estimates of rater severity that do not depend on differences in student achievement. When it is not possible to collect ratings using a fully crossed design, it is still possible to obtain rater- and student-invariant estimates, as long as the rating design contains sufficient connectivity. However, the type of rating design used to collect rater judgments has implications for the interpretation of calibrations, along with the corresponding indicators of reliability/precision. Rating designs that include more connections among raters (i.e., more commonly scored performances) result in greater reliability/precision for estimates of student achievement and rater severity (Wind, Wesolowski, & Engelhard, 2015). Chapter Twelve provides additional details related to rating designs and their implications for the interpretation of rater judgments in terms of rater-invariant measurement.

Summary and Discussion

> Whenever a test is administered, the test user would like some assurance that the results could be replicated if the same individuals were tested again under similar circumstances. This desired consistency (or reproducibility) of test scores is called reliability.
>
> *(Crocker & Algina, 1986, p. 105)*

In this chapter, we briefly described (1) the evolution of the concept of reliability during the 20th century, (2) the current consensus definition of reliability as represented by the *Standards for Educational and Psychological Testing*, and (3) the implications of these guiding principles of reliability for rater-mediated assessments. According to the *Standards for Educational and Psychological Testing*, reliability is defined as "the degree to which test scores for a group of test takers are consistent over repeated applications of a measurement procedure" (AERA, APA, & NCME, 2014, pp. 222–223). In this chapter, reliability was discussed in terms of measurement issues that arise within the context of rater-mediated assessments. As noted in the discussion of validity (Chapter Five), it is essential that rater-mediated assessments are evaluated in terms of the quality of rater judgments, and that all of the evidence of reliability/precision is based on rater judgments regarding the various facets included in the assessment system. Although it is possible to evaluate reliability/precision separately for different facets, all of these indices reflect the reliability/precision of rater judgments associated with these facets.

This chapter focused on how the eight thematic clusters of standards for reliability/precision (Figure 6.1, Table 6.1) can be conceptualized to guide the collection of evidence of reliability/precision related to rater-mediated assessments. The key idea in this chapter is that reliability/precision evidence for rater-mediated assessments should reflect a coherent measurement framework in which ratings are evaluated in terms of the requirements of a measurement model with useful properties. Specifically, the perspective put forth in this chapter is that adherence to the requirements for invariant measurement provides more meaningful evidence of rating quality than evidence of consistency among raters. This perspective stands in contrast to the view of reliability/

precision for rater-mediated assessments in the *Standards for Educational and Psychological Testing*:

> If raters are used to assign scores to responses, the variability in scores over qualified raters is a source of error.
>
> *(AERA, APA, & NCME, 2014, p. 33)*

In this chapter, we emphasized the idea that much of the historical and current concern with the concept of reliability can be recast in terms of facets of the quest for invariance in measurement in the human sciences. By viewing concerns with reliability, precision, and measurement error from the perspective of invariant measurement, the focus is placed on the signal and not the noise.

References

American Educational Research Association (AERA), American Psychological Association (APA), & National Council on Measurement in Education (NCME). (2014). *Standards for educational and psychological testing*. Washington, DC: AERA.

Brennan, R. L. (2001). An essay on the history and future of reliability from the perspective of replications. *Journal of Educational Measurement, 38*(4), 295–317.

Brookhart, S. M., & Nitko, A. J. (2014). *Educational assessment of students* (7th ed.). Boston, MA: Pearson.

Brown, W. (1910). Some experimental results in the correlation of mental abilities. *British Journal of Psychology, 1904–1920, 3*(3), 296–322. http://doi.org/10.1111/j.2044-8295.1910.tb00207.x

Clauser, B. E. (2000). Recurrent issues and recent advances in scoring performance assessments. *Applied Psychological Measurement, 24*(4), 310–324. http://doi.org/10.1177/01466210022031778

Coffman, W. E. (1971). Essay examinations. In R. L. Thorndike (Ed.), *Educational measurement* (2nd ed., pp. 271–302). Washington, DC: American Council on Education.

Crocker, L., & Algina, J. (1986). *Introduction to classical and modern test theory*. New York, NY: Holt, Rinehart and Winston.

Cronbach, L. J. (1951). Coefficient alpha and the internal structure of tests. *Psychometrika, 16*(3), 297–334. https://doi.org/10.1007/BF02310555

Cronbach, L. J., Gleser, G. C., Nanda, H., & Rajaratnam, N. (1972). *The dependability of behavioral measurements: Theory of generalizability for scores and profiles*. New York: John Wiley & Sons.

Embretson, S. E. (1996). The new rules of measurement. *Psychological Assessment, 8*(4), 341–349. http://doi.org/10.1037/1040-3590.8.4.341

Embretson, S. E., & Reise, S. P. (2000). *Item response theory for psychologists*. Mahwah, NJ: Lawrence Erlbaum Associates, Publishers.

Engelhard, G., & Myford, C. M. (2003). *Monitoring faculty consultant performance in the advanced placement English literature and composition program with a Many-Faceted Rasch model*. New York: College Entrance Examination Board.

Fisher, R. A. (1925). *Statistical methods for research workers*. Edinburgh: Oliver & Boyd.

Gulliksen, H. (1950). *Theory of mental tests*. New York, NY: Wiley.

Hardy, R. A. (1995). Examining the costs of performance assessment. *Applied Measurement in Education, 8,* 121–134.

Johnson, R. L., Penny, J. A., & Gordon, B. (2009). *Assessing performance: Designing, scoring, and validating performance tasks.* New York: The Guilford Press.

Kelley, T. L. (1923). *Statistical method.* New York, NY: Macmillan.

Kuder, G. F., & Richardson, M. W. (1937). The theory of the estimation of test reliability. *Psychometrika, 2*(3), 151–160. https://doi.org/10.1007/BF02288391

Linacre, J. M. (1989). *Many-Facet Rasch Measurement.* Chicago, IL: MESA Press.

Lunz, M., & Suanthong, S. (2011). Equating of multi-facet tests across administrations. *Journal of Applied Measurement, 12*(2), 124–134.

Mellenbergh, G. J. (1977). The replicability of measures. *Psychological Bulletin, 84*(2), 378. http://doi.org/10.1037/0033-2909.84.2.378

Myford, C. M., & Mislevy, R. J. (1995). *Monitoring and improving a portfolio assessment system* (No. ETS Center for Performance Assessment Report No. MS 94–05). Princeton, NJ: Educational Testing Service.

Rasch, G. (1960/1980). *Probabilistic models for some intelligence and achievement tests* (Expanded edition, 1980). Chicago: University of Chicago Press.

Spearman, C. (1904). The proof and measurement of association between two things. *American Journal of Psychology, 15,* 72–101.

Spearman, C. (1910). Correlation calculated from faulty data. *British Journal of Psychology, 1904–1920, 3*(3), 271–295. http://doi.org/10.1111/j.2044-8295.1910.tb00206.x

Stalnaker, J. M. (1951). The essay type of examination. In E. F. Lindquist (Ed.), *Educational measurement* (1st ed., pp. 495–530). Washington, DC: American Council on Education.

Wainer, H., & Thissen, D. (1993). Combining multiple-choice and constructed-response test scores: Toward a Marxist theory of test construction. *Applied Measurement in Education, 6,* 103–118.

Wind, S. A., Wesolowski, B., & Engelhard, G. (2015). *Exploring the effects of rater linking designs and rater fit on achievement estimates within the context of music performance assessments.* Presented at the American Educational Research Association, Chicago, IL.

7

FAIRNESS IN RATER-MEDIATED ASSESSMENT

Appropriate Interpretation and Use of Ratings

> Fairness to all individuals in the intended population of test takers is an overriding, foundational concern.
>
> *(AERA, APA, & NCME, 2014, p. 49)*

This chapter continues the discussion of the foundational areas described in the *Standards for Educational and Psychological Testing* (AERA, APA, & NCME, 2014). Specifically, this chapter addresses the foundational area of fairness with an emphasis on the role and implications of fairness issues in the context of rater-mediated assessments. Fairness is a validity issue focused on minimizing construct-irrelevant barriers in order to obtain accurate estimates of person locations on the latent variable.

The purposes of this chapter are to provide a brief summary of historical views of fairness, to describe the current consensus definition of fairness provided by the *Standards for Educational and Psychological Testing* (AERA, APA, & NCME, 2014), and to discuss the concept of fairness as it applies specifically to rater-mediated assessments.

Following the same structure as Chapter Five and Chapter Six, the current chapter is organized around the following questions and issues:

- What is fairness?
- What is the current consensus definition of fairness?
- How is fairness defined for rater-mediated assessments?
- What constitutes fairness evidence to support the interpretation and use of rater-mediated assessments?
- Summary and discussion

This chapter emphasizes how fairness can be viewed within the context of rater-mediated assessments.

What Is Fairness?

Fairness is the third foundational area in the recent revision of the *Standards for Educational and Psychological Testing* (AERA, APA, & NCME, 2014). Previous versions of the *Standards for Educational and Psychological Testing* have included topics related to fairness within other chapters, particularly in terms of issues related to validity and student language and disability subgroups. Although fairness is framed as a validity issue in the 2014 *Standards for Educational and Psychological Testing*, it is presented as a separate foundational area in a standalone chapter with an emphasis on measurement bias, accessibility, and universal design as fundamental issues that must be considered to ensure fairness for all test takers.

Similar to validity (see Chapter Five) and reliability (see Chapter Six), the definition of fairness, along with the methods used for investigating it in the human sciences, has been a contentious topic over time. In this book, we emphasize the idea that the underlying concept of much of the research on fairness in educational assessment reflects underlying concerns related to invariance. Although it is beyond the scope of this chapter to provide a thorough discussion of the historical development and current discussions of fairness, the next section provides a brief overview of some historical perspectives related to fairness in the context of educational assessment following the second half of the 20th century. A discussion in the next section of the current consensus definition of fairness, as reflected in the *Standards for Educational and Psychological Testing*, follows.

Summary of Historical Views of Fairness

As noted above, fairness is essentially a validity issue related to the comparability of test score interpretations for intended uses across groups of test takers. As a result, much of the historical development of conceptualizations of fairness is included in the development of the concept of validity (see Chapter Five). However, special attention related to fairness as a distinct concept can be found in discussions related to the concept of *bias* in testing. Throughout the development of classical and modern test theory, concerns related to observable differences in outcomes between groups of test takers have been persistent. Specifically, much attention has been devoted to developing methods for distinguishing between *true* differences related to underlying constructs and differences related to issues of fairness—i.e., bias.

In their summary of historical conceptualization of bias, Crocker and Algina (1986) observed that concerns with bias within the test-score tradition became particularly prominent in the psychometric literature around the late 1960s, especially related to the use of tests for selection purposes. Methods for detecting bias generally focused on identifying differences in overall test performance across *focal* and *reference* groups, where focal groups were generally defined as minority groups (i.e., groups with relatively fewer members for a given testing context) and reference groups were generally defined as majority groups (i.e., groups with a relatively larger number of members for a given testing context).

Crocker and Algina (1986) list a selection of definitions that reflect the progression of dominant perspectives of bias during the 1960s and 1970s, primarily concerned with differences across subgroups in prediction and classification based on observed total scores. For example, using a regression framework, Cleary (1968) defined bias as evidence of consistent prediction errors within a student subgroup, where

> the test is biased if the criterion score predicted from the common regression line is consistently too high or too low for members of the subgroup. With this definition of bias, there may be a connotation of "unfair," particularly if the use of the test produces a prediction that is too low. If the test is used for selection, members of a subgroup may be rejected when they were capable of adequate performance.
>
> *(p. 115)*

The use of a regression framework for defining bias remained prevalent in research on the use of tests for selection purposes. For example, Darlington (1971) proposed two definitions for bias: (1) The distribution of predictor scores varies across subgroups; and (2) the regression of the predictor scores on criterion scores varies across subgroups. In what can be seen as an extension of Cleary (1968) and Darlington (1971), McNemar (1975) proposed the use of separate regression lines for subgroups when differences in regression slopes were observed. This technique was aimed at reducing prediction errors within subgroups that resulted from the use of a single regression equation. Using a somewhat different perspective, Thorndike (1971) defined bias in selection procedures as evidence of a discrepancy between the proportions of subgroup members passing a cut score on the predictor scale and the proportions within these groups passing a cut score on the criterion scale.

Soon after the presentation of these definitions of bias within the context of selection procedures, concerns with fairness in testing began to switch to methods for detecting bias at the individual item level. Further, rather than describing any observed difference in achievement between subgroups as bias, researchers began to distinguish between *item bias* and *item impact*. Whereas *item bias* indicates differences in performance across subgroups related to construct-irrelevant components, *item impact* reflects true differences among subgroups in terms of locations on the latent variable. The term *differential item functioning* (DIF) describes situations in which test takers from different subgroups have differing probabilities of success on an item after they have been matched on the construct being measured. Evidence of DIF can alert researchers to potential bias.

Using the broad categories presented by Crocker and Algina (1986), efforts for detecting and quantifying indicators of DIF can be classified in terms of three major approaches: (A) methods based on item difficulty; (B) methods based on contingency tables (i.e., chi-square methods); and (C) methods based on IRT models.

In terms of the first category, methods for defining and detecting bias based on item difficulty are concerned with examining the degree to which item difficulty ordering is the same across subgroups, or the degree to which the difference in item difficulty between subgroups is the same across all items. For example, within the test-score tradition, Angoff and Ford (1973) proposed the use of the delta method, where transformations of proportion-correct statistics (e.g., p-values) to delta values are compared between subgroups using bivariate correlations and scatterplots. Additional techniques based on the delta method are available to determine the magnitude of differences between the delta-transformed values of item difficulty within subgroups. Because the delta–plot method may produce spurious results if item discrimination values vary across the subgroups of interest, improvements to the original delta technique have been proposed that incorporate matching variables, including external variables or total scores for the overall sample or within smaller groups (Crocker & Algina, 1986).

Next, contingency table approaches for detecting item bias include techniques aimed at comparing proportion-correct statistics for individual items across subgroups of test takers. Methods within this category use a sort of "matching" procedure where proportion-correct comparisons are made across groups of students who have comparable total scores within each subgroup. For example, Scheuneman (1979) and Camili (1979) proposed chi-square statistics that provide indicators of the magnitude and direction of differences in achievement for individual items that may warrant further investigation. Along the same lines, the Mantel-Haenszel procedure (Holland & Thayer, 1988) describes differences in item-level performance based on odds ratios. Essentially, the Mantel-Haenszel statistic provides an effect size and significance test that can be used to identify items for further analysis in bias studies. As pointed out by Clauser and Mazor (1998), this statistic "may be the most widely used of the contingency table procedures" (p. 35). Other contingency table approaches include Dorans and Kulick's (1986) standardization procedure, in which the standardized differences in proportion-correct values are examined within score groups.

Third, methods for detecting item bias based on latent trait models focus on identifying differences in student achievement on individual items after controlling for student locations on the latent variable. Embretson and Reise (2000) summarize this perspective as follows:

> A test item is measurement-invariant when it has the same relationship with a latent variable across groups. . . . As a consequence, examinee scores on the latent variable are comparable and mean differences between groups in raw scores legitimately reflect real mean differences on the latent variable and cannot be attributed to a measurement artifact.

(pp. 250–251)

Research on DIF has been widespread within the scaling tradition since the introduction of IRT, and numerous techniques have been proposed including indices of differences in between item calibrations and item characteristic curves. When DIF is explored in the context of models that meet the requirements for invariant measurement, these techniques are used to explore the degree to which invariance is observed across subgroups of test takers.

What Is the Current Consensus Definition of Fairness?

As noted in the previous two chapters, the *Standards for Educational and Psychological Testing* (AERA, APA, & NCME, 2014) can be viewed as a summary of the current consensus definition within the measurement community regarding psychometrically sound and legally defensible measurement principles and practices. The most recent version of the *Standards for Educational and Psychological Testing* defines fairness as:

> Responsiveness to individual characteristics and testing contexts so that test scores will yield valid interpretations for intended uses.
>
> *(p. 50)*

The perspective put forth in the current *Standards for Educational and Psychological Testing* reflects a view of fairness as an effort to maximize test takers' opportunity to demonstrate their standing on the construct of interest. This task involves identifying and minimizing barriers that can obstruct these opportunities for individual or groups of test takers. Specifically, threats to fairness include aspects of the testing procedure that produce systematic variance in test scores within subgroups that result in inappropriate interpretations and uses of test scores—i.e., construct-irrelevant variance.

The current *Standards for Educational and Psychological Testing* describes four major sources of construct-irrelevant variance whose influence must be minimized in order to ensure fair testing practices: (1) test content, (2) test context, (3) test response, and (4) opportunity to learn. First, *test content* is a potential source of construct-irrelevant variance when item content systematically favors or disadvantages some groups over others based on prior knowledge, experiences, level of interest or motivation, or other variables in a way that confounds the interpretation of test scores. In terms of *test context*, construct-irrelevant variance occurs when aspects of the testing environment systematically affect performance. Examples of construct-irrelevant aspects of a testing environment include the level of clarity provided in test instructions, language demands in assessment tasks, interpersonal issues in interactive assessments, and whether the language in which a test is administered represents a student's best language for academic tasks. Third, construct-irrelevant variance can be related to the *response types* elicited by assessment tasks that result in different score interpretations across test takers. For example, test takers may respond to assessment tasks differently based on characteristics unrelated to the construct being measured, such as perceptions of socially desirable responses, cultural views related to verbosity or rapid speech, or ability to communicate through writing or speech. The fourth major category of threats to fairness is related to *opportunity to learn*, which is defined as "the extent to which individuals have had exposure to instruction or knowledge that affords them the opportunity to learn the content and skills targeted by the test" (AERA, APA, & NCME, 2014, p. 56). Differences in opportunity to learn can influence the validity of test score interpretations for individual test takers, particularly when test scores are used to inform high-stakes decisions.

As given in the *Standards for Educational and Psychological Testing*, these threats to fairness can be minimized through test design and adaptations that reflect careful consideration of potential sources of construct-irrelevant variance. In particular, test construction practices that reflect principles of *universal design* facilitate the development of tests that are "as usable as possible for all test takers" (AERA, APA, & NCME, 2014, p. 56). In some cases, design principles are not sufficient to ensure fair testing practices for all test takers. As a result, adaptations to the testing procedure may be necessary for some test takers in order to maximize access to the construct being measured. These adaptations vary in terms of the degree to which the resulting test scores remain comparable with those obtained from the original procedure. Specifically, *accommodations* are relatively minimal changes to the testing procedure that maintain the intended construct, such as changes to the presentation, format, or response procedures. On the other hand, *modifications* are more substantial in terms of the construct; test scores obtained from modified testing procedures do not maintain the same interpretation in terms of the construct.

When evaluating and addressing threats to fairness, the *Standards for Educational and Psychological Testing* emphasize the importance of empirical evidence to support claims related to test score comparability for all test takers. The overarching and individual standards for fairness emphasize this general view:

STANDARD 3.0

All steps in the testing process . . . should be designed in such a manner as to *minimize construct irrelevant variance* and to *promote the validity of interpretations* for intended uses for all test takers in the intended population.

AERA, APA, & NCME (2014, p. 63, emphasis added)

The subsequent standards presented for fairness are organized in four thematic clusters of individual standards. Figure 7.1 illustrates the four clusters, which are named as follows:

I. Test Design, Development, Administration, and Scoring Procedures That Minimize Barriers to Valid Score Interpretations for the Widest Possible Range of Individuals and Relevant Subgroups

II. Validity of Test Score Interpretations for Intended Uses for the Intended Examinee Population

III. Accommodations to Remove Construct-Irrelevant Barriers and Support Valid Interpretations of Scores for Their Intended Uses

IV. Safeguards Against Inappropriate Score Interpretations for Intended Uses

The next section provides a brief overview of conceptualizations of fairness within performance assessment research in general. Then, each of the four clusters of fairness standards is explored from the perspective of rater-invariant measurement. The case study in Chapter Eight illustrates techniques based on Rasch

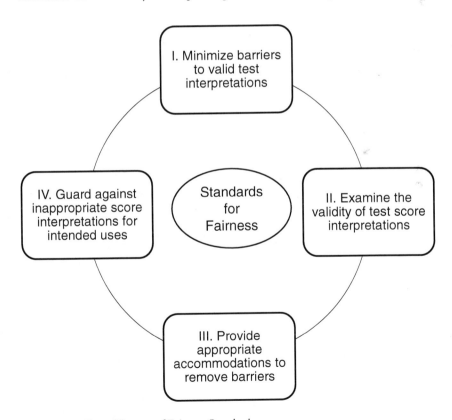

FIGURE 7.1 Four Clusters of Fairness Standards

Measurement Theory (Rasch, 1960/1980) that can be used to consider fairness issues within the framework of invariant measurement.

How Is Fairness Defined for Rater-Mediated Assessments?

As noted in the discussions of validity and reliability for rater-mediated assessments (Chapters Five and Six), a major theme emphasized throughout this book is the importance of considering the role of raters' judgmental process when evaluating the quality of rater-mediated assessments in terms of validity, reliability, and fairness. General discussions of fairness for performance assessments reflect the view of fairness as a validity issue that is emphasized in the *Standards for Educational and Psychological Testing*. Similar to the discussion of validity issues for performance assessments, general discussions of fairness for performance assessments often do not explicitly focus on the role of raters. In this book, we argue that the judgmental process is a central concern that must be considered in terms of validity, reliability, and fairness. The next section provides a brief summary of general discussions of fairness for performance assessments, followed by a consideration of fairness as it applies specifically to raters.

Fairness Issues for Performance Assessments in General

Similar to the treatment of fairness in previous editions of the *Standards for Educational and Psychological Testing*, most general discussions of fairness for performance assessments are included in discussions related to validity. In particular, research on the validity of performance assessments was prevalent during the 1980s and 1990s, when performance assessments grew in popularity. Similar to validity, one perspective during this period was that the use of performance assessment was itself a strategy for maximizing validity that also served to minimize threats to fairness. For example, Hambleton and Murphy (1992) contrasted the use of performance assessments with multiple-choice assessments:

> What is right to a majority-culture-test constructor may perhaps be perceived as ridiculous, unrealistic, or just plain unthinkable to a minority-group examinee; what is wrong may appear quite reasonable. At least with a free response, the examinee has a chance of explaining his or her nonmainstream viewpoint.
>
> *(p. 12)*

On the other hand, other researchers maintained that the performance assessment format was not a solution to fairness issues. Rather, these researchers claimed that the fairness issues that apply to "traditional" (i.e., multiple-choice) tests remain prevalent under the constructed-response format. For example, Linn, Baker, and Dunbar (1991) observed:

It would be a mistake to assume that shifting from fixed-response standardized tests to performance-based assessments will obviate concerns about biases against racial/ethnic minorities or that such a shift would necessarily lead to equality of performance . . . The key point is not dependent on the relative magnitude of group differences, however. Regardless of the relative size of the difference in performance between particular pairs of groups, it is clear that questions of fairness will loom as large for performance-based measures as they do for traditional tests.

(p. 18)

As pointed out by Linn, Baker, and Dunbar (1991), not only did fairness concerns persist within performance assessments, this assessment format introduced new fairness concerns related to methods used to obtain and score student responses. Using performance assessments that included reading passages as an example, these authors expressed concern related to differences in opportunity to learn across groups of test takers. In their words:

Although this trend may enhance the ecological validity of the tasks, it may also make it harder to achieve balance with regard to group differences in prior knowledge about the topics addressed in the passages.

(p. 18)

Reflecting similar concerns, Messick (1994) described threats to fairness in performance assessments in terms of unintended consequences that may arise related to constructed-response formats. Although advocates of performance assessments claim minimized threats of construct under-representation or construct-irrelevant variance, Messick observed that test developers and users must consider:

the possibility of unintended consequences of performance assessment, such as increased adverse impact for gender and racial/ethnic groups because of short-term misalignments in their educational experiences vis-a-vis the different cognitive demands of authentic testing and teaching.

(p. 22)

As with all assessment formats, Messick called for the careful consideration of potential threats to validity, including fairness throughout the test development, administration, scoring, and reporting processes.

Recently, several scholars have presented frameworks for fairness within the context of language testing that are applicable to performance assessments. For example, Kunnan (2004, 2010) presented another framework for test fairness based on two major principles: (1) the principle of justice and (2) the principle of beneficence. Essentially, these principles require tests to be free from construct-irrelevant variance and also result in benefits, rather than harm, to society. Later,

Xi (2010) presented another framework for exploring fairness considerations within the context of language performance assessments based on interpretive arguments. Specifically, this framework provides a structure for articulating a set of inferences, warrants, and assumptions that underlie the interpretation and use of an assessment. Using this framework, researchers and practitioners can articulate fairness arguments and evaluate evidence related to each element of the arguments in order to consider a variety of fairness issues related to the interpretation and use of an assessment. Reflecting validity arguments (Kane, 1992), Xi also encourages researchers to consider counter-arguments to fairness arguments and present rebuttals to these counter-arguments based on empirical evidence.

When evaluating performance assessments, we argue that it is essential to recognize that fairness is directly tied to the quality of ratings that result from rater interpretations of student performances, which are mediated by cues unique to the particular assessment context. Although several recent discussions of validity for performance assessments mention some fairness concerns related to the role of raters (e.g., Lane & Stone, 2006; Slomp, Corrigan, & Sugimoto, 2014), fairness issues related to the role of rater judgment have not been fully explored. In this book, we emphasize the central role of rating quality as a key component in evaluating the psychometric properties of rater-mediated assessments.

What Constitutes Fairness Evidence to Support the Interpretation and Use of Rater-Mediated Assessments?

This chapter contributes to the existing literature related to fairness for performance assessments through the exploration of a variety of concerns related to this foundational area from the perspective of rater-invariant measurement, particularly as these concerns relate to the fairness standards in the recent revision of the *Standards for Educational and Psychological Testing*. In this section, the four thematic clusters of fairness standards from the *Standards for Educational and Psychological Testing* are considered from the perspective of rater-mediated assessments, with an emphasis on the underlying issues related to invariant measurement. Table 7.1 summarizes the themes emphasized in the standards within each cluster. Table 7.2 summarizes the major concerns related to the four thematic clusters for fairness using questions that highlight concerns related to selected-response assessments and rater-mediated assessments. Whereas the underlying questions for selected-response assessments are specified to reflect the underlying concerns emphasized in the *Standards for Educational and Psychological Testing* for assessments in general, the questions presented for rater-mediated assessments are formulated to reflect the perspective of rater-invariant measurement.

TABLE 7.1 Four Thematic Clusters of Fairness Standards from the *Standards for Educational and Psychological Testing*

Cluster	Description from the Standards for Educational and Psychological Testing
I. Test Design, Development, Administration, and Scoring Procedures That Minimize Barriers to Valid Score Interpretations for the Widest Possible Range of Individuals and Relevant Subgroups	"A prime threat to fair and valid interpretation of test scores comes from aspects of the test or testing process that may produce construct-irrelevant variance in scores that systematically lowers or raises scores for identifiable groups of test takers and results in inappropriate score interpretations for intended uses" (p. 54)
II. Validity of Test Score Interpretations for Intended Uses for the Intended Examinee Population	"Fairness is a fundamental validity issue and requires attention throughout all stages of test development and use . . . Fairness to all individuals in the intended population of test takers is an overriding, foundational concern" (p. 49)
III. Accommodations to Remove Construct-Irrelevant Barriers and Support Valid Interpretations of Scores for Their Intended Uses	"Adaptation to individual characteristics and recognition of the heterogeneity within subgroups may be important to the validity of individual interpretations of test results in situations where the intent is to understand and respond to individual performance" (p. 53)
IV. Safeguards Against Inappropriate Score Interpretations for Intended Uses	"It is particularly important, when drawing inferences about an examinee's skills or abilities, to take into account the individual characteristics of the test taker and how these characteristics may interact with the contextual features of the testing situation" (p. 53)

1. Test Design, Development, Administration, and Scoring Procedures That Minimize Barriers to Valid Score Interpretations for the Widest Possible Range of Individuals and Relevant Subgroups

The first cluster of fairness standards focuses on methods to minimize barriers to the valid interpretation of test scores. As given in the *Standards for Educational and Psychological Testing* (AERA, APA, & NCME, 2014), barriers to valid test interpretations are sources of construct-irrelevant variance that systematically influence the interpretation and use of test scores:

A prime threat to fair and valid interpretation of test scores comes from aspects of the test or testing process that may produce construct–irrelevant

TABLE 7.2 Underlying Questions for the Four Fairness Clusters Based on Selected-Response and Rater-Mediated Assessments

Cluster	Selected-Response Assessments	Rater-Mediated Assessments
I. Test Design, Development, Administration, and Scoring Procedures That Minimize Barriers to Valid Score Interpretations for the Widest Possible Range of Individuals and Relevant Subgroups	What are the response characteristics central to the construct being measured? How do these align with the characteristics of the intended test takers? How can administration and scoring procedures be designed to remove construct-irrelevant barriers for relevant subgroups of intended test takers?	What are the potential unintended cues in the assessment system that could influence rater judgment in a construct–irrelevant way? How can rater training and monitoring procedures be designed to minimize construct-irrelevant barriers for relevant subgroups?
II. Validity of Test Score Interpretations for Intended Uses for the Intended Examinee Population	Is there evidence that test scores differ in meaning across test takers? What is the expected relationship between external criteria and test scores within all relevant subgroups?	Is there evidence to support the hypothesis of rater-invariant measurement for all intended test takers?
III. Accommodations to Remove Construct-Irrelevant Barriers and Support Valid Interpretations of Scores for Their Intended Uses	What adaptations are necessary in order to prevent features of the testing process (e.g., setting, delivery, response format) from presenting a construct-irrelevant barrier to some test takers? What evidence is there to support the equivalence of the construct between test scores obtained through the use of adaptations and test scores from the original procedure?	What adaptations are necessary in order to minimize the influence of construct-irrelevant cues on rater judgments? How do rater training procedures (e.g., rubrics and benchmarks) reflect the range of adaptations?
IV. Safeguards Against Inappropriate Score Interpretations for Intended Uses	What documentation is needed to reflect the scope of applicability of interpretations and uses of test scores for individual and subgroups of test takers? What additional sources of information can be used to support the use of a test score for placement, and/or high-stakes decisions?	What documentation is needed to reflect the scope of applicability of ratings for individual and subgroups of test takers? What additional sources of information can be used to support the use of ratings in a variety of contexts, including placement and/or high-stakes decisions?

variance in scores that systematically lowers or raises scores for identifiable groups of test takers and results in inappropriate score interpretations for intended uses.

(p. 54)

The first cluster of fairness standards emphasizes the need to carefully consider sources of construct-irrelevant variance throughout the test development, administration, and scoring processes. As given in Table 7.2, the fairness standards in this cluster reflect the following underlying questions for selected-response assessments:

- *What are the response characteristics central to the construct being measured? How do these align with the characteristics of the intended test takers?*
- *How can administration and scoring procedures be designed to remove construct-irrelevant barriers for relevant subgroups of intended test takers?*

Essentially, the first cluster of fairness standards emphasizes the importance of a clear definition of the response characteristics that reflect various locations on the construct and consideration of how these characteristics align with those of intended test takers. Specifically, assessment tasks, along with administration and scoring procedures, should be considered in terms of how they reflect the intended construct while also minimizing potential interactions with student characteristics that may result in construct-irrelevant barriers to a valid assessment process.

The underlying questions for rater-mediated assessments in Table 7.2 reflect essentially the same concerns as those identified for constructed-response items, with an emphasis on the role of raters' judgmental process for evaluating student responses in terms of the construct. From the perspective of rater-invariant measurement, the underlying concerns related to minimizing barriers to valid test interpretations can be summarized in terms of two questions:

- *What are the potential unintended cues in the assessment system that could influence rater judgment in a construct-irrelevant way?*
- *How can rater training and monitoring procedures be designed to minimize construct-irrelevant barriers for relevant subgroups?*

When rater judgment is involved in scoring procedures, it is necessary to consider how various aspects of the assessment process act as intended and unintended cues that influence rater judgment. Specifically, it is necessary to consider which characteristics are emphasized in materials presented during rater training and scoring guides (e.g., benchmark examples and rubrics), and the degree to which these characteristics may interact with student characteristics. The importance of developing scoring materials that reflect only the intended construct is emphasized in the *Standards for Educational and Psychological Testing* using the following example:

> A scoring rubric for a constructed response item might reserve the highest score level for test takers who provide more information or elaboration than was actually requested. In this situation, test takers who simply follow instructions, or test takers who value succinctness in responses will earn lower scores; thus, characteristics of the individuals have become construct-irrelevant components of the test scores.
>
> *(p. 56)*

From the perspective of rater-invariant measurement, efforts to ensure fairness must include the specification of the intended and potential unintended cues that inform raters' decision-making process. For example, cues that are intended to influence rater judgment may include response characteristics identified in a scoring rubric, rubric domains, or rating scale category exemplars. As noted in the example above, it is essential to consider whether these cues are central to the construct, along with the potential influence of other unintended cues. For example, unintended cues may include rater background characteristics or rater monitoring procedures in which employment decisions are based on agreement with other scorers. Hypotheses and empirical evidence related to these unintended cues should be used to inform rater training and monitoring procedures in order to minimize the influence of construct-irrelevant variance.

2. Validity of Test Score Interpretations for Intended Uses for the Intended Examinee Population

The second cluster of fairness standards focuses on the degree to which the validity of test score interpretations for intended uses is invariant across subgroups within a specified population of test takers. This cluster of standards focuses on identifying potential threats to validity related to subgroup membership. The standards in this cluster reflect the following perspective:

> Fairness is a fundamental validity issue and requires attention throughout all stages of test development and use . . . Fairness to all individuals in the intended population of test takers is an overriding, foundational concern.
>
> *(AERA, APA, & NCME, 2014, p. 49)*

As given in Table 7.2, the underlying concerns related to the second cluster of fairness standards can be summarized using two questions:

- *Is there evidence that test scores differ in meaning across test takers?*
- *What is the expected relationship between external criteria and test scores within all relevant subgroups?*

After the population of intended test takers is identified, it is essential to examine empirical evidence related to the equivalence of test score interpretations across subgroups within this population. Specifically, empirical evidence is necessary to determine whether observed differences in achievement levels across subgroups reflect true differences on the construct, or whether they indicate threats to fairness. Although differences in average achievement across student subgroups do not necessarily indicate fairness issues, observed differences should be examined from multiple perspectives in order to support the appropriateness of test score interpretations and uses across student subgroups. Further, the *Standards for Educational and Psychological Testing* call test developers and test users to explore evidence related to the equivalence of test-score-criterion relationships across subgroups as additional fairness evidence.

In terms of rater-mediated assessments, underlying fairness issues concerning the second cluster of standards are related to the invariance of rater judgments across subgroups of test takers. It should be noted that the *Standards for Educational and Psychological Testing* specifically address rater-mediated assessments in Standard 3.8, which is included in the second cluster:

Standard 3.8

When tests require the scoring of constructed responses, test developers and/or users should collect and report evidence of the validity of score interpretations for relevant subgroups in the intended population of test takers for the intended uses of the test scores.

(AERA, APA, & NCME, 2014, p. 66)

Evidence to support the claim of rater-invariant measurement across student subgroups is needed throughout the assessment process, including rater training procedures and monitoring raters during operational scoring. As given in Table 7.2, these underlying concerns related to rater-invariant measurement can be summarized in terms of the following question:

- *Is there evidence to support the hypothesis of rater-invariant measurement for all intended test takers?*

In practice, models that meet the requirements for invariant measurement can be used to obtain empirical evidence of rater-invariant measurement across student subgroups. Specifically, differential rater functioning analyses can be used to identify potential areas for further investigation, including qualitative studies, in order to more fully explore the quality of a rater-mediated assessment in terms of fairness. The case study in Chapter Eight illustrates methods based on Rasch Measurement Theory that can be used to obtain evidence related to fairness in the context of rater-mediated assessments.

3. Accommodations to Remove Construct-Irrelevant Barriers and Support Valid Interpretations of Scores for Their Intended Uses

The third cluster of fairness standards focuses on the appropriate use of accommodations to ensure that all test takers have an unobstructed opportunity to demonstrate their standing on the construct. As noted above, the *Standards for Educational and Psychological Testing* describe accommodations as a continuum of changes to the testing procedure that vary in terms of the degree to which resulting scores maintain the original construct interpretation, where accommodations are minor changes that retain the original construct interpretation and modifications result in scores that reflect a different construct. The individual fairness standards related to the concept of accommodations reflect the premise that changes to a testing procedure may be necessary in order to maximize access to the construct, and thus obtain the most accurate measure for individual test takers. This perspective is summarized in the *Standards for Educational and Psychological Testing* as follows:

> Adaptation to individual characteristics and recognition of the heterogeneity within subgroups may be important to the validity of individual interpretations of test results in situations where the intent is to understand and respond to individual performance.
>
> *(p. 53)*

As given in Table 7.2, underlying concerns for selected-response items related to the third cluster of fairness standards can be summarized in terms of two questions:

- *What adaptations are necessary in order to prevent features of the testing process (e.g., setting, delivery, response format) from presenting a construct-irrelevant barrier to some test takers?*
- *What evidence is there to support the equivalence of the construct between test scores obtained through the use of adaptations and test scores from the original procedure?*

Where appropriate, accommodations can be used to minimize threats to fairness that result from features of the testing procedure, such as the setting in which a test is administered or the response format through which students are required to demonstrate their standing on the construct. When changes to the testing procedure are made, empirical evidence is needed to determine the comparability of scores obtained with adaptations and scores from the original procedure.

In terms of rater-mediated assessments, fairness concerns related to changes in the testing procedure reflect the influence of these changes on raters' judgmental processes. As given in Table 7.2, two questions can be used to summarize the underlying concerns related to Cluster III for rater-mediated assessments:

- *What adaptations are necessary in order to minimize the influence of construct-irrelevant cues on rater judgments?*
- *How do rater training procedures (e.g., rubrics and benchmarks) reflect the range of adaptations?*

The first question reflects essentially the same concerns as the first question for selected-response questions within this cluster, with the additional consideration of the influence of rater judgment on the interpretation of student responses. In the context of rater-mediated assessments, threats to fairness can also include interactions between rater judgment and characteristics of student responses. When adaptations are used, it is necessary that rater training include efforts to "scaffold" rater judgment to ensure comparable scores between performances produced with and without adaptations. For example, if a testing adaptation allows some students to submit typed, rather than hand-written, essays, rater training materials should include appropriate benchmarks that illustrate student responses in the alternative format. Further, scoring rubrics should be applicable to both hand-written and typed response formats.

4. Safeguards Against Inappropriate Score Interpretations for Intended Uses

Similar to the discussions of fairness across subgroups of test takers, the standards in Cluster IV emphasize the need to identify and respond to the characteristics of test takers that may interact with aspects of the testing procedure. According to the *Standards for Educational and Psychological Testing,*

> It is particularly important, when drawing inferences about an examinee's skills or abilities, to take into account the individual characteristics of the test taker and how these characteristics may interact with the contextual features of the testing situation.
>
> *(p. 53)*

Whereas the standards in Cluster II emphasized the need to identify differences in the interpretation and use of test scores across subgroups of test takers, the standards in Cluster IV emphasize actions that test developers and test users must take in order to minimize threats to fairness for individual and subgroups of test takers. As given in Table 7.2, the underlying concerns for selected-response items can be summarized using two questions:

- *What documentation is needed to reflect the scope of applicability of interpretations and uses of test scores for individual and subgroups of test takers?*

- *What additional sources of information can be used to support the use of a test score for placement and/or high-stakes decisions?*

According to the individual fairness standards within Cluster IV, test developers and publishers must include evidence of applicability of test score interpretations for intended uses across test takers, with sufficient evidence for test users to identify individuals and subgroups for whom a given interpretation and use may not be appropriate. When evidence is not available regarding the applicability of a particular interpretation and use of test scores, sufficient cautionary statements are warranted to prevent unfair testing practices. Similarly, test users are cautioned to consider potential differences in the validity of test score interpretations for particular uses across individual and subgroups of test takers, and include multiple sources of evidence to inform high-stakes decisions.

In the context of rater-mediated assessments, fairness concerns related to Cluster IV reflect essentially the same concerns as those listed for selected-response items, with an emphasis on the appropriate interpretation of rater judgments for individual and subgroups of test takers:

- *What documentation is needed to reflect the scope of applicability of ratings for individual and subgroups of test takers?*
- *What additional sources of information can be used to support the use of ratings in a variety of contexts, including placement and/or high-stakes decisions?*

Similar to selected-response items, empirical evidence is needed that documents the applicability of rater judgment for test takers with a variety of characteristics. For example, technical documentations should include information about the characteristics of test takers from whom rater training and scoring materials were developed. Likewise, rater judgments should be supplemented with additional indicators of student standing on a construct, especially when ratings are used to inform high-stakes decisions.

Summary and Discussion

> Bias found for groups is never uniformly present among members of the group or uniformly absent among those not in the group. For the analysis of item bias to do individuals any good . . . it will have to be done at the individual level of the much more useful person fit analyses.
>
> *(Wright, 1984, p. 285)*

In this chapter, we briefly described (1) the evolution of the concept of fairness for educational assessments during the 20th century, (2) the current consensus definition of fairness as represented by the *Standards for Educational and Psychological Testing*, and (3) the implications of these guiding principles of fairness for rater-mediated assessments. The *Standards for Educational and Psychological Testing* summarize the requirements for ensuring fairness as follows:

> Fairness is a fundamental issue for valid test score interpretation, and it should therefore be the goal for all testing applications. Fairness is the responsibility of all parties involved in test development, administration, and score interpretation for the intended purposes of the test.
>
> *(AERA, APA, & NCME, 2014, p. 62)*

In this chapter, fairness was discussed in terms of measurement issues that arise within the context of rater-mediated assessments. As noted in the discussion of validity (Chapter Five) and reliability (Chapter Six), it is essential that evaluations of rater-mediated assessments in terms of fairness include evidence related to the quality of rater judgments.

This chapter focused on how the four thematic clusters of standards for fairness (Figure 7.1, Table 7.1) can be conceptualized to guide the collection of evidence of fairness related to rater-mediated assessments. The key idea in this chapter is that evidence of fairness in the context of rater-mediated assessments must be situated within a coherent measurement framework based on the requirements for invariant measurement.

The next chapter presents an illustrative case study in which data from a writing assessment are used to illustrate methods for exploring rating quality in terms of validity, reliability, and fairness from the perspective of rater-invariant measurement.

References

American Educational Research Association (AERA), American Psychological Association (APA), & National Council on Measurement in Education (NCME). (2014). *Standards for educational and psychological testing*. Washington, DC: AERA.

Angoff, W. H., & Ford, S. F. (1973). Item-race interaction on a test of scholastic aptitude. *Journal of Educational Measurement, 10*(2), 95–106.

Camili, G. (1979). *A critique of the chi-squared method for assessing item bias*. Unpublished paper, Laboratory of Educational Research, University of Colorado, Boulder.

Clauser, B. E., & Mazor, K. M. (1998). Using statistical procedures to identify differentially functioning test items. *Educational Measurement: Issues and Practice, 17*(1), 31–44. https://doi.org/10.1111/j.1745-3992.1998.tb00619.x

Cleary, T. A. (1968). Test bias: Prediction of grades of negro and white students in integrated colleges. *Journal of Educational Measurement, 5*(2), 115–124.

Crocker, L., & Algina, J. (1986). *Introduction to classical and modern test theory*. New York: Holt, Rinehart and Winston.

Darlington, R. B. (1971). Another look at "cultural fairness". *Journal of Educational Measurement, 8*(2), 71–82.

Dorans, N. J., & Kulick, E. (1986). Demonstrating the utility of the standardization approach to assessing unexpected differential item performance on the Scholastic Aptitude Test. *Journal of Educational Measurement, 23*(4), 355–368.

Embretson, S. E., & Reise, S. P. (2000). *Item response theory for psychologists*. Mahwah, NJ: Lawrence Erlbaum Associates, Publishers.

Hambleton, R. K., & Murphy, E. (1992). A psychometric perspective on authentic measurement. *Applied Measurement in Education, 5*(1), 1–16.

Holland, P. W., & Thayer, D. T. (1988). Differential item performance and the Mantel-Haenszel procedure. In H. Wainer & H. I. Braun (Eds.), *Test validity* (pp. 129–145). Hillsdale, NJ: Lawrence Erlbaum Associates.

Kane, M. T. (1992). An argument-based approach to validity. *Psychological Bulletin, 112*(3), 527–535. https://doi.org/10.1037/0033-2909.112.3.527

Kunnan, A. J. (2004). Test fairness. In M. Milanovic & C. Weir (Eds.), *European language testing in a global context* (pp. 27–48). Cambridge, UK: Cambridge University Press.

Kunnan, A. J. (2010). Test fairness and Toulmin's argument structure. *Language Testing, 27*(2), 183–189.

Lane, S., & Stone, C. (2006). Performance assessment. In R. Brennan (Ed.), *Educational measurement* (4th ed., pp. 387–431). Westport, CT: American Council on Education and Praeger.

Linn, R. L., Baker, E. L., & Dunbar, S. B. (1991). Complex, performance-based assessment: Expectations and validation criteria. *Educational Researcher, 20*(8), 15. https://doi.org/10.2307/1176232

McNemar, Q. (1975). On so-called test bias. *American Psychologist, 30*(8), 848–851. https://doi.org/10.1037/h0077026

Messick, S. (1994). The interplay of evidence and consequences in the validation of performance assessments. *Educational Researcher, 23*(2), 13–23. https://doi.org/10.2307/1176219

Rasch, G. (1960). *Probabilistic models for some intelligence and achievement tests*. Copenhagen, Denmark: Danish Institute for Educational Research. (Expanded edition, Chicago: University of Chicago Press, 1980).

Scheuneman, J. (1979). A method of assessing bias in test items. *Journal of Educational Measurement, 16*(3), 143–152.

Slomp, D. H., Corrigan, J. A., & Sugimoto, T. (2014). A framework for using consequential validity evidence in evaluating large-scale writing assessments: A Canadian study. *Research in the Teaching of English, 48*(3), 276–302.

Thorndike, R. L. (1971). Concepts of culture-fairness. *Journal of Educational Measurement, 8*(2), 63–70.

Wright, B. D. (1984). Despair and hope for educational measurement. *Contemporary Education Review, 1*, 281–288.

Xi, X. (2010). How do we go about investigating test fairness? *Language Testing, 27*(2), 147–170. https://doi.org/10.1177/0265532209349465

8

CASE STUDY

Evidence for the Validity, Reliability, and Fairness of Ratings on a Middle Grades Writing Assessment

> Better measurement leads to clearer thinking, and clearer thinking leads to improvements in both theory and practice.
>
> *(Linacre, 1989, p. iii)*

Chapters Five through Seven provided a theoretical overview of the three foundational areas for evaluating measurement procedures in the recent revision of the *Standards for Educational and Psychological Testing* (AERA, APA, & NCME, 2014): validity, reliability, and fairness. These chapters highlighted unique concerns related to these three concepts within the context of rater-mediated assessments. The current chapter summarizes the discussion of the foundational areas from the *Standards for Educational and Psychological Testing* by illustrating procedures for evaluating the quality of rater-mediated assessments using a case study. Specifically, an illustrative analysis of data from a middle grades writing assessment based on Rasch Measurement Theory is presented, and the results are discussed in terms of validity, reliability, and fairness issues.

This chapter is organized as follows:

- Methodology of case study

  o Participants
  o Analyses
  o Measurement model

- Results

  o Validity
  o Reliability
  o Fairness

- Summary and discussion

Methodology of Case Study

Participants

This chapter illustrates the use of Rasch Measurement Theory to explore the psychometric quality of a rater-mediated assessment. The illustrative data analyses in this chapter are based on a dataset that was previously examined by Gyagenda and Engelhard (2009). These data came from the Georgia High School Writing Test, and they include scores from 365 eighth-grade students whose persuasive essays were rated by 20 operational raters. The original ratings were obtained with a five-category rating scale (1 = *low* to 5 = *high*). However, due to a low frequency of ratings in the top category, the ratings were re-coded to a four-category scale (1 = *low* to 4 = *high*). Each essay was scored using analytic rubrics with four separate domains: Conventions, Organization, Sentence Formation, and Style. All 20 operational raters and a validity committee scored the entire set of 365 essays, yielding a fully crossed design with a high level of connectivity (Engelhard, 1997). Each essay received 21 ratings on each domain including an expert rater. The Facets computer program (Linacre, 2015) is used to conduct data analyses.

Analyses

The illustrative analyses in this chapter are based on the Many-Facet Rasch model (Linacre, 1989). The MFR model was originally developed as an approach to exploratory data analysis within the context of rater-mediated assessments. The MFR model can be specified as a generalization of either the Rating Scale (RS) or Partial Credit (PC) formulation of the Rasch model (Andrich, 1978; Masters, 1982) that incorporates additional explanatory variables, such as raters, tasks, and assessment occasions. These additional variables are called *facets*. Similar to a logistic regression model with fixed effects, the MFR model for ratings models observed ratings as the dependent variable with a single person parameter (θ) and additional researcher-specified facets as independent variables. When data fit the MFR model, invariant estimates of each of the facets on the logit scale can be obtained.

In contrast to traditional methods for evaluating rating quality that focus on indicators of rater agreement and reliability, the MFR model provides a method for evaluating rating quality that focuses on the degree to which ratings reflect a set of fundamental measurement properties. The contrast between the test-score and scaling approaches for evaluating rater-mediated assessments can be framed in terms of the view of ideal raters within each perspective. Within the test-score tradition, an ideal rater is one who produces ratings that are consistent with other members of a rater group—in other words, the goal is to produce reliable "rating machines." On the other hand, an ideal rater from the perspective of Rasch

Measurement Theory is one whose location on the construct can be defined and whose ratings match the expectations of a measurement model with useful properties. Specifically, if there is evidence that a rater approximates the requirements for invariant measurement, individual differences in rater severity do not affect the estimation of student locations on the latent variable—in other words, the goal is to estimate student locations using *rating experts*. Linacre (1989) summarized the usefulness of the MFR model as a method for going beyond observed ratings in order to facilitate inferences about a latent variable. In his words:

> In order to supersede the local particularities of the judging situation, each judge must be treated as though he has a unique severity, each examinee as though he has a unique ability, each item as though it has a unique difficulty, and the rating scale as though it has one formulation applied identically by all the judges . . . Thus each rating is considered to be the probabilistic result of only four interacting components: the ability of an examinee, the severity of a judge, the difficulty of an item, and the structure of the rating scale. With these assumptions, it is possible to obtain . . . an estimate of the ability of each examinee, freed from the level of severity of the particular judges who happened to rate the performance and also freed from the difficulty of the items and the arbitrary manner in which the categories of the rating scale has been defined.
>
> *(p. 41)*

Because it facilitates invariant measurement in situations involving multiple facets, the MFR model has been used to examine a variety of issues in educational assessments that require raters, judges, or panelists to assign polytomous ratings (e.g., Engelhard, 1994; Kaliski et al., 2013; Lunz, Wright, & Linacre, 1990; Wind & Engelhard, 2012).

Measurement Model

The illustrative analysis of the middle grades writing assessment data is based on a rating scale formulation of the MFR model that includes three facets: Students, Raters, and Domains. The model can be stated in log-odds format as follows:

$$\ln\left[\frac{P_{nijk}}{P_{nijk-1}}\right] = \theta_n - \lambda_i - \delta_j - \tau_k, \tag{8.1}$$

where:

θ_n = logit-scale location (i.e., writing achievement) of Student n,
λ_i = logit-scale location (i.e., severity) of Rater i,
δ_j = logit-scale location (i.e., difficulty) of Domain j, and
τ_k = difficulty of Category k relative to Category $k - 1$.

The dependent variable in this model is the log of the odds that a student receives a rating in Category k, rather than in Category $k - 1$, given their location on the latent variable, the severity of the rater, and the difficulty of the domain. τ_k reflects the structure of the rating scale, and it is not considered a facet in the model. As noted earlier in this book, each of the parameters in Model I are based on rater judgments. As a result, the student achievement parameter reflects rater judgments of each student's writing proficiency based on their essay. Similarly, the domain parameter reflects raters' judgments of the difficulty of each domain. The rater parameters reflect each rater's severity based on their judgments across students and domains.

Results

In this section, results from the MFR model analysis are presented in terms of the three foundational areas for evaluating rater-mediated assessments that were presented in Chapters Five through Seven: validity, reliability, and fairness. It should be noted that the general interpretation of the output from the Facets analysis of the illustrative data is essentially the same as the other illustrations of MFR model analyses presented earlier in this book. However, this chapter focuses on how the results can be interpreted with a specific focus on the foundational areas of validity, reliability, and fairness.

The presentation of results is organized as follows. For each foundational area, a brief summary of the current consensus definition from the *Standards for Educational and Psychological Testing* is presented and the major themes for evaluating rater-mediated assessments from the perspective of rater-invariant measurement are reviewed. Then, relevant results from the MFR model analysis are illustrated and discussed as they apply to the underlying questions for rater-mediated assessments that were presented in Chapters Five through Seven.

Validity

Chapter Five focused on the first foundational area in the recent revision of the *Standards for Educational and Psychological Testing* (AERA, APA, & NCME, 2014): Validity. As noted in Chapter Five, the current consensus definition of validity is as follows:

> The degree to which accumulated evidence and theory support a specific interpretation of test scores for a given use of a test.
>
> *(AERA, APA, & NCME, 2014, p. 11)*

Based on this definition, the *Standards for Educational and Psychological Testing* includes a set of validity standards organized in three thematic clusters: (1) establishing intended uses and interpretations; (2) issues regarding samples and settings used in validation; and (3) specific forms of validity evidence. The discussion of validity in the *Standards for Educational and Psychological Testing* focuses primarily on the third cluster of standards. Specifically, the *Standards for Educational and Psychological Testing* include an overview of five sources of validity evidence that can be used to support the interpretation and use of test scores: (A) test content, (B) response processes, (C) internal structure, (D) relations to external variables, and (E) consequences of testing (see Figure 5.1). For each of the three thematic clusters of validity standards, Chapter Five presented questions that reflect underlying concerns in the context of rater-mediated assessments, with an emphasis on the third cluster of standards. The following section presents results from the middle grades writing assessment related to the validity standards.

Validity Cluster I: Establishing Intended Uses and Interpretations

As given in Table 5.2, the underlying questions for rater-mediated assessments for the first cluster of validity standards is:

- *What is the intended interpretation and use of ratings?*

Similar to the underlying concerns for selected-response items, validity evidence for rater-mediated assessments must include a rationale to support each intended interpretation and use of ratings. Because of the role of rater judgment in obtaining scores from rater-mediated assessments, this evidence should include sufficient detail regarding the methods used to facilitate rater decision-making. For example, depending on the intended use and interpretation of ratings, different scoring designs (i.e., how many raters score each student), rater training and qualification procedures, and rater monitoring procedures may be necessary to support a particular interpretation and use.

The illustrative data used in this chapter were collected during an administration of the Georgia High School Writing Assessment. According to the Georgia Department of Education (2011), this assessment was designed to provide diagnostic information regarding students' strengths and weaknesses in persuasive and expository writing. Specifically, the interpretive guide for the writing assessment states: "the results are designed to inform students, parents, teachers, and school administrators of the extent to which students are able to demonstrate effective writing skills and to suggest areas of instruction where improvement could be made" (Georgia Department of Education, 2011, p. 5).

In order to support this interpretation of ratings, students receive scores from two raters who were required to complete a training program and earn passing scores on a qualifying test designed to assess their use of the rubric in terms of the specific requirements and intentions for prompts for the particular administration of the writing test.[1] As noted above, student scores are assigned using an analytic rubric that includes four separate domain areas. Separate domain-level scores are reported that reflect an average of the two ratings for each domain. These domain ratings are then weighted and transformed into a scale score. Student score reports include both the domain-level scores and scale score.

Validity Cluster II: Issues Regarding Samples and Settings Used in Validation

The second cluster of validity standards calls for the clear description of the samples and settings used to collect validity evidence. These standards also emphasize the shared responsibility between test developers and test users to evaluate the appropriateness of validity evidence for a particular assessment context. As noted in Table 5.2, the underlying question for this cluster of standards in the context of rater-mediated assessment is:

- *What samples and settings were used to obtain rater training materials (e.g., benchmark papers)?*

The technical manual should be consulted for information regarding the nature of rater training materials. Since this assessment is not currently used in Georgia, this information is not provided.

Validity Cluster III: Specific Forms of Validity Evidence

The third cluster of validity standards includes five specific forms of validity evidence: (A) test content, (B) response processes, (C) internal structure, (D) relations to external variables, and (E) consequences of testing. The *Standards for Educational and Psychological Testing* include separate discussions and standards related to each of these sources of evidence. However, the perspective on validity evidence set forth in the *Standards for Educational and Psychological Testing* is that validity evidence should include integrated evidence across the five sources that is appropriate for a particular assessment context.

A. Test Content

The first form of validity evidence is evidence related to test content. As given in the *Standards for Educational and Psychological Testing*, validity evidence related to test content is collected using "an analysis of the relationship between the content of a test and the construct it is intended to measure" (p. 14). From the perspective of invariant measurement, validity evidence related to test content can be conceptualized in terms of the Wright map. Specifically, examination of the observed and expected ordering of persons, items, or other facets on the Wright map can be used to support the interpretation of logit-scale locations as representing locations on the latent variable. In the context of rater-mediated assessments, the Wright map is a visual summary of the locations of raters, students, items, and other facets, based on rater judgments. Accordingly, the underlying question for the validity standards related to test content is:

• *What is the rater-mediated latent variable?*

Figure 8.1 shows the Wright map for the case study data. This visual display represents the overall shared understanding of student writing achievement, domain difficulty, and rating-scale categories for the writing assessment among the sample of raters. The first column is the logit scale that represents writing achievement, which is the latent variable examined in this study.

The next three columns display the logit-scale locations for the three facets: Students, Raters, and Domains. In order to provide a frame of reference for

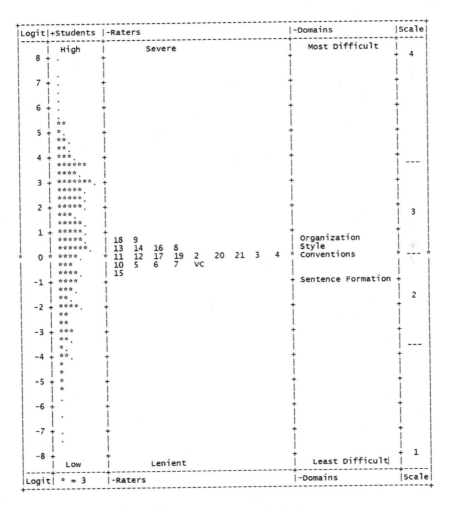

FIGURE 8.1 Rater-Mediated Latent Variable (Wright Map)

interpreting the logit-scale locations of the three facets, raters and domains are centered at zero (mean set to zero), and only the average location of the student facet is allowed to vary. The second column displays the student locations on the latent variable ($n = 365$). As can be seen in the variable map, there is a wide range in student locations on the latent variable, which suggests that the group of raters detected differences among these students in terms of writing achievement. Students who are located higher on the logit scale received higher ratings, and students who are located lower on the logit scale received lower ratings. Examination of the Rater column reveals that there is not much variation among the locations of the raters on the logit scale compared to the spread of students. Raters who are located higher on the logit scale were more severe (i.e., they assigned lower ratings more often). Raters who are located lower on the logit scale are less severe (i.e., they assigned higher ratings more often). Finally, the location of the domains on the logit scale reflects the judged difficulty of the style, organization, conventions, and sentence formation domains. Domains that are located higher on the logit scale are associated with more severe (i.e., lower) ratings, and domains that are located lower on the logit scale are associated with less severe (i.e., higher) ratings.

Table 8.1 includes summary statistics that correspond to the Wright map shown in Figure 8.1. This table summarizes the logit-scale locations for the

TABLE 8.1 Summary Statistics

	Students (θ)	Raters (λ)	Domains (δ)
Logit-Scale Measure			
M	0.80	0.00	0.00
SD	2.83	0.33	0.57
N	365	21	4
Infit MSE			
M	0.98	0.97	0.97
SD	0.22	0.17	0.04
Std. Infit MSE			
M	−0.20	−0.90	−2.00
SD	1.50	4.40	2.80
Outfit MSE			
M	0.98	0.98	0.98
SD	0.26	0.19	0.04
Std. Outfit MSE			
M	−0.20	−0.50	−0.80
SD	1.50	3.90	2.20
Separation Statistics			
Reliability of Separation	0.99	0.98	> 0.99
Chi-Squared	47,417.40*	846.70*	2,543.80*
Degrees of Freedom	364	20	3

* $p < 0.05$

Student, Rater, and Domain facets examined in the case study. Additional details regarding the model-data fit and separation statistics included in this table are discussed later in this chapter.

B. Response Processes

The second form of validity evidence described in the *Standards for Educational and Psychological Testing* includes evidence related to "the fit between the construct and the detailed nature of the performance or response actually engaged in by test takers" (AERA, APA, & NCME, 2014, p. 15). The validity standards related to response processes call for the use of theoretical and empirical analyses of student responses to assessment tasks, such as think-aloud interviews, to explore the alignment between observed and intended cognitive processes involved in responding to assessment tasks. In the context of rater-mediated assessments, it is also necessary to gather evidence related to the cognitive processes raters use while scoring student performances. Specifically, it is necessary to investigate rater interpretations of the performance tasks (i.e., prompts), scoring rubric(s), PLDs, and rating scale categories. As given in Chapter Five, the underlying question for validity evidence related to response processes in the context of rater-mediated assessments is:

- *How do rater interpretations of rubrics and performance-level descriptors lead to ratings of student achievement that define the rater-mediated latent variable?*

The scoring rubric and performance-level descriptors used during the collection of the case study data are given in Appendix 8.A at the end of this chapter. Raters used four separate rubrics that correspond to the four domains. Each rubric included the operational definition for each domain, components of writing associated with each domain, rating scale categories (1 = *Lack of control*, 2 = *Minimal control*; 3 = *Sufficient control*; 4 = *Consistent control*; 5 = *Full command*), and PLDs that included a list of characteristics of student writing at each level.

In order to gather validity evidence related to response processes for the case study data, qualitative interviews could be conducted during which raters are asked to describe their application of scoring rubrics to exemplar student responses. Several scholars have applied qualitative interview techniques as a method for exploring raters' cognitive processes (e.g., Lumley, 2002; Wolfe, Kao, & Ranney, 1998). As pointed out by Lumley (2002), these studies are aimed at exploring the process by which raters "reconcile their impression of the text, the specific features of the text, and the wordings of the rating scale" in order to rate a performance (p. 246). Lumley used think-aloud interviews to examine differences in raters' decision-making processes between experienced and novice raters within the context of second-language writing assessment. The think-aloud protocol asked raters to "vocalize your thoughts, and explain why you give the scores you give" (p. 274).

Depending on the nature of the assessment, a variety of qualitative coding schemes can be applied to these think-aloud interviews. In order to gather validity evidence related to raters' response process, the coding scheme should facilitate the exploration of raters' cognitive processes in terms of the types of cues that are informing their decision-making processes (see Chapter Four). Analyses of the alignment between observed and intended cues can be used to support the interpretation and use of ratings for a particular purpose.

C. Internal Structure

The third form of validity evidence is related to the internal structure of assessment tasks. As given in the *Standards for Educational and Psychological Testing*, this category of evidence is based on "the degree to which the relationships among test items and test components conform to the construct on which the proposed test score interpretations are based" (p. 16). Evidence in this category generally includes indicators of a positive relationship between item-level scores and total test scores, where evidence of a positive relationship provides support for the interpretation of item scores in terms of the construct.

Within the context of rater-mediated assessments, evidence in this category is used to support the interpretation of ratings as indices of the construct intended to be measured by the assessment. As given in Chapter Five, the underlying question for this category is:

• *How are rater interpretations of person locations, domain difficulties, and rating-scale categories mapped onto the rater-mediated latent variable?*

Several indicators can be used to examine the internal structure of rater-mediated assessments from the perspective of rater-invariant measurement, including indicators of model-data fit and differential rater functioning. One technique includes an examination of the degree to which observed ratings increase along with student locations on the latent variable. Specifically, it is possible to create a *test response function*, which is a plot of the average ratings on the raw-score scale across the range of student locations on the logit scale.

Figure 8.2 is a test response function based on the case study data. The *x*-axis displays student locations on the latent variable, and the *y*-axis displays average ratings on the raw score scale. The dashed line displays the observed correspondence between average ratings (*y*-axis) and student measures on the latent variable (*x*-axis), and the smooth line displays the model-expected response function. Inspection of the test response function indicates a positive relationship between latent variable locations and observed average ratings,

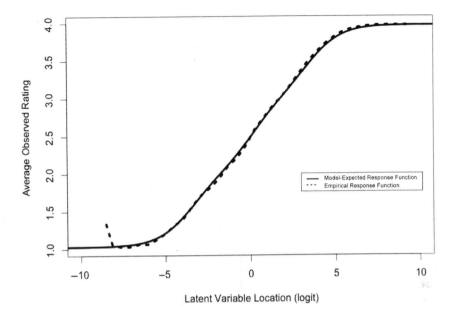

FIGURE 8.2   Test Response Function

along with a close match between the expected and empirical ratings across the range of the latent variable. Taken together, these findings provide support for the interpretation of observed ratings as indicators of student locations on the latent variable.

Additional evidence based on Rasch Measurement Theory related to the internal structure of rater-mediated assessments includes indicators of model–data fit and differential facet functioning. These indices are described later in this chapter in the discussions of reliability and fairness, respectively.

D. Relations to Other Variables

The fourth form of validity evidence described in the third cluster of validity standards is evidence based on relations between test scores and other variables. The *Standards for Educational and Psychological Testing* distinguish between *convergent relationships* that indicate that a test is measuring what it is intended to measure, and *divergent relationships* (i.e., null relationships) that indicate that a test is not measuring what it is not intended to measure. Depending on the nature of the assessment, convergent and divergent relationships with an assortment of variables may be of interest.

In the context of rater-mediated assessments, explorations of relations to other variables may also be valuable in order to inform the interpretation and use of ratings. Specifically, studies related to this form of validity evidence are used to explore the alignment between rater judgments of student achievement and indices based on other measures. As given in Chapter Five, the underlying question for this form of evidence for rater-mediated assessments is:

- *How does the alignment between ratings and relevant external variables support the interpretation of ratings in terms of the latent variable?*

It was noted in Chapter Five that relations between ratings and a variety of variables may be of interest that vary across assessment contexts, including studies of the correspondence between rater-assigned scores and scores from selected-response assessments of the same or similar domains. When the quality of ratings is the focus, another potentially relevant variable of interest is the match between operational rater-assigned scores and criterion scores that are assumed to reflect "true" or "accurate" ratings. One method for exploring this alignment within the framework of invariant measurement is to directly model indicators of rater accuracy using a Rasch model. Specifically, Engelhard (1996) proposed the use of a dichotomous model for rater accuracy. This model is based on dichotomous accuracy scores that result from the comparison of ratings assigned by operational raters to criterion ratings. For each performance, the score assigned by a given rater is compared to the criterion score. If the operational rating matches the criterion rating, the rater receives an accuracy score of "1"; otherwise, the rater receives an accuracy score of "0."

This model can be applied to the current case study using scores from the validity committee as criteria for evaluating the accuracy of each of the 20 operational raters on each of the 365 student essays. When applied to the writing data, the dichotomous model for accuracy is specified as follows:

$$\ln\left[\frac{P_{ji(x=1)}}{P_{ji(x=0)}}\right] = \delta_j - \beta_i, \tag{8.2}$$

where:

δ_j = the logit-scale location of Essay j on the logit scale that represents rater accuracy (i.e., the difficulty associated with assigning an accurate rating to Essay j), and

β_i = the logit-scale location of Rater i on the logit scale that represents rater accuracy (i.e., the accuracy level of Rater i).

The resulting estimates describe the locations of individual essays and raters on a linear scale that represents rater accuracy. Specifically, essay locations reflect the difficulty associated with providing an accurate rating to a particular essay, and rater locations describe overall accuracy levels for each rater.

Figure 8.3 is a variable map that illustrates rater accuracy for the case study data. In the context of accuracy ratings, the variable map represents rater accuracy in terms of the difficulty for raters to provide accurate ratings on each student essay, individual rater accuracy measures, and the difficulty for raters to provide accurate ratings within each of the writing domains. The first column is the logit scale that represents rater accuracy. The second column displays the location of each essay on the accuracy scale. The location of the essays on the logit scale represents the difficulty for operational raters to assign accurate scores. As can be seen in the variable map, there is a wide range in location of the 365 essays on the logit scale, which suggests that there are differences among the

```
+----------------------------------------------------------------------------------+
|Logit| Essays  |         Raters         |                Domains                  |
|-----+---------+------------------------+-----------------------------------------|
|     | Difficult|         Accurate       | Difficult to rate accurately           |
|     | to rate |                        |                                         |
| 5 + accurately+                        +                                         |
|     |         |                        |                                         |
|     |         |                        |                                         |
| 4 + |         +                        +                                         |
|     |         |                        |                                         |
|     |         |                        |                                         |
| 3 + |         +                        +                                         |
|     |         |                        |                                         |
|     |         |                        |                                         |
| 2 + |         +                        +                                         |
|     |         |                        |                                         |
|     |         |                        |                                         |
| 1 + |         +                        +                                         |
|     |         | 10                     |                                         |
|     |         | 2                      |                                         |
|     | .       | 4                      |                                         |
|     | .       | 6                      |                                         |
| *   0 + **,   * 11 12 13 14 16 17 20 8 9 * Conventions  Organization  Sentence Formation Style |
|     | ****,   | 15 18 3  5             |                                         |
|     | *****,  | 19 21 7               |                                         |
|     | ********* |                      |                                         |
|     | *******, |                        |                                         |
|-1 + ****,    +                        +                                         |
|     | ****    |                        |                                         |
|     | *,      |                        |                                         |
|     | *,      |                        |                                         |
|     | .       |                        |                                         |
|-2 + .       +                        +                                         |
|     | .       |                        |                                         |
|     | .       |                        |                                         |
|-3 + .       +                        +                                         |
|     | .       |                        |                                         |
|     |         |                        |                                         |
|-4 + |         +                        +                                         |
|     | .       |                        |                                         |
|     |         |                        |                                         |
|-5 + |         +                        +                                         |
|     | Easy    |                        |                                         |
|     | to rate |        Inaccurate      | Easy to rate accurately                |
|     | accurately|                      |                                         |
|-----+---------+------------------------+-----------------------------------------|
|Logit| * = 8   |         Raters         |                Domains                  |
+----------------------------------------------------------------------------------+
```

FIGURE 8.3 Variable Map for Rater Accuracy

essays in terms of difficulty for the operational raters to assign accurate scores. Essays that are located higher on the logit scale received inaccurate ratings more often, and essays that are located lower on the logit scale received accurate ratings more often. Examination of the Rater column reveals that there is some variation among the locations of the raters on the logit scale. Raters who are located higher on the logit scale were more accurate (i.e., their ratings matched expert ratings often). Raters who are located lower on the logit scale are less accurate (i.e., they assigned ratings that matched the expert less often). Finally, the location of the domains on the logit scale reflects the difficulty for raters to assign accurate ratings within each of the domains on the writing test examined in the case study. Domains that are located higher on the logit scale are associated with more accurate ratings, and domains that are located lower on the logit scale are associated with less accurate ratings.

Additional analyses related to rater accuracy are possible that include an examination of accuracy measures related to each individual student, rater, and domain. For a detailed illustration of rater accuracy analyses, please see Wind and Engelhard (2012, 2013).

E. Consequences of Testing

The final form of validity evidence described in the *Standards for Educational and Psychological Testing* is related to the consequences of testing. As noted in Chapter Five, the validity standards related to this form of evidence call test developers and users to look beyond the interpretation of a test score as an indicator of student achievement to also consider how tests may be used to inform decisions about educational systems, policy decisions, and other potential consequences not directly related to the construct being measured. In the context of rater-mediated assessments, the underlying concerns related to this form of validity evidence can be summarized using the following question:

- *What is the range of possible intended and unintended consequences of the rater-mediated assessment system?*

The major intended consequences for the writing assessment examined in this case study are made clear in the interpretive guide, which describes the assessment as follows:

> Student writing samples are evaluated on an analytic scoring system in all grades to *provide diagnostic feedback* to teachers, students, and parents about individual performance. The writing assessments *provide information to students about their writing performance* and *areas of strength and challenge*. This information is useful for *instruction and preparation for future writing assessments.*
> *(Georgia Department of Education, 2011, p. 5, emphasis added)*

This description highlights the intended consequences of the writing assessment as a method for informing writing instruction and test preparation. In addition to these intended consequences, it is necessary to consider potential unintended consequences of the writing assessment, which may include both positive and negative effects. When raters are considered specifically, these consequences may arise from differences in rating quality or differences in rater severity that affect individual students.

In practice, most large-scale assessment systems address these concerns by monitoring rating quality using indicators of rater agreement, errors, and accuracy based on the test-score tradition (Johnson, Penny, & Gordon, 2009). The perspective in this book is that additional indicators of rating quality based on the requirements for invariant measurement are necessary in order to identify the degree to which ratings are invariant across individual raters. Evidence of fit to models that meet the requirements for invariant measurement, such as Rasch models, provides evidence to support the claim that measures of student achievement are independent of the particular raters who scored their work, and that calibrations of raters are independent of the particular students they happened to score. Additional details about model-data fit are described in the discussion of reliability below.

Reliability

Chapter Six focused on the second foundational area in the recent revision of the *Standards for Educational and Psychological Testing* (AERA, APA, & NCME, 2014): Reliability. As noted in Chapter Six, the current consensus definition of reliability is as follows:

> The general notion of reliability/precision is defined in terms of *consistency over replications* of the testing procedure. Reliability/precision is high if the scores for each person are consistent over replications of the testing procedure and is low if the scores are not consistent over replications.
>
> *(p. 35, emphasis added)*

Based on this definition, the *Standards for Educational and Psychological Testing* includes a set of reliability standards organized in eight thematic clusters:

I. Specifications for replications of the testing procedure
II. Evaluating reliability/precision
III. Reliability/Generalizability coefficients
IV. Factors affecting reliability/precision
V. Standard errors of measurement
VI. Decision consistency
VII. Reliability/precision of group means
VIII. Documenting reliability/precision

For each of these clusters, Chapter Six presented questions that reflect underlying concerns in the context of rater-mediated assessments. The following section presents results from the middle grades writing assessment related to each of the clusters.

Clusters I and II: Specifying the Model to Represent Rater Judgment

The first two clusters of reliability standards reflect similar concerns related to the specification of aspects of the measurement procedure that constitute replications and the selection of appropriate reliability coefficients to reflect the replications. From the perspective of rater-invariant measurement, the underlying concerns for the first two clusters can be summarized using the following questions:

Cluster I: *Which aspects of the rater-mediated assessment system must be invariant?*
Cluster II: *Which cues in the judgmental process should be included in the measurement model?*

In terms of reliability evidence, indices related to the first two questions have to do with the specification of the measurement model. Specifically, the researcher must determine which aspects of the measurement procedure should be included as facets in the measurement model. In the current case study, the model was specified to include facets for students (θ), raters (λ), and domains (δ). Specifically, MF model estimates include logit-scale locations for individual students, raters, and domains on a linear scale that represents rater judgments of writing proficiency. These locations were summarized visually in Figure 8.1 and statistically in Table 8.1. Additional details regarding the logit-scale locations for individual students, raters, and domains are presented in Tables 8.2, 8.3, and 8.4, respectively.

Specifically, Table 8.2 summarizes the logit-scale locations for the students included in the case study data. Logit-scale locations for students represent their overall judged achievement level across the raters who scored their essays. As can be seen in the table, student locations range from –7.43 logits for Student 582, who had the lowest judged writing achievement (Average observed rating = 1.02) to 8.05 logits for Student 288, who had the highest judged writing achievement (Average observed rating = 3.99).

Similarly, Table 8.3 summarizes the calibrations of the 21 raters examined in the case study, including the validity committee. Rater calibrations on the logit scale represent their overall severity when judging student essays using the analytic rubric. As can be seen in the table, rater severity measures range from –0.55 logits for Rater 15, who is lenient (Average observed rating = 2.86), to 0.75 logits for Rater 9, who is severe (Average observed rating = 2.52).

TABLE 8.2 Judged Student Locations on the Rater-Mediated Latent Variable

Students	Average Rating	Judged Achievement (Logits)	SE	Infit MSE	Std. Infit	Outfit MSE	Std. Outfit
582	1.02	−7.43	0.71	1.00	0.23	2.16	1.32
444	1.04	−7.01	0.59	1.06	0.29	2.50	1.81
650	1.06	−6.46	0.46	0.99	0.12	0.91	−0.01
1099	1.13	−5.57	0.33	1.01	0.10	1.04	0.22
1208	1.13	−5.57	0.33	1.03	0.22	1.00	0.12
629	1.15	−5.36	0.31	1.34	1.52	1.81	2.51
1326	1.17	−5.27	0.30	0.95	−0.16	0.81	−0.69
225	1.18	−5.18	0.29	1.08	0.45	0.92	−0.27
1569	1.19	−5.10	0.28	0.95	−0.24	0.72	−1.24
150	1.21	−4.95	0.27	1.13	0.81	1.03	0.23
578	1.21	−4.95	0.27	1.13	0.82	1.34	1.54
519	1.24	−4.80	0.26	1.22	1.37	1.31	1.52
969	1.29	−4.54	0.25	1.16	1.16	1.25	1.45
1485	1.29	−4.54	0.25	1.42	2.75	1.39	2.15
1149	1.30	−4.48	0.24	0.90	−0.73	0.87	−0.82
1511	1.31	−4.42	0.24	0.99	−0.04	0.99	−0.01
1347	1.35	−4.25	0.23	0.79	−1.79	0.76	−1.79
1061	1.37	−4.14	0.23	1.12	1.00	1.11	0.88
...	...	...	...	...	...	...	...
1393	3.82	5.11	0.29	1.17	0.90	1.30	1.16
490	3.83	5.20	0.30	1.00	0.09	1.12	0.51
784	3.85	5.29	0.30	0.98	0.00	0.96	−0.05
839	3.85	5.29	0.30	1.10	0.51	1.32	1.15
1141	3.85	5.29	0.30	1.08	0.46	1.15	0.60
188	3.87	5.49	0.33	1.28	1.14	1.38	1.20
624	3.87	5.49	0.33	0.94	−0.15	0.83	−0.49
133	3.88	5.60	0.34	0.96	−0.06	0.83	−0.42
818	3.90	5.86	0.37	0.99	0.05	0.90	−0.13
377	3.92	6.01	0.40	0.97	0.02	0.80	−0.38
528	3.94	6.38	0.46	1.04	0.23	1.25	0.63
183	3.95	6.62	0.51	1.02	0.20	1.16	0.45
272	3.95	6.62	0.51	1.03	0.22	1.33	0.71
293	3.96	6.92	0.59	1.01	0.20	1.04	0.29
1128	3.96	6.92	0.59	1.00	0.17	0.83	−0.03
49	3.98	7.34	0.71	1.01	0.24	1.82	1.07
288	3.99	8.05	1.00	0.97	0.29	0.48	−0.13
Mean	2.71	0.80	0.23	0.98	−0.21	0.98	−0.22
SD	0.75	2.84	0.07	0.22	1.50	0.26	1.51

Note: This table shows a subset of the case study sample. Students are ordered by Achievement Measure from low judged achievement to high judged achievement. The Mean and Standard Deviations are calculated from the full sample ($N = 365$).

Table 8.4 includes logit-scale locations of the four domains from the analytic rubric. These locations represent the judged difficulty of each domain across the raters included in the case study data. As can be seen in the table, the domain calibrations range from −0.89 logits for the Sentence Formation

TABLE 8.3 Rater Locations on the Rater-Mediated Latent Variable

Raters	Average Rating	Severity (Logits)	SE	Infit MSE	Std. Infit	Outfit MSE	Std. Outfit
15	2.86	−0.55	0.05	1.00	0.14	1.10	1.87
7	2.84	−0.49	0.05	1.21	5.41	1.22	3.93
10	2.84	−0.48	0.05	1.05	1.46	1.07	1.28
6	2.83	−0.44	0.05	0.97	−0.75	0.98	−0.42
5	2.78	−0.26	0.05	1.17	4.53	1.16	3.20
VC	2.77	−0.19	0.05	0.58	−9.00	0.54	−9.00
12	2.76	−0.17	0.05	0.87	−3.82	0.89	−2.38
11	2.73	−0.08	0.05	0.82	−5.46	0.80	−4.43
21	2.73	−0.04	0.05	1.26	6.62	1.21	4.21
2	2.72	−0.02	0.05	0.80	−5.82	0.78	−5.09
3	2.72	−0.01	0.05	0.97	−0.75	1.05	1.09
19	2.70	0.07	0.05	1.24	6.25	1.21	4.17
4	2.69	0.10	0.05	0.81	−5.53	0.79	−4.80
17	2.69	0.11	0.05	0.81	−5.49	0.80	−4.60
20	2.68	0.15	0.05	1.00	−0.02	1.01	0.33
14	2.67	0.17	0.05	1.02	0.50	1.06	1.20
13	2.67	0.18	0.05	1.00	0.02	0.99	−0.11
8	2.65	0.27	0.05	0.93	−1.99	0.91	−1.99
16	2.61	0.41	0.05	0.92	−0.73	1.06	1.29
18	2.58	0.50	0.05	1.11	2.86	1.28	5.51
9	2.52	0.75	0.05	0.76	−7.07	0.73	−6.39
Mean	2.72	0.00	0.05	0.97	−0.89	0.98	−0.53
SD	0.09	0.34	0.00	0.17	4.49	0.19	3.98

Note: Raters are ordered by Severity Measure from low (lenient) to high (severe). "VC" refers to the ratings assigned by the validity committee.

TABLE 8.4 Judged Domain Locations on the Rater-Mediated Latent Variable

Domains	Average Rating	Judged Difficulty (Logits)	SE	Infit MSE	Std. Infit	Outfit MSE	Std. Outfit
Sentence Formation	2.94	−0.89	0.02	0.98	−1.36	0.97	−1.43
Conventions	2.74	−0.07	0.02	0.91	−6.17	0.93	−3.80
Style	2.64	0.31	0.02	1.02	1.54	1.05	2.36
Organization	2.54	0.65	0.02	0.97	−2.01	0.99	−0.38
Mean	2.72	0.00	0.02	0.97	−2.00	0.99	−0.81
SD	0.17	0.66	0.00	0.05	3.18	0.05	2.55

Note: Domains are ordered by judged difficulty from low (least difficult) to high (most difficult).

domain, which was judged easiest (Average observed rating = 2.94), to 0.65 logits for the Organization domain, which was judged most difficult (Average observed rating = 2.54).

Cluster III: Reliability Coefficients

The third cluster of reliability standards focuses on the lack of equivalence between different types and specifications of reliability coefficients. Reflecting the emphasis on the test-score tradition that characterizes the *Standards for Educational and Psychological Testing* for reliability, these standards highlight differences between G-theory coefficients that are calculated for different facets (e.g., items or raters) and emphasize the fact that these coefficients convey unique information about sources of measurement error, depending on their specification.

It is also possible to explore differences in reliability related to unique facets in a measurement procedure within the framework of Rasch Measurement Theory using reliability estimates based on the MF model. The underlying reliability concerns related to this facet can be summarized using the following question:

What is the reliability/precision of rater judgments related to various cues?

Reliability indices based on the Rasch model can be calculated separately for each facet in the model. Two indices of reliability are typically used: (1) reliability of separation (*Rel*) and (2) a chi-square statistic (χ^2).

Reliability of Separation Statistics

Reliability of separation statistics are used to describe the degree to which differences among individuals and items are realized in a measurement procedure. The *reliability of separation statistic* based on Rasch models indicates how well individual elements within a facet can be differentiated from one another, such as individual students, raters, or domains. When data fit the model, the reliability of separation statistics for the object of measurement (in this case, students) is comparable to classical reliability coefficients such as Cronbach's coefficient alpha and KR-20 because it reflects an estimate of true score to observed score variance. For the other facets, the reliability of separation statistic describes the spread or differences between elements within a facet, such as differences in rater severity. The statistic is calculated using the standard deviation (*SD*) and mean square error (*MSE*) as follows:

$$Rel = \frac{(SD^2 - MSE)}{SD^2},$$

(8.3)

where SD^2 is the observed variance of elements within a facet in logits and MSE is the mean square error. MSE is estimated as the average value of calibration error variances (squares of the standard errors) for each element within a facet. Andrich (1982) provides a detailed derivation of this reliability of separation index. In addition to the reliability of separation statistic, a chi-square statistic (χ^2) is calculated to test the null hypothesis that the differences between elements within a facet are not significantly different from zero. The chi-square test provides a method for determining whether the elements within a facet can be considered exchangeable.

Table 8.1 includes separation statistics for the case study data. As can be seen in the table, the overall differences between elements within the Student (θ), Rater (λ), and Domain (δ) facets are significant, based on the overall chi-square statistic ($p < 0.05$). The reliability of separation for students (equivalent to coefficient alpha) is quite high ($Rel_\theta = 0.99$). This finding of a high reliability of separation statistic for students suggests that there are reliable differences in the judged locations of each student's essay on the logit scale. For the Rater facet, the reliability of separation statistic describes the spread, or differences, between individual rater severity calibrations on the logit scale. In the case study example, a high reliability of separation statistic was observed for raters ($Rel_\lambda = 0.98$), which suggests that there are significant differences among the individual raters in terms of severity. Similarly, there is a high reliability of separation statistic for the domain facet ($Rel_\delta = 0.66$), which suggests meaningful differences in the difficulty locations of individual domains on the logit scale. This finding is reflected in the visual display of results for the domain calibrations in the Wright map (Figure 8.1).

Cluster IV: Factors Affecting Reliability/Precision

Reflecting the dominance of the test-score tradition in the recent revision of the *Standards for Educational and Psychological Testing* (AERA, APA, & NCME, 2014), the fourth cluster of reliability standards focuses on identifying sources of measurement error that affect the reliability/precision of measurement procedures. In this book, we emphasize that reliability/precision can be viewed as the flip side of invariance, and focus on evidence related to invariant measurement associated with various facets in a measurement procedure. The underlying concerns related to this cluster can be summarized from the perspective of rater-invariant measurement using the following question:

- *Is there evidence to support the inference of rater-invariant measurement?*

In terms of empirical evidence from a rater-mediated assessment, evidence related to the fourth cluster of standards can be obtained through the use of model-data fit statistics. Because the MFR model meets the requirements for invariant measurement, departures from model expectations, or residuals, are of interest for describing the quality of rater-mediated assessments. Thus, the Rasch-based approach to examining rating quality focuses on an examination of standardized residuals, summaries of residuals in the form of model-data fit statistics, and graphical displays of residuals.

The illustrative analysis in this study includes the mean square error (*MSE*) fit statistics and the standardized versions of these statistics that are calculated in the Facets computer program (Linacre, 2015). Infit and Outfit *MSE* statistics are summaries of residuals that describe departures from model expectations at the individual item level. Because it is unweighted, the Outfit statistic is useful because it is particularly sensitive to "outliers," or extreme unexpected observations. On the other hand, Infit *MSE* statistics are weighted by statistical information for a particular facet; as a result, they are not as sensitive to extreme outliers. Because the sampling distribution for the unstandardized *MSE* statistics is not known, several researchers encourage the use of standardized versions of these statistics when considering fit to the Rasch model (e.g., Smith, 2004; Smith, Schumacker, & Bush, 1998).

Overall summaries of fit statistics for the Student, Rater, and Domain facets are included in the summary statistics displayed in Table 8.1. Average values of the unstandardized and standardized *MSE* statistics for the three facets suggest that the MF model is generally functioning as intended for these rating data. Tables 8.2, 8.3, and 8.4 provide fit statistics for each of the individual students, raters, and domains, respectively. Overall, examination of the spread of fit statistics for each facet reveals acceptable fit to the model for all three facets, with unstandardized fit statistics around 1.00 and standardized fit statistics around 0.00. Additional details regarding the interpretation of model-data fit statistics based on Rasch models are provided in Chapter Eleven.

Cluster V: Standard Errors of Measurement

The fifth cluster of reliability standards deals with standard errors of measurement and the importance of these values as indicators of the precision of individual test scores. The underlying concerns related to this cluster can be summarized from the perspective of rater-invariant measurement using the following question:

- *What is the precision of estimates on the rater-mediated variable map?*

When the MFR model is estimated, it is possible to obtain standard error estimates for each element within a facet (e.g., individual raters, students, or domains) that describe the range within which the element (i.e., individual performance, rater, and item) would be expected to fall across replications of the measurement procedure. Smaller values of *SE* indicate more precise estimates, such that the logit-scale locations would be expected to remain stable across repeated administrations of an assessment. In the context of a rater-mediated assessment, standard errors for individual elements within a facet reflect the precision of rater judgments associated with the facet of interest.

Tables 8.2, 8.3, and 8.4 include standard errors associated with the logit-scale locations of each individual student, rater, and domain in the illustrative dataset, respectively. For individual students, standard errors can be interpreted as an indicator of the precision with which the group of raters interpreted its location on the construct. Higher values of standard errors suggest potential disagreement among raters regarding the logit-scale location for a given student that warrants further investigation. For individual raters, standard errors reflect the precision of rater severity calibrations on the logit scale, where larger standard errors suggest less precise calibrations. Likewise, standard errors for individual domains reflect the precision of rater judgments regarding the difficulty of each domain in terms of the latent variable. Similar to the Student facet, larger standard errors suggest potential disagreement among raters regarding the difficulty of a given domain that may warrant further investigation.

Cluster VI: Decision Consistency

The sixth cluster of reliability standards is related to decision consistency. As noted in Chapter Six, the *Standards for Educational and Psychological Testing* (AERA, APA, & NCME, 2014) distinguish between *decision consistency* and *decision accuracy*. Specifically, decision consistency is used to describe the degree to which classifications would remain consistent across replications of a measurement procedure, and decision accuracy is used to describe the alignment between observed and "true" classifications.

Major concerns related to decision consistency in the context of rater-mediated assessments are related to the exchangeability of raters in terms of rater severity, and the degree to which different classifications would result from differences in rater severity. These concerns can be summarized using the following question:

- *Is there sufficient evidence of adequate linking between raters and model-data fit to adjust student achievement estimates for differences in rater severity?*

When the MFR model is applied, student achievement estimates (θ) are adjusted for differences in rater severity. As noted in Chapter Six, these adjustments must be interpreted in light of model–data fit indicators for raters (Wind, Engelhard, & Wesolowski, 2016). Specifically, evidence of fit to the MFR model is necessary to permit interpretation of student achievement estimates as invariant across raters with different levels of severity. In order to illustrate the implications of model–data fit for adjustments based on the Rasch model, a theoretical example is presented. Then, the case study data are used in an empirical example.

Figure 8.4 includes a theoretical illustration of the influence of model-data fit on MFR model adjustments of student achievement. The theoretical illustration shows the consequence of adjustments for raters who fit the expectations of the Rasch model and for raters who do not fit the expectations of the Rasch model. Specifically, rater characteristic curves (RCCs) are presented for three illustrative raters. The RCCs show the relationship between student locations on the logit scale (θ) and the expected rating for a given rater based on the MFR model (Equation 8.1). Three illustrative raters are included in the illustration: Rater A is a lenient rater with adequate fit to the Rasch model; Rater B is a severe rater with

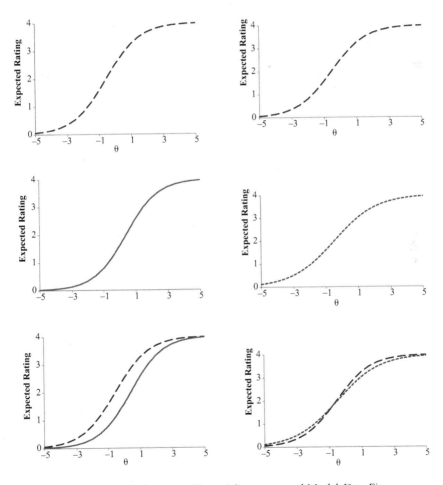

FIGURE 8.4 Theoretical Illustration: Rater Adjustments and Model–Data Fit

adequate fit to the Rasch model; and Rater C is a severe rater who does not fit the Rasch model. The top panel of Figure 8.4 displays conditional expected ratings for two raters who meet the expectations of the Rasch model: Rater A (lenient) and Rater B (severe). When raters display adequate model-data fit, it is possible to make a constant adjustment for differences in rater severity with the expected ratings using the MFR model. In other words, parallel response functions imply that student achievement can be interpreted on a common scale across severe and lenient raters. The bottom panel of Figure 8.4 displays conditional expected ratings for a lenient rater who meets the expectations of the Rasch model (Rater A) and a severe rater who displays misfit to the Rasch model (Rater C) with a slope parameter less than 1.00. When crossing rater response functions are observed, it is not possible to make a constant adjustment to account for differences in rater severity. In other words, there is no simple adjustment that can equate achievement estimates for students who were scored by Rater A and students who were scored by Rater C.

Similar results can be illustrated using the case study data. As noted above, there was a range of rater severity levels for the writing assessment data, ranging from −0.55 logits ($SE = 0.05$) for Rater 15, who was the most lenient rater (average rating = 2.86), to 0.75 logits ($SE = 0.05$) for Rater 9, who was the most severe rater (average rating = 2.52). If data fit the Rasch model, estimates of performance locations on the logit scale (θ) are adjusted for these differences in rater severity, such that rater-invariant measurement of performances is achieved.

An examination of model-data fit statistics for the raters in the case study indicates that, in general, values of the standardized Infit and Outfit statistics near their expected values. However, several raters demonstrate higher- and lower-than-expected fit statistics that suggest misfit to the MFR model. Figure 8.5 demonstrates an empirical example of the consequences of misfit to the MFR model for three illustrative raters from the case study data. Rater 15 is a lenient rater ($\delta = -0.55$) who demonstrated adequate fit to the MFR model (Infit $MSE = 1.00$, Std. Infit = −0.14; Outfit $MSE = 1.10$, Std. Outfit = 1.87), and Rater 16 is a severe rater ($\delta = 0.41$) who demonstrated adequate fit to the MFR model (Infit $MSE = 0.92$, Std. Infit = −0.73; Outfit $MSE = 1.06$, Std. Outfit = 1.29). On the other hand, Rater 7 is a lenient rater ($\delta = -0.49$) who demonstrated misfit to the MFR model (Infit $MSE = 1.21$, Std. Infit = 5.41; Outfit $MSE = 1.22$, Std. Outfit = 3.93). In the same manner as Figure 8.4, RCCs are displayed for each rater independently, and overlaid RCCs are used to illustrate the consequences of model-data fit for raters. As can be seen in the figure, it is possible to make a constant adjustment between Rater 15, who is a lenient rater, and Rater 16, who is a severe rater because both of these raters demonstrate adequate fit to the MFR model. On the other hand, it is not possible to make a constant adjustment between Rater 18 and Rater 7 (a lenient rater) because Rater 7 demonstrates misfit to the Rasch model—realized through

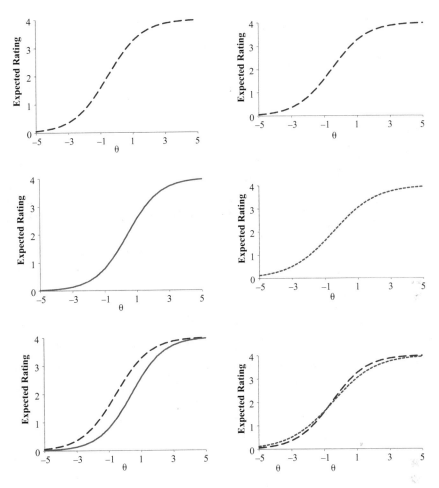

FIGURE 8.5   Empirical Illustration: Rater Adjustments and Model–Data Fit

higher-than-expected values of standardized fit statistics and a flatter-than-expected estimated discrimination parameter.

This illustration highlights the need to recognize the importance of model–data fit when the Rasch model is used to obtain estimates of student achievement that are adjusted for differences in rater severity. If good model–data fit is not observed, the resulting estimates may not reflect consistent adjustments for all students, such that performance estimates cannot be interpreted in the same way across raters. Further, the interpretation of student locations as adjusted for differences in rater severity depends on the degree to which the data collection design includes sufficient links among raters. Additional details regarding rater linking designs are given in Chapter Twelve.

Clusters VII and VIII: Documentation for Reliability Evidence

The final two clusters of reliability standards reflect similar concerns regarding documentation to support reliability evidence. Specifically, Cluster VII focuses on documentation of student characteristics from whom reliability of group mean estimates are obtained, and Cluster VIII focuses on documentation of methods used to collect reliability evidence. As noted in Chapter Six, details about characteristics of the raters, including background information and details about training and monitoring, are needed to inform the interpretation of reliability information. Further, information regarding the data collection design used to obtain ratings is also necessary for the interpretation of reliability/precision indices. Specifically, rating designs that include more connections among raters (i.e., more commonly scored performances) result in greater reliability/precision for estimates of student achievement and rater severity (Wind, Engelhard, & Wesolowski, 2016). Reflecting these concerns, the underlying questions for the final clusters of reliability standards can be summarized using the following questions:

- *Cluster VII: What are the characteristics of raters whose judgments are used to obtain scores?*
- *Cluster VIII: What type of rating design was used to collect rater judgments?*

The example dataset reflects a complete rating design, where every rater scored every student. However, practical constraints often limit the availability of complete rating designs in operational settings. Chapter Twelve provides additional details related to incomplete rating designs and their implications for the interpretation of rater judgments in terms of rater-invariant measurement.

Fairness

Chapter Seven focused on the third foundational area in the recent revision of the *Standards for Educational and Psychological Testing* (AERA, APA, & NCME, 2014): Fairness. As noted in Chapter Seven, the consolidation of fairness concerns into a single chapter is unique to the 2014 version of the *Standards for Educational and Psychological Testing*, and reflects an emphasis on fairness as a fundamental psychometric concern that must be addressed at all stages in the testing process. The current consensus definition of fairness is as follows:

> Responsiveness to individual characteristics and testing contexts so that test scores will yield valid interpretations for intended uses.
>
> *(p. 50)*

Based on this definition, the *Standards for Educational and Psychological Testing* includes a set of fairness standards organized in to four thematic clusters:

I. Test Design, Development, Administration, and Scoring Procedures That Minimize Barriers to Valid Score Interpretations for the Widest Possible Range of Individuals and Relevant Subgroups

II. Validity of Test Score Interpretations for Intended Uses for the Intended Examinee Population

III. Accommodations to Remove Construct-Irrelevant Barriers and Support Valid Interpretations of Scores for Their Intended Uses

IV. Safeguards Against Inappropriate Score Interpretations for Intended Uses

For each of these clusters, Chapter Seven presented questions that reflect underlying concerns in the context of rater-mediated assessments. The following section presents results from the middle grades writing assessment related to each of the clusters.

Cluster I: Test Design, Development, Administration, and Scoring Procedures That Minimize Barriers to Valid Score Interpretations for the Widest Possible Range of Individuals and Relevant Subgroups

The first cluster of fairness standards emphasizes the clear specification of the response characteristics that reflect various locations on the construct and consideration of how these characteristics align with those of intended test takers. According to the *Standards for Educational and Psychological Testing*, these considerations should be aimed at identifying and minimizing potential sources of construct-irrelevant variance throughout the test development, administration, and scoring processes. In the context of rater-mediated assessments, fairness efforts should include a consideration of potential construct-irrelevant variance related to raters' judgmental processes. As given in Chapter Seven, the underlying fairness concerns related to this cluster can be summarized using the following questions:

- *What are the potential unintended cues in the assessment system that could influence rater judgment in a construct-irrelevant way?*
- *How can rater training and monitoring procedures be designed to minimize construct-irrelevant barriers for relevant subgroups?*

In the context of the case study, unintended cues could potentially be introduced related to the use of cut scores for the writing assessment when it is used to inform promotion or placement decisions. For example, if students must earn an average rating of 3 across domains in order to receive a passing score on the assessment, raters might assign a higher frequency of scores in categories 2 and 3 in order to avoid being "flagged" in monitoring procedures.

It is likely that unintended cues will also be related to subgroup membership. For example, the grammatical structure of essays written by English Language

Learners may have an impact on various aspects of how a rater judges the quality of a writing assessment. It is also possible that a controversial essay may lead to unconscious biases from a rater. Many of these issues can also be identified and monitored in an operational writing assessment. Previously identified construct-irrelevant cues can be incorporated into rater training.

Cluster II: Validity of Test Score Interpretations for Intended Uses for the Intended Examinee Population

The second cluster of fairness standards includes calls for the consideration of potential threats to validity related to student subgroup membership. These standards emphasize the importance of clearly identifying the population of intended test takers in order to gather relevant empirical evidence related to the equivalence of test score interpretations across subgroups within this population. These standards also recommend examining differences in relationships between test scores and relevant variables across student subgroups. In the context of rater-mediated assessments, fairness concerns related to this cluster include the degree to which there is evidence to support the claim of rater-invariant measurement across student subgroups. Accordingly, the underlying concerns related to this cluster of standards can be summarized using the following question:

- *Is there evidence to support the hypothesis of rater-invariant measurement for all intended test takers?*

It is possible to examine this question for the case study by examining indicators of differential rater functioning (DRF) related to student subgroups. Within the context of Rasch Measurement Theory, DRF occurs when raters are systematically more or less severe when rating students with particular construct-irrelevant characteristics (Engelhard, 1994, 2002; Wolfe, Moulder, & Myford, 2001). Specifically, interaction terms can be added to MFR models in order to examine whether rater interpretation of the construct is consistent across facets. Tests for significant interactions based on the MFR model test the null hypothesis that the overall group of raters shares a common interpretation of the construct across student subgroups.

First, a facet that represents student gender can be added to the MFR model as follows:

$$\ln\left[\frac{P_{nimk}}{P_{nimk-1}}\right] = \theta_n - \lambda_i - \delta_j - \mu_m - \tau_k , \tag{8.4}$$

where μ_m represents student gender and the other terms are defined as they were in Equation 8.1.

Next, an interaction term between the two facets of interest (rater severity and student gender) is added to the model:

$$\ln\left[\frac{P_{nik}}{P_{nik-1}}\right] = (\theta_n - \lambda_i - \delta_j - \mu_m - \tau_k) - \lambda_i\delta_j , \tag{8.5}$$

where $\lambda_i\delta_j$ is the interaction between rater severity and student gender.

The Facets computer program (Linacre, 2015) can be used to compute an overall fixed chi-squared (χ^2) test for the significance of a set of interactions. This test statistic confirms or disconfirms the null hypothesis that the overall set of interactions is significantly different from zero, after allowing for measurement error. In other words, the significance test for this statistic answers the question: Is the overall set of interactions between these two facets significantly different from zero? A significant value for the chi-square statistic suggests that the interaction between the two specified facets is significant at an overall level. For the interaction between raters and student gender groups, the omnibus test examines the null hypothesis that the interactions between individual raters and the judged achievement of each student gender subgroup are not significant.

In addition to the overall test for significant interactions, it is possible to examine individual interactions between elements within two facets. These individual terms provide information about the direction and magnitude of each interaction, and they are useful for identifying patterns in data that can be used to inform the interpretation of measurement outcomes. Visual displays that illustrate these interaction terms are particularly useful for this purpose. Individual interaction terms are calibrated on the logit scale, and their precision is described using standard errors. The interaction terms are calculated as t-statistics, and they approximate the normal distribution (i.e., $M = 0$, $SD = 1$, or a z-score) with many observations. The significance tests for individual interaction terms can be used as a test for the statistical significance of the size of each pairwise interaction. A type of standardized effect size, these test statistics are primarily used as descriptors of patterns within rating data that may signal rater effects of substantive interest. As a result, significance tests are not of primary importance. However, a general practice in the interpretation of these statistics is to use an absolute value of 2.00 to identify interactions that may warrant further investigation. Furthermore, differences less than 0.30 logits do not carry substantive meaning (Engelhard & Myford, 2003). In this study, statistically significant interactions suggest that rater severity is meaningfully higher or lower than expected for a student subgroup based on its expected location on the logit scale (across the group of raters, based on the estimate under the MFR model).

When gender was added to the model, overall differences in student achievement were observed among the female and male students. Figure 8.6 is a Wright map that illustrates the locations for female and male students on the logit scale

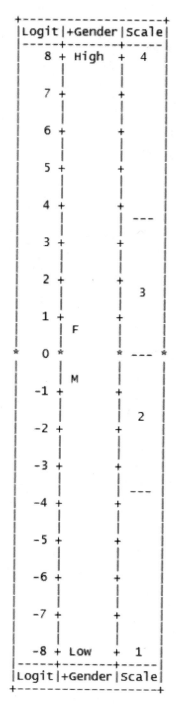

FIGURE 8.6 Judged Student Gender Subgroup Locations on the Rater-Mediated Latent Variable

Note: "F" indicates female students, and "M" indicates male students.

that reflects the construct for the writing assessment examined in the case study. Overall calibrations for the gender groups are given in Table 8.5 that correspond to the Wright map. These results indicate overall statistically significant group differences (χ^2 (1) = 2,005.8, $p < 0.001$). The judged differences in achievement levels for the gender subgroups were as follows: female students (0.51 logits, $n = 171$), male students (−0.51 logits, $n = 194$). The difference in logit-scale locations between the two subgroups exceeds the critical value of 0.30 logits proposed by Engelhard and Myford (2003) for identifying substantive significance.

Results from the interaction analysis revealed an overall significant interaction between rater severity and gender (χ^2 (42) = 173.8, $p < 0.001$). In terms of interactions between individual raters and gender subgroups, pairwise interaction analyses were conducted between all raters and the two gender subgroups (female and male students). As seen in Table 8.6, 43 interaction terms related to gender subgroups were detected. Of the 43 interaction terms, 20 were found to be significant ($| Z | > = 2.0$). Figure 8.7 depicts each rater's interaction term (Z) according to gender subgroups. Of the 21 raters, 10 raters (raters 3, 5, 7, 8, 9, 13, 15, 16, 18, and 20) demonstrated unexpected differential severity. For example, Rater 3 consistently underestimates writing achievement for female students ($Z = 3.16$), and Rater 5 consistently overestimates female students ($Z = −3.08$) and consistently underestimates male students ($Z = 3.00$).

TABLE 8.5 Judged Student Gender Subgroup Locations on the Rater-Mediated Latent Variable

Gender Subgroups	Average Rating	Judged Achievement (Logits)	SE	Infit MSE	Std. Infit	Outfit MSE	Std. Outfit
Male	2.47	−0.51	0.02	0.99	−1.04	1.01	0.66
Female	2.99	0.51	0.02	0.96	−4.01	0.96	−2.84
Mean	2.73	0.00	0.02	0.98	−2.53	0.99	−1.09
SD	0.37	0.72	0.00	0.02	2.10	0.04	2.47

Note: Gender groups are ordered by judged achievement from low to high.

TABLE 8.6 Summary of Interaction Terms by Gender Subgroup

Count of interaction terms	43
$|Z| \geq 2.0$	20
% Statistically significant	46.51
Chi-square	173.8*
df	42

Note: * $p < 0.001$

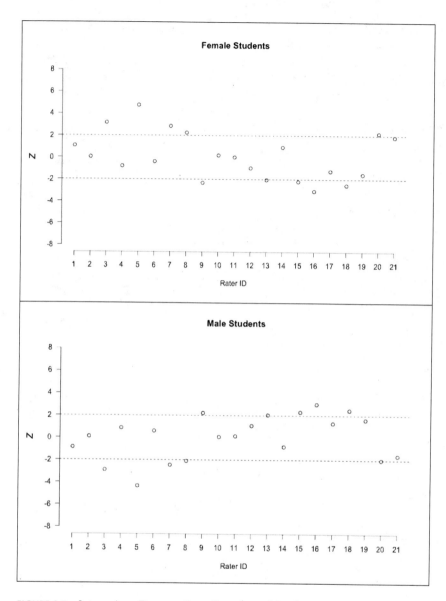

FIGURE 8.7 Interactions Between Rater Severity and Student Gender

Note: Rater 1 is the validity committee. *Z* values higher than +2.00 suggest that the rater assigned lower ratings (i.e., was more severe) than expected for a subgroup of students, based on the average measure for the subgroup across the raters. Test statistic values lower than −2.00 suggest that the rater assigned higher ratings (i.e., was more lenient) than expected for a subgroup of students.

Another method for exploring differences in rater severity across subgroups is through an examination of differences in rater severity based on separate calibrations within subgroups (Wright & Masters, 1982). It is important to note that rater severities are calibrated on a continuous scale, and that critical values related to differential rater functioning may limit the interpretation of the substantive significance of differences between rater calibrations. In this chapter, we illustrate the examination of "raw" differences between rater calibrations on the logit scale for the two gender subgroups using a visual display called a *DIF map* (Wind & Engelhard, 2012) as an additional method to gauge the direction and magnitude of differences in rater severity for female and male students. Essentially, a DIF map is a bar chart that emphasizes the conceptualization of differential item or rater functioning as a continuous variable.

Differences in rater severity between the two gender subgroups are displayed graphically in Figure 8.8, where each bar represents the logit differences between rater severities for female and male students. Rater numbers and values of the logit differences are used to label each bar.

As can be seen in the figure, differences in rater severity calibrations vary in terms of direction and magnitude, where positive differences indicate that a rater was more severe (higher logit-scale location) when scoring female students, and negative differences indicate that a rater was more severe (higher logit-scale location) when scoring male students.

Overall, these findings suggest that rater severity is not invariant across gender subgroups for the writing assessment examined in the case study. Additional analyses, including qualitative studies, may shed additional light on these results. Chapter Thirteen includes additional details regarding methods for detecting and exploring systematic biases in the context of rater-mediated assessments.

Cluster III: Accommodations to Remove Construct-Irrelevant Barriers and Support Valid Interpretations of Scores for Their Intended Uses

The third cluster of fairness standards focuses on the use of appropriate changes to a testing procedure to minimize construct-irrelevant barriers to valid testing procedures for all test takers. The *Standards for Educational and Psychological Testing* describe adaptations as a continuum of changes to the testing procedure, where accommodations are minor changes that retain the original construct interpretation and modifications result in scores that reflect a different construct. The perspective put forth in the fairness standards is that changes to a testing procedure may be necessary in order to maximize access to the construct, and thus obtain the most accurate measure for individual test takers.

In addition to considerations related to the equivalence of the construct between test administrations with and without adaptations, fairness efforts for rater-mediated

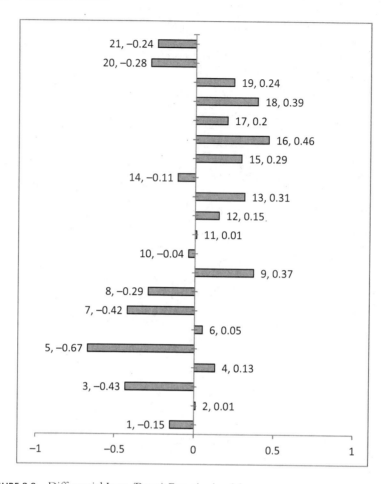

FIGURE 8.8 Differential Item (Rater) Functioning Map

Notes: Each bar represents the difference in rater severity calibrations between the female and male students. The labels indicate the rater ID (Rater 1 is the validity committee), followed by the value of the difference between logit-scale locations (female minus male). Negative differences (left side of the map) indicate that the rater was more severe (higher logit-scale value) when scoring male students, and positive differences (right side of the map) indicate that the rater was more severe (higher logit-scale value) when scoring female students.

assessments must also include considerations of the effect of adaptations on raters' judgmental process. The underlying concerns for rater-mediated assessments related to this cluster of standards can be summarized using two questions:

- *What adaptations are necessary in order to minimize the influence of construct-irrelevant cues on rater judgments?*
- *How do rater training procedures (e.g., rubrics and benchmarks) reflect the range of adaptations?*

The first question reflects concerns related to the nature of adaptations to a testing procedure. For example, a student may be better able to demonstrate their standing on the construct if the writing prompt is read aloud, or if they type, rather than hand-write their response. The second question highlights the implications of these adaptations on rater judgments. As was noted in Chapter Seven, if adaptations are included in the administration of a rater-mediated assessment, it is necessary that rater training materials include relevant exemplars and descriptions of student performance to ensure comparable scores between performances produced with and without adaptations

The case study data do not include details regarding the materials used in rater training procedures.

Cluster IV: Safeguards Against Inappropriate Score Interpretations for Intended Uses

The fairness standards in Cluster IV focus on the use of sufficient documentation that permits test users to determine the degree to which test scores are applicable for a given group of test takers. These standards also emphasize the importance of including additional sources of information beyond that provided by a single test to inform decisions about students, particularly when test scores are used to inform placement and/or high-stakes decisions.

In the context of rater-mediated assessments, fairness concerns related to documentation can be summarized using the following questions:

- *What documentation is needed to reflect the scope of applicability of ratings for individual and subgroups of test takers?*
- *What additional sources of information can be used to support the use of ratings in a variety of contexts, including placement and/or high-stakes decisions?*

It was noted in Chapter Seven that documentation for rater-mediated assessments should include sufficient detail for test users to determine the applicability of rater judgment for test takers with a variety of characteristics, including details about characteristics of test takers whose responses were used to develop rater training and scoring materials. Similarly, when rater judgments are used to inform high-stakes decisions, it is necessary to supplement rater judgments with additional sources of information.

The case study data do not include details regarding the development of rater training and scoring materials.

Summary and Discussion

> The Many-Facet Rasch Model is a powerful measurement tool . . . Rater training is transformed from inculcating mindless conformity into encouraging intelligent self consistency.
>
> *(Linacre, 1989, p. iii)*

This chapter provides a case study of how a researcher might approach a study of the psychometric quality of a writing assessment based on the *Standards for Educational and Psychological Testing*. Specifically, the purpose of the chapter was to illustrate procedures for evaluating the quality of rater-mediated assessments based on Rasch Measurement Theory. The recent revision of the *Standards for Educational and Psychological Testing* (AERA, APA, & NCME, 2014) was used as a framework to highlight a variety of concerns related to validity, reliability, and fairness, as they apply specifically to the context of rater-mediated assessments. It is important to note that the procedures described in this chapter reflect a range of potential analyses that can be used to explore the psychometric quality of a rater-mediated assessment, and they do not reflect an exhaustive list of requirements for all rater-mediated assessments. The specific assessment context and intended purposes of the assessment should guide the types of evidence needed to explore the validity, reliability, and fairness of a particular rater-mediated assessment system.

The key idea emphasized in the presentation of the three foundational areas in Chapters Five through Seven, and the case study in this chapter is that considerations of validity, reliability, and fairness for rater-mediated assessments are incomplete unless they include direct consideration of the judgmental processes from raters that characterize these assessments. In this book, we highlight the usefulness of invariant measurement as a framework in which to consider the quality of ratings that can be conceptualized in terms of the three foundational areas of validity, reliability, and fairness. Although validity, reliability, and fairness are described separately in the *Standards for Educational and Psychological Testing*, all three foundational areas can be conceptualized in terms of the requirements for invariant measurement. As pointed out by Cronbach (1988), "Validation will progress in proportion as we collectively do our damnedest—no holds barred—with our minds and our hearts" (p. 14). The same approach applies to the examination of the validity, reliability, and fairness of ratings obtained in rater-mediated writing assessment.

Note

1. Two raters assign scores in operational settings. The data used in the current study include additional ratings assigned to each essay.

References

American Educational Research Association (AERA), American Psychological Association (APA), & National Council on Measurement in Education (NCME). (2014). *Standards for educational and psychological testing*. Washington, DC: AERA.

Andrich, D. A. (1978). A rating formulation for ordered response categories. *Psychometrika*, *43*(4), 561–573. http://doi.org/10.1007/BF02293814

Andrich, D. A. (1982). An index of person separation in latent trait theory, the traditional KR.20 indices and the Guttman scale response pattern. *Education Research and Perspectives, 9,* 95–104.

Cronbach, L. J. (1988). Five perspectives on validation argument. In H. Wainer & H. Braun (Eds.), *Test validity* (pp. 34–35). Hillsdale, NJ: Erlbaum.

Engelhard, G., Jr. (1994). Examining rater errors in the assessment of written composition with a many-faceted Rasch model. *Journal of Educational Measurement, 31*(2), 93–112. http://doi.org/10.2307/1435170

Engelhard, G., Jr. (1996). Evaluating rater accuracy in performance assessments. *Journal of Educational Measurement, 33*(1), 56–70.

Engelhard, G. (1997). Constructing rater and task banks for performance assessments. *Journal of Outcome Measurement, 1*(1), 19–33.

Engelhard, G. (2002). Monitoring raters in performance assessments. In G. Tindal & G. Haladyna (Eds.), *Large-scale assessment programs for ALL students: Development, implementation, and analysis* (pp. 261–287). Mahwah, NJ: Erlbaum.

Engelhard, G., & Myford, C. M. (2003). *Monitoring faculty consultant performance in the advanced placement English literature and composition program with a many-faceted Rasch model.* New York: College Entrance Examination Board.

Georgia Department of Education. (2011). *Georgia middle grades writing test interpretive guide.* Atlanta, GA: Author.

Gyagenda, I. S., & Engelhard, G. (2009). Using classical and modern measurement theories to explore rater, domain, and gender influences on student writing ability. *Journal of Applied Measurement, 10*(3), 225–246.

Johnson, R. L., Penny, J. A., & Gordon, B. (2009). *Assessing performance: Designing, scoring, and validating performance tasks.* New York: The Guilford Press.

Kaliski, P. K., Wind, S. A., Engelhard, G., Morgan, D. L., Plake, B. S., & Reshetar, R. A. (2013). Using the many-faceted Rasch model to evaluate standard setting judgments: An illustration with the advanced placement environmental science exam. *Educational and Psychological Measurement, 73*(3), 386–411. http://doi.org/10.1177/0013164412468448

Linacre, J. M. (1989). *Many-facet Rasch measurement.* Chicago, IL: MESA Press.

Linacre, J. M. (2015). *Facets Rasch Measurement* (Version 3.71.4). Chicago, IL: Winsteps.com.

Lumley, T. (2002). Assessment criteria in a large-scale writing test: What do they really mean to the raters? *Language Testing, 19*(3), 246–276. http://doi.org/10.1191/0265532202lt230oa

Lunz, M. E., Wright, B. D., & Linacre, J. M. (1990). Measuring the impact of judge severity on examination scores. *Applied Measurement in Education, 3*(4), 331.

Masters, G. N. (1982). A Rasch model for partial credit scoring. *Psychometrika, 47*(2), 149–174. http://doi.org/10.1007/BF02296272

Smith, R. M. (2004). Fit analysis in latent trait models. In E. V. Smith & R. M. Smith (Eds.), *Introduction to Rasch measurement* (pp. 73–92). Maple Grove, MN: JAM Press.

Smith, R. M., Schumacker, R. E., & Bush, J. J. (1998). Using item mean squares to evaluate fit to the Rasch model. *Journal of Outcome Measurement, 2,* 66–78.

Wind, S. A., & Engelhard, G. (2012). Examining rating quality in writing assessment: Rater agreement, error, and accuracy. *Journal of Applied Measurement, 13*(4), 321–335.

Wind, S. A., & Engelhard, G. (2013). How invariant and accurate are domain ratings in writing assessment? *Assessing Writing, 18*(4), 278–299. http://doi.org/10.1016/j.asw.2013.09.002

Wind, S. A., Engelhard, G., & Wesolowski, B. (2016). Exploring the effects of rater linking designs and rater fit on achievement estimates within the context of music performance assessments. *Educational Assessment, 21*(4), 278–299. https://doi.org/10.1 080/10627197.2016.1236676

Wolfe, E. W., Kao, C.-W., & Ranney, M. (1998). Cognitive differences in proficient and nonproficient essay scorers. *Written Communication, 15*(4), 465–492. http://doi.org/ 10.1177/0741088398015004002

Wolfe, E. W., Moulder, B. C., & Myford, C. M. (2001). Detecting differential rater functioning over time (DRIFT) using a Rasch multi-faceted rating scale model. *Journal of Applied Measurement, 2*(3), 256–280.

Wright, B. D., & Masters, G. N. (1982). *Rating scale analysis: Rasch measurement.* Chicago, IL: MESA Press.

APPENDIX 8.A

Scoring Rubrics for Case Study Data

Domain 1: IDEAS. The degree to which the writer establishes a controlling idea and elaborates the main points with examples, illustrations, facts, or details that are appropriate to the assigned genre.

Components

- Controlling Idea/Focus
- Supporting Ideas
- Relevance of Detail

- Depth of Development
- Sense of Completeness
- Awareness of Genre

5	**Full command of the components of Ideas. The writing is characterized by most or all of the following:** • Consistent focus on the assigned topic and purpose • Fully developed controlling idea that addresses all aspects of the assigned writing task • Supporting ideas and elaboration are relevant to the writer's topic, assigned genre of writing, and audience • Supporting ideas are fully elaborated throughout the paper with logical examples and details • Response contains information that fully addresses reader concerns and perspectives • Uses genre-appropriate strategies to develop the writer's ideas
4	**Consistent control of the components of Ideas. The writing is characterized by most or all of the following:** • Consistent focus on the assigned topic and purpose • Well developed controlling idea that addresses the assigned writing task • Supporting ideas and elaboration are relevant to the writer's topic and assigned genre of writing • Supporting ideas are developed with specific examples and details • Response contains information that addresses reader concerns and perspectives • Response is appropriate to the assigned genre
3	**Sufficient control of the components of Ideas. The writing is characterized by most or all of the following:** • Generally consistent focus on the assigned topic and purpose • Developed controlling idea that addresses the assigned writing task • Most supporting ideas and elaboration are relevant to the writer's topic and assigned genre of writing • Supporting ideas are developed with some examples and details; some parts of the paper are well developed, but other parts of the paper are only partially developed • Response contains sufficient information to address the topic and some reader concerns and perspectives • Response is generally appropriate to the assigned genre
2	**Minimal control of the components of Ideas. The writing is characterized by most or all of the following:** • Limited focus on the assigned topic and purpose • Minimally developed controlling idea that addresses some aspect of the assigned writing task • Supporting ideas are vague, general, and/or undeveloped (or some ideas may be partially developed, while others are simply listed without development) • Response lacks sufficient information (due to brevity and/or repetition) to provide a sense of completeness and address reader concerns • Some points and details may be irrelevant or inappropriate for the writer's assigned topic, audience, and assigned genre of writing • Response does not demonstrate genre awareness
1	**Lack of control of the components of Ideas. The writing is characterized by most or all of the following:** • Lack of focus on the assigned topic and purpose • Lack of a controlling idea • Absence of supporting ideas (or unclear supporting ideas) • Development is lacking due to brevity of the response and/or repetition of ideas • Lacks a sense of completeness and fails to address reader concerns • Majority of details are irrelevant • Response is inappropriate to the assigned genre • Insufficient student writing (due to brevity or copying the prompt) to determine competence in Ideas

Domain 2: ORGANIZATION. The degree to which the writer's ideas are arranged in a clear order and the overall structure of the response is consistent with the assigned genre.

Components

- Overall Plan
- Introduction/Body/Conclusion
- Sequence of Ideas
- Grouping of Ideas within Paragraphs
- Genre-Specific Strategies
- Transitions

5	**Full command of the components of Organization. The writing is characterized by most or all of the following:** • Organizing strategy is appropriate to the writer's topic and the assigned genre of writing. The overall strategy facilitates the writer's communication of ideas • Logical and appropriate sequencing of ideas within paragraphs and across parts of the paper • Introduction engages and sets the stage, and conclusion provides a sense of resolution or closure • Both introduction and conclusion fit the writer's ideas and the purpose of the genre • Related ideas are grouped in a logical manner within paragraphs • Uses effective and varied transitional elements to link all elements of the response: parts of the paper, ideas, paragraphs, and sentences. Transitions extend beyond the use of transitional words and phrases
4	**Consistent control of the components of Organization. The writing is characterized by most or all of the following:** • Overall organizational strategy or structure is appropriate to the writer's ideas and purpose of the genre. Structure guides the reader through the text • Logical sequencing of ideas across parts of the paper • Introduction sets the stage, and conclusion ends the piece of writing without repetition • Logical grouping of ideas within paragraphs • Varied transitions link parts of the paper and link ideas within paragraphs
3	**Sufficient control of the components of Organization. The writing is characterized by most or all of the following:** • Organizational strategy is generally appropriate to the writer's ideas and purpose of the genre • Generally clear sequence of ideas • Introduction is clear and a conclusion provides closure • Related ideas generally grouped together within paragraphs • Transitions link parts of the paper
2	**Minimal control of the components of Organization. The writing is characterized by most or all of the following:** • Organizing strategy is formulaic and/or inappropriate to the assigned genre • Minimal evidence of sequencing • May lack an introduction or a conclusion or include an ineffective introduction or conclusion • Ideas within paragraphs are not arranged in a meaningful order • Limited use of transitions (transitions may be formulaic, ineffective or overused) • Demonstration of competence limited by the brevity of the response
1	**Lack of control of the components of Organization. The writing is characterized by most or all of the following:** • No evidence of an organizing strategy • Unclear sequence of ideas • Lacks an introduction and/or conclusion • Unrelated ideas included within paragraphs • Lack of transitions or inappropriate transitions • Insufficient writing (due to brevity or copying the prompt) to determine competence in Organization

	Domain 3: STYLE. The degree to which the writer controls language to engage the reader.

Components

- Word Choice
- Audience Awareness
- Voice

- Sentence Variety
- Strategies Appropriate to the Genre

5	**Full command of the components of Style. The writing is characterized by most or all of the following:** • Carefully crafted phrases and sentences create a sustained tone and advance the writer's purpose with respect to the intended audience • Varied, precise, and engaging language that is appropriate to the assigned genre • Word choice reflects an understanding of the denotative and connotative meaning of language • Figurative or technical language may be used for rhetorical effect • Sustained attention to the audience • Evocative or authoritative voice that is sustained throughout the response • An extensive variety of sentence lengths, structures, and beginnings • A variety of genre-appropriate strategies to engage the reader
4	**Consistent control of the components of Style. The writing is characterized by most or all of the following:** • Language and tone are consistent with the writer's purpose and appropriate to the assigned genre • Word choice is precise and engaging • Attention to audience in introduction, body, and conclusion • Consistent and distinctive voice • Sentences vary in length and structure • Some genre-appropriate strategies to engage the reader
3	**Sufficient control of the components of Style. The writing is characterized by most or all of the following:** • Language and tone are generally consistent with the writer's purpose and appropriate to the assigned genre • Word choice is generally engaging with occasional lapses into simple and ordinary language • Awareness of audience may be limited to introduction and/or conclusion • Writer's voice is clear and appropriate • Some variation in sentence length and structure • May include some genre-appropriate strategies
2	**Minimal control of the components of Style. The writing is characterized by most or all of the following:** • Language and tone are uneven (appropriate in some parts of the response, but flat throughout most of the response) • Word choice is simple, ordinary and/or repetitive • Limited awareness of audience • Minimal, inconsistent or indistinct voice • Little variation in sentence length and structure • Demonstration of competence limited by the brevity of the response
1	**Lack of control of the components of Style. The writing is characterized by most or all of the following:** • Language and tone are flat and/or inappropriate to the task and reader • Word choice is inaccurate, imprecise, and/or confusing • Little or no attention to audience • Writer's voice is not apparent • Lack of sentence variety • Insufficient student writing (due to brevity or copying the prompt) to determine competence in Style

Georgia Department of Education. (2010). Georgia grade 8 writing assessment interpretive guide. Atlanta, GA: Author.

Domain 4: CONVENTIONS. The degree to which the writer demonstrates control of sentence formation, usage, and mechanics. *Note: In general, sentence formation and usage are weighted more heavily than mechanics in determining the overall conventions score.*

Components

Sentence Formation	Usage	Mechanics
• correctness	• subject-verb agreement	• internal punctuation
• clarity of meaning	• standard word forms	• spelling
• complexity	• possessives	• paragraph breaks
• end punctuation	• contractions	• capitalization

5	**Full command of the components of Conventions. The writing is characterized by most or all of the following:** • Clear and correct simple, complex, and compound sentences with correct end punctuation • Variety of subordination and coordination strategies • Correct usage in a variety of contexts: subject-verb agreement, word forms (nouns, adjectives, adverbs), pronoun-antecedent agreement • Correct mechanics in a variety of contexts: punctuation within sentences, spelling, capitalization, and paragraph indentation • Infrequent, if any, errors
4	**Consistent control of the components of Conventions. The writing is characterized by most or all of the following:** • Correct simple, complex, and compound sentences with correct end punctuation and few errors • Correct usage with few errors • Correct mechanics with few errors • Errors are generally minor and do not interfere with meaning
3	**Sufficient control of the components of Conventions. The writing is characterized by most or all of the following:** • Sentences are generally correct with generally correct end punctuation • Some errors in complex and compound sentences, and occasional sentence fragments, run-ons, or awkward sentences. Few errors with simple sentences • Generally correct usage, but may contain some errors in subject-verb agreement, word forms, pronoun-antecedent agreement, verb tense, and commonly confused homonyms • Generally correct mechanics, but may contain some errors in spelling, capitalization, paragraph indentation, and punctuation within sentences • Few errors interfere with meaning
2	**Minimal control of the components of Conventions. The writing is characterized by most or all of the following:** • Minimal control in the three components of conventions or one component may be strong while the other two are weak • Simple sentences formed correctly, but other sentences may be incomplete or overloaded • Sentence structure is awkward and/or end punctuation may be missing or incorrect • May have frequent errors in usage and/or mechanics • Some errors may interfere with meaning • Demonstration of competence limited by the brevity of the response
1	**Lack of control of the components of Conventions. The writing is characterized by most or all of the following:** • Frequent sentence fragments, run-ons, and incorrect sentences • End punctuation incorrect or lacking • May contain frequent and severe errors in both usage and mechanics • Errors may interfere with or obscure meaning • Insufficient student writing (due to brevity or copying the prompt) to determine competence in Conventions

PART IV

Technical Issues and IRT Models for Ratings

9

MODELS FOR RATINGS BASED ON ITEM RESPONSE THEORY

This chapter focuses on two measurement theories for ratings within the scaling tradition based on Item Response Theory (IRT; DeAyala, 2009; Baker & Kim, 2004; Lord, 1980; Reise & Revicki, 2015; van der Linden, 2016a). Modern measurement research, theory, and practice are primarily conducted using IRT. IRT reflects what has been called the new rules of measurement (Embretson, 1996). Some researchers continue to use measurement theories based on the test-score tradition for ratings and rater-mediated assessments with much of this work based on Generalizability Theory (Brennan, 2001). As shown in Chapter Three, there are a number of advantages accrued from the use of IRT, including the potential to achieve invariant measurement within the context of rater-mediated assessment. In this chapter, the focus is on describing and comparing two major measurement models within the scaling tradition that have been proposed for ratings based on the research of Rasch (1960/1980) and Samejima (1969).

IRT models for ratings within the scaling tradition have been categorized in several different ways. In this chapter, we are guided by the conceptual notes of Mellenbergh (1995). Mellenbergh (1995) identified several approaches for thinking about ordered polytomous item responses: adjacent-category models, cumulative-probability models, and continuation-ratio models. This chapter focuses on the adjacent-category models using Rasch Measurement Theory (e.g., Partial Credit Model, PCM) and cumulative-probability models (e.g., Graded Response Model, GRM) because they are the most widely used in practice. These two models have also been called direct and indirect models (Embretson & Reise, 2000; Engelhard, 2005) and referred to as divide-by-total and difference models (Thissen & Steinberg, 1986). We have selected these two theoretical perspectives to highlight similarities and differences between models for adjacent and cumulative categories.

The specific issues and questions addressed in this chapter are as follows:

- Historical perspectives on polytomous data

  o What are the key historical advances for analyzing polytomous data?
  o How have polytomous ratings been conceptualized within the scaling tradition?

- Two Item Response Theory models for ratings

  o Partial Credit Model (PCM)
  o Graded Response Model (GRM)

- Empirical analyses of two IRT models for ratings
- Issues in modeling ordered categories within Rasch Measurement Theory

  o How are ratings conceptualized?
  o What are disordered thresholds?

- Summary and discussion

Readers who are interested in other polytomous models should consult Nering and Ostini (2010), who have edited a handbook that provides an overview of various models that are not included in this chapter. Penfield (2014) provides a training module on polytomous IRT models.

Historical Perspectives on Polytomous Data

> Statistical methodology for categorical data has only recently reached the level of sophistication achieved early in this century by methodology for continuous data.
>
> *(Agresti, 1990, p. 1)*

This section provides a brief and selective overview of some of the key advances related to the conceptualization and modeling of categorical and polytomous data.

What Are the Key Historical Advances for Analyzing Polytomous Data?

Agresti (1990) classifies categorical response data in terms of whether or not there are ordered levels for the variable. Since this book focuses on ratings, the categorical responses are intended to be ordered. A second classification issue relates to whether the ordinal responses are dichotomous with two ordered categories or polytomous with more than two ordered categories.

Several of the key figures in the modern development of models for analyzing categorical data are Goodman (1978); Haberman (1978); and Bishop, Fienberg, and Holland (1975). They developed and applied various log linear models to categorical and frequency data that are analogous to the use of regressions models for continuous variables. One of the major advances during the 20th century was the recognition that categorical data in the form of frequencies and contingency tables can be analyzed with various adaptations of the general linear model.

In addition to the use of log linear models, one of the major developments for analyzing categorical data was the introduction of generalized linear models by Nelder and Wedderburn (1972). Essentially, these models involve a set of non-linear transformations of categorical data with various link functions (McCullagh & Nelder, 1989). These transformations enable the use of the conceptual framework of standard linear models with categorical data (Bock, 1970, 1975).

As shown in the next section, there were parallel developments occurring in other fields with much of this work occurring within psychophysics and psychometrics. This is similar to the way in which the development of earlier statistical methodologies affected measurement models (and vice versa). For example, the development of correlation coefficients affected how reliability coefficients are defined in Classical Test Theory early in the 20th century. Another example is the application of Fisher's ANOVA framework and the design of experiments to conceptualize measurement issues within Generalizability Theory (Cronbach et al., 1972).

How Have Polytomous Ratings Been Conceptualized within the Scaling Tradition?

Hambleton, van der Linden, and Wells (2010) provide an historical perspective on how IRT models have evolved for analyzing polytomously scored data. Hambleton, van der Linden, and Wells (2010) highlight the connection between various dichotomous IRT models and their extensions to rating scales. For example, the PCM can be viewed as an extension of the dichotomous Rasch model, while the GRM is closely associated with the two-parameter logistic (2PL) model proposed by Birnbaum (1968).

Early work on polytomous data includes research by Thurstone and Chave (1929) with a selection of articles included in Thurstone (1959) within the scaling tradition. Thurstonian measurement explicitly connects psychophysics to research in psychometrics. Psychophysical models can be used to connect unobservable latent variables to probabilities of observing discrete and categorical responses. The research of Bock and Jones (1968) stands out as an important milestone in summarizing the statistical connections of psychophysical models to generalized linear models.

Mellenbergh (1995) provides a useful way of conceptualizing various models for polytomous item responses. Figure 9.1 provides a simple way to represent the PCM and the GRM models. Panel A of Figure 9.1 represents the underlying view of categories within the dichotomous Rasch model. The τ_1 parameter defines an item difficulty that represents the location of the item on the latent

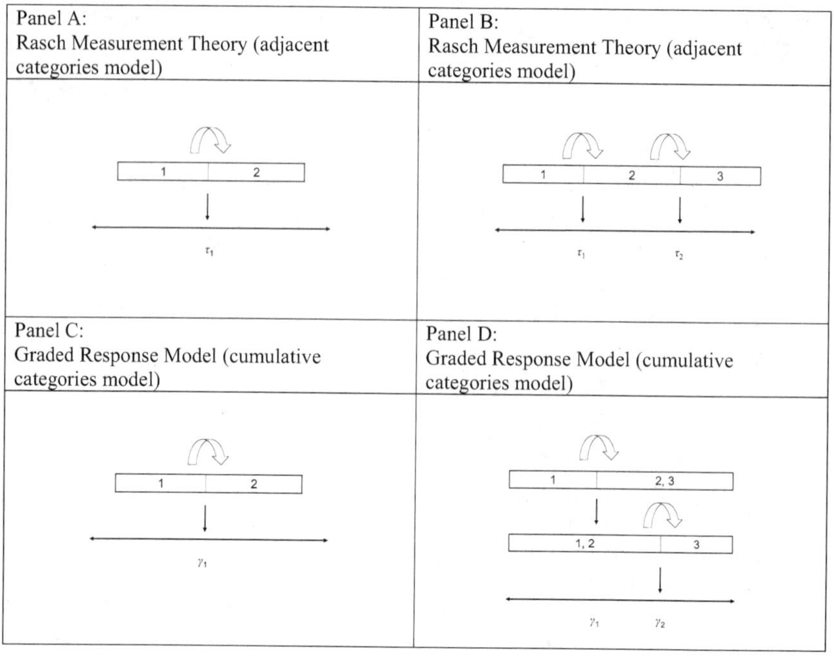

Panel A: Rasch Measurement Theory (adjacent categories model)	Panel B: Rasch Measurement Theory (adjacent categories model)
Panel C: Graded Response Model (cumulative categories model)	Panel D: Graded Response Model (cumulative categories model)

FIGURE 9.1 Two Perspectives on Ordered Categories: Adjacent and Cumulative Category Models

Note: The category coefficients (τ and γ) in each model have different substantive meanings.

variable. Persons that are above τ_1 on the line are expected to respond in Category 2, while persons below τ_1 are expected to respond in Category 1. As pointed out by Mellenbergh (1995), the extension of the dichotomous adjacent category model reflecting Rasch Measurement Theory can be represented in Panel B of Figure 9.1. For this three-category rating scale, the underlying process is viewed as two item locations (τ_1 and τ_2). Person locations on the line can be interpreted as indicating category thresholds that relate to the expected categories selected by each person. For example, persons with locations below τ_1 on the line are expected to respond in Category 1, persons between τ_1 and τ_2 are expected to respond in Category 2, and finally, persons with locations above τ_2 are expected to respond to the item in Category 3.

Turning now to the GRM, Panel C in Figure 9.1 represents a person responding to two categories defined by a single category coefficient (γ_1). If a person is below γ_1 on the line, then this person is expected to respond in Category 1. Persons who are above γ_1 on the line are expected to respond in Category 2. It should be noted that for the dichotomous case with one item, PCM and GRM are exchangeable. If two or more items are included, then the discrimination parameter included in the GRM leads to a lack of person invariant item calibration—in order words, crossing IRFs can occur that lead to interpretive problems regarding the simultaneous mapping of item and persons on the same line (Engelhard, 2013). Panel D in Figure 9.1 represents the generalization of the GRM to a three-category rating scale. In this case, the dichotomization of the categories is based on comparisons across cumulative categories.

Two Item Response Theory Models for Ratings: Partial Credit and Graded Response Models

In IRT, the latent variable is defined as an unobservable construct. The major purpose of measurement is to locate persons and items on the latent variable. We can visualize the latent variable as a line representing the construct. A central problem in psychometrics is the development of measurement models that connect person measures and item calibrations in a meaningful way to represent a construct as a line. The basic idea that motivates the use of IRT models for rating scale data is that the scoring of $m + 1$ ordered categories with ordered integers $(0,1, \ldots, m)$ based on the assumption that there are equal intervals between the category coefficients may not be justified. IRT models provide a framework to explicitly examine the category coefficients and parameterize the categories without this assumption of equal units. Specifically, IRT models for rating scale data are used to model category response functions that link the probability of a specific rating with person measures and a set of characteristics that reflect item and category calibrations. The category response function (CRF) represents the probability of obtaining a score of x on item i as a function of a person's location on the construct θ. The CRFs can be written as follows:

$$P_{xi}(\theta) = pr(X_i = x \mid \theta) \tag{9.1}$$

for $x = 0, 1, \ldots, m$. The IRT models for rating scale data vary in terms of how they define the operating characteristic functions (OCFs), and this in turn influences other characteristics of the models.

As pointed out earlier, there are several different ways to categorize IRT models for analyzing ratings. We have selected two models that represent adjacent category models (PCM) and cumulative category models (GRM). Adjacent category models focus on directly estimating category response functions, while cumulative category models require two steps that involve first estimating the operating characteristic functions, and then estimating the category response functions.

Partial Credit Model (PCM)

> The Partial Credit Model is a particular application of the model for dichotomies developed by Danish mathematician Georg Rasch.
>
> *(Masters, 2010, p. 109)*

The Partial Credit Model (PCM; Masters, 2016) is a unidimensional IRT model for ratings in two or more ordered categories. The PCM is a Rasch model, and therefore provides the opportunity to realize a variety of desirable measurement characteristics, such as separability of person and item parameters, sufficient statistics for parameters in the model, and specific objectivity (Rasch, 1977). When good model-data fit is obtained, then the PCM yields invariant measurement (Engelhard, 2013). The PCM is a straightforward generalization of the Rasch (1960/1980) model for dichotomous data applied to pairs of increasing adjacent categories.

The Rasch model for dichotomous data can be written as:

$$\phi_{i1} = \frac{P_{i1}(\theta)}{P_{i0}(\theta) + P_{i1}(\theta)} = \frac{\exp(\theta - \delta_{i1})}{1 + \exp(\theta - \delta_{i1})} \tag{9.2}$$

where $P(\theta)_{i1}$ is the probability of scoring 1 on item i, $P(\theta)_{i0}$ is the probability of scoring 0 on item i, θ is the location of the person on the construct, and δ_{i1} is the location on the construct where the probability of responding in adjacent categories, 0 and 1, is equal. The dichotomous case δ_{i1} is defined as the difficulty of item i. Equation 9.2 represents the operating characteristic function for the PCM. When the data are collected with more than two response categories, then the operating characteristic function can be generalized as

$$\phi_{ix} = \frac{P_{ix}(\theta)}{P_{ix} - 1(\theta) + P_{ix}(\theta)} = \frac{\exp(\theta - \delta_{ix})}{1 + \exp(\theta - \delta_{ix})} \tag{9.3}$$

where $P(\theta)_{ix}$ is the probability of scoring x on item i, $P(\theta)_{ix-1}$ is the probability of scoring $x - 1$ on item i, θ is the location of the person on the construct, and δ_{ix} is the location on the construct where the probability of responding in adjacent categories, $x - 1$ and 1, is equal.

The category response function (CRF) for the PCM is:

$$P_{ix}(\theta) = \frac{\exp\left[\sum_{j=0}^{x}(\theta - \delta_{ij})\right]}{\sum_{r=0}^{m_i}\exp\left[\sum_{j=0}^{r}(\theta - \delta_{ij})\right]} , \ x_i = 0, 1, \ldots, m_i \tag{9.4}$$

where $\sum_{j=0}^{0}(\theta - \delta_{ij}) \equiv 0$. The δ_{ij} parameter is still interpreted as the intersection between the two adjacent categories where the probabilities of responding in the adjacent categories are equal. The δ_{ij} term is described as a step difficulty by Wright and Masters (1982). Embretson and Reise (2000) have suggested calling the δ_{ij} term a *category intersection parameter*. Nering and Ostini (2010) suggest the term *boundary parameter*. It is important to recognize that the item parameter δ_{ij} represents the location on the construct where a person has the same probability of responding in categories x and $x - 1$. These conditional probabilities for adjacent categories are expected to increase, but the category coefficients are not necessarily ordered from low to high on the construct θ. By defining the item parameters locally, it is possible to verify that persons are using the categories as expected. The issue of disordered thresholds is discussed in more detail in a later section of this chapter.

Graded Response Model

> The principle behind the model and the set of accompanying assumptions (should) agree with the psychological nature that underlies the data.
>
> *(Samejima, 2010, p. 850)*

The Graded Response Model (GRM; Samejima, 2016) is another unidimensional IRT model for ordered responses. The GRM is a cumulative category model that requires first the estimation of the OCFs, and then the subtraction of the OCFs to obtain the CRFs. As pointed out by Samejima (1969) in describing the GRM:

> It is easily understood that any graded item can be reduced to a dichotomous item, if only we rescore a given graded item in such a way that any item score less than x_g is 0 and that more than or equal to x_g is 1 . . . Since there are m_g category bounds for a graded item, we can obtain m_g sets of $P_g(\theta)$ and $Q_g(\theta)$, the operating characteristics defined for a dichotomous item.
>
> *(p. 20)*

The OCFs for the GRM are defined using two-parameter IRT models (Birnbaum, 1968) for dichotomous data with slopes set equal within a rating scale item. The GRM treats four ordered response categories as a series of three dichotomies as follows: 0 vs. 1,2,3; 0,1 vs. 2,3; 0,1,2 vs. 3. The PCM examines adjacent categories to form three dichotomies: 0 vs. 1; 1 vs. 2; 2 vs. 3. This difference influences the substantive interpretations of the category parameters across the models, as well as the underlying definition of the latent variable. The OCFs for the GRM are modeling the probability of a person scoring x or greater on item i, while the PCM is modeling the probability of x or $x - 1$ for adjacent categories. The OCF for the GRM is

$$\pi_{ix}^{*} = P *_{ix}(\theta) = \frac{\exp[\alpha_i(\theta - \beta_{ij})]}{1 + \exp[\alpha_i(\theta - \beta_{ij})]} \tag{9.5}$$

The β_{ij} parameter is interpreted as the location on the construct necessary to respond above the j threshold on item i with a probability of .50, θ is the location of a person on the construct, and α_i is the slope parameter common across OCFs within item i. The slope parameter is constrained to be equal within item i, and this is called the *homogeneous case of the GRM*. The CRF for the GRM is

$$P_{ix}(\theta) = \frac{\exp[\alpha_i(\theta - \beta_{ix})]}{1 + \exp[\alpha_i(\theta - \beta_{ix})]} - \frac{\exp[\alpha_i(\theta - \beta_{i(x+1)})]}{1 + \exp[\alpha_i(\theta - \beta_{i(x+1)})]},$$

$$x_i = 1, \ldots, m_i$$

(9.6)

or

$$P_{ix}(\theta) = P*_{ix}(\theta) - P*_{i(x+1)}(\theta)$$

(9.7)

where $P*_{i(x=0)}(\theta) = 1.0$ and $P*_{i(x=mi+1)}(\theta) = 0.0$. It is important to highlight the substantive interpretations of category parameters β_{ij} of the GRM. The β_{ij} is not the location on the construct where a person has the same probability of being in adjacent categories—in other words, the GRM category parameter is not the point of intersection. This interpretation stands in contrast to the category parameters in the PCM, which represent the intersection points. Furthermore, the GRM category parameters β_{ij} are parameterized to be ordered within an item: $\beta_{i1} \leq \beta_{i2} \ldots \leq \beta_{im}$. The GRM has a historical connection to the earlier work of Thurstone (1959) on the method of successive intervals with the important distinction that a person parameter is added to the GRM model. The β_{ij} parameters are sometimes called *Thurstone thresholds*. These Thurstone thresholds represent the location on the construct where the probability of being rated j or above equals the probability of being in the categories below j, within item i.

Empirical Analyses of Two Item Response Theory Models for Ratings

In this section, we analyze the writing assessment data from Chapter One. The focus is on the ratings from Rater 1 using four domains (C = Conventions, I = Ideas , O = Organization, and S = Style). There are three rating categories: low, medium, and high quality of writing. These data are shown in Table 9.1 and summarized in Table 9.2.

The Facets computer program was used to obtain estimates of the parameters for a PC formulation of the Many-Facet Rasch Model (Linacre, 1989). Table 9.3 provides a summary of the Rasch analyses of these data by rating categories and the four domains.

The overall model-data fit is good as indicated by the Infit and Outfit mean square error (*MSE*) statistics. Both persons and domain fit the ratings for Rater 1 very well. The domains have Infit and Outfit mean square statistics close to the expected value of 1.00. The domains are centered at zero, and the average measure of writing achievement is −.40 logits (SD = 1.38). The reliability of person separation is .56. When good model-data fit is observed, the reliability of person separation is comparable to coefficient alpha within the test-score tradition. As would be expected, the reliability of person separation is low when only one rater is used to assess the quality of student writing.

TABLE 9.1 Observed Ratings by Rater 1 of Essay Quality ($N = 40$)

Person	C	O	I	S
1	1	2	2	2
2	3	2	3	3
3	2	1	2	1
4	2	3	3	3
5	1	2	1	1
6	2	2	1	1
7	2	3	3	2
8	1	2	3	1
9	1	1	1	2
10	2	3	1	1
11	1	1	2	1
12	3	1	1	1
13	1	3	2	1
14	1	2	2	2
15	1	1	1	3
16	2	1	3	2
17	2	1	2	2
18	2	2	2	2
19	1	1	1	2
20	2	3	2	2
21	1	2	1	2
22	1	1	2	2
23	1	1	2	2
24	2	1	1	1
25	2	2	2	3
26	3	2	2	3
27	2	2	3	3
28	2	1	3	2
29	1	1	1	3
30	2	2	1	3
31	2	1	2	2
32	3	1	3	3
33	1	2	2	1
34	3	3	3	2
35	1	2	1	1
36	2	3	3	3
37	2	3	1	2
38	1	3	3	3
39	1	1	1	2
40	1	2	1	2

Note: The data are based on Rater 1 from Table 1.2. The ratings are defined as 1 = Low, 2 = Medium, and 3 = High. The domains of writing quality are defined as C = Conventions, I = Ideas, O = Organization, and S = Style.

TABLE 9.2 Summary of Observed Ratings by Rater 1 of Essay Quality

Category	Conventions	Ideas	Organization	Style
Frequency:				
1	18	16	15	11
2	17	15	14	18
3	5	9	11	11 .
	40	40	40	40
Percentage:				
1	0.450	0.400	0.375	0.275
2	0.425	0.375	0.350	0.450
3	0.125	0.225	0.275	0.275
Cumulative Percentage:				
1	0.450	0.400	0.375	0.275
2	0.875	0.775	0.725	0.725
3	1.000	1.000	1.000	1.000

TABLE 9.3 Facets Summary Table for Rater 1

	Persons (N = 40)	Domains (N = 4)
Measure		
Mean	−.40	.00
SD	1.38	.46
Infit		
Mean	.99	1.00
SD	.59	.17
Outfit		
Mean	.98	.98
SD	.62	.20
Reliability of separation	.56	.63
Chi-squared statistic	73.2 (df = 39, p < .01)	7.6 (df = 3, p = .05)

Table 9.4 provides the calibration of the four domains. The domain locations range from Conventions (.62 logits) to Style (−.45 logits). The reliability of domain separation is statistically significant ($p < .05$). Table 9.5 gives the summary statistics for the rating structure within each domain. Again, the Outfit MSE statistic indicates good model-data fit for domains. Furthermore, the average judged student measures on the logit scale increase for each rating category within domains as expected.

The Wright map for these data is shown in Figure 9.2.

The first column in the Wright map represents the logit scale used to map the locations of persons, domains, and domain category thresholds on the latent variable. The second column presents the locations of the 40 persons, while the

TABLE 9.4 Summary Statistics for Partial Credit Model

Domain	Observed Average	Locations (Logits)	SE	Infit MSE	Outfit MSE
Conventions	1.70	0.62	0.30	0.98	1.01
Ideas	1.80	0.04	0.27	1.21	1.18
Organization	1.90	−0.20	0.27	0.79	0.71
Style	2.00	−0.45	0.28	1.00	1.01

TABLE 9.5 Summary Statistics for Rating Structure by Domain (PCM)

Rating Categories	Thresholds	SE	Outfit MSE	Average Measure
Conventions				
1			.9	−1.91
2	−1.28	.38	.8	−.54
3	1.28	.56	1.4	.52
Ideas				
1			1.3	−1.20
2	−.85	.39	1.2	−.44
3	.85	.48	1.0	.91
Organization				
1			.8	−1.23
2	−.68	.39	.7	−.37
3	.68	.45	.6	1.41
Style				
1			.9	−.98
2	−1.09	.41	1.1	−.11
3	1.09	.44	1.0	1.34

third column indicates the locations of the domains. The last column indicates the category thresholds estimated based on the PCM.

Figure 9.3 displays the category response functions for the four domains. The operating characteristic functions are shown in Figure 9.4, and they indicate the relationship between the latent variable (x-axis) and the expected score based on the PCM for each domain. The observed scores are also presented to give an indication of the correspondence between the observed and expected ratings for each domain. Figure 9.5 provides another way to see how the Rasch model appears as parallel (non-crossing) operating characteristics curves with the PCM for each domain.

In order to fit the GRM to these data, we used the IRT procedures available in Stata (StataCorp, 2015). Table 9.6 presents the summary statistics for these data based on the GRM.

```
+----------------------------------------------------------+
|                      |          Partial Credit(Domains)|
|Logit|+Persons    |Domains| S.1 | S.2 | S.3 | S.4 |
|-----+-----------+-------+-----+-----+-----+-----|
|  3 +   High      + Hard + (3) + (3) + (3) + (3) |
|    |             |       |     |     |     |     |
|    |             |       |     |     |     |     |
|    |             |       |     |     |     |     |
|    |   ****      |       |     |     |     |     |
|    |             |       |     |     |     |     |
|  2 +             +       +     +     +     +     |
|    |             |       |     |     |     |     |
|    |             |       |     |     |     |     |
|    |             |       |     | --- |     |     |
|    |   *****     |       |     |     |     | --- |
|    |             |       |     | --- | --- |     |
|  1 +             +       +     +     +     +     |
|    |             |       |     |     |     |     |
|    |   **        | 1     |     |     |     |     |
|    |             |       |     |     |     |     |
|    |             |       |     |     |     |     |
|    |             |       |     |     |     |     |
*  0 * *****       * 2     *  2  *  2  *  2  *  2  *
|    |             | 3     |     |     |     |     |
|    |             | 4     |     |     |     |     |
|    |   *******   |       |     |     |     |     |
|    |             |       |     |     |     |     |
| -1 +             +       +     +     +     +     |
|    |             |       |     | --- | --- |     |
|    |   ********** |       |     |     |     |     |
|    |             |       |     |     |     | --- |
|    |             |       | --- |     |     |     |
|    |             |       |     |     |     |     |
| -2 +             +       +     +     +     +     |
|    |             |       |     |     |     |     |
|    |   *******   |       |     |     |     |     |
|    |             |       |     |     |     |     |
|    |             |       |     |     |     |     |
|    |             |       |     |     |     |     |
| -3 +   Low       + Easy + (1) + (1) + (1) + (1) |
|-----+-----------+-------+-----+-----+-----+-----|
|     | * = 1      |Domains| S.1 | S.2 | S.3 | S.4 |
+----------------------------------------------------------+
```

FIGURE 9.2 Wright Map for Rater 1

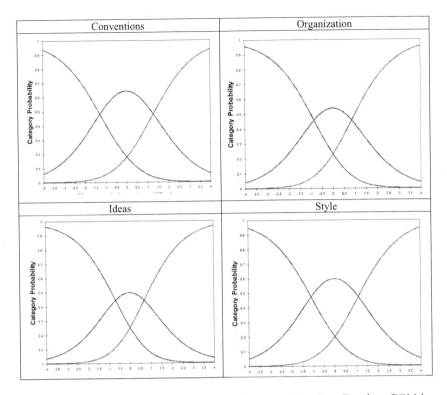

FIGURE 9.3   Graphical Displays of Category Response Functions Based on PCM by Domains

There are several important things to note in Table 9.6. First, the slope parameters are equal within a domain. Second, the reader should note that the slopes and category thresholds are parameterizing the cumulative category comparisons as shown in column three. The graphical displays for the GRM are shown in Figures 9.6 and 9.7. Figure 9.6 shows the category response functions for the GRM across domains.

As shown in Table 9.6, the slope is relatively high for the Ideas domain (slope = 2.71) and low for the Organization domain (slope = .59). Figure 9.7 shows the operating response functions for the GRM. Figure 9.7 provides another way to see how the use of the 2PL model for cumulative categories can lead to crossing category response functions within the GRM.

Figure 9.8 provides a matrix plot of three types of scores obtained for the 40 persons rated by Rater 1 on the four domains. When the sum score (Score) is plotted against the Partial Credit Score (PC Score), it is clear the there is a one-to-one relationship between the scores. This one-to-one correspondence occurs because the sum score is a sufficient statistic for estimating person achievement

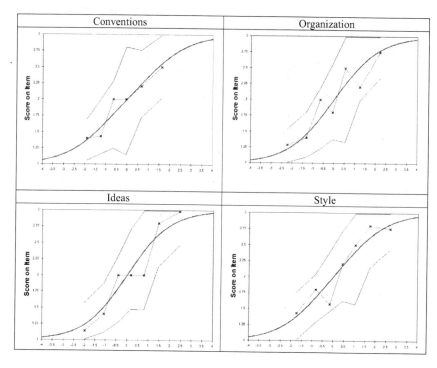

FIGURE 9.4 Graphical Displays of Operating Characteristic Functions Based on PCM by Domains (Observed and Expected Scores)

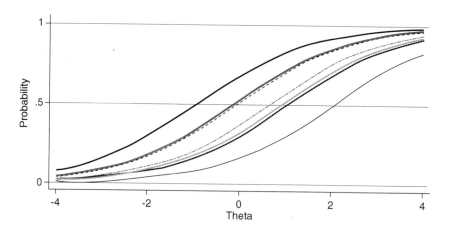

FIGURE 9.5 Operating Characteristic Functions for PCM

TABLE 9.6 Summary Statistics for Graded Response Model

Index	Domain	Category Comparisons	Discrimination	Difficulty
1	Conventions	1 to 2,3	1.02	−0.44
2	Conventions	1,2 to 3	1.02	2.13
3	Organization	1 to 2,3	0.59	−0.57
4	Organization	1,2 to 3	0.59	1.20
5	Ideas	1 to 2,3	2.71	−1.62
6	Ideas	1,2 to 3	2.71	1.39
7	Style	1 to 2,3	0.92	−1.30
8	Style	1,2 to 3	0.92	0.97

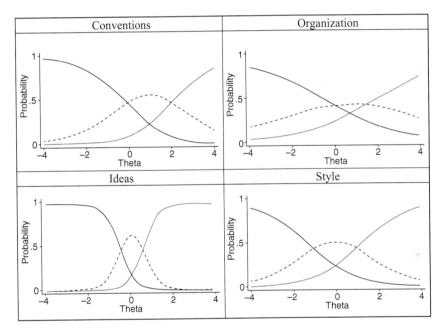

FIGURE 9.6 Graphical Displays of Category Response Functions Based on GRM

and location on the line representing the latent variable when the PCM is used. On the other hand, the plots of the GRM scores (GRM_Score) on both the sum scores (Score) and the PCM scores (PC_Score) indicate more scatter because the GRM scores do not have a one-to-one correspondence as a result of the parameterization of the slopes in the GRM.

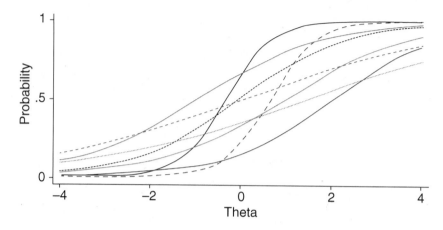

FIGURE 9.7   Operating Response Functions for GRM

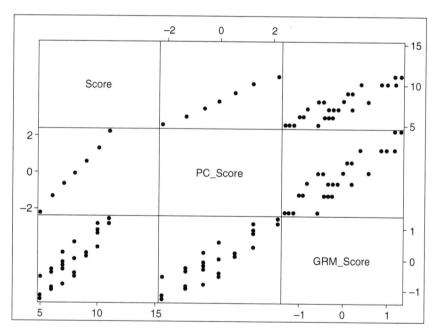

FIGURE 9.8   Matrix Plot: Sum Scores (Score), Partial Credit Model Scores (PC_Score), and Graded Response Model Score (GRM_Score)

Issues in Modeling Ordered Categories within Rasch Measurement Theory

In order to get a sense of several current issues related to rating scales, this section presents two important questions: (1) How ratings are conceptualized? and (2) What are disordered thresholds? Other issues related to how to evaluate the quality of rating scales are explored in Chapter Thirteen.

How Are Ratings Conceptualized?

Although the psychometric modeling of ordered categories has led to progress in how to approach rating scales (Nering & Ostini, 2010), there is still debate about the substantive and conceptual processes that undergird the use of rating scales. One of the key questions is as follows:

- What cognitive processes are engaged when a person or rater encounters a rating scale?

The initial development of the Partial Credit Model (Masters, 1982; Wright & Masters, 1982) used a step metaphor. Panel A of Figure 9.9 illustrates the item types that were used by Wright and Masters (1982) in their description of Partial Credit scoring. For example, the three-step mathematics item in Panel B of Figure 9.9 shows the mapping of three steps for a mathematics item onto the underlying latent variable. This perspective was used recently by Penfield (2014) in an instructional module to describe the hypothesized underlying cognitive processes used by persons when they respond polytomous items.

Andrich (2015) has argued that the step metaphor does not accurately reflect the underlying cognitive processes that occur when a person responds to a rating scale. In his words,

> the *step* characterization for dichotomous responses . . . is incompatible with the mathematical structure . . . the step metaphor leads to a superficial understanding of the models as mere descriptions of the data; at worst it leads to a misunderstanding of the models and how they can be used to assess if the empirical ordering of the categories is consistent with the intended ordering.
>
> *(p. 8)*

For example, Andrich (2015) points out:

> The correct generalization from the dichotomous to the polytomous responses is that, rather than a performance being classified in one of two ordered categories ($m = 1$), it is *classified* in one of $m + 1$ ordered categories ($m > 0$).
>
> *(p. 9)*

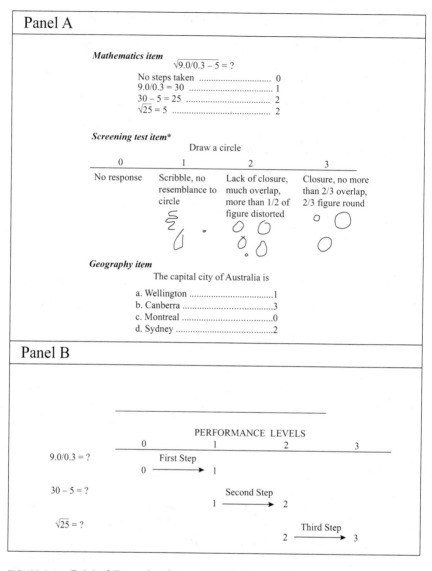

FIGURE 9.9 Original Example of Items Suitable for Partial Credit Model

Source: Wright & Masters (1982, p. 41).

The dichotomous responses across adjacent categories are a "latent dichotomous response between the categories" (Andrich, 2015, p. 9).

In conceptualizing the cognitive processes associated with the use of rating scales, researchers should think carefully about the congruence been the measurement model and the hypothesized cognitive processes. The best advice may be to match the terms used to describe person or rater thought processes to substantive context of the intended uses of the assessments. In many cases, it is plausible that raters are essentially selecting or choosing a category that best represents their judgments about the performance and person locations on the latent variable.

What Are Disordered Thresholds?

Another issue in modeling ordered categories within Rasch Measurement Theory is related to the measurement implications of disordered thresholds within an item. The PCM does not require the category coefficients to be ordered on the underlying latent variable. From one perspective, disordered thresholds can be viewed empirically as categories that are not used as frequently as the other categories. When these categories are modeled and mapped onto the latent variable, the modal values of the category probability distributions do not create a range of values on the line where each category is distinctive. Figure 9.10 illustrates the issue of disordered thresholds. In Panel A, the two thresholds are ordered $(\delta_1 = -1.00$ and $\delta_2 = 1.00)$ with each of the three categories defining distinct areas of the logit scale. The probability of being in Category 1 is highest for logit values below -1.00, the probability of being in Category 2 is highest from -1.00 to 1.00 logits, and the probability of being in Category 3 is highest above 1.00 logits. Panel B illustrates disordered thresholds $(\delta_1 = 1.00$ and $\delta_2 = -1.00)$. In this case, Category 2 is never the modal category along the logit scale.

Andrich (2013) has argued that the substantive implications for measurement are compromised when thresholds are disordered. In his words,

> Although the assumption that the ordering of the categories is working as intended is central to any interpretation that arises from such assessments, testing that this assumption is valid is not standard in psychometrics.
>
> *(p. 553)*

In contrast to this perspective, Adams, Wu, and Wilson (2012) do not reflect the same level of concern when disordered thresholds are encountered. They point out:

> When the data fit the Rasch rating model, the response categories are ordered regardless of the (order of the) values of the parameter estimates. In summary, reversed deltas [thresholds] are not necessarily evidence of a problem. In fact the reversed deltas [thresholds] phenomenon is indicative of specific patterns in the relative numbers of respondents in each category. When there are preferences about such relative numbers in categories, the patterns of deltas [thresholds] may be a useful diagnostic.
>
> *(p. 547)*

In taking a position on each issue, we are in agreement with the following observation by Mellenbergh (1995):

> The ordinal nature of the item response variable can be preserved by using adjacent-category, cumulative-probability, or continuation-ratio splittings.

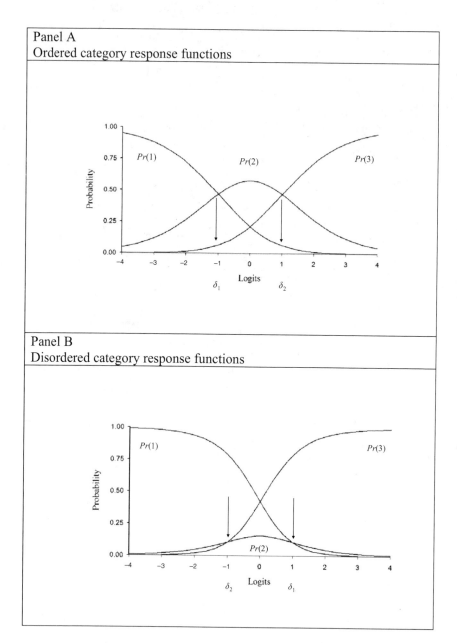

FIGURE 9.10   Ordered and Disordered Thresholds

The corresponding models have a similar structure, but the interpretation of the parameters is different. It seems plausible that the type of model used to preserve the ordinal nature should be determined by features of the item and by the cognitive processes involved in answering the item; however, the literature does not provide much support for preferring one model over another.

(p. 99)

These two issues are important because they highlight the connections between the underlying cognitive processes used to respond to rating scales, and the features of the measurement model used to represent essentially unobservable processes. Future research is needed on how persons respond to items and also on how raters actually use rating scales. One approach is to use various qualitative methodologies, such as think-aloud and stimulated recall (Wang et al., 2016), to obtain a deeper understanding of the correspondence between the measurement model and the substantive interpretation of the parameters in the model.

It is also important to stress that the model-data fit indices used within Rasch Measurement Theory, such as Infit and Outfit statistics, do not provide evidence regarding these two issues. The first issue is substantive and conceptual, while the second issue should be considered in conjunction with other psychometric criteria to evaluate the quality of the assessment system. Model-data fit issues are discussed in Chapter Eleven, while an additional array of indices for evaluating rating quality is introduced in Chapter Thirteen.

Summary and Discussion

This chapter described two approaches for analyzing ratings within the scaling tradition: the Partial Credit Model (PCM; Masters, 1982) and the Graded Response Model (GRM; Samejima, 1969). The PCM is based on the extension of the dichotomous Rasch model (Rasch, 1960/1980) to polytomous data, while the GRM can be viewed as the extension of the two-parameter logistic model (2PL; Birnbaum, 1968).

We have made several major points in this chapter:

- Polytomous data can be modeled as extensions of dichotomous IRT models. Two of the popular models are the PCM based on dichotomous Rasch model and the GRM based on dichotomous 2PL on the Birnbaum model.
- Classical Test Theory models ratings with equal units (score points), while IRT models in the scaling tradition explicitly model and estimate the units that define the sizes of the rating categories based on threshold and category coefficient parameters.
- Different IRT models for ratings have different substantive definitions of the latent variable when the thresholds and items are used to define adjacent versus cumulative categories.

- Substantive differences between models imply different cognitive processes from respondents and raters. These processes are unknown, but should be explicitly considered when selecting, estimating, and interpreting a rating scale model within a particular context.

It should be stressed that raters are not explicitly parameterized in the models discussed in this chapter. The PCM has been extended to include a rater parameter as shown in other chapters in this book. The Many-Facet Rasch Model (Linacre, 1989) is part of the family of models based on Rasch Measurement Theory (Rasch, 1960/1980) that specifically includes a rater facet. It is also important to note that principles of invariant measurement appear here "under the constraint that the a parameters [slopes] of polytomous item response models are equal between items, the log-odds differences of two different items are person invariant and the log-odds differences of two different persons are item invariant" (Mellenbergh, 1995, p. 99).

Developing and evaluating models for ratings based on IRT remains an area of active research in social, behavioral, and health sciences. There are several other important models for ratings that are not included in this chapter, and the reader should consult Nering and Ostini (2010), as well as recent handbooks on IRT (e.g., van der Linden, 2016a, 2016b), for descriptions of other models for ordered categorical data.

References

Adams, R. J., Wu, M. L., & Wilson, M. (2012). The Rasch rating model and the disordered threshold controversy. *Educational and Psychological Measurement, 72*(4), 547–573.

Agresti, A. (1990). *Categorical data analysis.* New York: John Wiley & Sons.

Andrich, D. A. (2013). The legacies of R. A. Fisher and K. Pearson in the application of the polytomous Rasch model for assessing the empirical ordering of categories. *Educational and Psychological Measurement, 73*(4), 553–580.

Andrich, D. A. (2015). The problem with the step metaphor for polytomous models for ordinal assessments. *Educational Measurement: Issues and Practice, 34*(2), 8–14.

Baker, F. B., & Kim, S. (2004). *Item response theory: Parameter estimation techniques* (2nd ed., Revised and Expanded). New York: Marcel Dekker.

Birnbaum, A. (1968). Some latent trait models and their use in inferring an examinee's ability, Part 5. In F. M. Lord & M. R. Novick (Eds.), *Statistical theories of mental test scores* (pp. 395–479). Reading, MA: Addison-Wesley.

Bishop, Y. V. V., Fienberg, S. E., & Holland, P. W. (1975). *Discrete multivariate analysis.* Cambridge, MA: MIT Press.

Bock, R. D. (1970). Estimating multinomial response relations. In R. C. Bose (Ed.), *Essays in probability and statistics* (pp. 111–132). Chapel Hill, NC: University of North Carolina Press.

Bock, R. D. (1972). Estimating item parameters and latent ability when responses are scored in two or more nominal categories. *Psychometrika, 37,* 29–51.

Bock, R. D. (1975). *Multivariate statistical methods in behavioral research.* New York: McGraw-Hill Book Company.

Bock, R. D., & Jones, L. V. (1968). *The measurement and prediction of judgment and choice.* San Francisco: Holden-Day.

Brennan, R. L. (2001). *Generalizability theory.* New York: Springer-Verlag.

Cronbach, L. J., Gleser, G. C., Nanda, H., & Rajaratnam, N. (1972). *The dependability of behavioral measurements: Theory of generalizability for scores and profiles.* New York: Wiley.

DeAyala, R. J. (2009). *The theory and practice of item response theory.* New York: The Guilford Press.

Embretson, S. E. (1996). The new rules of measurement. *Psychological Assessment, 8*(4), 341–349.

Embretson, S. E., & Reise, S. P. (2000). *Item response theory for psychologists.* Mahwah, NJ: Erlbaum.

Engelhard, G. (2005). Item Response Theory (IRT) models for rating scale data. *Encyclopedia of Statistics in Behavioral Science, 2,* 995–1003.

Engelhard, G. (2013). *Invariant measurement: Using Rasch models in the social, behavioral, and health sciences.* New York, NY: Routledge.

Goodman, L. A. (1978). *Analyzing qualitative/categorical data: Log-linear models and latent-structure analysis.* Cambridge, MA: Abt Books.

Haberman, S. J. (1978). *Analysis of qualitative data, volume one: Introductory topics.* New York: Academic Press.

Hambleton, R. K., van der Linden, W. J., & Wells, C. S. (2010). IRT models for the analysis of polytomously scored data: Brief and selected history of model building advances. In M. L. Nering & R. Ostini (Eds.), *Handbook of polytomous item response theory models.* New York, NY: Routledge.

Linacre, J. M. (1989). *Many-facet Rasch measurement.* Chicago: MESA Press.

Lord, F. M. (1980). *Applications of item response theory to practical testing problems.* Hillsdale, NJ: Erlbaum.

Masters, G. N. (1982). A Rasch model for partial credit scoring. *Psychometrika, 47,* 149–174.

Masters, G. N. (2010). The Partial Credit Model. In M. L. Nering & R. Ostini (Eds.), *Handbook of polytomous item response theory models* (pp. 109–122). New York, NY: Routledge.

Masters, G. N. (2016). Partial credit model. In W. J. van der Linden (Ed.), *Handbook of item response theory, volume one: Models* (pp. 109–126). Boca Raton, FL: CRC Press.

Masters, G. N., & Wright, B. D. (1984). The essential process in a family of measurement models. *Psychometrika, 49,* 529–544.

McCullagh, P., & Nelder, J. (1989). *Generalized linear models* (2nd ed.). Boca Raton: Chapman and Hall/CRC.

Mellenbergh, G. J. (1995). Conceptual notes on models for discrete polytomous item responses. *Applied Psychological Measurement, 19*(1), 91–100.

Nelder, J., & Wedderburn, R. W. M. (1972). Generalized linear models. *Journal of Royal Statistical Society A, 135,* 370–384.

Nering, M. L., & Ostini, R. (2010). *Handbook of polytomous item response theory models.* New York: Routledge.

Penfield, R. D. (2014). An NCME instructional module on polytomous item response theory models. *Educational Measurement: Issues and Practice, 33*(1), 36–48.

Rasch, G. (1960/1980). *Probabilistic models for some intelligence and attainment tests.* Copenhagen: Danish Institute for Educational Research. (Expanded edition, Chicago: University of Chicago Press, 1980).

Rasch, G. (1961). On general laws and meaning of measurement in psychology. In J. Neyman (Ed.), *Proceedings of the fourth Berkeley Symposium on mathematical statistics and probability* (pp. 321–333). Berkeley: University of California Press.

Rasch, G. (1977). On specific objectivity: An attempt at formalizing the request for generality and validity of scientific statements. *Danish Yearbook of Philosophy, 14*, 58–94.

Reise, S. P., & Revicki, D. A. (Eds.). (2015). *Handbook of item response theory modeling: Applications to typical performance assessment.* New York: Routledge.

Samejima, F. (1969). Estimation of latent ability using a response pattern of graded scores. *Psychometrika Monograph, 34*(4, pt. 2), 100.

Samejima, F. (1983). Some methods and approaches for estimating the operating characteristics of discrete item responses. In H. Wainer & S. Messick (Eds.), *Principle of modern psychological measurement: A festschrift for Frederic M. Lord* (pp. 159–182). Hillsdale, NJ: Erlbaum.

Samejima, F. (1997). Graded response models. In W. J. van der Linder & R. K. Hambleton (Eds.), *Handbook of modern item response theory* (pp. 85–100). New York: Springer.

Samejima, F. (2010). The general Graded Response Model. In M. L. Nering & R. Ostini (Eds.), *Handbook of polytomous item response theory models* (pp. 77–108). New York, NY: Routledge.

Samejima, F. (2016). The graded response model. In W. J. van der Linden (Ed.), *Handbook of item response theory, volume one: Models* (pp. 95–108). Boca Raton, FL: CRC Press.

StataCorp. (2015). *Stata: Release 14: Statistical software.* College Station, TX: StataCorp LP.

Thissen, D., & Steinberg, L. (1986). A taxonomy of item response models. *Psychometrika, 51*(4), 567–577.

Thurstone, L. L. (1959). *The measurement of values.* Chicago: University of Chicago Press.

Thurstone, L. L., & Chave, E. J. (1929). *The measurement of attitude.* Chicago: University of Chicago Press.

van der Linden, W. J. (2016a). *Handbook of item response theory, volume one: Models.* Boca Raton, FL: CRC Press.

van der Linden, W. J. (2016b). *Handbook of item response theory, volume two: Statistical tools.* Boca Raton, FL: CRC Press.

van der Linden, W. J. (2016c). *Handbook of item response theory, volume three: Applications.* Boca Raton, FL: CRC Press.

Wang, J., Engelhard, G., Razynski, K., Song, T., & Wolfe, E. (2016, April). *Evaluating rater accuracy and cognition for document-based literacy assessments using IRT and stimulated-recall method.* Paper presented at annual meeting of the American Educational Research Association, Washington, DC.

Wright, B. D., & Masters, G. N. (1982). *Rating scale analysis: Rasch measurement.* Chicago: MESA Press.

10
PARAMETER ESTIMATION FOR THE POLYTOMOUS RASCH MODEL

> In order to put a measurement model to work, methods for estimating its parameters from suitable data must be developed.
>
> *(Wright, 1980, p. 188)*

This chapter focuses on selected methods for estimating parameters used with the polytomous Rasch model. As pointed out by Andrich (2015),

> the polytomous Rasch model (PRM), [is] the simplest special case of the class of adjacent category models. It has two common parameterizations, the *partial credit* and *rating scale*, which at the level of the response process of a single person to a single item are identical.
>
> *(p. 8)*

We focus on the PRM because it provides the opportunity to obtain invariant parameters when good model-data fit is obtained, and it is the preferred model for measurement that seeks to create meaningful and useful measures that can support Wright maps. The reader should recall that Wright maps are visual displays that represent the locations of persons, raters, and cues simultaneously on the same continuum that defines a latent variable or construct.

Within the context of statistical inference, estimation can be defined simply as "using data to estimate an unknown quantity" (Wasserman, 2010, p. xi). In measurement, the unknown quantities are the parameters in our measurement models. A key question is how to obtain the estimated parameters in our measurement models. There have been numerous methods suggested for estimating the parameters of IRT models. Each of the estimation methods reflects a variety of assumptions. When model-data fit is good, then the different estimation procedures tend to converge on comparable estimates of the parameters. In this book, estimation is viewed as a set of statistical procedures for locating persons and cues (e.g., domains, items, and thresholds) on the line that represents the rater-mediated latent variable. Of all of the topics in measurement, estimation depends most heavily on statistical methodology.

It should be stressed at the outset that estimation is an area of active research by many psychometricians using advanced statistical methodologies that are beyond the scope of this chapter. Our intent is to provide readers with an overview of the underlying principles and concepts that can help develop an understanding of the role of estimation in measurement. Van der Linden (2016) should be consulted for some of the latest applications of modern statistical tools to the estimation of IRT parameters. Baker and Kim (2004) offer detailed descriptions of many of the common approaches to parameter estimation. Another important point to stress is that measurement is not solely about the estimation of parameters, although it appears that statistical issues dominate much of the research in psychometrics. As pointed out by Linacre (2004a), "the challenge is no longer to estimate measures, it is to understand and communicate their meaning" (p. 69).

The basic problem in measurement is centered on the connections between observed data (e.g., ratings) and a measurement model (e.g., polytomous Rasch model) that can be used to obtain parameter estimates that reflect person locations on a construct or latent variable of interest. Figure 1.1 in Chapter One presented a visual representation of the role that measurement models play in connecting observations to inferences regarding person locations (measures) on the underlying continuum that defines the construct being measured. When rater-mediated assessments are of interest, the calibration of the cues (e.g., domains or generalized items) provides assessment opportunities for defining the construct for persons as mediated through rater judgments.

The specific issues and questions addressed in this chapter are organized as follows:

- What is parameter estimation?
- Illustration of a pairwise algorithm for rating scales
- Estimation of person locations
- Summary and discussion

What Is Parameter Estimation?

Measurement theories play a central role in guiding researchers and practitioners by defining the underlying latent variables that we are using in our research and practice. In this book, we highlight the use of Rasch Measurement Theory as the basis for models that provide a framework for achieving invariant measurement within the context of rater-mediated assessments. Once a model is specified, then the next step is to estimate the parameters in the model in order to consider how well the model-based representation of the assessment process is reflected in our observed data. Methods of estimation are designed to provide values for the parameters in our measurement models that meet criteria for maximizing the fit between the model-based expected ratings and observed ratings.

Figure 10.1 shows a way to conceptualize the role of estimation as a set of rules (numerical and statistical methods) for connecting observed data and a measurement model. Figure 10.1 illustrates how observed data on four dichotomous items can be mapped onto a line representing a continuum. The mapping of the item difficulties is called *calibration* based on the estimation of the locations of the four item parameters through a measurement model. In this case, once the item locations are estimated, then we want to infer the location of Person A on the line. Person A answered two items correctly with a score of two that reflects four observations: [1 1 0 0]. Based on the item calibrations, we can infer that Person A is located on the line between Items 2 and 3. The estimation of person location is described in detail later in this chapter.

There have been quite a few methods proposed for estimating item locations on the line used to represent the construct being measured. Engelhard (2013) described a variety of estimation methods for the dichotomous Rasch model. These methods can also be applied to the polytomous Rasch model for ratings. Linacre (2004a, 2004b) provides a detailed overview of methods for estimating parameters for both dichotomous and polytomous Rasch models. In this section, we briefly describe several estimation methods: LOG, PAIR, CMLE, MMLE, JMLE, and BAYES.

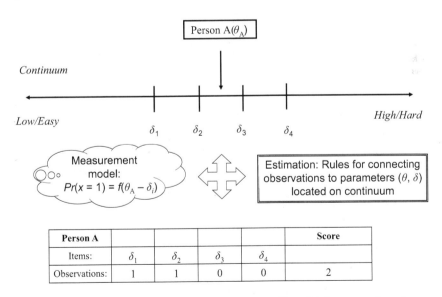

FIGURE 10.1   Location of Person A on a Continuum (Four Dichotomous Items)

LOG Method

One of the first methods of estimation proposed by Rasch (1960/1980) was presented in his chapter called *Control of the Model* (Chapter VI). Wright (1980) called this the LOG method. Rasch took the logs of the ratios of successes to failures on each test item, and then fit a linear model with no interactions to the item and score groups logits. The LOG method was the basis for graphical model-data fit analyses used by Rasch, and these displays provided an intuitively obvious way to display the invariance of item calibrations (Engelhard, 1994). As far as we know this method has not been extended for ratings, and it has not been used as an operational method for estimating the parameters of the Rasch model.

PAIR Method

The second method for item calibration proposed by Rasch (1960/1980) was the PAIR method. This method focuses on item calibration with the desirable property that "person parameters are completely removed by conditioning" (Wright, 1980, p. 188). The PAIR method analyzes items in pairs as its name suggests. Further, the method involves the creation of a pairwise count matrix (adjacency matrix) that can be used to estimate item locations by fitting a linear model using least squares or maximum likelihood estimation. The PAIR method has been extended for ratings, and it is implemented in the RUMM2030 computer program (www.rummlab.com). This method is also implemented in a simple R program called *Everyone's Rasch Measurement Analyzer* (ERMA) that has been developed by Wang and Engelhard (2014). The PAIR method is described in detail in the next section.

CMLE Method

Another method suggested by Rasch (1960/1980) for estimating item parameters is based on conditional maximum likelihood estimation (CMLE). CMLE provides a numerical approach that fully conditions out the persons from the calibration of the items. CMLE takes full advantage of the invariance properties of Rasch Measurement Theory. Andersen (1973) was a major contributor to the development of the CMLE method for estimating item parameters in Rasch Measurement Theory. The CMLE method is currently available in an R package: *Extended Rasch Modeling* (eRm).

MMLE Method

Marginal maximum likelihood estimation (MMLE) is another widely used method for item calibration. MMLE uses numerical methods, such as Gaussian quadrature, to condition out of the estimation equations an assumed distribution of persons on the latent variable. A normal distribution is typically assumed for persons, although it is also possible to use empirical estimates of the person distribution. This removes persons from the calibration of items by assuming a prior distribution of persons on the latent variable. As pointed out by Baker and Kim (2004), MMLE "involves a change from working with individual examinee data to using *artificial data*" (p. 185) based on the assumed prior distribution. A normal prior is typically used, but it is possible to use other prior distributions. Thissen (1982) describes MMLE estimation for the dichotomous Rasch model, and MMLE is used in the Conquest program (www.acer.edu.au/conquest).

JMLE Method

The most popular method for estimating parameters of the Rasch model is joint maximum likelihood estimation (JMLE). The JMLE method for Rasch Measurement Theory was introduced by Wright and Panchapakesan (1969). This estimation method iterates between item calibration and person measurement using numerical methods (e.g., Newton-Raphson) to jointly obtain parameter estimates. JMLE method is the estimation method used in the Winsteps and Facets computer programs (www.winsteps.com). When other estimation methods are used, such as PAIR and CMLE, these programs are typically used to calibrate items, and then JMLE (or more accurately MLE since the item parameters are treated as fixed) is used as separate step to estimate the person parameters.

BAYES Methods

Bayesian (BAYES) methods have emerged as a popular approach for estimating parameters in item response models. BAYES methods differ from other estimation methods because they are based on the use of prior information about the distribution of parameters in the measurement model. Essentially, BAYES methods provided a weighted combination of prior knowledge and current empirical data to obtain parameter estimates. BAYES methods are similar to JMLE methods with a uniform prior assumed for the distribution of the parameters. Johnson and Sinharay (2016) provide descriptions of various BAYES methods that have been proposed.

In summary, there are a variety of estimation methods that can be used to obtain calibrations for items, persons, and other facets. Some of the methods focus primarily on the calibration of items (PAIR, CMLE, and MMLE). Other methods provide for the simultaneous estimation of item and person parameters (JMLE and BAYES). The most commonly used method for the estimation of person parameters is JMLE with BAYES methods emerging in current theoretical work. We illustrate JMLE and BAYES estimation of person locations in a later section of this chapter.

Illustration of a Pairwise Algorithm for Rating Scales

The pairwise algorithm provides a useful approach for illustrating the estimation of item parameters within Rasch Measurement Theory. It is one of the earliest estimation methods proposed by Rasch (1960/1980), and it has been studied and used by several measurement researchers since Rasch first suggested this approach to estimation for parameters in his measurement model. Rasch (1960/1980) attributed an early pairwise algorithm to Leunbach (1976, pp. 171–172). Early research by Choppin (1968, 1985, 1987) demonstrated the desirable properties of the pairwise algorithm. It has been extended to polytomous Rasch models by Wright and Masters (1982). Garner and Engelhard (2009, 2010) extended the algorithm to estimate parameters for rater-mediated assessments. Wang and Engelhard (2014) have developed an R program using the pairwise algorithm based on the pairwise algorithm for item calibration. In this section, we provide an empirical example using the data from Chapter Nine.

Figure 10.2 shows how the dichotomization of rating scale data can also be viewed in terms of estimating and mapping item locations. In this case, we can view the ratings as generalized (G) items that are recoded based on a latent Guttman scale. For example, Person B has a score of 6 that reflects the idea that his

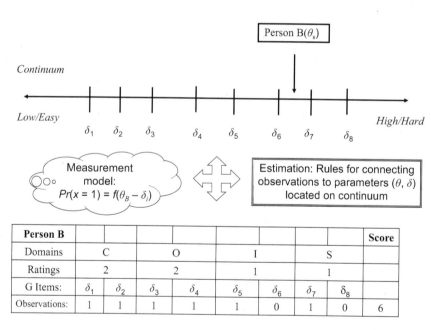

Person B									Score
Domains	C		O		I		S		
Ratings	2		2		1		1		
G Items:	δ_1	δ_2	δ_3	δ_4	δ_5	δ_6	δ_7	δ_8	
Observations:	1	1	1	1	1	0	1	0	6

FIGURE 10.2 Location of Person B on a Continuum (Four Domains with Eight Generalized Items)

Note: G items = generalized items recoded from ratings. Domains: C = Conventions, O = Organization, I = Ideas, and S = Style.

location is higher than the six generalized items. Person B received ratings of 2, 2, 1, and 1 on four domains (Conventions, Organization, Ideas, and Style), and this yields the following response pattern on the G items [1 1 1 1 0 1 0 1]. In this case, Person B is located between G items 6 and 7.

It is not necessary to actually go through the process of recoding the ratings because it "is a latent dichotomous response between the categories . . . it is the building block of adjacent category models [although] this response is never observed" (Andrich, 2015, p. 9). However, the creation of Guttman recoded G items provides a useful visualization of the calibration process to aid in understanding the pairwise approach used to estimate item parameters in this chapter.

Rasch Measurement Theory is fundamentally based on the concept of comparisons. Rasch (1977) argued that all scientific statements "deal with comparisons, and the comparisons should be objective" (p. 68). A pairwise algorithm has the didactic value and simple elegance for demonstrating the invariance properties of Rasch Measurement Theory through a comparative process. In this chapter, a program written in R (Wang & Engelhard, 2014) is used to estimate the parameters of the polytomous Rasch model that includes Partial Credit (Masters, 1982; Masters, in press), Rating Scale (Andrich, 1978), and Many-Facet (Linacre, 1989) Rasch models as special cases.

One of the advantages of the pairwise approach to estimation is that a simple counting algorithm can be used to illustrate the idea of invariant comparisons and objectivity that is fundamental to Rasch Measurement Theory (Rasch, 1977; Engelhard, 2013). In order to illustrate the pairwise algorithm, Table 10.1 shows the ratings from a single rater on four domains. These ratings can be recoded as follows:

Rating		G Items	
	Recoded	δ_1	δ_2
2		1	1
1	⟹	1	0
0		0	0

Table 10.2 shows the Guttman recoded generalized items (G matrix) based on the ordered ratings. Essentially, each ordered rating is conceptualized as a generalized item scored as separate dichotomous observations. For example, a rating of 0 is recoded as [0 0], a rating of 1 is recoded as [1 0], and a rating of 2 as [1 1].

Wilson (2005) described a framework for constructing measures that provides a description of how to develop scales based on four building blocks. Engelhard (2013) labeled these building blocks as (1) latent variable, (2) observational design, (3) scoring rules, and (4) Rasch model. The extension of these building blocks for rater-mediated assessments is presented in Chapter Twelve. The Guttman recoding used in this chapter reflects the third building block: scoring

TABLE 10.1 Observed Ratings from Table 9.1 Minus 1

Person	C	O	I	S	Sum Score
1	0	1	1	1	3
2	2	1	2	2	7
3	1	0	1	0	2
4	1	2	2	2	7
5	0	1	0	0	1
6	1	1	0	0	2
7	1	2	2	1	6
8	0	1	2	0	3
9	0	0	0	1	1
10	1	2	0	0	3
11	0	0	1	0	1
12	2	0	0	0	2
13	0	2	1	0	3
14	0	1	1	1	3
15	0	0	0	2	2
16	1	0	2	1	4
17	1	0	1	1	3
18	1	1	1	1	4
19	0	0	0	1	1
20	1	2	1	1	5
21	0	1	0	1	2
22	0	0	1	1	2
23	0	0	1	1	2
24	1	0	0	0	1
25	1	1	1	2	5
26	2	1	1	2	6
27	1	1	2	2	6
28	1	0	2	1	4
29	0	0	0	2	2
30	1	1	0	2	4
31	1	0	1	1	3
32	2	0	2	2	6
33	0	1	1	0	2
34	2	2	2	1	7
35	0	1	0	0	1
36	1	2	2	2	7
37	1	2	0	1	4
38	0	2	2	2	6
39	0	0	0	1	1
40	0	1	0	1	2

Note: Domains: C = Conventions, O = Organization, I = Ideas, and S = Style.

TABLE 10.2 Guttman Recoding of Ratings from Table 10.1 to Generalized (G) Items

Domain:	C	C	O	O	I	I	S	S	
Thresholds:	τ_{C1}	τ_{C2}	τ_{O1}	τ_{O2}	τ_{I1}	τ_{I2}	τ_{S1}	τ_{S2}	
G Items:	δ_1	δ_2	δ_3	δ_4	δ_5	δ_6	δ_7	δ_8	Sum Score
1	0	0	1	0	1	0	1	0	3
2	1	1	1	0	1	1	1	1	7
3	1	0	0	0	1	0	0	0	2
4	1	0	1	1	1	1	1	1	7
5	0	0	1	0	0	0	0	0	1
6	1	0	1	0	0	0	0	0	2
7	1	0	1	1	1	1	1	0	6
8	0	0	1	0	1	1	0	0	3
9	0	0	0	0	0	0	1	0	1
10	1	0	1	1	0	0	0	0	3
11	0	0	0	0	1	0	0	0	1
12	1	1	0	0	0	0	0	0	2
13	0	0	1	1	1	0	0	0	3
14	0	0	1	0	1	0	1	0	3
15	0	0	0	0	0	0	1	1	2
16	1	0	0	0	1	1	1	0	4
17	1	0	0	0	1	0	1	0	3
18	1	0	1	0	1	0	1	0	4
19	0	0	0	0	0	0	1	0	1
20	1	0	1	1	1	0	1	0	5
21	0	0	1	0	0	0	1	0	2
22	0	0	0	0	1	0	1	0	2
23	0	0	0	0	1	0	1	0	2
24	1	0	0	0	0	0	0	0	1
25	1	0	1	0	1	0	1	1	5
26	1	1	1	0	1	0	1	1	6
27	1	0	1	0	1	1	1	1	6
28	1	0	0	0	1	1	1	0	4
29	0	0	0	0	0	0	1	1	2
30	1	0	1	0	0	0	1	1	4
31	1	0	0	0	1	0	1	0	3
32	1	1	0	0	1	1	1	1	6
33	0	0	1	0	1	0	0	0	2
34	1	1	1	1	1	1	1	0	7
35	0	0	1	0	0	0	0	0	1
36	1	0	1	1	1	1	1	1	7
37	1	0	1	1	0	0	1	0	4
38	0	0	1	1	1	1	1	1	6
39	0	0	0	0	0	0	1	0	1
40	0	0	1	0	0	0	1	0	2

Note: G items = generalized items recoded from ratings. Domains: C = Conventions, O = Organization, I = Ideas, and S = Style.

rules extended to consider ratings. We use this Guttman recoded summary of polytomous ratings in our pairwise comparison algorithm. The basic counting algorithm underlying the pairwise algorithm, as well as least square estimates of generalized item locations, can be written in R (see Appendix 10.A).

According to Choppin (1968, 1985), if the total score of individuals is one on items i and j, b_{ij} of them get item i correct and item j wrong, and b_{ji} of them get item j correct and item i wrong, then a paired comparison matrix B can be created. The B matrix is an adjacency matrix that can be constructed with entries b_{ij}, and the transpose of matrix B is composed of entries b_{ji}.

For example in Table 10.2, there are 17 people with a rating of 1 on generalized Item 1 and a rating of 0 on generalized Item 2 based on the Guttman recoded data [1 0]. This count is shown in the adjacency matrix in Table 10.3 (Panel A). The other values in Panel A are obtained in a similar way. It is important to note that some of the non-diagonal values are zero, and that this indicates that direct comparisons do not yield useable information. Garner and Engelhard (2002) recognized that powers of the adjacency matrix (B) can be used to increase connectivity through indirect comparisons. If the adjacency matrix has zeros, then the B matrix can be raised to successive powers in order to eliminate zeroes in the adjacency matrix. This process can be continued until all of the generalized items have direct or indirect connections with each other. Panel B in Table 10.3 shows the B^2 matrix. After squaring the B matrix, there are no longer any zeros in the off diagonals of the B^2 matrix.

The D matrix (Panel C in Table 10.3) is obtained by dividing the transpose of the B^2 matrix by B^2, which is the ratio of b_{ji}/b_{ij}. By taking the logarithm of these ratios, a logit matrix (Table 10.4) is created with all the relative difficulties between each pair of generalized items as entries. The generalized item difficulties can then be summarized by calculating the means across the rows. The rater severities, item difficulties, and threshold values can be estimated by taking average values of these generalized item difficulties across items, raters, and thresholds, respectively.

Table 10.5 provides a summary of the ERMA analyses for the generalized items. In order to validate the algorithm implemented in R, we compared the ERMA analyses with the results from the Facets computer program. Table 10.6 shows the unstandardized and standardized estimates of the rater, item, and threshold parameters from both computer programs. The differences in the obtained estimates are quite small (mean is zero), and this indicates good conformity between parameters estimated from ERMA and the Facets computer program.

The pairwise algorithm provides an elegant and effective approach for teaching the basic principles of Rasch Measurement Theory. By simply counting the number of comparisons between observations, an adjacency matrix can be formed that can be used to obtain parameter estimates for raters, items, and thresholds. When there is good model-data fit, then there is a close correspondence between the item locations obtained with ERMA and the Facets computer program.

TABLE 10.3 Pairwise Matrices for Generalized Items

Panel A
Adjacency Matrix: B

G Items:	1	2	3	4	5	6	7	8
1	0	17	8	15	6	13	5	14
2	0	0	2	4	1	2	1	2
3	10	21	0	15	8	16	7	16
4	2	8	0	0	2	4	2	6
5	9	21	9	18	0	14	5	17
6	2	8	3	6	0	0	1	5
7	12	25	12	22	9	19	0	18
8	3	8	3	8	3	5	0	0

Panel B
Adjacency Matrix Squared: B^2

G Items:	1	2	3	4	5	6	7	8
1	292	755	229	596	198	471	146	509
2	59	152	33	98	39	91	29	101
3	266	889	374	756	222	557	157	614
4	68	206	104	214	56	138	32	134
5	265	859	267	684	279	555	179	580
6	69	210	59	169	80	158	51	146
7	337	1117	338	880	291	702	277	790
8	83	281	82	206	66	177	80	230

Panel C
Ratio Matrix: $D = (B^2)'/B^2$

G Items:	1	2	3	4	5	6	7	8
1	1.000	0.078	1.162	0.114	1.338	0.146	2.31	0.163
2	12.797	1.000	26.939	2.102	22.026	2.308	38.52	2.782
3	0.861	0.037	1.000	0.138	1.203	0.106	2.15	0.134
4	8.765	0.476	7.269	1.000	12.214	1.225	27.50	1.537
5	0.747	0.045	0.831	0.082	1.000	0.144	1.63	0.114
6	6.826	0.433	9.441	0.817	6.938	1.000	13.76	1.212
7	0.433	0.026	0.464	0.036	0.615	0.073	1.00	0.101
8	6.133	0.359	7.488	0.650	8.788	0.825	9.88	1.000

Estimation of Person Locations

Measurement can be defined as the procedures used for estimating person locations on a continuum developed to represent the latent variable. In this section, several approaches that are commonly used for estimating person locations are described. All of the estimation methods in this section treat the generalized (G) item locations as defined in advance. It is also important to note that G item locations are usually estimated with more precision than person parameters because there is

TABLE 10.4 Pairwise Estimates from ERMA Computer Program

	C		O		I		S		
G Items:	δ_1	δ_2	δ_3	δ_4	δ_5	δ_6	δ_7	δ_8	
Thresholds:	τ_{C1}	τ_{C2}	τ_{O1}	τ_{O2}	τ_{I1}	τ_{I2}	τ_{S1}	τ_{S2}	
	1	2	3	4	5	6	7	8	Mean
1	0.000	−2.549	0.150	−2.171	0.291	−1.921	0.836	−1.814	−0.897
2	2.549	0.000	3.294	0.743	3.092	0.836	3.651	1.023	1.899
3	−0.150	−3.294	0.000	−1.984	0.185	−2.245	0.767	−2.013	−1.092
4	2.171	−0.743	1.984	0.000	2.503	0.203	3.314	0.430	1.233
5	−0.291	−3.092	−0.185	−2.503	0.000	−1.937	0.486	−2.173	−1.212
6	1.921	−0.836	2.245	−0.203	1.937	0.000	2.622	0.193	0.985
7	−0.836	−3.651	−0.767	−3.314	−0.486	−2.622	0.000	−2.290	−1.746
8	1.814	−1.023	2.013	−0.430	2.173	−0.193	2.290	0.000	0.831

Note: Cell entries are $ln(D)$. C = Conventions, O = Organization, I = Ideas, and S = Style.

TABLE 10.5 Summary of ERMA Analyses

G Items	Domain	Threshold	Measures	SEM	Infit	Outfit
1	C	1	−0.897	0.383	0.902	0.917
2		2	1.899	0.508	0.894	1.050
3	O	1	−1.092	0.383	1.124	1.169
4		2	1.233	0.460	1.073	0.813
5	I	1	−1.212	0.384	0.878	0.718
6		2	0.985	0.445	0.725	0.516
7	S	1	−1.746	0.396	0.980	0.728
8		2	0.831	0.437	0.949	0.977

Note: C = Conventions, O = Organization, I = Ideas, and S = Style.

typically more information (number of persons) available for G item parameter estimation as compared to the estimation of person measures (number of G items).

Glas (2016) has identified two broad categories of estimators that reflect two major paradigms in statistics: frequentist and Bayesian approaches. Frequentist approaches are based on observed data, while Bayesian approaches typically include prior distributions based on the researcher judgments. The two most common frequentist approaches for estimating person locations are the maximum likelihood estimation (MLE; Wright & Panchapakesan, 1969) and weighted maximum likelihood estimation (WMLE; Warm, 1989). The two most common Bayesian approaches are maximum *a posteriori* (MAP) estimation and expected *a posteriori* (EAP) estimation. Bock and Mislevy (1982) provide an excellent description of these Bayesian estimation methods in the context of computer adaptive testing. The reader should be

TABLE 10.6 Comparison of Estimates from Facets and ERMA Computer Programs

	Domains		Domains Centered		Difference
	ERMA	Facets	ERMA	Facets	
Conventions	0.50	0.62	1.45	1.56	−0.11
Organization	0.07	0.04	0.20	0.10	0.10
Ideas	−0.11	−0.20	−0.32	−0.50	0.18
Style	−0.46	−0.45	−1.33	−1.14	−0.19
Mean	0.00	0.00	0.00	0.01	−0.00
SD	0.35	0.40	1.00	1.00	0.17
	Thresholds		Thresholds Centered		Difference
	ERMA	Facets	ERMA	Facets	
Conventions	−1.40	−1.28	−1.05	−1.20	0.15
Organization	1.40	1.28	1.05	1.20	−0.15
	−1.16	−0.85	−0.87	−0.79	−0.08
Ideas	1.16	0.85	0.87	0.79	0.08
	−1.10	−0.68	−0.83	−0.64	−0.19
Style	1.10	0.68	0.83	0.64	0.19
	−1.29	−1.09	−0.97	−1.02	0.05
	1.29	1.09	0.97	1.02	−0.05
Mean	0.00	0.00	0.00	0.00	0.00
SD	1.33	1.07	1.00	1.00	0.14

Note: Mean overall differences are .00.

cautious about the strict categorization of estimation methods as frequentist or Bayesian approaches because the numerical methods are similar. Even though there are some strong philosophical differences between these two approaches, actual assessment practices freely borrow and use both frequentist and Bayesian ideas.

MLE Method

Maximum likelihood estimation uses an iterative process for estimating person locations. Person estimation is the person part of the *joint* maximum likelihood estimation of person and item locations. In this section, the item locations are treated as known a priori.

Generalized item response functions can be used to obtain a likelihood function. Since the Rasch model requires local independence given each person's location, the probabilities of a correct or positive response can be multiplied to obtain the likelihood function. For the generalized items, the conditional probability of observing a response pattern (*P*) is

$$P = \prod_{i=1}^{L} P_i^{x_i} \left(1 - P_i\right)^{1-x_i} \tag{10.1}$$

where x_i represents the rating for a person to generalized item i with $x = 1$ for a positive response and $x = 0$ for a negative response, P_i is the conditional probability of a correct response ($x = 1$) based on the Rasch model, and L is the number of generalized items. Since the generalized item parameters are defined as known in this section, the likelihood of observing a particular response pattern can be obtained from Equation 10.1. There are several numerical approaches for estimating parameters, and Baker and Kim (2004) describe in great detail many of these approaches for estimating item and person parameters.

Figure 10.3 provides a graphical display of the MLE method with the eight generalized items. The top panel in Figure 10.4 shows the generalized item response functions, while the lower panel in Figure 10.4 shows the likelihood based on the product of these functions. Essentially, MLE of person locations involves summarizing this likelihood function shown in the lower panel of the figure. For example, a good estimate for location of Person A is to use the mode of the likelihood distribution shown in the lower panel in Figure 10.4. The amount of spread in the likelihood distribution can also be used to estimate the standard error of measurement.

WMLE (Warm, 1989) is also frequently used to estimate person locations. In this case, a weighted likelihood function is used.

Bayesian Methods

As pointed out by Glas (2016), the second broad category of estimators utilizes Bayesian methods. The two approaches to estimation illustrated here are MAP and EAP. Once suitable estimates are available to define the locations of the generalized items on the line, the next measurement task is to obtain estimates of person locations on the line. In general, the calibration of items is based on many more data points (number of persons) than the measurement of persons (number of items). In this section, we treat item locations as known with the measurement

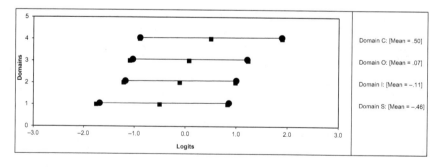

FIGURE 10.3 Maximum Likelihood Estimation: Generalized Item Response Functions and Likelihood Function

Note: Domains: C = Conventions, O = Organization, I = Ideas, and S = Style

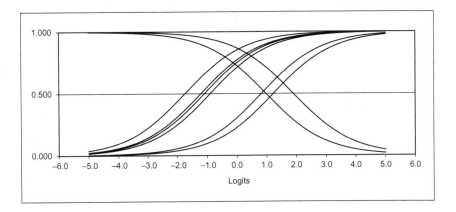

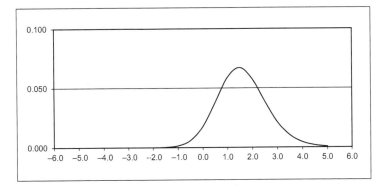

FIGURE 10.4 Maximum Likelihood Estimation: Generalized Item Response Functions and Likelihood Function

task defined as locating a person on the line. As pointed out by Wainer and Mislevy (1990), the "maximum likelihood estimator is just a Bayes Modal estimator with a uniform prior" (p. 72).

The MAP estimator follows a form that is similar to MLE. Figure 10.5 illustrates the relationship between the estimators. In Panel A of Figure 10.4, the researcher specifies a prior distribution for a person's location, while Panel B shows the generalized item response functions. Panel C shows the likelihood function based on the responses to a set of calibrated items. The posterior distribution in Panel D is based on the product of the prior and likelihood functions. As pointed out earlier, the MAP estimates are equivalent to the MLE with a uniform prior. The last aspect of the estimation task is to summarize the posterior distribution, and the expected mode is used for the MAP estimator.

Probably the most commonly used estimator of person locations is the EAP estimator. EAP differs from MAP in terms of how the posterior distribution in Panel D is summarized. For EAP, the mean of the posterior distribution is used as the estimate for a person's location on the continuum. Bock and Mislevy (1982)

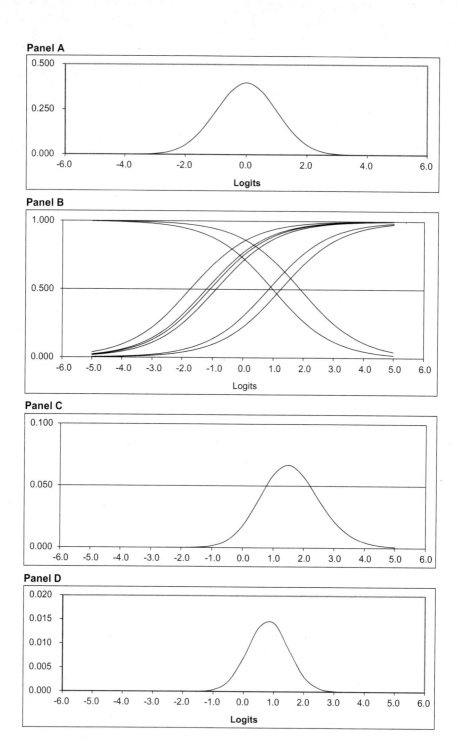

FIGURE 10.5 Bayesian Estimation: Prior, Generalized Item Response Functions, Likelihood Function and Posterior

provide a clear treatment of the numerical methods that can be used for both MAP and EAP estimation.

In summary, there are a variety of estimation methods that can be adapted for estimating the location of a person on the line when the calibrations of the item difficulties are fixed and viewed as known values. In this chapter, we briefly focused on the most popular methods: maximum likelihood (ML), weighted maximum likelihood (WML), maxiumum a posteriori (MAP; Bock & Aitkin, 1981), and expected a posteriori (EAP; Bock & Aitkin, 1981) estimators.

Summary and Discussion

> The implementation of item response theory rests on the statistical techniques for estimating the parameters of test items and of examinee ability.
>
> *(Baker & Kim, 2004, p. xi)*

There are several major points that we would like to stress related to this chapter. First of all, various methods of parameter estimation draw heavily on statistical methods. There are many recent advances in statistical methods, with many new approaches being invented for use with Item Response Theory, and this remains an area of active research in psychometrics. Second, it is important to note that various statistical methods tend to produce comparable parameter estimates under conditions where good model-data fit is achieved. The estimation of parameters for the polytomous Rasch model can be approached by several different statistical procedures. The estimation of item locations is typically called *item calibration*, while the estimation of person locations is usually labeled *measurement*. We view estimation as a set of rules used to estimate parameters in measurement models that reflect the locations of generalized items and persons on a latent continuum.

Another point that we would like to stress is that within the context of rater-mediated assessments, it is important to highlight that we are actually modeling the judgments of raters. It is essential that researchers be careful in their language related to rater-mediated assessments because all of the facets of the measurement model are based on ratings obtained from a human rater. For example, the difficulty of a generalized item is based on a rater's perspective, and it is more accurate to refer to the locations as *judged difficulties*. If the raters had been trained in a different way, then the locations can vary based on the cognitive frame of reference embedded in the assessment system. Theoretically, expert raters should be able to move between different frames of reference.

In closing this chapter, it should be recognized that estimation is closely connected to methods for examining model-data fit described in the next chapter. Chapter Eleven describes the next steps in the process regarding how well the data fit the model. Model-data fit provides guidance on aspects of the assessment system that may have failed to function as intended.

References

Andersen, E. B. (1973). A goodness of fit test for the Rasch model. *Psychometrika, 38*(1), 123–140. https://doi.org/10.1007/BF02291180

Andrich, D. A. (1978). A rating formulation for ordered response categories. *Psychometrika, 43*, 561–573.

Andrich, D. A. (2015). The problem with the step metaphor for polytomous models for ordinal assessments. *Educational Measurement Issues and Practice, 34*(2), 8–14.

Baker, F. B., & Kim, S. (2004). *Item response theory: Parameter estimation techniques* (2nd ed., Revised and Expanded). New York: Marcel Dekker.

Bock, R. D., & Aitkin, M. (1981). Marginal maximum likelihood estimation of item parameters: Application of an EM algorithm. *Psychometrika, 46*, 443–459.

Bock, R. D., & Mislevy, R. J. (1982). Adaptive EAP estimation of ability in a microcomputer environment. *Applied Psychological Measurement, 6*, 431–444.

Choppin, B. (1968). Item banking using sample free calibration. *Nature, 219*, 870–872.

Choppin, B. (1985). A fully conditional estimation procedure for Rasch model parameters. *Evaluation in Education, 9*, 29–42.

Choppin, B. (1987). The Rasch model for item analysis. In D. I. McArthur (Ed.), *Alternative approaches to the assessment of achievement* (pp. 99–127). Norwell, MA: Kluwer.

Engelhard, G. (1994). Historical views of the concept of invariance in measurement theory. In M. Wilson (Ed.), *Objective measurement: Theory into practice* (Vol. 2, pp. 73–99). Norwood, NJ: Ablex.

Engelhard, G. (2013). *Invariant measurement: Using Rasch models in the social, behavioral, and health sciences.* New York: Routledge.

Garner, M., & Engelhard, G. (2002). An eigenvector method for estimating item parameters of the dichotomous and polytomous Rasch models. *Journal of Applied Measurement, 3*(2), 107–128.

Garner, M., & Engelhard, G. (2009). Using paired comparison matrices to estimate parameters of the partial credit Rasch measurement model for rater-mediated assessments. *Journal of Applied Measurement, 10*(1), 30–41.

Garner, M., & Engelhard, G. (2010). Extension of the pairwise algorithm to the rating scale and partial credit models. In M. Garner, G. Engelhard, M. Wilson, & W. Fisher (Eds.), *Advances in Rasch measurement* (Vol. 1, pp. 45–63). Maple Grove, MN: JAM Press.

Glas, C.A.W. (2016). Frequentist model-fit tests. In W. J. van der Linden (Ed.), *Handbook of item response theory, volume two: Statistical tools* (pp. 343–361). Boca Raton, FL: CRC Press.

Johnson, M. S., & Sinharay, S. (2016). Bayesian estimation. In W. J. van der Linden (Ed.), *Handbook of item response theory, volume two: Statistical tools* (pp. 237–257). Boca Raton, FL: CRC Press.

Leunbach, G. (1976). *A probabilistic measurement model for assessing whether two tests measure the same personal factor (Technical report 1976.19).* Copenhagen, Denmark: The Danish Institute of Educational Research.

Linacre, J. M. (1989). *Many-facet Rasch measurement.* Chicago: MESA Press.

Linacre, J. M. (2004a). Estimation methods for Rasch measures. In E. V. Smith & R. M. Smith (Eds.), *Introduction to Rasch measurement: Theory, models, and applications* (pp. 25–47). Maple Grove, MN: JAM Press.

Linacre, J. M. (2004b). Rasch model estimation: Further topics. In E. V. Smith & R. M. Smith (Eds.), *Introduction to Rasch measurement: Theory, models, and applications* (pp. 48–72). Maple Grove, MN: JAM Press.

Linacre, J. M. (2015). *Facets Rasch Measurement* (Version 3.71.4). Chicago, IL: Winsteps.com.

Masters, G. N. (1982). A Rasch model for partial credit scoring. *Psychometrika, 47*, 149–174.

Masters, G. N. (2016). Partial credit model. In W. J. van der Linden (Ed.), *Handbook of item response theory, volume two: Models* (pp. 109–137). Boca Raton, FL: CRC Press.

Mislevy, R. J. (1986). Bayes modal estimation in item response models. *Psychometrika, 51*, 177–195.

Rasch, G. (1960/1980). *Probabilistic models for some intelligence and attainment tests.* Copenhagen: Danish Institute for Education Research. (Reprinted, Chicago: University of Chicago Press, 1980).

Rasch, G. (1977). On specific objectivity: An attempt at formalizing the request for generality and validity of scientific statements. *Danish Yearbook of Philosophy, 14*, 58–94.

Thissen, D. (1982). Marginal maximum likelihood estimation for the one-parameter logistic model. *Psychometrika, 47*, 175–186.

van der Linden, W. J. (2016). *Handbook of item response theory, volume two: Statistical tools.* Boca Raton, FL: CRC Press.

Wainer, H., & Mislevy, R. J. (1990). Item response theory, item calibration, and proficiency estimation. In H. Wainer (Ed.), *Computerized adaptive testing: A primer* (pp. 65–102). Hillsdale, NJ: Erlbaum.

Wang, J., & Engelhard, G. (2014). A pairwise algorithm in *R* for rater-mediated assessments. *Rasch Measurement Transactions, 28*(1), 1457–1459.

Warm, T. A. (1989). Weighted likelihood estimation of ability in item response theory. *Psychometrika, 54*(23), 427–450.

Wasserman, L. (2010). *All of statistics: A concise course on statistical inference.* New York, NY: Springer.

Wilson, M. (2005). *Constructing measures: An item response modeling approach* (2nd ed.). Mahwah, NJ: Erlbaum.

Wright, B. D. (1980). Afterword. *Probabilistic models for some intelligence and attainment tests* (Expanded ed., pp. 185–196). Chicago: University of Chicago Press.

Wright, B. D., & Masters, G. N. (1982). *Rating scale analysis: Rasch measurement.* Chicago: MESA Press.

Wright, B. D., & Panchapakesan, N. (1969). A procedure for sample-free item analysis. *Educational and Psychological Measurement, 29*, 23–48.

APPENDIX 10.A

R syntax

```
#Clear variables
rm(list=ls())

x <- read.table ("c:\\Users/George/Dropbox/Data/C10 Guttman recoded.csv",header=
  TRUE,sep=",")
x <- x[,-1]

Nperson <- dim(x)[1]
Nitem <- dim(x)[2]

B <- matrix(0, Nitem, Nitem)
for(k in 1:Nperson){
  for(i in 1:Nitem){
    for(j in 1:Nitem){
      if(is.na(x[k,i])==FALSE & is.na(x[k,j])==FALSE){
      if(x[k,i]>x[k,j]){B[i,j] <- B[i,j]+1} } } } }

B2 <- B %*% B

D <- t(B2)/B2
Logit <- log(D)
Items <-colMeans(Logit)
Items
```

PART V
Practical Issues

11

MODEL-DATA FIT FOR POLYTOMOUS RATING SCALE MODELS

A model is never true, but only more or less adequate.

(Rasch, 1960/1980, p. 92)

A framework for evaluating model-data fit can be built on residual analyses (Wells & Hambleton, 2016). The idea of residual analyses has a long history in statistics (Anscombe & Tukey, 1963). The basic structure for rater-mediated assessments with ratings can be presented as follows:

Observed ratings = Expected ratings + Residual ratings

The observed ratings are obtained from rater judgments based on a set of person performances (e.g., written essays) with expected ratings obtained from fitting a measurement model (e.g., polytomous Rasch model). The residual ratings reflect the differences between observed ratings and the model-based expectations based on the measurement model for the ratings. A variety of analytic methods have been proposed for summarizing these differences, including numerical and graphical approaches. For example, the traditional chi-squared statistic (Pearson, 1900) has been adapted to quantify the significance of the differences between observed and expected responses in Item Response Theory (Glas, 2016).

Engelhard (2013) described model-data fit analyses for dichotomous items, and this chapter extends many of these ideas for ratings. The situation is more complex within the context of measurement based on rater-mediated assessments. Rater-mediated assessments are multifaceted (e.g., domains, tasks, and raters), and the locations of the parameters reflecting these multiple facets are based on rater judgments. It is essential to recognize that the locations are *judged locations*, and that different rater training protocols may lead to different locations yielding different definitions of the construct.

The specific issues and questions addressed in this chapter are organized as follows:

- What is model-data fit?
- Conceptual framework for model-data fit with rater-mediated assessments

    1. What are the requirements of invariant measurement for raters?
    2. How can we diagnose model-data misfit?

- Approaches for augmenting residual analyses of model-data fit
- Illustrative analyses
- Summary and discussion

What Is Model-Data Fit?

> All models are wrong; the practical question is how wrong do they have to be not to be useful.
>
> *(Box & Draper, 1987, p. 74)*

In Item Response Theory, it is widely recognized that good model-data fit is essential in order to obtain the invariant properties that are the hallmark of these measurement models. As pointed out by Wells and Hambleton (2016),

> The advantages and attractive features of IRT are based on the invariance property . . . the invariance property only holds when the assumptions of the specific IRT model are satisfied. As a result, evaluating the fit of an IRT model is an important step in any situation where an IRT model is being applied.
>
> *(p. 395)*

Although there are a variety of approaches for examining model-data fit, this book focuses on the use of residual analyses. Anscombe and Tukey (1963) point out several additional steps that are possible after the individual residuals are calculated:

(1) The relationship of the residuals to external variables [can be examined],
(2) All the residuals from a given body of data can be examined en bloc,
(3) The individual residuals can be plotted against individual fitted values . . . or against values computed from the whole table of fitted values, and
(4) Groups of residuals from different parts of the data can be used to indicate differences in variability of response in these parts.

> *(p. 142)*

In this chapter, we focus primarily on the procedure outlined in Step (4), which provides diagnostic information regarding different facets of rater-mediated assessments that define parts of the data that may not be functioning as intended.

There are at least three components to consider when discussing model-data fit from the perspective of residual analyses. These include the measurement model, the data, and the analytic procedures used to summarize the correspondence between the expected ratings obtained based on a measurement model and observed rating data.

Measurement Model

In this book, we have stressed the requirements for obtaining invariant measurement with raters. Chapter One described these requirements, and we have focused on the polytomous Rasch model (Chapter Ten) as an example of a measurement model that provides the opportunity for invariant rater-mediated assessments. The requirements reflect the quest for scales that define a continuum representing a latent variable of interest—this latent variable or construct is visually represented as a Wright map. For example, Figure 1.8 illustrated an intended Wright map for writing assessment, while Figure 1.10 presents an implemented (i.e., empirical) Wright map that is revisited in this chapter. The overall goal of rater-mediated assessments is to provide a rater-invariant Wright map with persons, cues (items), rating categories, and raters simultaneously located on the line.

Once the parameters of the measurement model have been estimated and used to construct a Wright map, the next component involves determining if the measurement model, including the visual representation embodied in the Wright map, is *a good fit* for understanding the observed data. It is important to recognize that the Rasch model was developed to define invariant measurement, and that model-data fit is inherently sample-dependent. Within the context of invariant measurement with raters, it is also important to recognize that the invariance properties are built into the Rasch model by definition.

Data

In measurement situations with raters, the data represent observed ratings that are collected based on a careful design to obtain information regarding person locations on the latent variable (see Chapter Twelve for guidelines on building rater-mediated assessment systems). Even when rating designs are carefully planned and implemented, there may still be quality control issues encountered with observed ratings. In fact, it is important to recognize that the observed data may not support our inferences based on the model. As pointed out by Wright and Stone (1979),

> The model is constructed to govern our use of data according to the characteristics we require of a measure and to show us, through the exposure of discrepancies between intention and experience, where our efforts to measure are threatened.
>
> *(p. 91)*

The discrepancies between *intention* and *experience* are exactly what residual analyses are intended to reveal. The process of diagnosing misfit situations requires a deep understanding of the construct as well as the context for obtaining the ratings. In order to diagnosis sources of misfit, there are a variety of tools that can be used, such as the residual analyses described in this chapter. However, the interpretation of the residuals as reflecting misfit cannot be accomplished without a grounded understanding of the assessment system and its context.

Procedures for Examining Model-Data Fit

Turning now to the third component, the field of statistics includes a long history of procedures, such as chi-squared statistics, that can be used to summarize the correspondence or fit between models with expected ratings, and observations or ratings based upon fallible data (Pearson, 1900; Stigler, 1999). There are two major ways to present model-data fit: numerical and graphical displays. Although chi-squared statistics are used in psychometric contexts, it is well known there are several drawbacks to the use of chi-squared statistics (Wells & Hambleton, 2016). It is our considered judgment that residual-based approaches are promising for diagnosing misfit, and that developing meaningful and useful interpretations of residual ratings can lead to improvements in the quality of ratings obtained in rater-mediated assessments.

Figure 11.1 (Panel A) displays the basic structure of the decomposition of the observed ratings. Panel B in Figure 11.1 shows the definitions of the matrices.

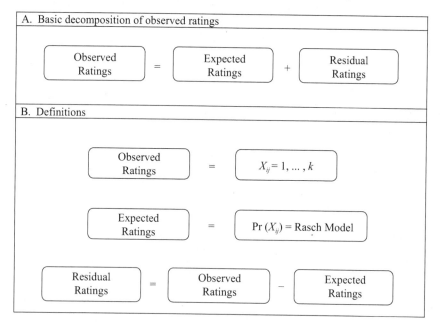

FIGURE 11.1   Conceptual Framework for Model-Data Fit

Note: X_{ij} is the rating for person i on generalized item j.

The observed ratings can be represented as a row-by-column table with rows representing the persons being measured and columns representing various combinations of assessment components (cues) used by the raters to form their judgments reflected in the observed ratings. The expected ratings are based on the polytomous Rasch model with a variety of facets added as required by the particular assessment system. Finally, the residual ratings are obtained by subtracting residual ratings from the observed ratings.

Once the residuals are obtained, there are a variety of strategies that can be used for examining them. In some cases, it is informative to consider the use of standardized residuals obtained by dividing the residual ratings by estimates of the standard errors of the residuals. Residual analyses form the framework for examining the requirements of invariant measurement and diagnosing aspects of the assessment system that may not be functioning as intended by the researchers.

Wells and Hambleton (2016) focused on residuals related to items, but the same principles can be extended to raters within rater-mediated assessment systems. In order to illustrate the basic idea, we use Person 33 (MSE = 1.54, Fit Category = C) from Table 11.8. The observed, expected, residual, and standardized residuals (Z) ratings are shown below:

Observed	1	2	2	1	3	2	3	2	2	2	3	2
Expected	2.05	2.22	2.14	2.27	1.88	2.05	1.97	2.10	1.95	2.13	2.04	2.17
Residual	−1.05	−0.22	−0.14	−1.27	1.12	−0.05	1.03	−0.10	0.05	−0.13	0.96	−0.17
Z		−1.83	−0.39	−0.24	−2.22	1.96	−0.09	1.79	−0.17	0.09	−0.22	1.67	−0.30

For example, the largest standardized residual (Z) is − 2.22 for Person 33, and this unexpected rating was obtained from Rater 1 on the Domain of Style. These data are explored in more detail later in the section on data analyses.

Different rules of thumb have been proposed for evaluating model-data fit indices based on mean square errors. For example, Wright and Linacre (1994) have proposed two sets of guidelines for reasonable mean-square fit values. Based on these recommendations and our experiences with rater-mediated assessment in a variety of contexts, we propose the guidelines and labels for mean square error statistics for rater-mediated assessments shown in Table 11.1. We also propose category labels that can be used to provide a shorthand way to summarize model-data fit.

It should be noted that several researchers have highlighted the limitations of Rasch residual fit statistics (Karabatsos, 2000). There are other forms of residuals that can be used with improved statistical properties (Haberman, 2009), but the general approach advocated in this chapter is comparable regardless of the exact form of the standardized residuals. It is also important to note once more that no single model-data fit statistic can detect all the ways that measurement

TABLE 11.1 Requirements of Invariant Measurement with Raters

Requirements	Questions	Evidence
1. Rater-Invariant Measurement of Persons		
The measurement of persons must be independent of the particular raters that happen to be used in the assessment.	Does a more able person always have a better chance of a higher rating than a less able person?	MSE statistics Non-crossing person response functions
2. Rater-Invariant Calibration of Cues		
The calibration of the cues must be independent of the particular raters used in the assessment.	Does every person have a better chance of a higher rating on an easy cue than on a more difficult cue?	MSE statistics Non-crossing cue response functions
3. Rater-Invariant Calibration of Rating Scales		
The structure of the rating categories must be independent of the particular raters used in the assessment.	Does every person have a better chance of a higher rating on a lower category than on a higher category?	MSE statistics Non-crossing category functions
4. Invariant Locations of Raters		
The locations of raters must be independent of the particular persons, cues, and rating scales used in the assessment.	Does every person have a better chance of success from a lenient rater than a more severe rater?	MSE statistics Non-crossing rater response functions
5. Rater-Invariant Wright Map		
Persons, cues, and rating scales must be simultaneously located on the Wright map regardless of raters.	Do raters share a common interpretation and use of persons, cues, and rating scales represented by the Wright map?	MSE statistics Non-crossing response functions for all facets

can go wrong. Karabatsos (2000) makes a sound recommendation based on using counts of Guttman responses errors, but he does not recognize that Rasch fit statistics also reflect Guttman's ideal-type perspective by using a probabilistic rather than using Guttman's deterministic framework. Infit and Outfit are essentially summaries of probabilistic Guttman error counts as shown in Engelhard and Perkins (2013).

Wells and Hambleton (2016) point out that "since no parametric model will fit real data, testing a null hypothesis without any specific alternative is often meaningless" (p. 411). If a formal statistical test is desired, then current research suggests that the root integrated squared error (RISE) statistic is a promising approach (Douglas & Cohen, 2001; Wells & Hambleton, 2016). The RISE statistic is a non-parametric approach for diagnosing misfit that includes both numerical and graphical approaches with empirical sampling distributions for statistically testing fit. It is beyond the scope of this chapter to describe this approach in detail.

In the next section, we focus on how this conception of residuals can be used to evaluate model-data fit within the context of rater-mediated assessments.

Model-Data Fit for Rater-Mediated Assessments

> There is no reason to suppose that the ideal conditions are ever satisfied exactly in practice . . . we are concerned with detecting and measuring certain sorts of departure from the ideal conditions, conveniently labeled "misbehaviors."
>
> *(Anscombe & Tukey, 1963, p. 144)*

We conceptualize model-data fit in terms of how well each of the requirements for invariant measurement are met within the observed dataset. The Rasch model reflects what can be considered *ideal conditions* for achieving invariant measurement. In this case, we are using the concept of ideal type in the sense of the German sociologist and methodologist Max Weber (Engelhard & Perkins, 2013). In other words, we start with a model and theory that describes measurement with desirable properties based on invariant measurement (e.g., rater-invariant person measurement), and then we determine how well the data fit the model that embodies these optimal characteristics. Table 11.1 presents the ideal requirements for rater-invariant measurement, the underlying questions reflected in these requirements, and graphical displays that can be used to evaluate invariance related to various facets of the assessment system. These requirements were also presented in Chapter One. Residual analyses (numerical/statistical and graphical) can be used to provide evidence regarding *misbehaviors* related to each requirement for invariant measurement.

The first requirement is related to the measurement of persons. As pointed out frequently in this book, person measures in the context of a rater-mediated assessment system reflect *judged locations* of persons on the linear continuum that reflects the latent variable. In order to inform the interpretation and use of estimates of judged person locations, it is important to evaluate model-data fit for persons. Ultimately, rater-mediated assessments are used to make decisions about individuals, and it is important to evaluate person fit. Assessment systems are designed to provide information about persons that define their locations on a latent variable. Person locations represent the measures that we use when applying the scores obtained on the basis of our assessment system. There are four key aspects of person measurement. Specifically, these are the:

- Estimation of a person's location,
- Estimation of uncertainty in a person's location,

- Examination of person fit (numerically), and
- Diagnosis of potential sources of person misfit (graphically).

The second requirement is to explore whether or not the locations of the cues are invariant across raters. This requirement can be evaluated using both numerical (MSE statistics) and graphical techniques. The discussion of rater fit can be extended to look at how raters interpret and use the cues intended to define the construct. It is important to remember that the data being modeled are actually rater judgments.

The third requirement reflects the invariant functioning of the structure of the rating scale. As with other components of the assessment system, it is required that each of the raters interpret the meaning of the rating categories in the same way. As with other approaches to examining aspects of model-data fit, we can use both numerical and graphical methods for exploring how raters interpret the rating structure. Chapter Twelve describes a variety of additional ways for exploring the functioning of rating scales that augment the use of model-data fit described in this chapter.

The fourth requirement is related to invariant locations of raters across persons, cues, and rating scales used in the assessment. This requirement can be evaluated using MSE statistics for raters, as well as graphical techniques based on response functions for individual raters. When raters are used to define the construct, it is important that different raters share the same conceptualization of the cues and other indicators that are used to define the line. One way to obtain this evidence is examine whether or not rater response functions cross (Engelhard & Perkins, 2013; Wind & Engelhard, 2014). Individual fit plots of each rater that include observed and expected ratings as well as residual plots can provide diagnostic tools to evaluate the quality of the Wright map across raters. For example, model-data fit can be an issue when considering adjustments for differences in rater severity. Wind and Engelhard (2014) have illustrated how rater adjustments may not be valid when rater response functions cross.

The fifth requirement is related to the development of a *rater-invariant Wright map*. As pointed out frequently in this book, measurement can be viewed as the development and use of a line that is designed to represent a construct or latent variable of interest. The Wright map embodies the calibration of the persons, cues, rating scale categories, and raters on the logit scale that represents the construct. Accordingly, evidence of model-data fit for each of the facets provides evidence to support the interpretation and use of the Wright map.

In the next section, we illustrate model-data fit analyses for rater-mediated assessments using data from Chapter One.

Data Analyses

The data analyzed in this section are shown in Table 11.2. The log-odds format for the polytomous Rasch model with three facets for these data can be written as:

TABLE 11.2 Guidelines for Interpreting *Mean Square Error (MSE)*

Mean Square Error (MSE)	*Interpretation*	*Fit Category*
$50 \leq MSE < 1.50$	Productive for measurement	A
$MSE < .50$	Less productive for measurement, but not distorting of measures	B
$1.50 \leq MSE < 2.00$	Unproductive for measurement, but not distorting of measures	C
$MSE \geq 2.00$	Unproductive for measurement, distorting of measures	D

$$ln\left(\frac{P_{nmik}}{P_{nmik-1}}\right) = \theta_n - \lambda_m - \delta_i - \tau_k \tag{11.1}$$

where

P_{nmik} = probability of person n being rated k on domain i by rater m,
P_{nmik-1} = probability of person n being rated $k - 1$ on domain i by rater m,
θ_n = judged location of person n,
λ_m = severity of rater m,
δ_i = judged difficulty of domain i, and
τ_k = judged difficulty of rating category k relative to category $k - 1$.

The data analyses were conducted using the Facets computer program (Linacre, 2015). The Facets syntax for conducting this analysis is given in Appendix 11.A.

Table 11.3 provides a summary of the Facets analyses for these data. There are several things that the reader should note about this table. First of all, the raters and domains are centered at zero. In Many-Faceted Rasch models, the object of measurement (persons in this case) does not have a mean measure of zero, while the other facets are centered at zero. The reliability of separation is significant for all of the facets with a value of .81 for reliability of person separation (comparable to coefficient alpha in traditional analyses). The estimated Wright map corresponding to this analysis is shown in Chapter One (Figure 1.10).

Table 11.4 provides a summary for the four raters included in these analyses. Using the guidelines shown in Table 11.2, it appears that Rater 1 ($MSE = 1.67$, Fit Category = C) is not functioning well based on the measurement model. Panel A in Figure 11.2 shows the rater response functions for these four raters. It is clear in this figure that Rater 1 has a flatter slope than the other raters, and that this leads to crossing person response functions.

The analyses suggest that the ratings are not invariant over raters, and that there appears to be differential rater functioning.

TABLE 11.3 Summary of Facets Analyses

	Raters (N = 4)	Domains (N = 4)	Persons (N = 40)
Measure (Logits)			
M	.00	.00	−.63
SD	.34	.30	1.28
Infit			
M	.90	1.00	.99
SD	.54	.03	.47
Outfit			
M	.89	.98	.98
SD	.53	.02	.47
Separation Statistics			
Reliability of Separation	.72	.68	.81
Chi-Square	9.1*	9.2*	165.5*
Degrees of Freedom	3	3	39

* $p < .05$

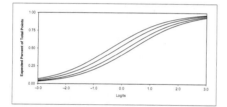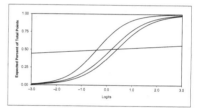

FIGURE 11.2 Differential Rater, Domain and Person Functioning

TABLE 11.4 Rater Fit (ordered by measure)

Raters	Observed Average	Measure	SE	Infit MS	Outfit MS	Slope	Fit Category
2509	1.64	0.38	0.21	0.70	0.67	1.41	A
2606	1.76	0.16	0.15	0.69	0.69	1.42	A
1	1.85	−0.13	0.14	1.69	1.67	0.08	C
698	1.98	−0.40	0.20	0.50	0.52	1.65	B

The analyses can also be summarized by domains. Table 11.5 provides the summary of the Facets analyses by domain. The domains range from a judged difficulty of −.30 logits for Style domain to judged difficulty of .37 logits for Conventions. The *MSE* statistics indicate good fit to the measurement model with all domains exhibiting Fit Category A. The domain response functions do not cross as shown in Panel B of Figure 11.2.

Table 11.6 summarizes the functioning of the categories over the combined raters, and also for individual raters. As was found in Table 11.4, Rater 1 appears

TABLE 11.5 Domain Fit (ordered by measure)

Domains	Observed Average	Measure	SE	Infit MS	Outfit MS	Slope	Fit Category
C	1.70	0.37	0.17	0.99	0.97	1.00	A
I	1.78	0.09	0.17	1.04	0.98	1.02	A
O	1.86	−0.16	0.17	0.97	1.01	1.02	A
S	1.90	−0.30	0.17	0.98	0.97	1.01	A

TABLE 11.6 Category Characteristics by Rater

Rating	Count	Percentage	Observed Average	Measure	SE	Outfit MS	Fit Category
Combined							
1	161	33.54	−1.54			1.0	A
2	249	51.88	−.43	−1.41	.11	.9	A
3	70	14.58	.80	1.41	.15	1.0	A
Individual Raters							
Rater 1							
1	60	37.50	−.97			1.4	A
2	64	40.00	−.28	−.82	.19	1.7	C
3	36	22.50	.37	.62	.23	1.6	C
Rater 698							
1	16	19.05	−1.91			.7	A
2	54	64.29	−.19	−2.05	.32	.6	A
3	14	16.67	2.12	2.05	.35	.5	A
Rater 2509							
1	31	40.79	−2.02			.8	A
2	41	53.95	−.84	−1.64	.26	.6	A
3	4	5.26	−.02	1.64	.53	.8	A
Rater 2606							
1	54	33.75	−1.94			.8	A
2	90	56.25	−.62	−1.72	.19	.8	A
3	16	10.00	1.13	1.72	.30	.7	A

to be using the rating categories in an idiosyncratic way with categories 2 and 3 both falling in Fit Category C.

Finally, Table 11.7 provides a summary of person fit. The distribution over fit quality is as follows: A ($N = 30$), B ($N = 4$), C ($N = 2$), and D ($N = 4$). Seventy-five percent of the persons fall in Fit Category A; this indicates good model-data fit. We have selected four persons to illustrate how person response functions can be used to identify misfit.

TABLE 11.7 Person Fit (ordered by measure)

Persons	Observed Average	Measure	SE	Infit MS	Outfit MS	Slope	Fit Category
1	1.50	−1.68	0.53	0.74	0.73	1.49	A
2	2.75	2.45	0.66	0.89	0.86	1.12	A
3	1.67	−1.14	0.51	0.71	0.71	1.44	A
4	2.67	2.06	0.59	0.88	0.93	1.13	A
5	1.08	−3.98	1.04	0.97	0.87	1.02	A
6	1.58	−1.40	0.52	0.81	0.82	1.30	A
7	2.17	0.38	0.50	0.45	0.45	1.67	B
8	1.92	−0.37	0.50	0.78	0.78	1.24	A
9	1.50	−1.68	0.53	0.72	0.73	1.52	A
10	1.92	−0.37	0.50	0.79	0.79	1.23	A
11	1.58	−1.40	0.52	0.81	0.82	1.30	A
12	1.75	−0.63	0.51	1.28	1.27	0.60	A
13	1.92	−0.12	0.50	0.78	0.78	1.24	A
14	1.92	−0.12	0.50	0.25	0.25	1.85	B
15	1.50	−1.43	0.53	1.30	1.25	0.50	A
16	1.75	−0.63	0.51	1.08	1.08	0.89	A
17	1.83	−0.37	0.50	0.48	0.48	1.63	B
18	1.83	−0.37	0.50	0.29	0.30	1.88	B
19	1.25	−2.44	0.65	0.90	0.91	1.09	A
20	1.92	−0.12	0.50	0.63	0.63	1.43	A
21	1.67	−0.88	0.51	0.70	0.70	1.46	A
22	1.33	−2.05	0.59	0.83	0.80	1.25	A
23	1.67	−1.14	0.51	0.71	0.72	1.43	A
24	1.75	−0.88	0.51	0.68	0.68	1.42	A
25	2.50	1.43	0.53	0.72	0.72	1.52	A
26	1.50	−1.68	0.53	2.04	2.05	-0.81	D
27	2.33	0.89	0.51	1.05	1.04	0.95	A
28	2.00	−0.12	0.50	0.59	0.59	1.45	A
29	1.58	−1.40	0.52	1.10	1.08	0.88	A
30	1.67	−1.14	0.51	1.04	1.03	0.97	A
31	2.33	0.89	0.51	1.26	1.26	0.59	A
32	2.08	0.13	0.50	1.23	1.23	0.74	A
33	2.08	0.38	0.50	1.54	1.54	0.36	C
34	1.58	−1.15	0.52	2.18	2.14	-0.97	D
35	2.17	0.63	0.50	2.10	2.10	-0.37	D
36	1.67	−0.88	0.51	2.02	2.00	-0.56	D
37	2.17	0.63	0.50	0.95	0.95	1.06	A
38	1.83	−0.37	0.50	1.71	1.71	0.15	C
39	1.33	−2.05	0.59	0.88	0.88	1.16	A
40	1.17	−2.94	0.77	0.81	0.64	1.18	A

Specifically, we selected Persons 4, 23, 28, and 33. The residual analyses for these persons are shown in Table 11.8. The person response functions with and without estimated slope parameters are shown in Figure 11.2. A graphical display of the residuals for Persons 4 and 33 are shown in Figure 11.3. Standardized residuals with values greater than 2.0 suggest unexpected ratings, and it is clear that Person 33 (Fit Category = C) has more disagreement about ratings than Person 4 (Fit Category = A).

In summary, the analyses suggest that Rater 1 is not interpreting and using the facets of the assessment system as intended by the test developers. Other facets of the rater-mediated assessment system vary in terms of the impact that Rater 1 has on the invariance of ratings related to each facet.

TABLE 11.8 Detailed Analyses of Person Fit

Person	Index	Rater	Domain	Observed	Expected	Residual	Variance	Standardized Residual
Person 4 (Outfit MS = .93, Fit Category = A)								
4	1	1	C	2	2.58	−0.58	0.27	−1.10
4	2	1	O	3	2.71	0.29	0.22	0.62
4	3	1	I	3	2.65	0.35	0.25	0.70
4	4	1	S	3	2.74	0.26	0.20	0.58
4	5	698	C	3	2.65	0.35	0.25	0.71
4	6	698	O	3	2.76	0.24	0.19	0.54
4	7	698	I	3	2.71	0.29	0.22	0.62
4	8	698	S	2	2.79	−0.79	0.17	−1.90
4	9	2606	C	2	2.49	−0.49	0.30	−0.90
4	10	2606	O	3	2.64	0.36	0.25	0.72
4	11	2606	I	3	2.58	0.42	0.28	0.81
4	12	2606	S	2	2.67	−0.67	0.24	−1.39
Person 23 (Outfit MS = .72, Fit Category = A)								
23	1	1	C	1	1.55	−0.55	0.31	−1.00
23	2	1	O	1	1.72	−0.72	0.33	−1.27
23	3	1	I	2	1.64	0.36	0.32	0.63
23	4	1	S	2	1.77	0.23	0.33	0.40
23	5	698	C	2	1.64	0.36	0.32	0.64
23	6	698	O	1	1.81	−0.81	0.33	−1.42
23	7	698	I	2	1.73	0.27	0.33	0.47
23	8	698	S	2	1.86	0.14	0.33	0.25
23	9	2606	C	2	1.47	0.53	0.29	0.99
23	10	2606	O	2	1.63	0.37	0.32	0.66
23	11	2606	I	1	1.55	−0.55	0.31	−0.99
23	12	2606	S	2	1.67	0.33	0.32	0.57

(Continued)

TABLE 11.8 (Continued)

Person	Index	Rater	Domain	Observed	Expected	Residual	Variance	Standardized Residual
Person 28 (Outfit MS = .59, Fit Category = A)								
28	1	1	C	2	1.88	0.12	0.33	0.21
28	2	1	O	1	2.06	−1.06	0.33	−1.84
28	3	1	I	3	1.97	1.03	0.33	1.79
28	4	1	S	2	2.10	−0.10	0.33	−0.18
28	5	698	C	2	1.97	0.03	0.33	0.05
28	6	698	O	2	2.14	−0.14	0.33	−0.25
28	7	698	I	2	2.06	−0.06	0.33	−0.11
28	8	698	S	2	2.19	−0.19	0.33	−0.33
28	9	2606	C	2	1.79	0.21	0.33	0.37
28	10	2606	O	2	1.96	0.04	0.33	0.07
28	11	2606	I	2	1.88	0.12	0.33	0.21
28	12	2606	S	2	2.01	−0.01	0.33	−0.01
Person 33 (Outfit MS = 1.54, Fit Category = C)								
33	1	1	C	1	2.05	−1.05	0.33	−1.83
33	2	1	O	2	2.22	−0.22	0.33	−0.39
33	3	1	I	2	2.14	−0.14	0.33	−0.24
33	4	1	S	1	2.27	−1.27	0.33	−2.22
33	5	2509	C	3	1.88	1.12	0.33	1.96
33	6	2509	O	2	2.05	−0.05	0.33	−0.09
33	7	2509	I	3	1.97	1.03	0.33	1.79
33	8	2509	S	2	2.10	−0.10	0.33	−0.17
33	9	2606	C	2	1.95	0.05	0.33	0.09
33	10	2606	O	2	2.13	−0.13	0.33	−0.22
33	11	2606	I	3	2.04	0.96	0.33	1.67
33	12	2606	S	2	2.17	−0.17	0.33	−0.30

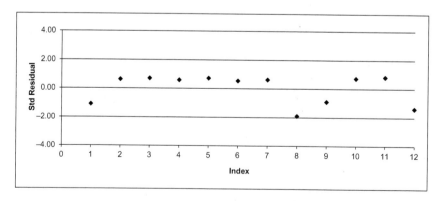

FIGURE 11.3 Residual Analyses for Persons 4 and 33

Summary and Discussion

> Models should not be true, but it is important that they are applicable.
>
> *(Rasch, 1960/1980, pp. 37–38)*

This chapter focused on residual-based approaches for examining model-data fit. This approach provides detailed diagnostic information that can be used to explore the psychometric quality of the ratings. As pointed out by Engelhard and Perkins (2013), in research on invariant measurement, there are several issues that are of perennial concern related to model-data fit:

- Since the interpretations of model-data fit indices require judgments, how do we answer the fundamental question: How good is good enough?
- What are the appropriate sampling distributions to use with various model-data fit indices? Are rules of thumb and experience-based interpretations *good enough* for determining substantive significance of results?
- If there is no single index of model-data fit that will detect all of the possible disturbances that may affect the measurements encountered in the human sciences, then how do we integrate the different approaches into a systematic set of activities to evaluate model-data fit?
- What graphical and statistical displays of fit indices are useful devices for interpreting lack of model-data fit?

(p. 115)

Our view of the question of *How good is good enough?* is that the answer should be based on a careful consideration of model-data fit with a strong emphasis on the substantive context and decisions that the assessment system was designed to address. The interpretation of misfit is inherently an art that is dependent on researchers with a deep understanding of the latent variable represented by the line. It also depends on the broader theoretical and applied context for identifying how the construct is related to other variables within the assessment system. Researchers should also consider how the latent variable fits into a broader program of substantive research utilizing the construct.

In terms of the second question, the quest for exact sampling distributions is not practical based on the current state of the field, and rules of thumb combined with experience and research-based rules of thumb can be useful in improving operational assessment systems based on rater-mediated judgments.

In answering the question posed in the third bullet, researchers and practitioners develop communities of practice that provide guidance regarding the most useful indices of model-data fit. In coming to a consensus on the guidelines, it is important to explore and estimate model-data misfit. This matters because misfit can affect the decisions made about persons. Finally, the numerical summaries of fit indices combined with graphical displays described in this chapter can form a starting point for interpreting lack of model-data fit.

One of the earliest systematic approaches to residual analyses with the Rasch model was developed by Mead (1976). He highlighted how misfit provides diagnostic information about violation of Rasch requirements. He also highlighted that most disturbances in the measurement process are related to multidimensionality.

Recently, Haberman and Sinharay (2013) have proposed a new residual-based approach that in theory may lead to improved summary statistics, but as pointed out by (Wells & Hambleton, 2016), this approach may have inflated Type I error rates. There are other approaches that can be used for evaluating model-data fit with rater-mediated assessments, such as Bayesian model-data fit (Sinharay, 2016). If there is an interest in comparing the fit of non-nested models, then a variety of information-based criteria are also available (Cohen & Cho, 2016). It is beyond the scope of this chapter to discuss these other approaches.

References

Anscombe, F. J., & Tukey, J. W. (1963). The examination and analysis of residuals. *Technometrics, 5*(2), 141–160.

Box, G. E. P., & Draper, N. R. (1987). *Empirical model building and response surfaces.* New York, NY: Wiley.

Cohen, A. S., & Cho, S. J. (2016). Information criteria. In W. J. van der Linden (Ed.), *Handbook of item response theory, volume two: Models* (pp. 363–378). Boca Raton, FL: CRC Press.

Douglas, J., & Cohen, A. (2001). Nonparametric item response function estimation for assessing parametric model fit. *Applied Psychological Measurement, 25*(3), 234–243.

Engelhard, G., Jr., & Perkins, A. (2013). Goodness of model-data fit and invariant measurement. *Measurement: Interdisciplinary Research and Perspectives, 11*(3), 112–116.

Glas, C. A. W. (2016). Frequentist model-fait tests. In W. J. van der Linden (Ed.), *Handbook of item response theory, volume two: Models* (pp. 343–361). Boca Raton, FL: CRC Press.

Haberman, S. J. (2009). *Use of generalized residuals to examine goodness of fit of item response models* (Research Rep. No. RR-09–15). Princeton: ETS.

Haberman, S. J., & Sinharay, S. (2013). Assessing item fit for unidimensional item response theory models using residuals from estimated item response functions. *Psychometrika, 78,* 417–440.

Karabatsos, G. (2000). A critique of Rasch residual fit statistics. *Journal of Applied Measurement, 1,* 152–176.

Linacre, J. M. (2015). *Facets Rasch Measurement* (Version 3.71.4). Chicago, IL: Winsteps.com.

Mead, R. (1976). *Assessment of fit of data to the Rasch model through analysis of residuals.* Unpublished doctoral dissertation, University of Chicago, Chicago.

Pearson, K. (1900). On the criterion that a given system of deviations from the probable in the case of a correlated system of variables is such that it can be reasonably supposed to have arisen from random sampling. *Philosophy Magazine, 50,* 157–172.

Rasch, G. (1960/1980). *Probabilistic models for some intelligence and attainment tests.* Copenhagen: Danish Institute for Educational Research. (Expanded edition, Chicago: University of Chicago Press, 1980).

Sinharay, S. (2016). Bayesian model fit and model comparison. In W. J. van der Linden (Ed.), *Handbook of item response theory, volume two: Models* (pp. 379–394). Boca Raton, FL: CRC Press.

Stigler, S. M. (1999). *Statistics on the table: The history of statistical concepts and methods.* Cambridge, MA: Harvard University Press.

Walker, A. A., & Engelhard, G. (2015). Exploring person fit with an approach based on multilevel logistic regression. *Applied Measurement in Education, 28*(4), 274–291.

Wells, C. S., & Hambleton, R. K. (2016). Model fit with residual analyses. In W. J. van der Linden (Ed.), *Handbook of item response theory, volume two: Models* (pp. 395–413). Boca Raton, FL: CRC Press.

Wind, S. A., & Engelhard, G., Jr. (2014). Model-data fit and adjustments for rater effects. *Rasch Measurement Transactions, 28*(3), 1483–1484.

Wright, B. D., & Linacre, J. M. (1994). Reasonable mean-square fit values. *Rasch Measurement Transactions, 8*(3), 37.

Wright, B. D., & Stone, M. (1979). *Best test design: Rasch measurement.* Chicago, IL: MESA Press.

APPENDIX 11.A

Facet syntax

Title= GA Middle School Writing (N=40) with four raters
Facets=3
Arrange=M   ; arrange tables in (n)umber, (m)easure, (f)it order
Unexpected=3   ; flag residuals greater than 3
Barchart=no
Iterations=50   ; default is 100 iterations
Dvalue=3,1-4
Models
?,?,?,r3
*
Labels=
1,Persons
1-40=
*
2,Raters
1= ;Expert
698= ;Rater C
2509= ; Rater B
2606= ;Rater A; Anchor
*
3,Domain
1= C
2= O
3= I
4= S
*
Data=
1,1,1,2,2,2
2,1,3,2,3,3
3,1,2,1,2,1
4,1,2,3,3,3
5,1,1,2,1,1

...

35,2606,3,3,2,3
36,2606,1,1,1,1
37,2606,3,2,2,3
38,2606,2,1,1,2
39,2606,2,1,1,2
40,2606,1,1,1,1

Note: Complete data shown in Table 1.2.

12

DESIGNING RATER-MEDIATED ASSESSMENT SYSTEMS

This chapter continues the discussion of practical issues for rater-mediated assessments, with a focus on issues related to designing rater-mediated assessment systems from the perspective of invariant measurement. A set of *four building blocks* for constructing rater-mediated assessments serves as an organizing framework for the various design considerations. These building blocks are adapted from the frameworks for constructing measures presented by Wilson (2005) and adapted by Engelhard (2013). These frameworks describe a series of essential considerations for constructing measures in the social sciences, including the conceptualization of a latent variable, designs for collecting relevant observations, scoring rules, and the measurement model used to connect scored observations to a linear continuum that represents the latent variable.

Specifically, this chapter extends the constructing measures framework (Wilson, 2005) and its adapted version (Engelhard, 2013) to the context of rater-mediated assessments. As given in Figure 12.1, the four building blocks for rater-mediated assessments are (A) rater-mediated latent variable, (B) observational design for ratings, (C) scoring rules for ratings, and (D) measurement model for ratings. Table 12.1 summarizes the four building blocks in terms of the underlying questions related to the design of rater-mediated assessment systems. As is the case with assessment design in general, the design of rater-mediated assessments is an iterative and non-linear process. Nonetheless, the concept of building blocks serves as a useful conceptual model to illustrate a variety of considerations central to the design of rater-mediated assessment systems.

The chapter is organized as follows. For each building block, an overview of the key concepts from the constructing measures framework (Engelhard, 2013; Wilson, 2005) is presented. Next, considerations specific to the design of rater-mediated assessments are presented and illustrated. Special attention is

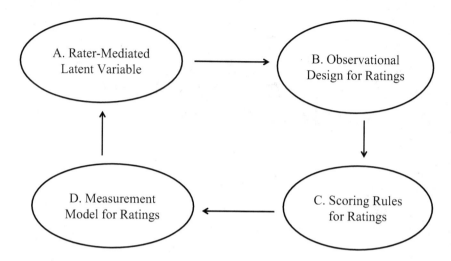

FIGURE 12.1 Building Blocks for Rater-Mediated Assessments

TABLE 12.1 Building Blocks for Rater-Mediated Assessments

Building Block	Underlying Questions for Designing Rater-Mediated Assessments
A. Rater-Mediated Latent Variable	What is the rater-mediated latent variable? How do raters interpret the construct being measured?
B. Observational Design for Ratings	What is the procedure for collecting ratings on cues obtained from persons in order to define the rater-mediated latent variable?
C. Scoring Rules for Ratings	How do rater interpretations of rubrics and performance-level descriptors lead to ratings of student achievement that define the rater-mediated latent variable?
D. Measurement Model for Ratings	How are rater interpretations of person locations, domain difficulties, and rating-scale categories mapped onto the rater-mediated latent variable?

Note: Adapted from Engelhard (2013) and Wilson (2005).

directed toward the second building block (B. Observational design for ratings), and empirical data are used to illustrate various data collection systems for rater-mediated assessments related to this building block. The chapter concludes with a summary and discussion. The major headings for this chapter are:

- Building blocks for rater-mediated assessments

    A. Rater-mediated latent variable
    B. Observational design for ratings
    C. Scoring rules for ratings
    D. Measurement model for ratings

- Rasch models as equating models for rater-mediated assessments
  - o Rater fit
  - o Theoretical illustration
  - o Empirical illustration
- Summary and discussion

Building Blocks for Rater-Mediated Assessments

1. Rater-Mediated Latent Variable

The first building block for designing rater-mediated assessments is the *rater-mediated latent variable.* When constructing any scale in social science measurement, researchers must begin by conceptualizing the underlying continuum in terms of a qualitative order from low to high (i.e., fail/pass; strongly disagree/disagree/agree/strongly agree; etc.). As noted in Chapter One, Wright maps are visual representations of the latent variable that facilitate the interpretation of locations of individual persons, cues, raters, rating categories, and other facets in terms of this underlying continuum. When there is good model-data fit, the locations can be interpreted as representing locations on the latent variable based on observations collected during the measurement process.

When this building block is applied to the context of rater-mediated assessments, these procedures involve defining the *rater-mediated latent variable.* As given in Table 12.1, this building block can be summarized using two underlying questions:

- What is the rater-mediated latent variable?
- How do raters interpret the cues used to define the latent variable?

The distinction between the first building block presented in this chapter and the first building block included in the original presentation of the constructing measures framework is related to the definition of the construct as rater-mediated. This distinction highlights the central role that raters play in defining the latent variable in a rater-mediated assessment system. In particular, it is essential to recognize that locations on the Wright map are estimated based on rater interpretations and judgments of person locations, cue difficulties, and rating-scale categories that are mediated by the unique decision-making process for the raters assigning scores based on the cues unique to the assessment context. In a rater-mediated assessment, cues may take on the form of tasks, prompts, or domains in analytic scoring.

Chapter Four presented a detailed discussion of a lens model framework that characterizes the underlying concepts related to rater-mediated latent variables. This lens model framework was adapted from early research on decision-making presented by Brunswik (1956) and Hammond (e.g., Hammond, Stewart, Brehmer, & Steinmann, 1975). Essentially, this framework is based on the idea that a person's performance is scored using a set of cues, such as rubric domains and rating scale categories, by a rater whose judgment is used to reveal the person's judged location on the latent variable. Evidence of rating quality supports the interpretation and use of these judgments as indicators of student locations on the latent variable; additional details regarding the evaluation of rating quality are provided in Chapter Thirteen. In some chapters in this book, the cues are referred to as generalized items with ratings recoded to reflect the underlying latent Guttman process (see Chapters Ten and Eleven).

2. Observational Design for Ratings

The second building block is the *observational design for ratings*. Essentially, an observational design is the set of assessment opportunities that are used to define the latent variable. For selected-response assessments, the observational design is often summarized using tables of specifications or test blueprints that describe the content to be assessed, the level at which the content is aimed, and the process for interpreting and using assessment results (Engelhard, 2013).

In the context of rater-mediated assessments, assessment opportunities consist of the combination of student performances related to a particular cue (e.g., prompt or domain) with raters. Accordingly, observational designs for ratings involve specifying *rating designs*, or the procedures with which individual raters or groups of raters are assigned to score student performances. Design considerations for rater-mediated assessments related to this building block can be summarized using the following underlying question:

- What is the procedure for collecting ratings on cues obtained from persons in order to define the rater-mediated latent variable?

Practical constraints in most operational assessment settings limit the possibility for every rater to score every performance. As a result, observational designs must be specified that define the procedure with which student performances are assigned to raters. When different raters are assigned to different student performances, fairness issues are a potential concern. Recognizing issues related to rater exchangeability, many performance assessment systems include training programs with qualification requirements prior to operational scoring. These training programs aim to establish a common interpretation and use of rubrics and rating scales among raters. Nonetheless, research on performance assessments indicates that differences in rater severity persist beyond training (e.g., Lunz & Stahl, 1990; Lunz, Stahl, & Wright, 1996; O'Neill & Lunz, 2000; Raymond, Webb, & Houston, 1991).

Recognizing persistent differences in rater severity, several post-hoc procedures have been proposed that can be used to account for differences in rater severity. In particular, methods have been proposed based on ANOVA (Braun, 1988), regression models (Lance, LaPointe, & Stewart, 1994; Raymond & Viswesvaran, 1993; Raymond, Webb, & Houston, 1991; H. G. Wilson, 1988), and measurement models such as the Many-Facet Rasch Model (Engelhard, Myford, & Cline, 2000; Lunz & Suanthong, 2011; Myford & Mislevy, 1995). These methods reflect the same general aims as test equating in selected-response assessments, but with the goal of adjusting estimates of student achievement for differences in rater severity.

In the context of rater-mediated assessments, equating procedures are based on data collection designs that involve creating links between raters in order to perform transformations that control for differences in rater severity. These data collection designs can be considered within the framework of experimental design and analysis of variance (ANOVA; Kirk, 1995), and can be viewed as block designs in which ratings are replications within each cell of a rater-by-task design. The next section describes three major types of rating designs that are commonly applied in research and practice (Wind & Peterson, 2017), along with their implications: (1) fully crossed designs, (2) linked designs, and (3) disconnected designs.

1. Fully Crossed Rating Designs

The first major observational design for ratings is a *fully crossed* rating design. These designs have also been described as *complete assessment networks* (Engelhard, 1997; Wind, Engelhard, & Wesolowski, 2016). Within the context of test equating based on Classical Test Theory (CTT), these designs are comparable to single group designs.

Fully crossed rating designs are characterized by complete connectivity across all facets in an assessment system. Figure 12.2 illustrates two examples of fully crossed rating designs. For each design, a matrix is displayed in which a check mark (✓) indicates that a rater scored a student's performance. A graphical display is also used to illustrate connectivity among facets, where a solid line indicates a direct link established through common assessment components.

Panel A is an example of a rating design with two facets: Raters and Students. This design is fully crossed because every rater scores every student. As a result, all three raters are directly connected. Similarly, the three-facet rater-mediated assessment system illustrated in Panel B involves a fully crossed rating design because every rater scores every student on every domain.

A: Two-Facet Rater-Mediated Assessment System	Rater	Domain	Student										Graphical Illustration
			1	2	3	4	5	6	7	8	9	10	
	1		✓	✓	✓	✓	✓	✓	✓	✓	✓	✓	
	2		✓	✓	✓	✓	✓	✓	✓	✓	✓	✓	
	3		✓	✓	✓	✓	✓	✓	✓	✓	✓	✓	
B. Three-Facet Rater-Mediated Assessment System	1	1	✓	✓	✓	✓	✓	✓	✓	✓	✓	✓	
	1	2	✓	✓	✓	✓	✓	✓	✓	✓	✓	✓	
	2	1	✓	✓	✓	✓	✓	✓	✓	✓	✓	✓	
	2	2	✓	✓	✓	✓	✓	✓	✓	✓	✓	✓	
	3	1	✓	✓	✓	✓	✓	✓	✓	✓	✓	✓	
	3	2	✓	✓	✓	✓	✓	✓	✓	✓	✓	✓	

FIGURE 12.2 Fully Crossed Rating Designs

Note: Raters are abbreviated using "R" and domains are abbreviated using "D." Solid lines in the graphical illustrations indicate direct links established through common assessment components.

2. Linked Rating Designs

The second major observational design for ratings is a *linked rating design*. These designs have also been described as incomplete assessment networks (e.g., Engelhard, 1997; Wind, Engelhard, & Wesolowski, 2016). Within the context of test equating based on CTT, these designs reflect anchor test designs. In the context of rater-mediated assessments, linked designs are methods for collecting ratings that involve the systematic use of common assessment components through which uncommon assessment components are connected.

Numerous data collection designs for linked rating designs can be specified based on matrix sampling techniques for balanced incomplete block and partially unbalanced incomplete block designs (Kirk, 1995). Figure 12.3 illustrates four examples of linked rating designs that reflect different methods for establishing connectivity among facets in rater-mediated assessments.

First, Panel A illustrates a rating design in which common student performances are used to establish connectivity. This rating design can be described as an *anchor student design*. In this design, Student 4 and Student 5 provide links between all three raters. Along the same lines, Panel B illustrates a linked rating design in which connectivity is established using a common rater. This rating design can be described as an *anchor rater design*. In this design, Rater 2 scores five performances in common with Rater 1 (Students 1–5) and five performances in common with Rater 2 (Students 6–10). Although Rater 1 and Rater 3 do not score any performances in common, an indirect link is established between these two raters as a result of each of their links to Rater 2.

	Rater	Domain	Student										Graphical Illustration
			1	2	3	4	5	6	7	8	9	10	
A: Two-Facet Linked Design (Anchor Students)	1					✓	✓	✓	✓	✓			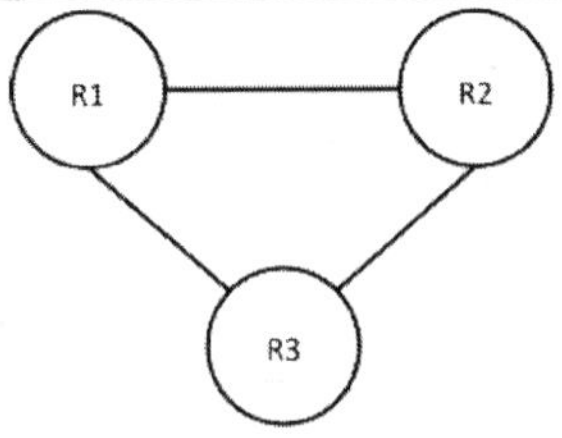
	2		✓	✓	✓	✓	✓						
	3					✓	✓				✓	✓	
B. Two-Facet Linked Design (Anchor Rater)	1		✓	✓	✓	✓	✓						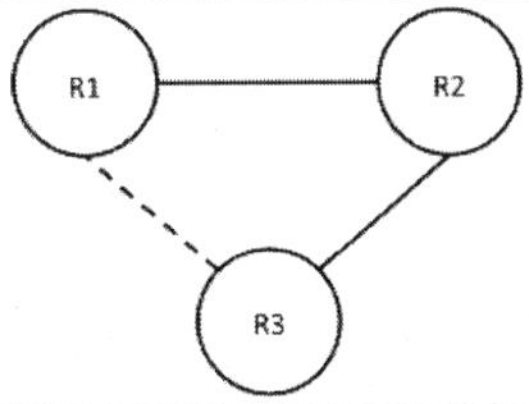
	2		✓	✓	✓	✓	✓	✓	✓	✓	✓	✓	
	3								✓	✓	✓	✓	
C. Three-Facet Linked Design (Anchor Raters and Anchor Domains)	1	1	✓	✓	✓	✓	✓						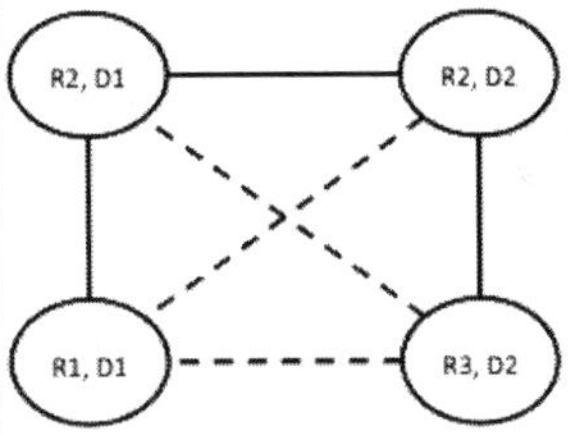
	1	2											
	2	1	✓	✓	✓	✓	✓	✓	✓	✓	✓	✓	
	2	2	✓	✓	✓	✓	✓	✓	✓	✓	✓	✓	
	3	1											
	3	2						✓	✓	✓	✓	✓	
D. Two-Facet Linked Design (Anchor Multiple-Choice Items)	1		✓	✓	✓	✓							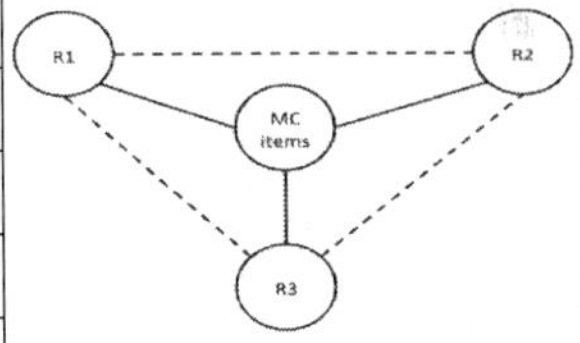
	2						✓	✓	✓	✓			
	3										✓	✓	
	Multiple Choice Items	1	✓	✓	✓	✓	✓	✓	✓	✓	✓	✓	
		2	✓	✓	✓	✓	✓	✓	✓	✓	✓	✓	
		3	✓	✓	✓	✓	✓	✓	✓	✓	✓	✓	
		4	✓	✓	✓	✓	✓	✓	✓	✓	✓	✓	
		5	✓	✓	✓	✓	✓	✓	✓	✓	✓	✓	
		6	✓	✓	✓	✓	✓	✓	✓	✓	✓	✓	
		7	✓	✓	✓	✓	✓	✓	✓	✓	✓	✓	
		8	✓	✓	✓	✓	✓	✓	✓	✓	✓	✓	
		9	✓	✓	✓	✓	✓	✓	✓	✓	✓	✓	
		10	✓	✓	✓	✓	✓	✓	✓	✓	✓	✓	

FIGURE 12.3 Linked Rating Designs

Note: Raters are abbreviated using "R" and domains are abbreviated using "D." Solid lines in the graphical illustrations indicate direct links established through common assessment components, and dashed lines indicate indirect links.

Panel C illustrates a linked rating design in which connectivity is established using a common rater and common domains. In this design, Rater 2 acts as an anchor rater to connect Rater 1 to Rater 3. Although Rater 1 and Rater 3 do not score any common performances or domains, they are linked because Rater 2 scores five students in common with each rater on the same domain.

Finally, Panel D illustrates a linked rating design in which connectivity is established using an anchor set of multiple-choice (MC) items. This design could also be illustrated using an anchor set of additional performance tasks or a variety of other assessment types, as long as there is theoretical justification to support the interpretation of the anchor in terms of the same construct as the performance task(s). In this design, each of the three raters is fully nested within student performances. However, because each of the 10 students responded to the entire set of MC items, connectivity is established among the three raters.

3. Disconnected Rating Designs

Third, *disconnected* rating designs (i.e., non-linked assessment networks; Engelhard, 1997; Wind, Engelhard, & Wesolowski, 2016) do not include systematic links between assessment components. These designs are comparable to equivalent group designs based on CTT test equating. Because these designs do not involve connectivity among facets in an assessment system, estimates for individual facets cannot be interpreted independently from other facets in the assessment system. Rather, the interpretation of estimates from these designs depends upon the degree to which the hypothesis of random equivalence of assessment components (e.g., randomly equivalent raters and students) can be supported.

Figure 12.4 illustrates two examples of disconnected rating designs. Panel A is a two-facet, rater-mediated assessment system in which raters are nested within

	Rater	Domain	Student										Graphical Illustration
			1	2	3	4	5	6	7	8	9	10	
A. Two-Facet Non-Linked Design (Raters nested within Students)	1		✓	✓	✓								R1 R2
	2					✓	✓	✓	✓				
	3								✓	✓	✓		R3
B. Three-Facet Non-Linked Design (Raters nested within Students and Domains)	1	1	✓	✓	✓	✓							R1, D1 R2, D2
	2	2					✓	✓	✓				
	3	3							✓	✓	✓		R3, D3

FIGURE 12.4 Disconnected Rating Designs

Note: Raters are abbreviated using "R" and domains are abbreviated using "D." Solid lines in the graphical illustrations indicate direct links established through common assessment components, and dashed lines indicate indirect links.

student performances. As a result, student achievement estimates cannot be interpreted separately from rater severity, and the interpretation of rater severity estimates cannot be separated from student achievement. Similarly, Panel B illustrates a three-facet disconnected rating design in which raters are nested within student performances and domains. As a result, student achievement estimates cannot be interpreted separately from rater severity, and the interpretation of rater severity estimates cannot be separated from student achievement. Furthermore, domain difficulty cannot be interpreted separately from rater severity and student achievement.

Illustration: Observational Designs for a Rater-Mediated Writing Assessment

Next, an illustrative analysis of data from a rater-mediated writing assessment is used to illustrate the implications of different observational designs for ratings in terms of the interpretation of student achievement estimates. The illustrative dataset used in this chapter was also explored in the case study presented in Chapter Eight. As noted in Chapter Eight, the original data were collected during an administration of the Georgia High School Writing Assessment and include three facets: Essays (N = 365), Raters (N = 21), and Domains (N = 4). The original observational design for the illustrative dataset was fully crossed, such that all 21 raters scored each of the 365 essays on all four domains in the analytic rubric.

For illustrative purposes, the dataset is modified from the original version to construct four datasets that reflect rating designs commonly used in operational assessment settings. Each modified dataset includes 360 randomly selected essays, 20 randomly selected raters, and the complete set of four domains from the original dataset. The four designs are illustrated in Figure 12.5. Design One is the original data collection design, in which all raters scored all essays on all four domains. Design Two is a linked rating design in which two raters scored each essay on all four domains, and each rater scored 18 essays in common with one other rater, thus establishing direct links between each rater and one other rater, and indirect links through common performances and domains. Design Three is a linked rating design in which direct links are established between each rater and one other rater through 18 common essays, along with direct links to an anchor rater (Rater 1) who scored the entire set of essays on all four domains. Finally, Design Four is a linked rating design that only includes indirect links among raters. In this design, each rater scores a unique set of 18 essays on all four domains. As a result, indirect links are established among all 20 raters through the common set of domains.

Stability of Essay Ordering

When the observational design contains sufficient links between raters, models based on Rasch Measurement Theory can be used to obtain estimates of student achievement that are adjusted for differences in rater severity. As a result, Rasch

Design One: Fully Crossed

Essays	Raters (All Domains)																			
	1	2	3	4	5	6	7	8	9	10	11	12	13	14	15	16	17	18	19	20
1–18	✔	✔	✔	✔	✔	✔	✔	✔	✔	✔	✔	✔	✔	✔	✔	✔	✔	✔	✔	✔
19–36	✔	✔	✔	✔	✔	✔	✔	✔	✔	✔	✔	✔	✔	✔	✔	✔	✔	✔	✔	✔
37–54	✔	✔	✔	✔	✔	✔	✔	✔	✔	✔	✔	✔	✔	✔	✔	✔	✔	✔	✔	✔
55–72	✔	✔	✔	✔	✔	✔	✔	✔	✔	✔	✔	✔	✔	✔	✔	✔	✔	✔	✔	✔
. . .	✔	✔	✔	✔	✔	✔	✔	✔	✔	✔	✔	✔	✔	✔	✔	✔	✔	✔	✔	✔
343–360	✔	✔	✔	✔	✔	✔	✔	✔	✔	✔	✔	✔	✔	✔	✔	✔	✔	✔	✔	✔

Design Two: Linked (Common Performance and Domains)

Essays	Raters (All Domains)																			
	1	2	3	4	5	6	7	8	9	10	11	12	13	14	15	16	17	18	19	20
1–18	✔	✔																		
19–36		✔	✔																	
37–54			✔	✔																
55–72				✔	✔															
. . .																				
343–360	✔																			

Design Three: Linked (Common Performance and Domains + Anchor Rater)

Essays	Raters (All Domains)																			
	1	2	3	4	5	6	7	8	9	10	11	12	13	14	15	16	17	18	19	20
1–18	✔	✔																		
19–36	✔	✔	✔																	
37–54	✔		✔	✔																
55–72	✔			✔	✔															
. . .	✔																			
343–360	✔																			

Design Four: Linked (Common Domains)

Essays	Raters (All Domains)																			
	1	2	3	4	5	6	7	8	9	10	11	12	13	14	15	16	17	18	19	20
1–18	✔																			
19–36		✔																		
37–54			✔																	
55–72				✔																
. . .																				
343–360																				✔

FIGURE 12.5 Illustrative Observational Designs

models for ratings (discussed further below in building block D) can be seen as a method for obtaining a concurrent calibration of student achievement across different raters.

In the illustrative analysis, estimates of essay locations on the logit scale (θ) were estimated using a Rating Scale formulation of the Many-Facet Rasch (MFR) model with three facets:

$$\ln\left[\frac{P_{nijk}}{P_{nijk-1}}\right] = \theta_n - \lambda_i - \delta_j - \tau_k, \tag{12.1}$$

where

θ_n = the judged location (i.e., achievement) of Essay n,
λ_i = the location (i.e., severity) of Rater i,
δ_j = the judged location (i.e., difficulty) of Domain j, and
τ_k = the judged location on the logit scale where rating scale categories k and $k-1$ are equally probable.

The MFR model in Equation 12.1 was applied separately to each observational design in order to obtain four sets of logit-scale location estimates (θ) for the essays. These estimates were compared between the original rating design (Design One) and the three modified designs. The correlation of essay ordering based on the original design with the ordering based on the other designs was of interest in order to examine differences in MFR model adjustments related to differences in rater linking patterns.

Results from the comparison are presented in Figure 12.6. Overall, examination of the scatterplots reveals a positive linear relationship between performance ordering for the essays based on the original data collection design (Design One; x-axis) and the three modified designs. However, each comparison reveals differences in the relative ordering of performances across the designs, with decreasing magnitudes of correlations observed as the level of connectivity decreases.

Examination of results in terms of individual essays further highlights the consequences of different linking designs. Figure 12.7 shows discrepancies in logit-scale locations between the original rating design (Design One) and each of the modified designs for the 360 essays. A discrepancy of zero (horizontal line) indicates no change in the essay achievement measure between designs. Positive values indicate that the student had a higher judged location (theta) in the modified design, whereas negative values indicate that the student had a lower judged location in the modified design. Overall, these results indicate variation in the direction and magnitude of discrepancies between the original and modified rating designs across the sample of students.

Overall, results from the correlation analysis indicate that, as connectivity decreases in rating designs, the correspondence between performance ordering decreases. The comparison between the original rating design and the modified

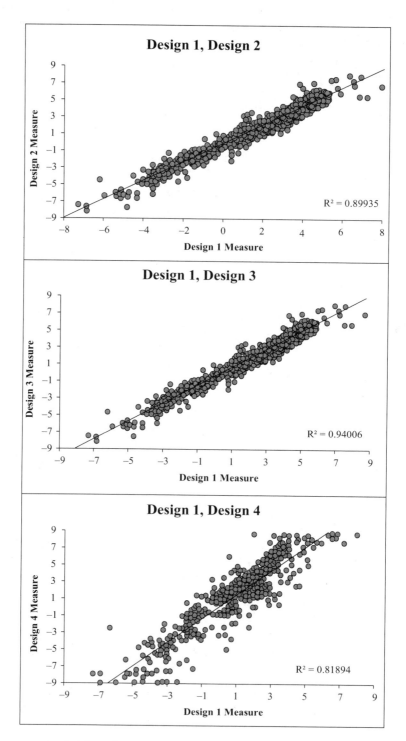

FIGURE 12.6 Stability of Performance Ordering across Observational Designs

Discrepancies between Essay Measures from Design 1 and Modified Rating Design

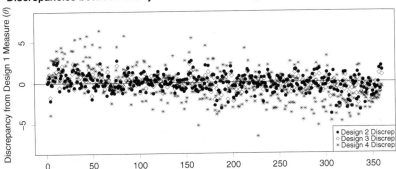

FIGURE 12.7   Discrepancies in Performance Estimates

designs illustrates the degree to which the conclusions about relative ordering of essays would change when different observational designs are used in rater-mediated assessments. The finding of closer correspondence when strong links between facets in an assessment system are maintained highlights the importance of establishing adequate links between raters in order to obtain rater-invariant performance estimates.

3. Scoring Rules for Ratings

The third building block for rater-mediated assessments is *scoring rules for ratings*. This building block is analogous to the *outcome space* building block presented by Wilson (2005) and the *scoring rules* building block presented by Engelhard (2013). Essentially, this building block describes the system with which rater judgments are categorized to reflect the directionality of the latent variable. As given in Table 12.1, the rating rules building block can be summarized using the following question:

- How do rater interpretations of rubrics and performance-level descriptors lead to ratings of student achievement that define the rater-mediated latent variable?

Rater-mediated assessments usually include rubrics in which performance-level descriptors or exemplars describe the distinction between rating scale categories in terms of essential features of student responses. Rubrics are often created in conjunction with tasks or prompts, and include a specification of the specific aspects of a response that reflect the construct being measured. Rubrics may be *holistic*, where all aspects of a response are used to assign an overall score. Holistic ratings may reflect multiple components of a response, but a single score is used to reflect the overall level of the performance. Holistic rubrics may be preferred in cases where unique aspects of a domain cannot be distinguished or in cases in which an overall picture of performance is desired, rather than a detailed analysis of specific strengths and weaknesses related to different aspects of a domain (Arter & McTighe, 2001; Johnson, Penny, & Gordon, 2009). On the other hand, *analytic* rubrics are used to gather separate scores for distinct components of a response. For example, in the context of a writing assessment, an analytic rubric might include separate domain areas in which students receive distinct scores for the *meaning* and *mechanics* of their writing. The major motivation for the use of analytic rubrics is that they provide "valuable information for diagnostic purposes . . . [that] lends itself to evaluating strengths and weaknesses of test takers" (AERA, APA, & NCME, 2014, p. 79). Johnson et al. noted that analytic rubrics are particularly useful in assessment contexts in which students have the opportunity to re-take the assessment after receiving feedback. However, as noted in the *Standards for Educational and Psychological Testing*, "validation will be required for diagnostic interpretations for particular uses of the separate scores" (p. 79). When both an overall summary score and diagnostic, domain-level scores are desired, it is also possible to collect both holistic and analytic scores (Johnson, Penny, & Gordon, 2009; Mullis, 1984); however, this approach is costly in terms of scoring resources.

In most cases, the sequence of these performance-level descriptors implies an ordinal level of measurement for the rating scale categories, where increasing ratings are associated with increasing locations on the latent variable. When polytomous formulations of the Rasch model are applied, it is possible to empirically verify the realization of the expected category ordering in operational ratings (Andrich, 2016; Linacre, 2002). Specifically, estimates of threshold parameters (τ) can be examined for each category for evidence of non-decreasing locations on the logit scale in order to verify the alignment between raters' use of rating scale categories and the latent variable. This diagnostic feature of polytomous Rasch models is not available in polytomous Item Response Theory models in which thresholds are defined using cumulative probabilities, such as the Graded Response Model. As pointed out by Andrich (2016), the empirical examination of category ordering is distinct from indicators of model-data fit, and is essential for improving measurement procedures and informing the interpretation and use of ratings. In his words:

> With the ubiquitous application of rating scales in the social sciences, the facility to test the empirical ordering of categories is critical. Otherwise, decisions, ranging from those of policy to individual diagnoses, may be misleading.
>
> *(p. 78)*

4. Measurement Model for Ratings

The final building block for rater-mediated assessments is the *measurement model for ratings*. As described in the original constructing measures framework, the measurement model serves as a tool "to relate the scored outcomes from the items design and the outcome space back to the construct that was the original inspiration of the items" (Wilson, 2005, p. 85). Although a variety of measurement models are available for use with selected-response items and ratings, this book focuses on measurement models based on Rasch Measurement Theory. A major theme that has been emphasized throughout the book is the use of Rasch models to obtain estimates that can be used to describe persons, items, raters, and other facets on a linear continuum that represents the construct. Within the context of rater-mediated assessments, the measurement model serves as a tool through which to connect rater judgments collected using rating designs and rating rules to the rater-mediated latent variable. Rasch models for ratings facilitate the mapping of individual raters, students, and other facets onto a single linear continuum that represents a rater-mediated latent variable. The underlying concerns related to this building block can be summarized using the following question:

- How are rater interpretations of person locations, domain difficulties, and rating-scale categories mapped onto the rater-mediated latent variable?

As was noted in Chapter Nine, a variety of polytomous Item Response Theory (IRT) models have been proposed that can be applied to polytomous ratings (Nering & Ostini, 2010). Each of these models offers unique diagnostic information related to items, persons, rating scale categories, and other facets included in the model. Within the framework of Rasch Measurement Theory, two formulations of the polytomous Rasch model are widely used: The Rating Scale Model (RSM) (Andrich, 1978) and the Partial Credit Model (PCM) (Masters, 1982). The major difference between these two models can be seen in the way the rating scale category thresholds are defined. When the RS model is applied, the distance between rating scale categories is fixed across all items, such that the interpretation of a rating in each category is constant across the set of items. On the other hand, when the PC model is applied, rating scale category thresholds are estimated separately for each item. As a result, the distance between and interpretation of rating scale categories is not necessarily equivalent across items.

The difference between the RS and PC models can be seen in the expression of the threshold parameter across the two models. For example, the RS model can be stated as:

$$\ln\left(\frac{P_{ni(x=k)}}{P_{ni(x=k-1)}}\right) = \theta_n - \lambda_i - \tau_k \tag{12.2}$$

where

θ_n = the judged location of person n,
λ_i = the severity of rater i, and
τ_k = the logit-scale location at which a rating in category k and category $k-1$ are equally probable.

In Equation 12.2, the threshold parameter is defined for the overall set of raters, such that a common rating scale structure is estimated across raters.

On the other hand, the PC model can be stated as follows:

$$\ln\left(\frac{P_{ni(x=k)}}{P_{ni(x=k-1)}}\right) = \theta_n - \lambda_i - \tau_{ik}, \tag{12.3}$$

where

θ_n = the judged location of person n,

λ_i = the severity of rater i, and

τ_k = the logit-scale location at which a rating in category k and category $k-1$ are equally probable specific to rater i.

In Equation 12.3, the threshold parameter includes an additional subscript that indicates the facet for which thresholds are allowed to vary. In this example, thresholds are allowed to vary across the rater facet. However, it is also possible to allow thresholds to vary across other facets in the model, such as items, domains, or prompts. Because the rating scale thresholds are estimated separately for individual elements within a given facet, the PC model can be used to empirically verify the comparability of a rating scale structure across these elements. Additional details about the use of the PC model to explore rating scale category functioning are provided in Chapter Thirteen.

Rasch Models as Equating Models for Rater-Mediated Assessments

As noted in the discussion of the observational design building block above, measurement models based on Rasch models can be used to obtain estimates of student achievement that are adjusted for differences in rater severity. Essentially, these models serve as methods for equating student achievement across raters with different levels of severity. As a result of this useful property, the Many-Facet Rasch (MFR) model has become increasingly prevalent in the context of performance assessments because it facilitates adjustments for rater differences in the presence of incomplete data.

Although the use of the MFR model has gained popularity as a scaling technique for performance assessments, several key considerations related to model-data fit are often overlooked that have implications for the interpretation of adjusted student estimates. Specifically, it is essential to recognize that evidence of adequate model-data fit is a prerequisite to the interpretation of estimates on the logit scale in terms of the construct. In particular, the interpretation of student achievement estimates on the logit scale as adjusted for differences in rater severity depends on the degree to which there is evidence of model-data fit for the rater facet.

Rater Fit

Rater misfit to the Rasch model can occur in several different ways (Linacre & Wright, 1994), and a variety of Rasch-based indices are frequently used to identify rater effects, including Infit and Outfit statistics (Engelhard, 2013). In addition to statistical summaries expressed using a coefficient, Schumacker (2015) observed the usefulness of examining expected and empirical Item Response Functions (IRFs) as an indicator of model-data fit. He also pointed out the relationship between the slope of IRFs and standardized fit statistics: items with higher-than-expected fit statistics tend to have steeper IRFs, whereas items with lower-than-expected fit statistics tend to have flatter IRFs. These graphical displays can also be used in the context of rater-mediated assessments by examining the slope of rater response functions (RRFs), which describe model-expected ratings for a given rater across the range of the logit scale.

Although the Rasch model does not include a direct estimate of a discrimination (i.e., slope) parameter, it is possible to estimate discrimination for persons, items, and other facets using Rasch measurement software (Linacre, 2015). For polytomous items, an estimate of the discrimination parameter for raters can be calculated as:

$$\hat{a} = 1 + \left[\frac{\sum_N (M_{niX_{nij}} - \sum_{k=1}^{m} P_{nijk} M_{nijk})}{\sum_n \left(\sum_{k=1}^{m} M^2_{nijk} P_{nijk} - \left(\sum_{k=1}^{m} M_{nijk} P_{nijk} \right)^2 \right)} \right] \qquad (12.4)$$

with

$$M_{nik} = k(\theta_n - \lambda_i) - \sum_{l=1}^{k} \tau_{ij} \qquad (12.5)$$

where

M_{nik} = the value of M in Equation 12.4 for the observation, $k = X_{nij}$, that was observed when person n encountered rater i on item j.

The next section includes a brief illustration of the impact of one type of rater misfit on the interpretation of student achievement estimates that are adjusted using the MFR model. Graphical displays are used to illustrate the consequences of variation in model-data fit using a theoretical and empirical illustration.

Theoretical Illustration

As noted earlier, estimates of rater discrimination around 1.00 serve as one indicator of adequate fit to the MFR model. Figure 12.8 illustrates the influence of

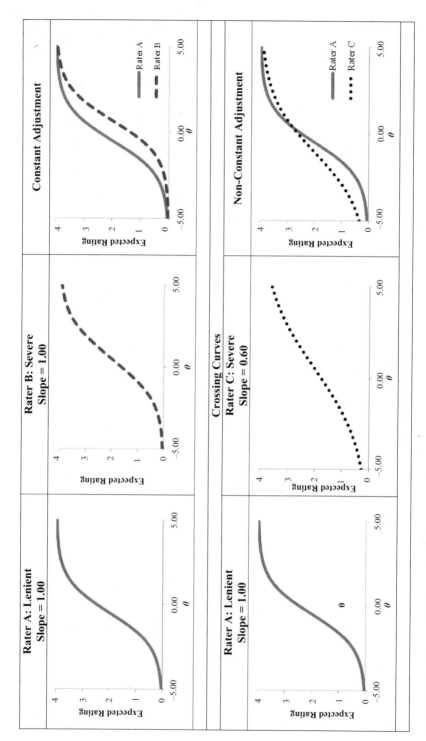

FIGURE 12.8 Theoretical Illustration: Adjustments for Rater Severity

model–data fit on MFR model adjustments of student achievement estimates using three illustrative raters. For each rater, an expected response function (i.e., rater response function, RRF) is presented that illustrates the relationship between student achievement estimates on the logit scale (θ) and the expected rating based on the rating scale formulation of the MFR model. In the top panel, Rater A and Rater B display adequate fit to the MFR model, but demonstrate different levels of severity. When the RRFs for these two raters are overlaid, their parallel slopes result in a constant adjustment for differences in rater severity using the expected ratings from the MFR model, such that student achievement can be interpreted on a common scale across raters with different levels of severity. On the other hand, Rater C is severe and displays misfit to the MFR model (slope = 0.60). When the RRFs for Rater C and Rater A are overlaid, the non-parallel slopes indicate that it is not possible to make a constant adjustment in student achievement estimates to account for the severity differences between these two raters.

Empirical Illustration

Figure 12.9 illustrates the same principles as Figure 12.8, but with empirical results from the empirical analysis of Design One using three raters with different severity estimates. Rater 14 is lenient ($\delta = -0.55$, $SE = 0.05$) and demonstrates adequate fit to the MFR model (slope = 0.99); Rater 15 is severe ($\delta = 0.37$, $SE = 0.05$) and also demonstrates adequate fit to the MFR model (slope = 1.01). On the other hand, Rater 20 is a moderate rater ($\delta = -0.04$, $SE = 0.05$) who has a lower-than-expected slope estimate (slope = 0.75). The overlaid RRFs indicate that, although it is possible to make a constant adjustment between Rater 14 (lenient) and Rater 15 (severe), it is not possible to make a constant adjustment between Rater 15 (severe) and Rater 20 (moderate).

Summary and Discussion

Using an adaptation of Wilson's (2005) constructing measures framework, this chapter provided an overview of key issues related to the design of rater-mediated assessment systems within the framework of rater-invariant measurement. Specifically, a set of building blocks for rater-mediated assessments were used to organize the presentation of key issues related to the definition of the rater-mediated latent variable, observational designs for ratings, rating rules, and measurement models for ratings. A set of guiding questions was presented that reflect these key considerations across various stages in the design of rater-mediated assessment systems.

A key message emphasized throughout this chapter is the central role of design decisions in the interpretation and use of results from rater-mediated assessment systems. Further, the design of rater-mediated assessment systems should be

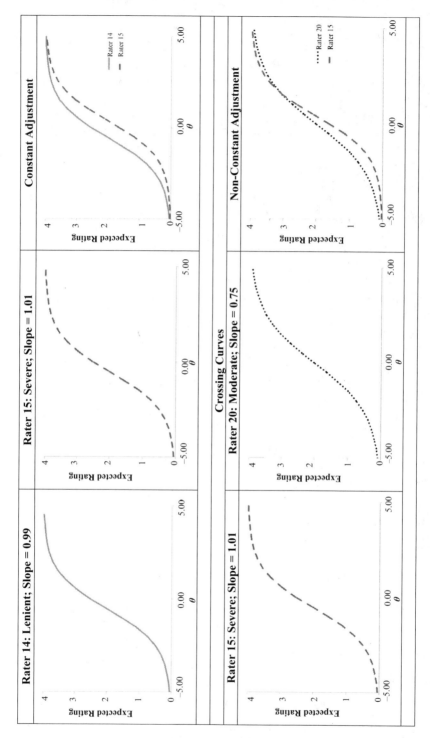

FIGURE 12.9 Empirical Illustration: Adjustments for Rater Severity

viewed as an iterative process in which empirical results inform subsequent iterations, including rater training procedures, the development of scoring materials, and rating designs. Although models based on Rasch Measurement Theory have been frequently applied in research related to rater-mediated assessments, it has not been widely recognized that design considerations, particularly related to connectivity within observational designs, category ordering, and model-data fit, are prerequisites to the invariance properties that motivate the use of this approach.

The consideration of practical issues for rater-mediated assessments concludes with the presentation of methods for evaluating rating quality in the next chapter.

References

American Educational Research Association (AERA), American Psychological Association (APA), & National Council on Measurement in Education (NCME). (2014). *Standards for educational and psychological testing.* Washington, DC: AERA.

Andrich, D. A. (1978). A rating formulation for ordered response categories. *Psychometrika, 43*(4), 561–573. https://doi.org/10.1007/BF02293814

Andrich, D. A. (2016). Rasch rating-scale model. In W. J. van der Linden (Ed.), *Handbook of item response theory, volume one: Models* (pp. 75–94). Boca Raton, FL: CRC Press.

Arter, J., & McTighe, J. (2001). *Scoring rubrics in the classroom.* Thousand Oaks, CA: Corwin Press.

Braun, H. I. (1988). Understanding scoring reliability: Experiments in calibrating essay readers. *Journal of Educational and Behavioral Statistics, 13*(1), 1–18. https://doi.org/10.3102/10769986013001001

Brunswik, E. (1956). *Perception and the representative design of psychological experiments* (2nd ed.). Berkeley, CA: University of California Press.

Engelhard, G. (1997). Constructing rater and task banks for performance assessments. *Journal of Outcome Measurement, 1*(1), 19–33.

Engelhard, G. (2013). *Invariant measurement: Using Rasch models in the social, behavioral, and health sciences.* New York, NY: Routledge.

Engelhard, G., Myford, C. M., & Cline, F. (2000). *Investigating assessor effects in National Board for Teaching Standards assessments for early childhood/generalist and middle childhood/generalist certification* (ETS Research Report No. RR-00–13). Princeton, NJ: Educational Testing Service.

Hammond, K. R., Stewart, T. R., Brehmer, B., & Steinmann, D. (1975). Social judgment theory. In M. F. Kaplan & S. Schwartz (Eds.), *Human judgment and decision processes.* New York, NY: Academic Press.

Johnson, R. L., Penny, J. A., & Gordon, B. (2009). *Assessing performance: Designing, scoring, and validating performance tasks.* New York: The Guilford Press.

Kirk, R. E. (1995). *Experimental design: Procedures for the behavioral sciences* (3rd ed.). Pacific Grove, CA: Brooks/Cole.

Lance, C. E., LaPointe, J. A., & Stewart, A. M. (1994). A test of the context dependency of three causal models of halo rater error. *Journal of Applied Psychology, 79*(3), 332–340. https://doi.org/10.1037/00219010.79.3.332

Linacre, J. M. (2002). Optimizing rating scale category effectiveness. *Journal of Applied Measurement, 3*(1), 85–106.

Linacre, J. M. (2015). *Facets Rasch Measurement* (Version 3.71.4). Chicago, IL: Winsteps.com.

Linacre, J. M., & Wright, B. D. (1994). Chi-square fit statistics. *Rasch Measurement Transactions, 8*(2), 350.

Lunz, M. E., & Stahl, J. A. (1990). Judge consistency and severity across grading periods. *Evaluation & the Health Professions, 13*(4), 425–444. https://doi.org/10.1177/016327879001300405

Lunz, M. E., Stahl, J. A., & Wright, B. D. (1996). The invariance of rater severity calibrations. In G. Engelhard & M. Wilson (Eds.), *Objective measurement: Theory into practice* (Vol. 3, pp. 99–112). Stamford, CT: Ablex.

Lunz, M., & Suanthong, S. (2011). Equating of multi-facet tests across administrations. *Journal of Applied Measurement, 12*(2), 124–134.

Masters, G. N. (1982). A Rasch model for partial credit scoring. *Psychometrika, 47*(2), 149–174. https://doi.org/10.1007/BF02296272

Mullis, I. V. S. (1984). Scoring direct writing assessments: What are the alternatives? *Educational Measurement: Issues and Practice, 3*(1), 16–18. https://doi.org/10.1111/j.17453992.1984.tb00728.x

Myford, C. M., & Mislevy, R. J. (1995). *Monitoring and improving a portfolio assessment system* (No. ETS Center for Performance Assessment Report No. MS 94–05). Princeton, NJ: Educational Testing Service.

Nering, M. L., & Ostini, R. (Eds.). (2010). *Handbook of polytomous item response theory models.* New York, NY: Routledge.

O'Niell, T. R., & Lunz, M. E. (2000). A method to study rater severity across several administrations. In M. Wilson & G. Engelhard (Eds.), *Objective measurement: Theory into practice* (Vol. 5, pp. 135–146). Stamford, CT: Ablex.

Raymond, M. R., & Viswesvaran, C. (1993). Least squares models to correct for rater effects in performance assessment. *Journal of Educational Measurement, 30*(3), 253–268.

Raymond, M. R., Webb, L. C., & Houston, W. M. (1991). Correcting performance-rating errors in oral examinations. *Evaluation & the Health Professions, 14*(1), 100–122. https://doi.org/10.1177/016327879101400107

Schumacker, R. E. (2015). Detecting measurement disturbance effects: The graphical display of item characteristics. *Journal of Applied Measurement, 16*(1), 76–81.

Wilson, H. G. (1988). Parameter estimation for peer grading under incomplete design. *Educational and Psychological Measurement, 48*(1), 69–81. https://doi.org/10.1177/001316448804800109

Wilson, M. (2005). *Constructing measures: An item response modeling approach.* New York, NY: Taylor & Francis.

Wind, S. A., Engelhard, G., & Wesolowski, B. (2016). Exploring the effects of rater linking designs and rater fit on achievement estimates within the context of music performance assessments. *Educational Assessment, 21*(4), 278–299. https://doi.org/10.1080/10627197.2016.1236676

Wind, S. A., & Peterson, M. E. (2017). A systematic review of methods for evaluating rating quality in language assessment. *Language Testing.* https://doi.org/10.1177/0265532216686999

13

EXAMINING RATING SCALE FUNCTIONING

> Since the analyst is always uncertain of the exact manner in which a particular rating scale will be used by a particular sample, investigation of the functioning of the rating scale is always merited.
>
> *(Linacre, 2002, p. 86)*

This chapter focuses on methods for exploring the empirical functioning of rating scales that provide evidence to inform the interpretation and use of ratings. Whereas the indicators of rating quality discussed in previous chapters focused on patterns of ratings specific to *individual raters*, the methods presented in this chapter describe the degree to which individual *rating scale categories* are actually functioning across various facets of a rater-mediated assessment system. *Rating scale functioning* provides additional information beyond indicators at the individual rater level related to how the categories are interpreted and used. This information is particularly useful in the development and revision of scoring materials, such as rubrics and performance-level descriptors, as well as rater training.

In polytomous Rasch models, it is possible to obtain a variety of diagnostic indicators regarding the empirical functioning of rating scale categories that are not available when other models are applied. Several scholars have proposed guidelines for evaluating the quality of rating scale functioning within the framework of polytomous Rasch Measurement Theory models (Engelhard & Wind, 2013; Linacre, 2002). These guidelines include both statistical (numerical) and graphical summaries that highlight a variety of empirical characteristics of rating scale category functioning. These guidelines support the quest for invariant measurement with rating scales.

The purpose of this chapter is to describe and illustrate methods for evaluating the empirical functioning of rating scales based on polytomous Rasch models. The specific issues and questions addressed in this chapter are organized as follows:

- How can polytomous Rasch models be used to examine rating scale functioning?
  - o Guidelines for rating scale functioning
- Empirical illustration
  - o Data analysis
- Evidence of rating scale functioning
- Summary and discussion

How Can Polytomous Rasch Models Be Used to Examine Rating Scale Functioning?

In previous chapters, we highlighted the implications of adjacent-categories probabilities as the underlying probability formulation for polytomous Rasch models, including the Rating Scale Model (RSM) (Andrich, 1978) and the Partial Credit Model (PCM) (Masters, 1982). Specifically, the definition of rating scale category thresholds in both models is based on the probability of a rating in a given category, rather than the category just below it. This *adjacent-categories* formulation stands in contrast to other threshold formulations for polytomous Item Response Theory models, such as the Graded Response Model (Samejima, 1969, 1997), in which thresholds are defined using cumulative probabilities.

An important consequence of this formulation of rating scale thresholds in the polytomous Rasch model is that it is possible to evaluate the empirical functioning of rating scale categories independently of the other categories in the scale. Similar to empirical investigations of model-data fit, the empirical investigation of rating scale category functioning can reveal discrepancies between expectations based on the underlying measurement theory and the operational use and interpretation of rating scale categories. These results are an essential component providing validity evidence for regarding the appropriate interpretation and use of scores. This information is also useful for guiding revision of scoring materials and training procedures.

Guidelines for Rating Scale Functioning

Several scholars have proposed guidelines and recommendations for evaluating rating scale functioning that include both numerical summaries and graphical displays. The information based on polytomous Rasch models has diagnostic value for exploring the empirical properties of rating scales. These guidelines can be viewed as criteria that can inform the interpretation and revision of rating scales.

Linacre (2002) proposed a set of guidelines for rating scales that can be evaluated using empirical results from both the RS and PC models. These guidelines include a general prerequisite that rating scale ordering is aligned with orientation of the latent variable, and eight specific guidelines that describe a variety of aspects of rating scale functioning. Building upon these guidelines, Engelhard and Wind (2013) described a systematic approach to evaluating rating scale functioning using numerical and graphical evidence based on polytomous Rasch models. In this chapter, these guidelines and sources of evidence are considered in terms of four major categories: (A) category structure; (B) directional orientation with the latent variable; (C) category precision; and (D) model-data fit (see Table 13.1). This section includes a summary of the numerical and graphical sources of evidence related to each of the categories in Table 13.1. An empirical illustration using data from a rater-mediated writing assessment follows.

TABLE 13.1 Guidelines and Evidence of Rating Scale Category Functioning

Guidelines	Evidence of Intended Rating Scale Functioning	Numerical Evidence	Graphical Evidence
Rating scale category structure	The distance between rating scale category thresholds is invariant within cues in the assessment system	The distance between thresholds is equivalent within cues in the assessment system	Wright map shows similar threshold locations within cues
Directional orientation with the latent variable	Increasing locations on the latent variable correspond to increasing categories on the rating scale	Increasing average logit-scale locations for the object of measurement within increasing rating scale categories. Increasing rating scale category thresholds across increasing rating scale categories	Expected response functions are monotonic
Category precision	Rating scale categories are distinct	Ratings are normally or uniformly distributed across scale categories. The absolute value of the difference between rating scale category thresholds is between 1.4 and 5.0 logits	Category probability functions are multimodal. Conditional probability curves are distinct. Information functions support the inference of distinct categories

(Continued)

TABLE 13.1 (Continued)

Guidelines	Evidence of Intended Rating Scale Functioning	Numerical Evidence	Graphical Evidence
Model-data fit	Rating scale categories meet model expectations	Model-data fit statistics for rating scale categories fall within the range of expected values when data fit the model	Acceptable match between empirical and expected response functions

A. Rating Scale Category Structure

The first guideline including presentation of evidence for evaluating rating scale functioning is related to the structure of the rating scale categories based on the polytomous Rasch model. Across both the RS and PC formulations of the polytomous Rasch model, the distance between rating scale category thresholds is determined empirically. In other words, the distance between any two adjacent rating scale categories is not constrained to be equivalent to the distance between any other two adjacent rating scale categories. However, when the RS model is applied, the empirical structure of the rating scale categories is fixed across elements within each of the cues included in the model, such that a single set of rating scale thresholds is obtained. On the other hand, the PC model results in separate sets of threshold estimates that describe the structure of the rating scale specific to individual elements within a cue of interest, such as items or raters. These estimates are not required to maintain a common structure across the individual rating scales.

In many applications of rating scales, the structure of the scale categories (i.e., the distances between categories) is intended to be equivalent across cues, such that the interpretation of ratings is invariant across individual raters, items, or other facets. This hypothesized rating scale structure is illustrated in Figure 13.1, Panel A for a group of three raters who share a common interpretation of the rating scale category structure for a five-category scale. Because the PC model results in empirical estimates of thresholds specific to cues of interest, this model is particularly useful for evaluating the hypothesis of a common rating scale structure. As shown in Figure 13.1, Panel B, estimates based on the PC model can reveal differences in the empirical structure of rating scales across cues.

As given in Table 13.1, evidence of rating scale functioning related to this category describes the degree to which the distance between rating scale category thresholds is invariant across elements within cues in the assessment system. When the PC model is applied, numerical and graphical evidence can be examined for evidence that the structure of the rating scale is invariant across these elements.

A. Rating Scale Model				
Rater 1 $X = 1$	$X = 2$	$X = 3$	$X = 4$	$X = 5$
Rater 2 $X = 1$	$X = 2$	$X = 3$	$X = 4$	$X = 5$
Rater 3 $X = 1$	$X = 2$	$X = 3$	$X = 4$	$X = 5$

B. Partial Credit Model				
Rater 1 $X = 1$	$X = 2$	$X = 3$	$X = 4$	$X = 5$
Rater 2 $X = 1$	$X = 2$	$X = 3$	$X = 4$	$X = 5$
Rater 3 $X = 1$	$X = 2$	$X = 3$	$X = 4$	$X = 5$

FIGURE 13.1   Rating Scale and Partial Credit Models

Note: The dashed vertical lines illustrate rating scale category thresholds (τ) that define the structure of the rating scale.

Numerical Evidence

First, the distance between PC model threshold estimates (τ_{ik}) on the logit scale provides numerical evidence regarding the invariance of the rating scale structure across elements within cues in an assessment system. Specifically, the absolute value of the distance between threshold estimates can be compared across elements within a cue. Large discrepancies in the rating scale structure across elements provide evidence that rater interpretations of the rating scale categories are not invariant across these elements.

Graphical Evidence

The distance between rating scale category thresholds based on the PC model can also be evaluated using graphical evidence. When the PC model is applied, the corresponding Wright map includes estimates of threshold locations specific to the set of rating scales specified across elements of a particular cue. These locations can be compared visually in order to gauge the comparability of the rating scale structures.

B. Directional Orientation with the Latent Variable

The second category of evidence is related to the orientation of the rating scale categories with the direction of the latent variable. Essentially, evidence in this category describes the degree to which higher rating scale categories correspond to higher locations on the construct. As noted above, the order of rating scale category thresholds is determined empirically when polytomous Rasch models are applied in practice. These estimates can be examined empirically to determine whether their ordering corresponds to the intended ordering of the rating scale. Category directionality can be evaluated using both the PC and RS formulation of the polytomous Rasch model. When the PC model is applied, category directionality can be evaluated separately for each of the separate rating scales that are estimated; when the RS model is applied, category ordering can be evaluated for the overall set of cues.

Numerical Evidence

Table 13.1 lists two major sources of numerical evidence regarding the directional orientation of the rating scale with the latent variable. First, the average logit-scale locations of the object of measurement (e.g., students) observed within rating scale categories can be examined. Increasing average values across increasing categories suggest that the rating scale categories are oriented in the same direction as the latent variable. Second, the values of threshold estimates obtained from the PC or RS model can be examined for evidence of increasing logit-scale locations across increasing categories.

Graphical Evidence

In terms of graphical evidence, the directional orientation of the rating scale can also be evaluated using expected response functions, which are graphical displays that illustrate the relationship between expected ratings based on the polytomous Rasch model and logit-scale locations. Non-decreasing IRFs provide evidence that the empirical ordering of rating scale categories is congruent with the intended order.

C. Category Precision

The second category of evidence for evaluating rating scale functioning is related to the precision with which categories describe unique locations on the latent variable. Essentially, evidence of category precision suggests that each of the categories included in the rating scale is being used to meaningfully distinguish persons in terms of the latent variable. These indicators can be calculated using both the PC and RS formulations of the polytomous Rasch model.

Numerical Evidence

Table 13.1 includes two sources of numerical evidence related to category precision. First, numerical indicators of category precision include the distribution of observed ratings across categories. In order to obtain stable estimates of category thresholds, Linacre (2002) recommended a minimum of 10 observations within each rating scale category. Second, the overall distribution of ratings across categories should be approximately normal or uniform. In order to ensure that rating scale categories describe distinct locations on the construct, Linacre recommended that the thresholds between rating scale categories range between about 1.4 and 5 logits for most scales.

Graphical Evidence

Results from polytomous Rasch models can also be used to create a variety of graphical displays to evaluate category precision. First, category probability curves (i.e., category response functions) can be drawn that represent the conditional probability for a rating in a given category across the range of the latent variable, where the peak of each curve (i.e., the mode) reflects the location at which a rating in a particular category is most probable. Distinct modes for each rating scale category provide evidence of category precision.

Second, conditional probability curves illustrate the relationship between probabilities for observed ratings in pairs of adjacent rating scale categories and locations on the latent variable. Specifically, each curve displays the conditional probability for a rating in a given category and the category just below it (y-axis), given person locations on the latent variable (x-axis). Distinct (non-overlapping) conditional probability curves provide evidence of category precision.

Finally, statistical information functions can be calculated that reflect the overall precision across rating scale categories. In the context of IRT, information functions reflect the targeting between person locations and item difficulty, as well as the standard error of measurement (Fisher, 1958). Well-targeted rating scale categories and smaller standard errors provide more information than poorly targeted items and larger standard errors. Graphical displays of information in the form of *information functions* display values of statistical information (y-axis) within a category across logit-scale locations (x-axis). Evidence of category precision is provided by peaked (i.e., maximized) information in lower categories at the lower end of the logit scale, and peaked information in higher categories at the higher end of the logit scale.

D. Model-Data Fit

The third category of evidence for evaluating rating scale functioning is model-data fit. Essentially, indices of model-data fit describe the match between empirical observations and underlying model requirements. In addition to indicators of model-data fit for items, persons, and other cues, it is also possible to explore model-data fit for rating scale categories using numerical and graphical evidence. These indicators of model-data fit can be evaluated using both the PC and RS formulations of the polytomous Rasch model.

Numerical Evidence

First, model-data fit can be evaluated for rating scale categories using summaries of residuals for observations within a particular category. When the polytomous Rasch model is estimated, the Facets computer program (Linacre, 2015) provides Outfit mean square error (*MSE*) statistics that are specific to each rating scale category. These Outfit *MSE* statistics for categories are calculated using the same general form as Outfit *MSE* statistics for items, persons, and other facets. Specifically, Outfit *MSE* for categories is calculated as:

$$U_{ik} = \frac{\sum_{n}^{N} Z_{nik}^2}{N_{ik}},$$

(13.1)

where

Z^2_{nik} = the standardized residual between the observed rating and the expected rating for Person n who receives a rating in category k on item i, based on the polytomous Rasch model, and

N_{ik} = the number of persons who receive a rating in category k on item i.

Values of the Outfit MSE statistic for rating scale categories are interpreted in the same general manner as Rasch fit statistics for persons, items, and other facets.

Graphical Evidence

Graphical displays can also be used to evaluate model-data fit for rating scale categories. Specifically, the expected item response functions and category probability curves discussed related to Category C can be overlaid with empirical observations in order to explore the alignment between model expectations and empirical responses. Evidence of close correspondence between expected and empirical response functions provides evidence of model-data fit for rating scale categories.

Empirical Illustration

In this section, empirical data from a large-scale, rater-mediated writing assessment are used to illustrate the investigation of rating scale functioning using polytomous Rasch models. The data were collected during an administration of the Alaska High School Graduation Qualification Examination (HSGQE) for writing. The HSGQE includes a combination of multiple-choice items and extended constructed-response (ECR) items that are scored by raters. The current illustration focuses on the ratings assigned to three ECR items that are scored using a four-category scale (1 = *low*; 4 = *high*). The illustrative dataset includes 8,620 students and 39 raters.

Data Analysis

In order to explore rating scale functioning in the HSGQE, two PC formulations of the MFR model were estimated using the Facets program (Linacre, 2015). Model I was specified in order to allow the structure of the rating scale to vary across the ECR items as follows:

$$\ln\left[\frac{P_{nij=k}}{P_{nij=(k-1)}}\right] = \theta_n - \lambda_i - \delta_j - \tau_{nk}, \tag{13.1}$$

where

θ_n = the judged logit-scale location of Student n,
λ_i = the logit-scale location of Rater i,

δ_j = the judged logit-scale location of ECR item j, and
τ_{nk} = the location on the logit scale at which a rating in Category
k is equally probable as a rating in Category $k - 1$ for ECR item j.

Model II is specified in order to allow the rating scale to vary across raters:

$$\ln\left[\frac{P_{nij=k}}{P_{nij=(k-1)}}\right] = \theta_n - \lambda_i - \delta_j - \tau_{nk} \tag{13.2}$$

where all of the terms are defined as in Equation 13.2 except the threshold parameter. In Model II, the threshold is defined as the location on the logit scale at which a rating in Category k is equally probable as a rating in Category $k - 1$ specific to Rater i.

Evidence of Rating Scale Functioning

This section includes results from Model I and Model II related to the four categories of rating scale functioning described above: (A) Category Structure, (B) Directional Orientation with the Latent Variable, (C) Category Precision, and (D) Model-Data Fit.

1. Category Structure

As noted above, the first category of evidence of rating scale functioning is related to the overall structure of the rating scale categories. In the illustrative analysis, two PC models were specified that allow for the examination of category structure across the ECR items (Model I) and across the raters (Model II).

Numerical Evidence

Numerical evidence related to the structure of rating scale categories includes the absolute value of the difference between thresholds. In general, similar values of these distances within cues provides evidence that a rating scale is functioning as intended. Table 13.2, Panel A includes the absolute values of the distances between thresholds for the individual rating scales estimated for the three ECR items using Model I. Examination of these results suggests a similar overall rating scale category structure across these items, providing evidence that raters' interpretation of the rating scale category structure was comparable for the three items.

Table 13.2, Panel B includes the absolute values of the distances between thresholds for the rating scales estimated for each of the 39 raters using Model II. Although the values are generally comparable across raters, the results indicate some variation in the interpretation of the categories for individual raters. Specifically, the absolute value of the distance between the first two thresholds

TABLE 13.2 Numerical Evidence for Category A (Rating Scale Structure)

Panel A: Model I

Item	$|\tau_2-\tau_1|$	$|\tau_3-\tau_2|$
ECR1	5.71	2.95
ECR2	5.46	3.21
ECR3	5.08	3.13

Panel B: Model II

Rater	$|\tau_2-\tau_1|$	$|\tau_3-\tau_2|$
1	6.37	4.12
2	5.17	3.11
3	6.48	2.61
4	6.98	2.93
5	4.94	3.71
6	5.37	3.91
7	6.14	4.22
8	5.73	2.37
9	4.75	4.57
10	4.92	2.70
11	4.73	2.54
12	4.96	3.31
13	5.96	2.60
14	5.45	3.16
15	4.47	3.39
16	4.47	2.97
17	5.68	2.23
18	6.20	2.51
19	5.20	2.50
20	4.22	2.75
21	5.93	4.07
22	5.01	3.30
23	5.33	3.47
24	5.84	3.08
25	4.86	2.77
26	5.60	4.09
27	5.37	2.31
28	5.66	2.72
29	6.40	2.30
30	6.14	3.47
31	5.77	2.92
32	5.69	3.38
33	6.22	3.63
34	5.65	2.89
35	5.69	3.11
36	3.97	3.61
37	4.84	3.88
38	6.09	3.21
39	5.25	3.42

($|\tau_1 - \tau_2|$) ranges from 3.97 logits for Rater 36 to 6.98 logits for Rater 4—a distance of about 3 logits. Similarly, the absolute value of the distance between the second two thresholds ($|\tau_3 - \tau_2|$) ranges from 2.23 logits for Rater 17 to 4.57 logits for Rater 9.

Graphical Evidence

Graphical evidence related to category structure includes the threshold locations on the Wright map. When the Facets program is used to estimate the PC model, it is possible to output a Wright map that shows the estimated threshold locations for each rating scale. For example, Figure 13.2A is a Wright map that shows the rating scale structure for the three ECR items based on Model I. The first column is the logit scale, and the three subsequent columns show the rating scale calibrations for ECR1, ECR2, and ECR3. Horizontal lines are used to illustrate the locations of rating scale thresholds, such that the horizontal line between rating scale Category 1 and rating scale Category 2 reflects the location of τ_1 on the logit scale, and the horizontal line between rating scale Category 2 and rating scale Category 3 reflects the location of τ_2 on the logit scale. Visual inspection of this display confirms the finding from the numerical evidence that the rating scale structure is comparable across the three ECR items.

Figure 13.2B is a Wright map that shows the rating scale structure for the 39 raters based on Model II. Following the same format as Figure 13.2A, the first column is the logit scale, and the subsequent columns show the rating scale structure for each of the raters included in the example dataset. As was noted in the inspection of the distances between thresholds using numerical evidence, the results from Model II suggest some differences in the interpretation of the rating scale across individual raters. These differences suggest that individual raters may rate student performances that have the same logit-scale location within different categories. For example, a student located at $\theta = 4.7$ would be rated within Category 4 by Rater 4 and within Category 3 by Rater 7.

2. Directional Orientation with the Latent Variable

The second category of evidence is related to the degree to which the rating scale categories are oriented in the same direction as the latent variable. In this section, the illustrative dataset is examined for evidence of directional orientation with the latent variable for the three ECR items (Model I) and the 39 raters (Model II).

Numerical Evidence

As noted above, there are two main sources of numerical evidence that can be used to evaluate the directional orientation of rating scale categories with the latent variable. First, average logit-scale locations for the object of measurement

```
+-----------------------+
|Logit|ECR1 |ECR2 |ECR3 |
|-----+-----+-----+-----|
|  7 + (4) + (4) + (4) |
|     |     |     |     |
|     |     |     |     |
|  6 +     +     +     |
|     |     |     |     |
|     |     |     |     |
|  5 +     +     +     |
|     |     |     |     |
|     |     |     |     |
|  4 + --- + --- + --- |
|     |     |     |     |
|  3 +     +     +     |
|     |     |     |     |
|     | 3   | 3   | 3   |
|  2 +     +     +     |
|     |     |     |     |
|     |     |     |     |
|  1 +     +     +     |
|     | --- | --- | --- |
|     |     |     |     |
* 0 *     *     *         *
|     |     |     |     |
|     |     |     |     |
| -1 +     +     +     |
|     |     |     |     |
|     |     |     |     |
| -2 + 2   + 2   + 2   |
|     |     |     |     |
|     |     |     |     |
| -3 +     +     +     |
|     |     |     |     |
|     |     |     |     |
| -4 +     +     +     |
|     |     |     | --- |
|     | --- | --- |     |
| -5 +     +     +     |
|     |     |     |     |
|     |     |     |     |
| -6 +     +     +     |
|     |     |     |     |
|     |     |     |     |
| -7 + (1) + (1) + (1) |
|-----+-----+-----+-----|
|Logit|ECR1 |ECR2 |ECR3 |
+-----------------------+
```

FIGURE 13.2A Graphical Evidence for Category A, Model I

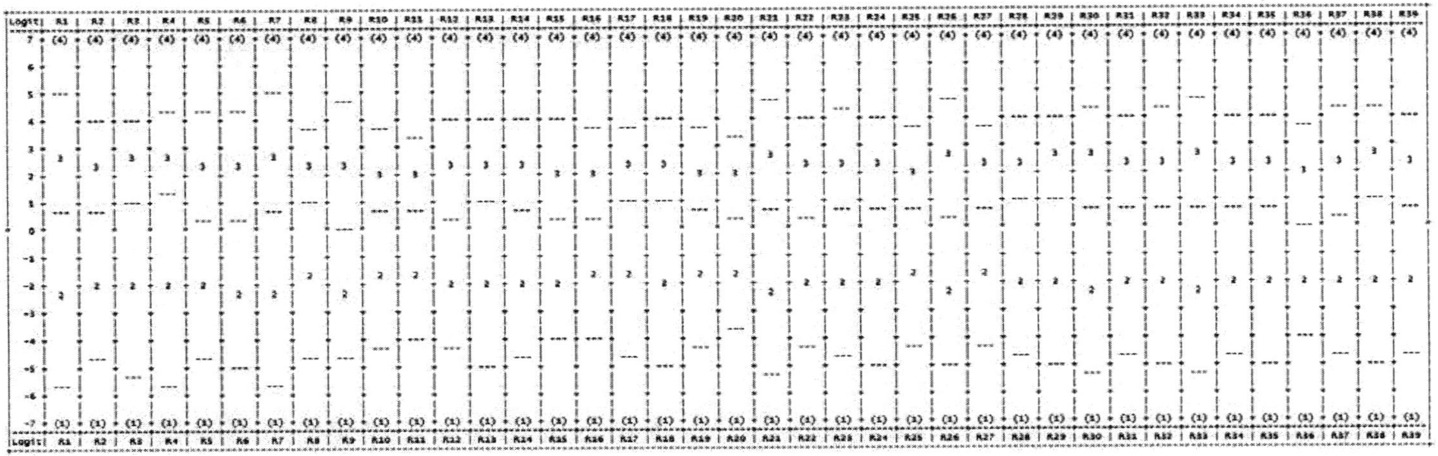

FIGURE 13.2B Graphical Evidence for Category A, Model II

can be examined within each rating scale category. When the rating scale is oriented in the same direction as the latent variable, these average values will increase within increasing categories. In the context of the illustrative dataset, students are the object of measurement. Accordingly, estimates of average judged logit-scale locations for students within each rating scale category provide numerical evidence to evaluate the directional orientation of the rating scale. Second, threshold locations on the logit scale can be examined; these values suggest directional orientation with the latent variable when the values of threshold locations increase with increasing rating scale categories.

Table 13.3 includes average logit-scale locations for students within the four rating scale categories based on Model I (Panel A) and Model II (Panel B). These results indicate monotonic increasing judged locations within increasing rating scale categories for each of the ECR items and each of the raters in the Alaska writing data.

Table 13.3 also includes the three estimated locations of the three thresholds for the four-category rating scale based on Model I (Panel A) and Model II (Panel B). Similar to the average logit-scale locations, these results also suggest directional orientation with the latent variable for each of the ECR items and each of the raters in the Alaska writing data.

Graphical Evidence

Graphical evidence related to the orientation of rating scale categories with the latent variable includes graphical displays of expected response functions. As noted above, these response functions illustrate the expected ratings based on the model across the range of the latent variable. When the rating scale categories are oriented in the same direction as the latent variable, expected ratings will increase across increasing rating scale categories. In the illustrative analysis, response functions are examined for ECR items related to Model I and for raters related to Model II.

Figure 13.3 Panel A includes expected item response functions (IRFs) for the three ECR items based on Model I. In each plot, the logit scale that represents the latent variable is plotted along the x-axis, and the expected ratings based on Model I are plotted along the y-axis. Because each of the IRFs is increasing as the logit scale moves from low to high (left to right), these results suggest that the rating scale categories are oriented as expected for the three ECR items.

Along the same lines, Figure 13.3 Panel B includes expected item response functions based on Model II. Because the rating scale was allowed to vary across raters, the response functions based on this model are drawn for each of the 39 raters included in the illustrative dataset. For illustrative purposes, three raters were selected to illustrate graphical evidence related to this category: Rater 4, Rater 15, and Rater 36. Similar to the findings from Model I, these rater response functions (RRFs) suggest that, although there are some differences across individual raters, the rating scale categories are oriented in the same direction as the latent variable because the expected ratings are increasing across increasing values of the logit scale.

TABLE 13.3 Numerical Evidence for Category B (Directional Orientation with the Latent Variable)

Panel A: Model I

Item	Average θ within Categories				Threshold Estimates		
	$X = 1$	$X = 2$	$X = 3$	$X = 4$	τ_1	τ_2	τ_3
ECR1	−4.39	−1.48	1.21	3.03	−4.79	0.92	3.87
ECR2	−4.34	−1.52	1.28	3.08	−4.71	0.75	3.96
ECR3	−4.28	−1.51	1.22	3.08	−4.43	0.65	3.78

Panel B: Model II

Rater	Average θ within Categories				Threshold Estimates		
	$X = 1$	$X = 2$	$X = 3$	$X = 4$	τ_1	τ_2	τ_3
1	−4.38	−1.53	1.58	3.38	−5.62	0.75	4.87
2	−3.88	−1.11	1.63	3.29	−4.48	0.69	3.80
3	−3.87	−1.12	1.82	3.67	−5.19	1.29	3.90
4	−4.65	−1.47	1.42	3.65	−5.63	1.35	4.28
5	−3.64	−1.58	1.57	3.49	−4.53	0.41	4.12
6	−3.92	−1.19	1.71	3.95	−4.88	0.49	4.40
7	−4.24	−1.51	1.49	3.80	−5.50	0.64	4.86
8	−4.47	−1.30	1.25	3.31	−4.61	1.12	3.49
9	−4.50	−1.57	1.21	3.53	−4.69	0.06	4.63
10	−3.97	−1.31	1.34	2.87	−4.18	0.74	3.44
11	−4.05	−1.33	1.30	3.00	−4.00	0.73	3.27
12	−4.28	−1.55	0.80	3.01	−4.41	0.55	3.86
13	−3.68	−1.36	1.57	3.62	−4.84	1.12	3.72
14	−4.26	−1.43	1.17	2.99	−4.69	0.76	3.92
15	−4.11	−1.39	1.23	3.26	−4.11	0.36	3.75
16	−3.50	−1.26	1.12	3.03	−3.97	0.50	3.47
17	−4.76	−1.41	1.41	2.68	−4.53	1.15	3.38
18	−4.52	−1.45	1.29	2.93	−4.97	1.23	3.74
19	−3.92	−1.21	1.09	3.18	−4.30	0.90	3.40
20	−3.51	−1.51	1.17	2.79	−3.73	0.49	3.24
21	−4.19	−1.41	1.39	3.25	−5.31	0.62	4.69
22	−4.34	−1.41	1.39	2.98	−4.44	0.57	3.87
23	−4.65	−1.72	1.02	2.55	−4.71	0.62	4.09
24	−4.47	−1.56	1.17	3.28	−4.92	0.92	4.00
25	−4.15	−1.37	1.18	2.79	−4.16	0.70	3.47
26	−4.54	−2.24	0.63	2.49	−5.10	0.50	4.59
27	−4.43	−1.44	1.17	2.67	−4.35	1.02	3.33
28	−4.73	−1.69	0.87	2.37	−4.68	0.98	3.70
29	−4.49	−1.28	1.50	3.01	−5.03	1.37	3.67
30	−4.51	−1.45	1.25	3.16	−5.25	0.89	4.36
31	−4.38	−1.56	1.34	3.08	−4.82	0.95	3.87
32	−3.68	−1.04	1.57	4.05	−4.92	0.77	4.15
33	−4.08	−1.34	1.72	3.86	−5.36	0.86	4.49
34	−4.67	−1.49	1.28	3.12	−4.73	0.92	3.81
35	−4.40	−1.40	1.34	3.01	−4.83	0.86	3.97
36	−4.30	−1.63	0.99	2.93	−3.85	0.12	3.73
37	−4.58	−1.89	0.76	2.25	−4.52	0.32	4.20
38	−5.05	−1.85	0.97	3.16	−5.13	0.96	4.17
39	−4.06	−1.43	1.59	3.49	−4.64	0.61	4.03

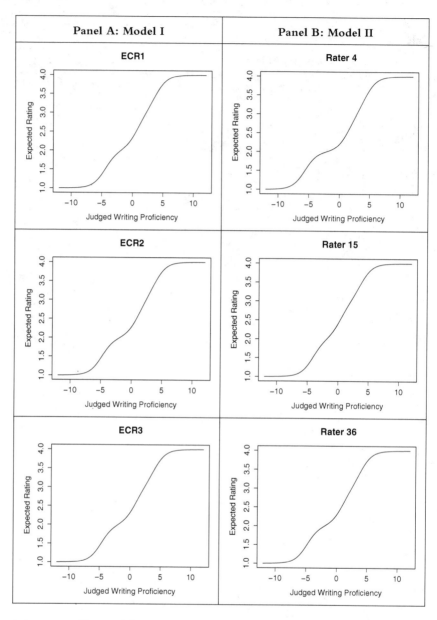

FIGURE 13.3 Expected Response Functions

3. Category Precision

Next, evidence of category precision is used to evaluate the degree to which the operational use of rating scale categories reflects distinct locations on the latent variable. Using the illustrative dataset, evidence of category precision is examined for each of the ECR items using Model I and for each rater using Model II.

Numerical Evidence

There are two main sources of numerical evidence related to category precision. First, the frequency of ratings can be examined within each category for evidence that each of the categories is being used, where an approximately normal or uniform distribution of ratings across categories provides evidence of category precision. In the context of the illustrative dataset, these frequencies are examined as they relate to ECR items (Model I) and raters (Model II). Table 13.4, Panel A, includes the observed frequencies of ratings within each of the four rating scale categories for the three ECR items. These results indicate a similar distribution of ratings across categories for the three items, where most of the ratings were assigned in Category 2 or Category 3. Furthermore, Category 4 appears to be relatively infrequently used across all three items. A similar result is also evident in the distribution of ratings across categories for the raters. As can be seen in Table 13.4, Panel B, most of the raters tended to use Category 2 or Category 3 most frequently, with notably fewer ratings assigned in the extreme categories.

In addition to the distribution of ratings across categories, numerical evidence related to category precision also includes the absolute value of the difference between rating scale category thresholds. These values were examined for the illustrative dataset as evidence of the category structure above, where they were examined for evidence that the difference between thresholds was comparable across rating scales. For the purpose of evaluating category precision, these values are examined for evidence that the distance between categories is within an acceptable range to describe a distinct set of locations on the latent variable. As noted above, Linacre (2002) recommended a distance between 1.4 and 5.0 logits as evidence that rating scale categories are being used operationally to describe a unique range of the latent variable.

Examination of the values in Table 13.2 suggests that the rating scale categories in the illustrative dataset may not reflect distinct values on the logit scale for all three ECR items (Panel A) and many of the raters (Panel B). Specifically, the absolute value of the distance between the first two thresholds exceeds Linacre's (2002) recommended maximum value of 5 logits for all three ECR items and for 29 of the raters. This finding suggests that the operational use of Category 2 may not reflect a distinct set of locations on the latent variable.

Graphical Evidence

As given in Table 13.1, three graphical displays are particularly useful for exploring the degree to which rating scale categories describe distinct locations on the

TABLE 13.4 Numerical Evidence for Category C (Category Precision)

Panel A: Model I

Item	X = 1		X = 2		X = 3		X = 4	
	f	%	*f*	%	*f*	%	*f*	%
ECR1	1,676	10	9,905	62	3,778	24	651	4
ECR2	1,487	11	7,936	58	3,607	26	622	5
ECR3	1,957	12	8,811	56	4,214	27	787	5

Distribution of Ratings Across Categories (for Panel A)

Panel B: Model II

Rater	X = 1		X = 2		X = 3		X = 4	
	Freq	%	Freq	%	Freq	%	Freq	%
1	29	5	330	59	182	33	19	3
2	37	7	268	49	190	35	53	10
3	26	5	308	60	134	26	44	9
4	44	6	500	70	150	21	25	3
5	41	8	258	51	174	34	35	7
6	22	5	225	47	193	40	40	8
7	28	5	336	58	197	34	19	3
8	33	11	189	61	65	21	21	7
9	167	9	914	48	748	39	72	4
10	113	12	506	54	255	27	67	7
11	145	14	545	53	264	26	79	8
12	282	14	1,123	57	499	25	72	4
13	30	7	249	61	100	25	28	7
14	53	11	280	58	131	27	21	4
15	83	12	347	50	228	33	42	6
16	147	12	628	50	389	31	95	8
17	283	14	1,259	61	399	19	107	5
18	156	10	996	65	312	20	65	4
19	139	11	681	56	306	25	85	7
20	76	16	234	50	127	27	33	7
21	54	5	567	57	336	34	31	3
22	74	10	385	54	216	30	37	5
23	202	13	914	61	354	23	37	2
24	313	11	1,872	63	683	23	108	4
25	227	14	909	54	434	26	100	6
26	310	16	1,254	63	404	20	21	1
27	287	15	1,147	60	378	20	93	5
28	202	16	785	64	219	18	29	2
29	123	8	984	66	312	21	78	5
30	128	7	1,097	63	461	26	55	3
31	236	11	1,377	62	510	23	94	4
32	26	5	293	52	201	36	46	8
33	25	5	293	57	167	33	28	5
34	263	12	1,362	61	524	23	97	4
35	145	9	949	59	432	27	69	4
36	95	18	255	48	155	29	23	4
37	232	17	753	56	325	24	28	2
38	204	13	1,041	67	285	18	31	2
39	39	8	239	51	156	33	32	7

Distribution of Ratings Across Categories (for Panel B)

latent variable: category probability curves, conditional probability curves, and information functions.

Figure 13.4 includes category probability curves for the three ECR items based on Model I (Panel A) and three selected raters based on Model II (Panel B).

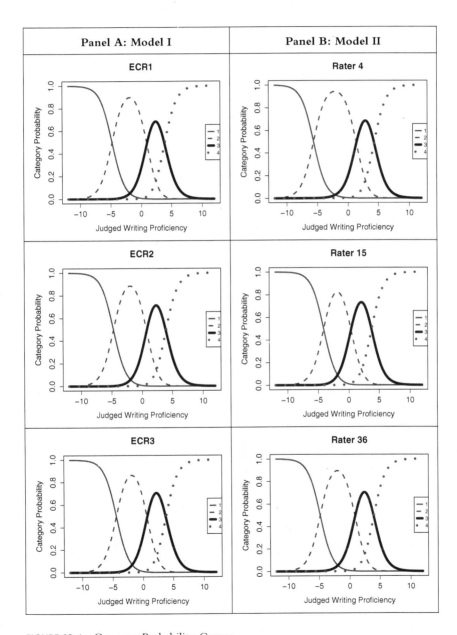

FIGURE 13.4 Category Probability Curves

In each plot, the x-axis shows the logit scale that represents the latent variable of judged writing proficiency, and the y-axis shows the probability that a rating is assigned in category k, rather than in category $k-1$. Different lines are used to show the probabilities associated with each category in the rating scale. These plots provide evidence of category precision when they are multimodal—that is, when the curve representing each category in the rating scale has a distinct peak. Inspection of the category probability curves for the three ECR items in Panel A suggests that the categories represent distinct locations on the latent variable, but that there are some differences across categories with regard to the range of values on the latent variable at which the category is most probable. Similarly, the category probability curves for Raters 4, 15, and 36 (Panel B) indicate distinct categories for all three raters, but also suggest differences in the operational use of the categories across raters.

The second source of graphical evidence related to category precision is conditional probability curves. As noted above, these curves display the conditional probability that a rating is assigned in pairs of adjacent categories across values of the latent variable. These curves are useful for exploring the degree to which rating scale categories are used operationally to describe distinct locations on the logit scale. Figure 13.5 includes conditional probability curves for the three ECR items based on Model I (Panel A) and three selected raters based on Model II (Panel B). In each plot, the x-axis shows the logit scale that represents the latent variable of judged writing proficiency, and the y-axis shows the probability that a rating is assigned in category k or category $k-1$. These plots provide evidence of category precision when the curves that represent each pair of adjacent categories are non-overlapping. Inspection of the category probability curves for the three ECR items in Panel A suggests that the raters are distinguishing between categories in their operational application of the rating scale. Similarly, the conditional probability curves for Raters 4, 15, and 36 (Panel B) indicate distinct categories for all three raters, but also suggest differences in the operational use of the categories across raters.

Third, information functions can be examined for evidence of category precision. As noted above, information functions are graphical displays that illustrate the targeting between student locations and item difficulty, as well as the standard error of measurement (Fisher, 1958). Higher values of statistical information suggest more precise measurement (i.e., better targeting and lower standard errors). Using the Facets program (Linacre, 2015), information functions can be drawn for an overall rating scale and within rating scale categories. In keeping with the focus of this chapter on rating scale categories, information functions for rating scale categories are illustrated using the example dataset. These displays provide evidence of category precision when the information for each category is maximized across a distinct range on the latent variable.

Figure 13.6 includes category information functions for the three ECR items based on Model I (Panel A) and three selected raters based on Model II (Panel B).

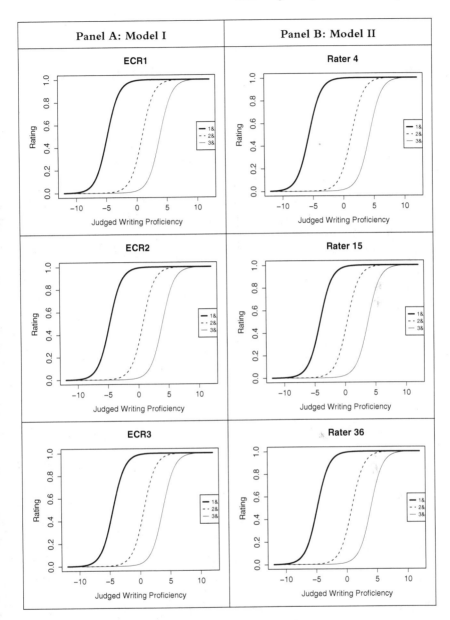

FIGURE 13.5 Conditional Probability Curves

In each plot, the *x*-axis shows the logit scale that represents the latent variable of judged writing proficiency, and the *y*-axis shows values of statistical information. Separate lines are used to show the information specific to each category in the rating scale. Inspection of these plots suggests that, for all three ECR items

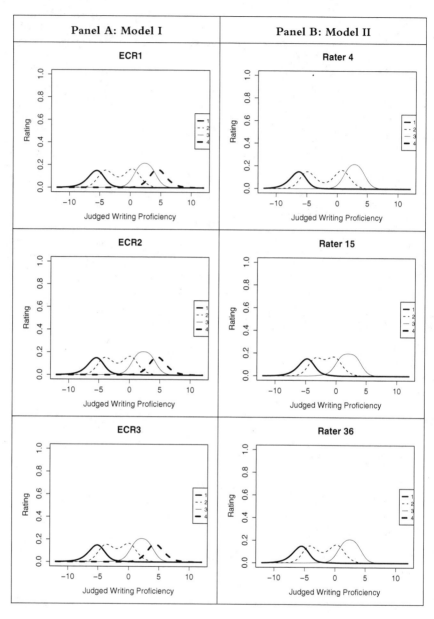

FIGURE 13.6 Category Information Functions

and across the illustrative raters, there is a decrease in statistical information within the second rating scale category. Whereas the information functions for Categories 1, 3, and 4 show clear peaks at distinct locations on the latent variable, there are "dips" or decreases in statistical information related to Category 2. This finding suggests that students who receive a rating of 2 may display meaningful differences in writing ability that are not adequately distinguished in the raters' operational use of the rating scale categories. In other words, there are potentially substantively meaningful differences in the writing achievement among the group of students who received a rating of 2.

4. Model-Data Fit

Finally, evidence of model-data fit is used to evaluate the match between raters' operational use of rating scale categories and the expectations of the measurement model. In the context of the illustrative dataset, model-data fit is examined for rating scale categories in terms of the ECR items (Model I) and the individual raters (Model II).

Numerical Evidence

Numerical evidence of model-data fit for rating scale categories includes summaries of residuals that describe differences between raters' operational use of rating scale categories and the expected ratings based on the model. When the Facets program (Linacre, 2015) is used to explore rating scale functioning, these summaries are presented in the form of Outfit *MSE* statistics for each category. As noted above, values of Outfit *MSE* around 1.00 are usually interpreted as evidence of adequate model-data fit to support the interpretation and use of results from the Rasch model.

Table 13.5 includes Outfit *MSE* statistics for rating scale categories specific to each ECR item (Model I, Panel A) and to each rater (Model II, Panel B). In general, results from both models suggest generally acceptable fit for the rating scale categories across items and raters.

Graphical Evidence

In addition to numerical evidence, it is also possible to explore model-data fit using empirical response functions overlaid with expected response functions based on the Rasch model. As noted above, these plots can be used to identify specific ranges on the logit scale at which notable departures from model expectations are observed in the form of higher-than-expected or lower-than-expected ratings that may warrant further investigation.

Figure 13.7 includes expected and empirical response functions for the three ECR items based on Model I (Panel A) and three selected raters based on Model II (Panel B). In each plot, the *x*-axis shows the logit scale that represents the latent variable of judged writing proficiency, and the *y*-axis shows the rating scale. A solid black line shows the expected ratings based on the model, and a dashed line shows the empirical observations for each item or rater. Inspection of these

TABLE 13.5 Numerical Evidence for Category D (Model-Data Fit)

Model I

Item	Outfit MSE for Categories			
	X = 1	X = 2	X = 3	X = 4
ECR1	0.90	1.00	0.90	1.00
ECR2	1.00	1.00	0.90	1.10
ECR3	0.90	0.90	0.80	0.90

Model II

Rater	Outfit MSE for Categories			
	X = 1	X = 2	X = 3	X = 4
1	1.10	1.00	1.00	1.20
2	0.80	0.90	1.00	1.30
3	1.10	0.90	1.00	1.00
4	0.90	1.00	1.00	0.80
5	1.10	0.70	0.80	1.00
6	0.90	0.90	0.90	1.00
7	1.10	1.00	0.80	0.90
8	0.60	0.90	1.10	0.80
9	0.80	0.90	0.90	0.90
10	1.00	1.00	0.80	0.90
11	0.80	0.90	0.80	0.90
12	1.00	1.10	1.10	0.90
13	1.20	0.90	0.80	0.70
14	1.00	1.10	0.90	1.00
15	0.80	0.80	0.70	0.80
16	1.10	1.00	1.00	0.90
17	0.60	0.80	0.80	1.00
18	0.90	1.00	1.00	1.00
19	0.90	1.00	1.10	0.80
20	1.20	0.90	0.70	0.90
21	1.10	1.00	0.90	0.90
22	0.80	0.80	0.70	0.90
23	0.90	0.90	0.80	1.10
24	0.90	1.00	0.90	0.90
25	0.90	0.90	0.90	1.00
26	1.40	1.20	1.00	1.00
27	0.90	0.90	0.90	0.90
28	1.10	1.00	1.00	1.10
29	0.90	1.00	0.90	1.20
30	1.00	1.00	1.00	1.00
31	0.90	0.90	0.80	1.00
32	1.20	1.00	1.00	0.70
33	1.20	0.90	0.80	0.90
34	0.80	0.90	0.80	0.90
35	0.90	1.00	0.90	0.90
36	0.70	0.80	0.70	0.80
37	1.00	1.10	1.00	1.20
38	0.80	1.00	1.00	0.80
39	1.00	0.90	0.80	0.80

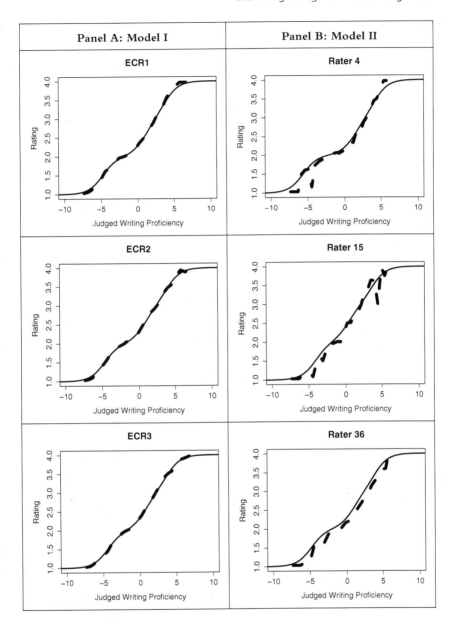

FIGURE 13.7 Empirical and Expected Response Functions

response functions suggests that there is a good match between raters' empirical use of the rating scale categories and model expectations across the three ECR items. Similarly, the results for the three selected raters suggest generally close correspondence between empirical and expected ratings, with some minor departures from model expectations. For example, the plot for Rater 4 indicates some unexpected ratings for students with low judged locations on the latent variable that may warrant further investigation.

Summary and Discussion

The purpose of this chapter was to describe and illustrate the use of polytomous Rasch models as a method for evaluating the empirical functioning of rating scales. *Rating scale functioning* was presented as a set of evidence that describes the operational application of rating scale categories in order to guide the improvement and interpretation of ratings in practice. Because polytomous formulations of the Rasch model are based on adjacent-categories probabilities, it is possible to empirically investigate individual rating scale categories for evidence that they are used as expected. Four categories of numerical and graphical evidence of rating scale functioning were presented as a systematic method for exploring rating scale functioning that can be applied based on the Rating Scale and Partial Credit formulations of the polytomous Rasch model: (A) category structure, (B) directional orientation with the latent variable, (C) category precision, and (D) model-data fit. An illustrative analysis of data from an administration of the Alaska High School Graduation Qualification Examination for writing was used to demonstrate the investigation of rating scale functioning in terms of these categories of evidence.

Throughout this book, we have emphasized the central role of rater judgments in mediating the results of rater-mediated assessments, such that it is necessary to explicitly examine raters' interpretations of cues in the assessment system in order to inform the interpretation and use of their ratings. In this chapter, we presented an additional set of diagnostic evidence that provides researchers with tools for exploring raters' operational use of rating scale categories. These numerical and graphical indicators of rating scale provide insight into the empirical use of rating scale categories that is not captured in overall indicators of model-data fit for raters, students, and other cues. Rather than providing a set of critical values for evaluating rating scales, the overall aim of this chapter was to demonstrate the diagnostic value of polytomous Rasch models for exploring the operational application of rating scale categories that has direct practical implications for the improvement and interpretation of ratings. In particular, results from analyses of rating scale functioning can be used to investigate the degree to which rating scales are functioning as intended in operational settings. This information can then be used to identify areas for improvement, such as rating scale category descriptors and rater training procedures. The unique context in which rating scales are applied will determine the relative importance of each piece of information and the extent to which revisions are necessary.

Acceptable model-data fit is essential for achieving the invariant properties connected to the use of Rasch Measurement Theory within the context of rater-mediated assessments. The guidelines and methods described in this chapter provide additional evidence and requirements for evaluating the quality of ratings. Inferences about whether or not invariant measurement has been achieved depends on a variety of sources of evidence, and no single numerical or graphical display can fully reflect the various ways that rater-mediated assessments can go wrong.

References

Andrich, D. A. (1978). A rating formulation for ordered response categories. *Psychometrika, 43*(4), 561–573. http://doi.org/10.1007/BF02293814

Engelhard, G., & Wind, S. A. (2013). *Rating quality studies using Rasch measurement theory* (Research Report No. 2013–3). New York, NY: The College Board.

Fisher, R. A. (1958). *Statistical methods for research workers.* New York, NY: Hafner Publishing Company.

Linacre, J. M. (2002). Optimizing rating scale category effectiveness. *Journal of Applied Measurement, 3*(1), 85–106.

Linacre, J. M. (2015). *Facets Rasch Measurement* (Version 3.71.4). Chicago, IL: Winsteps. com.

Masters, G. N. (1982). A Rasch model for partial credit scoring. *Psychometrika, 47*(2), 149–174. http://doi.org/10.1007/BF02296272

Samejima, F. (1969). Estimation of latent ability using a response pattern of graded scores. *Psychometrika Monograph Supplement, 34*(2, No. 17), 100.

Samejima, F. (1997). Graded response model. In W. J. van der Linden & R. K. Hambleton (Eds.), *Handbook of modern item response theory* (pp. 139–152). New York, NY: Springer.

PART VI
Final Word

14
INVARIANT MEASUREMENT WITH RATERS AND RATING SCALES

Summary and Discussion

> Raters are human and they are therefore subject to all of the errors to which humankind must plead guilty.
>
> *(Guilford, 1936, p. 272)*

We started our book with a quote from Guilford (1936) that stresses the idea of a continuum in conceiving rater-mediated assessments:

> The essence of all forms of rating devices is the same. Some particular psychological continuum is defined . . . [cues] landmarks or guideposts are supplied along this continuum to aid a judge in the evaluations of samples to be placed on that continuum . . . a straight horizontal line is drawn to represent the continuum . . . the judge merely checks . . . that point on the continuum where he believes the sample should fall.
>
> *(Guilford, 1936, p. 263)*

It seems appropriate to start this last chapter with a Guilford quote regarding the potential limits inherent in assessments that include raters. If raters are error prone, then it is important to consider how to identify and minimize as many of these potential rater effects as possible. This book focused on using Rasch Measurement Theory in combination with a lens model for human judgment to develop, evaluate, and maintain rater-mediated assessments. Rater-mediated assessments pose several unique problems because the observed data are ratings obtained from human judgments of performances (e.g., writing assessment) that may include both conscious and unconscious biases. As pointed out by Saal, Downey, and Lahey (1980), "most of the reservations, regardless of how elegantly phrased, reflect fears that rating scale data are subjective (emphasizing, of course, the undesirable connotations of subjectivity), biased, and at worst, purposefully distorted" (p. 143). Without a doubt, we recognize the potential limits of our ratings, but strongly support human judgments as a basis for assessing many aspects of human performance.

There are quite a few traditional methods for examining rating quality, including rater agreement indices, intraclass correlations, kappa coefficients, and generalizability coefficients (Cronbach et al., 1972; von Eye & Mun, 2005). However, each of these methods provides a piecemeal look at selected aspects of rating quality without being guided by a measurement theory that incorporates the variety of rater effects discussed in this book. None of these other methods for examining rating quality are explicitly based on the important concept of invariant measurement. Invariant measurement based on Rasch Measurement Theory provides a set of standards that can guide high-quality, rater-mediated assessment systems. The overall goal is to create valid, reliable, and fair ratings. In addition to the benefits of invariant measurement, we would like to stress the value of the Wright map that defines the continuum indicated by Guilford (1936) and that provides the opportunity to visualize and understand rater-mediated measurement as a line representing the construct or latent variable of interest.

It is important to recognize that the measurement theory developed by Rasch (1960/1980) reflects a paradigm shift from earlier research traditions in measurement. The statistics obtained from Classical Test Theory within the test-score tradition are person, cue, and rater dependent (Crocker & Algina, 1986), while Rasch Measurement Theory offers the possibility of rater-invariant assessment systems (Engelhard, 2013). This paradigm shift has important implications for the rater-mediated assessments that we highlight in this book. As pointed out by van der Linden (2016), "one of the best introductions to this change of paradigm is Rasch (1960, Chapter 1), which is mandatory reading" (p. xvii). Andrich (1989) has highlighted the importance of making a distinction between assumptions used in statistical models with the requirements of measurement reflected in Rasch Measurement Theory.

We have proposed five requirements for invariant measurement with raters that are briefly restated here from Figure 1.4:

1. The measurement of persons must be independent of the particular raters that happen to be used in the assessment.
2. The calibration of the cues must be independent of the particular raters used in the assessment.
3. The structure of the rating categories must be independent of the particular raters used in the assessment.
4. The locations of raters must be independent of the particular persons, cues, and rating scales used in the assessment.

5. Persons, cues, rating scales, and raters must be simultaneously located on an underlying latent continuum used in an assessment system.

In this final chapter, we summarize major sections of our book and discuss areas for future research. Specifically, this chapter is outlined as follows:

- Theories of measurement and judgment for rating scales
- Foundational areas for rating scales
- Technical issues and IRT models for ratings
- Practical issues
- Future trends and promising areas for new developments
- Final word

Theories of Measurement and Judgment for Rating Scales

In the first major section of our book, we introduced several key ideas related to invariance as a general principle in science including a discussion of its role in defining scientific progress. We also introduced a set of measurement issues based on the three foundational areas identified in the *Standards for Educational and Psychological Testing* (American Educational Research Association, American Psychological Association, and National Council on Measurement in Education, 2014): validity, reliability, and fairness. Next, we focused specifically on one of our major themes: Rater-mediated assessment requires strong theories of both measurement and human judgment.

Measurement theories can be broadly classified into two research traditions that have been called the *test score* and *scaling traditions* (Engelhard, 2013). As it label implies, the test-score tradition models observed ratings, while models in the scaling tradition (e.g., Rasch model) focus on development of scales to represent latent variables. In this second major section, we compare Generalizability Theory (Cronbach et al., 1972) with Rasch Measurement Theory. We highlight the advantages of using the Facets Model for rater-mediated assessments.

Chapter Four provides an overview of lens models originally proposed by Brunswik (1952) and the use of lens models for understanding human judgments (Cooksey, 1996). The main point is that the development and maintenance of rater-mediated assessments can be guided by a lens model that includes suggestions for training raters.

Given the importance of rater cognition, it is appropriate to note that there was a special issue of *Educational Measurement: Issues and Practice* devoted to rater cognition and score validity (Leighton, 2012). Cognitive psychology offers a variety of options for improving judgment and decision-making tasks related to rater-mediated assessments. Several of the articles in this special issue highlight promising areas for future research (Myford, 2012).

Foundational Areas for Rating Scales

Part III in our book summarizes the foundational areas identified in the *Standards for Educational and Psychological Testing* and their implications for rater-mediated assessments. The three foundational areas are validity, reliability, and fairness. There are four chapters in this section with one chapter for each foundational area, as well as Chapter Eight that illustrates how these foundational areas play a role in evaluating a rater-mediated assessment for a middle grades writing assessment.

Validity is typically viewed as the umbrella concept that encompasses reliability and fairness issues. In particular, Standard 1.9 in the validity section of the *Standards for Educational and Psychological Testing* states:

Standard 1.9

When a validation rests in part on the opinions or decision of expert judges, observers, or raters, procedures for selecting such experts and for eliciting judgments or ratings should be fully described. The qualifications and experience of the judges should be presented. The description of procedures should be include any training and instructions provided, should indicate whether participants reach their decisions independently, and should report the level of agreement reached. If participants interacted with one another or exchanged information the procedures which they may have influenced one another should be set forth.

(AERA, APA, & NCME, 2014, p. 25)

There is still a great deal of work to be done on developing strategies based on the *Standards for Educational and Psychological Testing* for developing, evaluating, and maintaining rater-mediated assessment. We believe that explicit connections between models of human judgment and measurement models open up many opportunities for future research. Many current methods for evaluating assessments can be adapted and productively used to examine the psychometric quality of rater-mediated assessments. In other areas, researchers will need to be creative in developing procedures to apply to rater-mediated assessments.

Technical Issues and IRT Models for Ratings

In Part IV, we examine several technical issues including the description of two popular models from the scaling tradition that are based on Item Response Theory: the Graded Response Model (GRM) and the Partial Credit Model (PCM). The GRM was developed by Samejima (1997), while the PCM was developed by Masters (1982). The empirical analyses in Chapter Nine highlight the potential advantages of using PCM when the goal is to guide the interpretation of ratings and identify areas for improving the psychometric quality of rater-mediated assessments.

This section of our book briefly provides an overview of parameter estimation. From our perspective, parameter estimation is basically the assignment of persons, cues, and raters to locations on a Wright map.

Research on technical issues is one of the most active areas in psychometrics. New methods of estimation are continuously being proposed and explored. It is fortunate indeed that most estimation methods converge on similar parameter estimates when there is good model-data fit. Baker and Kim (2004) and the new handbooks of IRT (van der Linden, 2016) provide additional resources for future technical developments.

Practical Issues

Part V discusses what we consider critical practical issues that emerge in the operational administration and analysis of data from rater-mediated assessments. First of all, in order to use various measurement models, we need to address several practical issues, including issues related to model-data fit. It cannot be stressed enough that the properties of invariant measurement are only met with good model-data fit. There are a variety of methods for examining model-data fit, including our preference for residual-based analyses (Wells & Hambleton, 2016). However, none of the current methods for examining model-data fit provide unequivocal rules for answering the question, How do we evaluate how good is "good enough"? This is an important area for future research.

As pointed out several times throughout this book, rater-invariant measurement is obtained when there is good model-data fit. In fact, the Rasch Measurement Theory is based on an ideal-type model that exhibits invariant measurement by definition. The practical problem is to evaluate how well our observed data fit our ideal view of invariant measurement. We can view model-data fit issues as a process for evaluating the quality of Wright map that we want to use as a meaningful representation of the latent variable or construct. Figure 1.8 in Chapter One presents a hypothesized Wright map to represent writing proficiency, while Figure 8.3 in Chapter Eight represents the operational Wright map that reflects the construct based on our specific dataset.

Another practical issue arises related to the design of rater-mediated assessment. Chapter Twelve describes several observational designs for linking raters in rater-mediated assessments. Most operational rater-mediated assessments include incomplete rater linking designs, and it is important to consider how to develop and maintain appropriate linkages among various facets of the assessment system.

The last practical issue discussed in this major section relates to the examination of how raters are using the rating scales. This topic is discussed in Chapter Thirteen. One of the essential differences between measurement models in the test score and scaling traditions is that test score models view scores as having equal units based on score points, while models in the scaling tradition estimate the size of the rating categories on the Wright map based on how the rating scale is actually used by the raters. This property allows researchers to empirically evaluate rating scale functioning, as well as the comparability of rating scales across various facets of the assessment system such as raters or domains in an analytic scoring rubric.

Future Trends and Promising Areas for New Developments

There are a variety of areas for future research, and we would like to briefly mention a few in this section. First of all, the *Standards for Educational and Psychological Testing* focus on three separate foundational areas (validity, reliability, and fairness). We believe that future research on evaluating the psychometric quality of rater-mediated assessments should consider the use of *fairness* as the umbrella term. Most psychometricians consider *validity* as the umbrella term, although it is still a widely debated construct (Engelhard & Behizadeh, 2012). We feel that the use of fairness as an overarching concept for the psychometric quality of rater-mediated assessments has the potential to communicate concepts related to the quality of these assessments to the public in a clearer way. In particular, fairness is strongly related to concerns about systematic rater biases. Previously, rater bias has typically been addressed as a validity concern. Systematic biases can also be viewed as a source of measurement error that results in inconsistent ratings for particular student subgroups across raters—thus influencing the reliability and precision of ratings. Viewing rater biases as a threat to fairness encompasses both of these perspectives.

Although automated scoring procedures have been available for some time (Page, 1966), there has been a recent increase in interest in the use of *automated scoring* for performance assessments (e.g., Foltz et al., 2012). As these scoring procedures become more prevalent, particularly in conjunction with high-stakes assessments, it is critically important to examine the correspondence between the ratings obtained from human and machine scoring, along with other indices of psychometric quality. In particular, it is especially important to identify aspects of performances that are problematic for machine scoring in order to ensure that construct-irrelevant characteristics of student responses do not unduly influence the scoring procedures for these performances. As with any rater-mediated assessment, it is critical to evaluate the quality of each aspect of the automated scoring process, including the procedures used to develop the prediction model (e.g., Wind et al., in press), the quality of the scores obtained from the model, and the intended and unintended consequences that result from the operational use of the scoring procedures.

Somewhat related, the *adaptive training* and evaluation of operational raters represents an exciting approach for monitoring and maintaining rater-mediated assessments. C. Wang et al. (2017) have described many of the issues involved in this process. Based on principles related to computer adaptive testing (CAT), adaptive training procedures for raters use real-time analyses of rating quality to identify raters in need of remediation. As computer-based formats for both the administration and scoring of educational performance assessments become increasingly prevalent, this application of CAT is particularly promising.

Relatively little research has been conducted on the impact of various data collection and *rater linking designs*. In particular, details regarding rating designs are not frequently provided in research on rater-mediated performance assessments, regardless of the measurement approach that is used to evaluate ratings (Wind & Peterson, 2017). This lack of concern for the design of rating systems suggests that most researchers do not recognize the importance of establishing connectivity in order to ensure that ratings are comparable across facets of the rater-mediated assessment system. We anticipate this to be another promising area for future research that will contribute to the improvement of rater-mediated assessments. For example, Wind, Ooi, and Engelhard, G. (in review) have examined how various designs affect decision consistency within the context of musical performances. Along the same lines, Wind and Jones (2017, in review) recently examined the influence of the characteristics of the common performances (e.g., anchor sets) that are used to establish connectivity in performance assessments in which there is very little overlap across raters, such as teacher evaluation systems based on classroom observations. More work is needed in this area that highlights both the practical consequences of limited connectivity in rating designs as well as practical solutions for establishing psychometrically sound rating designs.

Rater accuracy is another important concept that warrants additional research. Scholars have used the term *rater accuracy* in numerous ways to describe a variety of characteristics of ratings, including agreement, reliability, and model-data fit (e.g., Wolfe & McVay, 2012). However, we feel that a criterion-referenced approach to evaluating rater accuracy based on the match between operational (i.e., observed) ratings and criterion ratings, such as ratings assigned by an expert, leads to a clearer interpretation of rater accuracy that can be incorporated into rater training and remediation activities. There have been several recent applications of this criterion-referenced approach to evaluating rater accuracy that reflect different measurement frameworks. For example, adapting the Rasch model for rater accuracy presented by Engelhard (1996), Wesolowski and Wind (2017), and Bergin et al. (2017) used the match between operational and expert ratings as the dependent variable in a Many-Facet Rasch Model in order to evaluate rater accuracy in music assessments and teacher evaluations, respectively. Using a different approach, Patterson, Wind, and Engelhard (2017) presented a method for incorporating criterion ratings into signal detection theory procedures for evaluating rating quality. Furthermore, Wang, Engelhard, and Wolfe (2015) have proposed an unfolding model for examining rater accuracy that takes into account the direction of inaccuracy (e.g., ratings that are too severe or too lenient). Additional research on rater accuracy is needed in order to more clearly understand the practical utility of feedback based on rater accuracy models for individual raters during training and operational scoring.

Finally, we would like to see researchers generalize the *concept of invariance* as a philosophy of science for social science measurement in general and rater-mediated assessments in particular. In this book, we have stressed how this concept can be useful in thinking about assessments, but invariance can also be broadly conceived as a general principle in science. In order to improve the psychometric quality of rater-mediated assessments, it is necessary that researchers and practitioners identify those aspects of assessment systems across which invariance is a prerequisite for fairness. It is essential to evaluate invariance related to rater severity across student subgroups, assessment tasks, or domains in the scoring rubric. Researchers should empirically evaluate the degree to which invariance is observed across these facets.

Final Word

> It is no great exaggeration to compare the power of testing on human affairs with the power of atomic energy. Both are capable of great positive benefit to all of mankind and both contain equally great potential for destroying mankind. If mankind is to survive, we must continually search for the former and seek ways of controlling or limiting the later.
>
> *(Bloom, 1970, p. 26)*

Rater-mediated assessments are used around the world, and it is important to recognize the value of building assessment systems that yield valid, reliable, and fair scores for informing our decisions. We strongly argue that psychometrically sound assessments based on human judgments can be developed and maintained following the suggestions we have made in this book. In particular, Rasch Measurement Theory and a lens model of human judgment offer a sound approach to solving some problems related to rater-mediated assessments. We hope that the Wright maps can form a unifying concept in various communities of practice. In particular, we view measurement as defining a continuum or line that operationally defines a construct with the requirements of invariant measurement used to guide the creation of a scale. These scales have a certain degree of consistency and stability across various facets of assessment situations. Further, we view invariance as a set of hypotheses that can be critically examined by researchers in order to produce meaningful and useful scales. We also accept that if invariance is not achieved within a particular context, then sources of variance can be explored to gain a deeper understanding of the construct that is represented by the scale.

Bloom (1970) stated that "Testing is a two-edged sword that can do incalculable good as well as great harm to the individual" (p. 25). We hope that this book contributes to the "good" and appropriate uses of rater-mediated assessments.

References

American Educational Research Association [AERA], American Psychological Association [APA], & National Council on Measurement in Education [NCME]. (2014). *Standards for educational and psychological testing.* Washington, DC: AERA.

Andrich, D. (1989). Distinctions between assumptions and requirements in measurement in the social sciences. In J. A. Keats, R. Taft, R. A. Heath, & S. H. Lovibond (Eds.), *Mathematical and theoretical systems* (pp. 7–16). North Holland: Elsevier Science.

Baker, F. B., & Kim, S. (2004). *Item response theory: Parameter estimation techniques* (2nd ed., Revised and Expanded). New York: Marcel Dekker.

Bergin, C., Wind, S. A., Grajeda, S., & Tsai, C.-L. (2017). Teacher evaluation: Are principals? Classroom observations accurate at the conclusion of training? *Studies in Educational Evaluation, 55*, 19–26. https://doi.org/10.1016/j.stueduc.2017.05.002

Bloom, B. S. (1970). Toward a theory of testing which includes measurement-evaluation-assessment. In M. C. Wittrock & D. Wiley (Eds.), *Evaluation of instruction: Issues and practices* (pp. 25–50). New York, NY: Holt, Rinehart and Winston.

Brunswik, E. (1952). *The conceptual framework of psychology.* Chicago: University of Chicago Press.

Cooksey, R. W. (1996). *Judgment analysis: Theory, methods and applications.* Bingley, UK: Emerald Group Publishing Limited.

Crocker, L., & Algina, J. (1986). *Introduction to classical and modern test theory.* New York: Holt, Rinehart and Winston.

Cronbach, L. J., Gleser, G. C., Nanda, H., & Rajaratnam, N. (1972). *The dependability of behavioral measurements: Theory of generalizability for scores and profiles.* New York: Wiley.

Engelhard, G., Jr. (1996). Evaluating rater accuracy in performance assessments. *Journal of Educational Measurement, 33*(1), 56–70.

Engelhard, G. (2013). *Invariant measurement: Using Rasch models in the social, behavioral, and health sciences.* New York: Routledge.

Engelhard, G., & Behizadeh, N. (2012). Epistemic iterations and consensus definitions of validity. *Measurement: Interdisciplinary Research and Perspectives, 10*(1), 55–58.

Guilford, J. P. (1936). *Psychometric methods.* New York: McGraw-Hill.

Foltz, P., Rosenstein, M., Lochbaum, K., & Davis, L. (2012). *Improving reliability throughout the automated scoring development process.* Presented at the National Council on Measurement in Education, Vancouver, BC, Canada.

Leighton, J. P. (2012). Editorial. *Educational Measurement: Issues & Practice, 31*(3), 48–49.

Masters, G. N. (1982). A Rasch model for partial credit scoring. *Psychometrika, 47*, 149–174.

Myford, C. M. (2012). Rater cognition research: Some possible directions for the future. *Educational Measurement: Issues & Practice, 31*(3), 48–49.

Page, E. B. (1966). The imminence of grading essays by computer. *Phi Delta Kappan, 47*, 238–243.

Patterson, B. F., Wind, S. A., & Engelhard, G. (2017). Incorporating criterion ratings into model-based rater monitoring procedures using latent-class signal detection theory. *Applied Psychological Measurement*, 014662161769845. https://doi.org/10.1177/01466 21617698452

Rasch, G. (1960/1980). *Probabilistic models for some intelligence and attainment tests.* Copenhagen: Danish Institute for Educational Research. (Expanded edition, Chicago: University of Chicago Press, 1980).

Saal, F. E., Downey, R. G., & Lahey, M. A. (1980). Rating the ratings: Assessing the psychometric quality rating data. *Psychological Bulletin, 88*(2), 413–428.

Samejima, F. (1997). The graded response model. In W. J. van der Linder & R. K. Hambleton (Eds.), *Handbook of modern item response theory* (pp. 85–100). New York: Springer.

van der Linden, W. J. (Ed.). (2016). *Handbook of item response theory, volume two: Models* (pp. 395–413). Boca Raton, FL: CRC Press.

von Eye, A., & Mun, E. Y. (2005). *Analyzing rater agreement: Manifest variable methods.* Mahwah, NJ: Lawrence Erlbaum Associates.

Wang, C., Song, T., Wang, Z., & Wolfe, E. (2017). Essay selection methods for adaptive rater monitoring. *Applied Psychological Measurement, 41*(1), 60–79. https://doi.org/10.1177/0146621616672855

Wang, J., Engelhard, G., & Wolfe, E. W. (2015). Evaluating rater accuracy in rater-mediated assessments with an unfolding model. *Educational and Psychological Measurement, 76*(6), 1005-1025.

Wells, C. S., & Hambleton, R. K. (2016). Model fit with residual analyses. In W. J. van der Linden (Ed.), *Handbook of item response theory, volume two: Models* (pp. 395–413). Boca Raton, FL: CRC Press.

Wesolowski, B. W., & Wind, S. A. (2017). Investigating rater accuracy in the context of secondary-level solo instrumental music. (Advance online publication). https://doi.org/10.1177/1029864917713805

Wind, S. A., & Jones, E. (2017). The stabilizing influences of linking set size and model-data fit in sparse rater-mediated assessment networks. *Educational and Psychological Measurement,* 001316441770373. https://doi.org/10.1177/0013164417703733

Wind, S. A., & Jones, E. (in review). Exploring the influence of range restrictions on connectivity in sparse assessment networks: An illustration and exploration within the context of classroom observations.

Wind, S. A., Ooi, P. S., & Engelhard, G. (in review). Exploring decision consistency across rating designs in rater-mediated assessments.

Wind, S. A. & Peterson, M. E. (2017). A systematic review of methods for evaluating rating quality in language assessment. *Language Testing.* Advance online publication. doi: 10.1177/0265532216686999

Wind, S. A., Wolfe, E. W., Engelhard, G., Jr., Foltz, P., & Rosenstein, M. (in press). The influence of rater effects in training sets on the psychometric quality of automated scoring for writing assessments. *International Journal of Testing.*

Wolfe, E. W., & McVay, A. (2012). Application of latent trait models to identifying substantively interesting raters. *Educational Measurement: Issues and Practice, 31*(3), 31–37. https://doi.org/10.1111/j.17453992.2012.00241.x

GLOSSARY

Ability   The generic term used to describe the level of performance of a person on a latent variable or construct.

Accommodations   Changes to the testing procedure that are relatively minimal and maintain the construct being measured, such as changes to the presentation, format, or response procedures.

Accurate ratings   Ratings that match a person's known or "true" score, such as criterion ratings based on expert judgment.

Adaptations   Changes to a testing procedure that may include accommodations and modifications to the presentation, format, or response procedures.

Adjacent-Category Model   Polytomous model in which the dichotomization of the rating scale categories is based on comparisons between categories that are next to each other.

Analytic ratings   Ratings in which separate scores are assigned to distinct components of a response.

Anchor rater   A rater used to connect otherwise disconnected components of an assessment system.

Anchor students   A group of students used to connect otherwise disconnected components of an assessment system.

Attenuation paradox   A phenomenon that occurs when the psychometric guidelines for maximizing reliability coefficients yields a decrease in validity coefficients.

Birnbaum Models (2PL, 3PL)   Measurement models proposed by Birnbaum (1968) using the logistic item response function that include a two parameter logistic (2PL) model with item and slope parameters, as well as a three parameter logistic (3PL) model that adds a guessing parameter.

Bloom's Taxonomy   A classification of learning objectives developed by Professor Ben Bloom based on six cognitive levels: knowledge, comprehension, application, analysis, synthesis, and evaluation.

Category response function   A function that represents the relationship between the probability of selecting a response category and the underlying latent variable.

Complementary science   An approach to science that illuminates facets of a disciplinary area that are not examined within the context of normal science. A complementary science can guide us in reconsidering the underlying assumptions that are frequently taken for granted in the current practice of measurement.

Conditional probability curve   Graphical representations of the relationship between probabilities for observed ratings in pairs of adjacent rating scale categories and locations on the latent variable.

Construct   Underlying latent variable that is represented by the Wright map.

Constructed-response tasks   The directions that are given to persons regarding the responses to a performance assessments (e.g., essay prompt).

Cues   The indicators (e.g., items and domains) that are used to define the latent variable.

Cumulative Probability Model   Polytomous model in which the dichotomization of the rating scale categories is based on comparisons across cumulative categories.

Dichotomous data   Response outcomes that are divided into two non-overlapping categories (e.g., not present/present, yes/no, and wrong/right).

Dichotomous Rasch Model   Rasch measurement model used to analyze dichotomous data.

Differential rater functioning   Systematic differences in rater severity related to construct-irrelevant characteristics of performances.

Disconnected rating design   Rating designs that do not include systematic links between assessment components.

Domains   The aspects of a performance task that are used as cues to define the latent variables (e.g., mechanics of writing).

Epistemic iterations   A problem-solving technique for clarifying foundational concepts in measurement and selecting among competing measurement theories based on an iterative process that is evaluated in terms of key goals, such as the requirements for invariant measurement.

Equating   The procedures used to develop equivalent and comparable scores across different tests or assessment systems.

Estimation of parameters   Statistical procedures for connecting parameters in a measurement model to observed data.

Facets   A computer program designed to apply Rasch Measurement Theory to person–item response data (http://winsteps.com/facets.htm).

Facets Model   A Rasch model that typically includes more than two facets (e.g., persons and items) such as a rater facet.

Fairness   Guidelines for developing and using assessment systems that lead to comparable measures of persons regardless of construct-irrelevant characteristics.

Fully crossed rating design   A rating design characterized by complete connectivity across all facets in an assessment system.

Generalizability Theory   An approach to measurement that extends Classical Test Theory to include multiple sources of measurement error.

Generalized Linear Model   Extensions of the linear model to include ordinal dependent variables.

Goodness of fit   A judgment of how well a dataset fits a measurement model.

Graded Response Model   A measurement model proposed for rating scale data that is based on cumulative categories rather than adjacent categories.

Guttman scaling   A technique for examining response patterns to determine whether or not a set of items administered to a group of persons is unidimensional.

Holistic ratings   Ratings in which all aspects of a response are used to assign an overall score. Holistic ratings may reflect multiple components of a response, but a single score is used to reflect the overall level of the performance.

Ideal-Type Model   A measurement model that specifies the requirements to be met in order to realize desirable measurement properties, such as invariant measurement.

Infit statistics   Weighted mean square error statistics that summarize the fit between the observed and expected responses based on residual analyses.

Information function   Graphical representations of statistical information (y-axis) within a category across logit-scale locations (x-axis).

Inter-rater reliability   The correlation between the ratings of two independent raters. Focuses on relative ordering rather than exact agreement of persons on the latent variable.

Invariance   Stability and consistency across different contexts that can be defined and studied from different perspectives.

Invariant measurement   A philosophical approach to measurement that supports item-invariant measurement of persons and person-invariant calibration of items that can be simultaneously represented on a Wright map.

Invariant measurement with raters   A philosophical approach to measurement with raters that supports rater-invariant measurement of persons and person-invariant calibration of raters that can be simultaneously represented by a rater-mediated Wright map.

Item difficulty   The location of the item on the latent variable in log-odds units (logits).

Item response function   A function that represents the relationship between person locations on the latent variable and probability of a positive response on an item.

Judged locations (theta estimates)   Estimated location of persons on the Wright map based on a rater-mediated assessment.

Latent variable The underlying construct that is being measured or represented by the Wright map.

Lens model for rater-mediated assessment A conceptual model of human judgment that illustrates how rater perception of student locations on a latent variable is made visible by cues (intervening variables) such that the observed rating reflects rater judgment of the student locations that are mediated by various cues.

Linked rating design A rating design characterized by the systematic use of common assessment components through which uncommon assessment components are connected.

Logits (logit scale) Underlying scale units that are obtained by a logistic transformation of item response probabilities.

Many-Facet Rasch Model A Rasch measurement model that can be used to model data that has multiple facets (Linacre, 1989).

Mean square error fit statistics Summaries of residuals that describe departures from model expectations. Infit and Outfit formulations of mean square error fit statistics are available in most Rasch software programs.

Measurement The systematic process of locating both persons and items on a Wright map that represents a latent variable (construct).

Measurement models Statistical models that provide the underlying conceptual and theoretical frameworks that guide the theory and practice of assessment in the social sciences.

Misfit Lack of correspondence between observed responses and model-based expectations based on the measurement model.

Model–data fit A judgment of the degree to which the data under investigation meet the requirements of a measurement model.

Modifications Changes to a testing procedure that are substantial and modify the construct being measured. Test scores obtained from modified testing procedures do not maintain the same interpretation in terms of the construct.

Normal science Scientific practice that is guided by the paradigms that are found in various handbooks and textbooks that serve to guide scientific practice.

Objective measurement The phrase used by Professor Benjamin Wright to describe Rasch's concept of specific objectivity. Objective measurement is essentially equivalent to the concept of invariant measurement as described in this book.

Operating characteristic function (OCF) The OCF represents the general form of the item or person response functions that are used to stochastically model measurement data.

Operational definition A detailed description of a latent variable represented in invariant measurement by the Wright map.

Ordinal Observed ratings that order persons on the latent variable with meaningful directionality without the assumption of equal intervals or equal units.

Outfit statistics Mean square error statistics that summarize the fit between the observed and expected responses based on residual analyses.

Parameter separation A property of Rasch measurement models that allows the conditional separation of item and person locations on the latent variable.

Partial Credit Model A unidimensional Rasch model for ratings in two or more ordered categories.

Performance assessments Testing systems that require a person to create or construct a response (e.g., essay) that is scored by a rater using a rating scale.

Performance-level descriptor Verbal or written description of representative persons ordered at critical points along the Wright map used to guide the assignment and interpretation of ratings.

Person fit A summary statistic that represents the agreement between a person's observed and expected responses based on a measurement model.

Person response function The function that represents the relationship between response probabilities and a set of items for a person.

Polytomous data Response outcomes that are divided into more than two non-overlapping categories (e.g., low/medium/high; strongly disagree/disagree/agree/strongly agree.

Polytomous Rasch Model Rasch measurement models designed to model rating scale data, such as the Rating Scale Model and Partial Credit Model.

Probabilistic model A statistical model used to estimate the probability of an event occurring based on a set of data.

Psychometrics The application of statistical methods to measurement problems in the social and behavioral sciences.

Rasch measurement models A family of measurement models developed by Georg Rasch that provides an opportunity to meet the requirements of invariant measurement including the following models: Dichotomous Model, Partial Credit Model, Rating Scale Model, and Many-Facet Model.

Rasch Measurement Theory A measurement theory based on the measurement models proposed by Georg Rasch and based on the requirements for invariant measurement.

Rater agreement The congruence between two raters in terms of their ratings of a group of persons.

Rater response function The function that represents the relationship between response probabilities and a set of items for a person based on rater judgments.

Rater severity Location of the rater on the Wright map.

Rater-mediated assessment Any assessment or test that consists of constructed responses that require a rater, reader, judge, or examiner to interpret the performance and to assign a rating based on their judgment.

Rater-mediated Wright map An instantiation of an operational definition mediated and interpreted by a set of raters of a continuum designed to represent a construct. Wright maps are also called variable maps, item maps, and curriculum maps.

Rating design   Procedures with which individual raters or groups of raters are assigned to score student performances.

Rating scale   Structure of the format used to collect numerical ratings (e.g., Likert scale).

Rating scale functioning   Information related to how rating scale categories are interpreted and used.

Rating Scale Model   A unidimensional Rasch model that can be used to analyze ratings in two or more ordered categories.

Reliability coefficient   A statistical index that represents the consistency of the ordering of persons over different situations.

Reliability of separation statistic   A value between 0.00 and 1.00 that indicates how well individual elements within a facet can be differentiated from one another, such as individual students, raters, or domains. This statistic is comparable to classical reliability coefficients under many conditions when estimated for person facet.

Research traditions   A concept developed by Laudan (1977) to describe the underlying paradigms that guide the practice of science in a variety of disciplines.

Residual   The difference between observed data and the model-based expectations based on the measurement model.

Residual analysis   Numeric and graphical summaries of residuals.

Response format   The method used to collect responses from persons (e.g., multiple-choice and constructed-response items).

Rubric (i.e., scoring rubric)   The guidelines used to define and score responses to constructed-response items such as essays.

Scaling tradition   A set of measurement theories, such as Rasch Measurement Theory and Item Response Theory, that focuses on item and person responses with the goal of achieving invariant measurement.

Science   A system of disciplined inquiry that embodies a set of procedures for solving a variety of problems that can be evaluated by a community of scholars.

Selected-response items   An item response format that provides a limited number of predetermined responses for a person (e.g., multiple-choice items).

Specific objectivity   Rasch (1960/1980) used this term to describe his version of invariant measurement. The concept is similar to objective measurement as used by Wright (1968).

Standard error of measurement   An indication of the amount of uncertainty in an estimated statistic or parameter in a measurement model.

Standardized residuals   Residuals transformed to a scale with a specified distribution, such as a normal distribution.

Sum score   A score based on the summation of the observed responses (e.g., correct responses or ratings).

Test response function   A function that represents the relationship between person locations on the latent variable and the expected score based on the measurement model.

Test-score tradition A set of measurement theories, such as Classical Test Theory and Generalizability Theory, that focuses on test scores and the sources of error variance that may affect the interpretation and use of test scores.

Threshold (for rating scale categories) Locations on the latent variable associated with the probability of a rating in a particular category.

Unidimensional A term used to describe a meaningful mapping of persons and items onto a single construct represented by a Wright map.

Validity An evaluative judgment based on evidence to support whether or not an assessment system supports the intended meaning and use of scores.

Wright map A visual representation of the construct being measured. Wright maps have also been called variable maps, construct maps, item maps, and curriculum maps.

INDEX

Page numbers in *italic* indicate a figure and page numbers in **bold** indicate a table on the corresponding page.